Unfolding Bodymind

Exploring Possibility Through Education

Edited by

Brent Hocking
Johnna Haskell
Warren Linds

Unfolding Bodymind

ISBN: 1-885580-08-8

Library of Congress Card Number: 00-110983

Copyright © 2001 by the Foundation for Educational Renewal
P.O. Box 328, Brandon, VT 05733-0328
1-800-639-4122
www.great-ideas.org

Printed in Rutland, Vermont, USA

*In memory of
"Tsimilano,"
known to us as Vince Stogan
(1918-2000)
who honored our presence on
Musqueum First Nation Land.*

Los puentes colgantes

¡Oh qué gran muchedumbre,
invisible y renovada,
la que viene a este jardín
a descansar para siempre!

Cada paso en la Tierra
nos lleva a un mundo nuevo.
Cada pie lo apoyamos
sobre un puente colgante.

Comprendo que no existe
el camino derecho.
Sólo un gran laberinto
de encrucijadas múltiples.

Constantemente crean
nuestros pies al andar
inmensos abanicos
de senderos en germen,

¡Oh jardín de la blancas
teorías! ¡Oh jardín
de lo que no soy pero
pude y debí haber sido!

—*Federico García Lorca*
(1899-1936)

Floating Bridges

Oh what tremendous multitudes,
invisible and ever-changing,
come to this garden
and linger forever!

Every step we take on Earth
takes us to a new world.
Every single footstep
lands on a floating bridge.

I know that there is no such thing
as a straight road.
Only a vast labyrinth
of intricate crossroads.

Our steps incessantly
create as we go
immense spirals
of unfolding pathways.

Oh garden of fresh
possibilities! Oh garden
of all I still am not
but could and should have been!

—*translation by Kate Farrell*

Table of Contents

Section One.
Turning Together on Paths of Awareness

Explores notions of unfoldment. Worlds of possibility open paths of
unexpected entanglements through teaching and learning. Pedagogy is
free-flowing and dynamic, caught in spaces where the whole body is
washed in sensory interplay between individual educators and their
encompassing worlds.

Section Two.
Embodying "Pedagogical Possibilities":
Teaching Being, Being Teaching

Intertwines languages and understandings of *bodymind* with those of
embodiment to present contrasting views of mindful awareness. These views
are never fixed, but always unfolding, always seeking to catch the ephemeral
and possible worlds that emerge through bodies of teaching and educational
inquiry.

Section Three.
Education and Culture:
Experiencing Im/possibility

Explores curriculum and instruction as cultural and human artifacts. Classroom relationships cannot blossom without understanding the place of these artifacts. A critical analysis of culture highlights the values, beliefs, and assumptions that enable, exclude, and disrupt embodied learning in formal education.

Section Four.
Ecological Interplay—Humans/Nature in Freefall

Identifies ecological interplay as a path for renewing humans/nature relationships. Interplay speaks to different senses of connectedness and passion that allow us to experience the environment and our bodies as living, breathing phenomena.

Acknowledgments

We would like to acknowledge the following individuals for their support:

Dr. Brent Davis at York University and **Dr. Karen Meyer** at the University of British Columbia who started us on this journey;

Dr. Ron Miller whose patience, insight, and ongoing support have made our project a reality;

The diverse group of contributors whose words illuminate the pages of this collection;

The reviewers who evaluated manuscripts;

Amy Kirtley, Charles Jakiela, and **Norma Montaigne** for their roles respectively as copyeditor, production coordinator, and cover designer.

The Faculty of Graduate Studies, the **Walter Gage Memorial Fund**, the **Department of Curriculum Studies**, and the **Centre for the Study of Curriculum and Instruction at the University of British Columbia** for funding our *Bodymind Conference* in May 1999;

Dr. David Abram and **Dr. David Jardine** whose love of language and eloquent presentations graced the above conference;

Dr. Carl Leggo and **Dr. Patrick Verriour**, Department of Language and Literacy Education, University of British Columbia, who introduced us to narrative and poetic forms of inquiry in education and encouraged us to lay down our own paths as writers;

Dr. Ted Aoki of the University of British Columbia who has inspired our thinking;

And **Kevin, John**, and **Rachel** who encouraged and enlivened the unfolding of this book as a labor of love.

P R E F A C E

Ron Miller, Ph.D.

I was immediately intrigued when I heard that a conference was going to be held in Vancouver on "embodied learning," calling together scholars who had been influenced by phenomenology, Buddhism, ecological theory and the holistic biology of Humberto Maturana and Francisco Varela to raise probing questions about how modern education defines learning and knowledge. It was apparent that here was a rare opportunity to deepen the intellectual foundations of the emerging field of holistic education, and I contacted the organizers of the conference—three energetic graduate students at the University of British Columbia—and offered to publish the papers that would be presented. After many, many hours of planning, editing, revising, selecting, and more editing, the result is the remarkable book that follows. It is a gathering of truly provocative ideas, and in my opinion it does, indeed, offer a deeper dimension to our thinking in holistic education.

As a recognizable movement, holistic education is still young, dating back to a couple of conferences held in California (where else?) in 1979 and 1980 that drew together some of the main writers on humanistic psychology and the human potential movement who had an interest in education (among them were Joseph Chilton Pearce, George Leonard, Theodore Roszak, Beverly Galyean, and Jack Canfield). During the 1980s, educators attracted to "human potential" and "New Age" ideas (because of their emphasis on the wholeness of the human being, including spirituality and embodied wisdom) began to identify with this new "paradigm" in education. We (holistic educators) quickly recognized that many of its core principles had been expressed by earlier romantic and dissident educators like Pestalozzi, Froebel, Alcott, Montessori, Krishnamurti and Steiner, but that as a guiding theory it required a more contemporary, comprehensive elaboration (John P. Miller 1988; Ron Miller 1990).

We began to trace the theoretical outlines of this emerging field, stating in broad generalities that it provided a uniquely *spiritual* orientation to education as well as an *ecological* worldview. Drawing upon popular presentations of post-Cartesian/Newtonian science, such as the useful work of Fritjof Capra (1976, 1982; see also Capra 1996), we knew that holism had to do with healing the alienation between mind and body, between spirit and matter, that has dominated the modern Western worldview, but for several years our explication of this emerging theory was still rather primitive; we were satisfied to simply proclaim boldly: "Modern education separates mind and body; holistic education reconnects them." But what exactly does this *mean*? What makes an ecological worldview *epistemologically* different from the dominant technocratic culture? A few intrepid scholars, like Douglas Sloan (1983) and C.A. Bowers (1993), addressed these questions, but for the most part "new paradigm" educators remained satisfied with the broad vision. It is only in the last few years that a serious interest in the philosophical foundations of holistic education has emerged. Now, spirituality and ecological wisdom are commonly addressed at academic conferences and in the professional education literature.

Yet, even as we have begun to provide holistic education with a coherent, intellectually rigorous theory, we have found that most of the available academic discourses are inadequate for our purpose. The literature of "critical pedagogy," for example, while offering a powerful tool for deconstructing modernist assumptions, is plagued with an esoteric jargon that fails to speak to holistic educators' primary interest in *meaning known through experience*. One would think that John Dewey's work addressed just this point, but Dewey's investigation, although a useful foundation, stopped short of the transpersonal (archetypal, supra-rational) domain of experience that is the gateway to spirituality. Holistic theorists have begun to look more closely at the literature of phenomenology (exemplified by Maurice Merleau-Ponty's work), at Buddhist philosophy, and at sophisticated expressions of deep ecology, and it is just these intellectual sources that inform the essays in this book. *Unfolding Bodymind* represents the leading edge of holistic education theorizing. The authors are clearly concerned with meaning derived through experience, and they describe lived experiences in vital detail, while they investigate the philosophical implications of such meanings.

This book challenges the linear, narrowly rational form of discourse that we are conditioned to using. Many of the authors play with language, using free verse, unusual typography, or unexpected punctuation to dramatize how ambiguous and inexact our verbal representations of experienced reality can be. The authors invite the reader to experience "knowing-through-action" along with them. Their theory is never far removed from the dynamic relationships between knower and known, between teacher and learner, that all holistic educators place at the heart of the educational endeavor. Yet these authors reflect on what such relationships mean; they attempt to describe the nature of learning with the senses keenly alive, with feelings and desires informing rational thought, with the whole bodymind open to uncharted *possibilities* of experience; in a word, they explore just how we might educate the *soul* of the human being, as Jack Miller (1999) and Rachael Kessler (2000) have recently emphasized as the essence of holistic education.

Unfolding Bodymind is the fourth volume in a new series published by the Foundation for Educational Renewal on the philosophical foundations of holistic education. This series brings together authors with diverse perspectives on the cultural, moral, ecological and spiritual dimensions of this emerging field. Our aim is to establish "holistic education" as a serious and legitimate discourse in its own right. *Unfolding Bodymind,* like the other books in the series, demonstrates that this postmodern (or perhaps we could say "transmodern") way of thinking about education and human development offers one way out of the dehumanized technotopia of the modern world. As I wrote in *Caring for New Life,* the first volume of this series, "The vision of holism is a vision of healing. It is a vision of atonement between humanity and nature. It is a vision of peace. And it is a vision of love." I think all the authors on the following pages would agree that our work is not merely theoretical or academic, that it aims passionately to transform the world.

Ron Miller, Ph.D.
President, Foundation for Educational Renewal

References

Bowers, C.A. 1993 *Education, cultural myths, and the ecological crisis: toward deep changes.* Albany: State University of New York Press.

Capra, Fritjof. 1976 *The Tao of physics: An exploration of the parallels between modern physics and eastern mysticism.* Boulder, CO: Shambhala.

Capra, Fritjof. 1982 *The turning point: Science, society and the rising culture.* New York: Simon and Schuster.

Capra, Fritjof. 1996 *The web of life: A new scientific understanding of living systems.* New York: Anchor/Doubleday.

Kessler, Rachael. 2000 *The soul of education: helping students find connection, compassion, and character at school.* Alexandria, VA: Association for Supervision and Curriculum Development.

Miller, John P. 1988 *The holistic curriculum.* Toronto: Ontario Institute for Studies in Education Press. (2nd revised edition, 1996)

Miller, John P. 1999 *Education and the soul: Toward a spiritual curriculum.* Albany: State University of New York Press.

Miller, Ron. 1990 *What are schools for? Holistic education in American culture.* Brandon, VT: Holistic Education Press. (2nd edition, 1992; 3rd revised edition, 1997)

Sloan, Douglas. 1983. *Insight-imagination: The emancipation of thought and the modern world.* Westport, CT: Greenwood Press. (paperback edition 1993, Brandon, VT: Resource Center for Redesigning Education)

Re-imag(e)ining Worlds through Education: An Overview of the Book and Its Influences

Brent Hocking
Johnna Haskell
Warren Linds

I watch Maggie, our cat, accustomed to spending the winter
indoors, reluctant now to go out of doors. I leave the screen
door open. She sits, watches what seems like the possibility of
going outside (a risky endeavor?), sniffs, eyes wide open,
watching the birds, the trees waving in the breeze, surveying
the landscape of the unknown and…tentatively places herself
just on the doorstep and stops. She returns indoors and starts the
process over again. Five minutes later I look for her. I see she is
across the yard, slinking like a tiger as she and the landscape
explore each other. (Warren, May 1999)

Like Warren's cat, this book is placed at a twinkling of possibility, one that
will unfold through the bodies of its writers and readers. The possibilities
available to us as humans may or may not emulate those embodied by
Maggie: the possibility to wake during and after sleep, to act carefully or in
haste, to work and play, to love and be loved. When we eat we satisfy cravings
and cultivate desires for the ordinary and exotic. When we move limbs or
dream we change our sense of place. When we speak we immerse ourselves in
the mysteries of language. When we sing our skin tingles with the sounds of
music, a melody shaped through years of practice and improvisation.
Possibilities vary according to organism and circumstance, yet all beings experience the world as a series of unfolding interactions. Whether as cats or educators, our bodies implicate us in the world in particular ways. These are the
energies and relationships that identify our evolutions and ecologies as individuals and as species.

Reflections on bodymind and bodyworld connections have persisted since
Classical Antiquity, giving rise to animated discussions about knowing, thinking, and doing as well as questions about moral agency and autonomy. This collection of writings flows from a need to understand embodied forms of knowing
and participating with the world as *possibilities arise through relationship.*

Such possibilities are underscored by contemporary disciplinary and cross-
disciplinary studies. These may include, to name a few, biological sciences,
cultural studies, feminist theories, Buddhism, gay and lesbian studies, envi-

ronmental ethics, language studies, performative inquiry, hermeneutics, and phenomenological traditions. Each of these brings different considerations to bear on education as a intricate web of relations. For us, the significance of these discussions emerges through their dynamic interactions; that is, the ways in which they envelop one another. Additionally, they provide all of the authors in this volume with inspiration and guidance.

Our primary interest as teachers, learners, and researchers is to concentrate on the possibilities offered for education by holistic[1] and ecophilosophical schools of thought. Most notably, our work is influenced by the writings of Dewey (1929), Merleau-Ponty (1962), Bateson (1972), Varela, Thompson, and Rosch (1991), and Abram (1996). We also believe that the sacred and spiritual dimensions of enacting new possibilities are addressed by different authors in this collection. It is the unfolding interactions among the authors that open spaces of possibility for us as editors. Each of us embraces different questions of language, environmental ethics and outdoor education, spirituality, and performance. It is the resonance of these webs of being that entwines us in this work.

Embodying Possibility through Language

The translation of possibilities into language has been a significant challenge for us as writers and academics. Since this volume is based on a 1999 conference, *Bodymind: Holistic Explorations of Cognition, Action, and Interaction in Education,* that we organized in Vancouver, Canada, the term *bodymind* occupies a central role in the chapters that follow. You will notice that this word is not separated, hyphenated, or linked by *and.* Some readers might take our combining of the words as a Cartesian view of the dualistic nature of our body—that we still have bodies and minds that are separate and it is only in language that we may combine them. But to us this term is symbolic of moving "beyond" such an atomistic and binary view of the human being.

The idea of combining body and mind into one word is not new. John Dewey (1929, 232), using a hyphenated version of the term, argued that

> [B]ody-mind simply designates what actually takes place
> when a living body is implicated in situations of discourse,
> communication and participation...."body" designates the
> continued and conserved, the registered and cumulative opera-
> tion of factors continuous with the rest of nature, inanimate as
> well as animate; while "mind" designates the characters and
> consequences which are differential, indicative of features
> which emerge when "body" is engaged in a wider, more com-
> plex and interdependent situation.

Many advertisements for alternative health therapies and New Age workshops combine body, mind and spirit[2] to indicate their holistic emphases. In this book we include material from some of these orientations, but have expanded our use of the word to include other ways bodymind may unfold through education.

Another key term is *embodiment*. By *embodiment* we mean the integration of the physical or biological body and the phenomenal or experiential body (Varela, Thompson, and Rosch 1991, xvi). For us, as for other contributors, embodiment suggests a seamless though often elusive matrix of bodymind-world, a web that integrates thinking, being, doing and interacting within worlds. How this seamlessness emerges through education and under what conditions it flourishes are critical questions of this project. *Embodiment* moves us away from the Cartesian legacy of how we view knowing and knowledge not as concrete things that reside in the body or mind but that emerge through our interactions with/in the world.

Bodymind is something we all strive for, a way of being through which our embodied awareness unfolds through engaging/embracing our experiencing. We hope this also happens in the living experiencing of reading. We do not consider language to be secondary to or a derivative of the possibilities announced by this book, but rather to flow through them. Before discussing the Bodymind Conference and the organization of chapters in this collection, we would like to focus on the language of the title we have chosen as a way to enter into and illuminate influential aspects of our work.

Unfolding Our Title

How might we describe a book that unfolds intricate possibilities emerging through bodymind intertwining with/in a world that is constantly changing?

Perhaps an exploration of the words in our title, *Unfolding Bodymind: Exploring Possibility through Education,* will help. In this section we unfold the words and then consider the implications of their intertwining within the flow of the book. Let's follow a route between and amongst the webbing of these words. We will do this not in a linear fashion as the title is written but through concepts that con/di/verge as they meet one another.

Unfolding...

When thinking of unfolding, imag(e)ine the miracle of plant growth. A tiny seed sown in the earth suddenly unfolds, first into a shoot, then a stalk, then a bud, then a flower, and finally an unfolding of beautiful, perfumed sensuousness. This is the magic of transformation. "Unfolding is to increase, to grow"...to fold is to diminish, to reduce, to withdraw into the recesses of a world" (Deleuze 1993, 8-9). Every being is a double of itself: the bud is folded into the flower that will soon unfold to be and become.

The idea of *fold* disrupts the binary notion that there is an inside and an outside, that there is a separate mind, separate body and separate world. Think of a Mobius strip[3] which has one continuous surface of interconnected sides. We make such a strip by folding the outside into the inside. This conflates subject-object, inside-outside binaries (St. Pierre 1997). Folding disrupts our conventional ideas of the binary because "the outside is an exact reversion or 'membrane,' of the inside" (Badiou 1997, 61). In other words, through diffusion, the inside and outside of the Mobius strip are not opposite sides but are flowing one into the other and the surface/border becomes a place of interaction and transformation.

Opening Spaces of Possibility

Biologist Jack Cohen and mathematician Ian Stewart (1994) write about the space of the possible as an ever-evolving, ever-dynamic web of interrelationships. The space of the possible doesn't so much exist but evolves through our interactions with/in the wor(l)d. The text of words interplays with the text of the world being written, opening spaces. When the spaces interact, delightful possibilities spring forth. This space is dynamic because the living world, our bodyminds, are always evolving and developing through interaction with one another.

> The separate beings of audience and performers can disappear, and at such moments there is a kind of secret complicity between us. (Nachmanovitch 1990, 101)

This idea of complicity that Nachmanovitch identifies arises when simple systems interact in ways that change one another. The whole extends beyond the sum of its parts. Although there are patterns, the interrelationships of the parts within the whole are such an intricate and convoluted ball of intertwined threads that "any attempt to dissect its internal workings and past history just leads to a reductionist nightmare" (Cohen and Stewart 1994). We need to look at the parts and the spaces as systems that are reiterated like fractals[4]. These systems include our living experiences with/in the world.

Complicity doesn't fit with fixed binary distinctions. It alerts us to their contrived and over-determined simplicity, emphasizing instead relations that are intertwined and fluid. Complicity—being implicated in/with—moves us as educators from managing a simplistic system of outcome-based reading towards engaging through reading *this* text. This requires an attentiveness to our participation through events, engaging in knowing/being/doing a complex and forever unfolding world.

As educators we cannot think of ourselves as just "operating in" educational settings, planning, theorizing, leading, learning, teaching and then leaving the cultures of which we are part. Educational practices informed by and respectful of the complex worlds of schools/community are not just "interventions" but instances of complicity in which educators unfold with cultures-in-the-making through dynamic individual and collective interactions.

We have a responsibility to embody awareness of our intentions, values, and beliefs emerging through worlds of interaction. Complicity alerts us to an engaging which arises as a transformative process revitalizing the space of the possible. Education no longer characterizes or announces what is, but takes on a participating role, intertwining with all learning bodies, including educators. Imagine a series of the same Mobius strips we mentioned earlier, but this time interconnected, interlocked, so that a whole view of the Mobius strip is reproduced in the individual strips. In other words, they would not only interconnect but also interlink so there is one continuous surface.

We have been limiting ourselves by referring to the Mobius strip as a series of surfaces, but it is also a series of spaces, the spaces of possibility, which incorporate the "more-than-human world" (Abram 1996). The educator/writer is part of all this, operating "in an open space throughout which things-flows are distributed rather than plotting out a close space for linear and solid things" (Deleuze and Guattari 1987, 361). Spaces of this type exist within education. Or perhaps it is more accurate to say that spaces emerge in/through educational experiencing?

Interstanding[5] "through" Education

Mary Catherine Bateson (1994) has written, "the quality of recognition in any experience suggests a meeting of something already present with/in the environment" (201). But that isn't quite it. The "meeting" she describes is actually an intertwining of human bodies and landscape bodies. This intertwining is evocatively illustrated in the following example:

> To draw a carp, Chinese masters warn, it is not enough
> to know the animal's morphology, study its anatomy or
> understand the physiological functions of its existence.
> They tell us it is also necessary to consider the reed
> against which the carp brushes each morning while
> seeking its nourishment, the oblong stone behind
> which it conceals itself, or the rippling water when it
> springs toward the surface. These elements should in

no way be treated as the fish's environment, the milieu
in which it evolves or the natural background against
which it can be drawn. They belong to the carp itself....
The carp must be apprehended as a certain power to
affect and be affected by the world. (Morley 1992, 183)

This metaphor captures different senses of what Varela, Thompson, and
Rosch call structural coupling, a co-emerging of a bodily entity with its encompassing world. One does not exist without the other as "organism and environment enfold into each other and unfold from one another in the fundamental circularity that is life itself" (1991, 217). This is true of interactive systems
that have evolved historically over time as much as it is for systems emerging
with/in moments. We see the flow of structural coupling, for example, in the
image of a tightrope walker maintaining balance by means of the exquisite
structural dynamics of bodywork intertwining with the precise behavioral
dynamics of footwork on the rope. The tightrope walker and rope change
together. There are times when the relationship is shaky and times when it is
slick and smooth. A similar path is laid down through our manner of living. It
is sometimes narrow and uneven, sometimes broad and straight, and sometimes appears as invisible, only a trace on the landscape.

Life, like tightrope walking, is scary and risky. It involves a bodymind full
of unfamiliar learning. This risk speaks to our histories of embodiment (that is,
to our processes of living and becoming) and to the ways in which our bodies
unfold through and are complicit within our language as educators. For Varela
and his fellow authors, the emphasis on structural coupling means shifting
from an instrumentalist orientation (e.g., how can bodymind help solve educational problems?) to one that allows us as humans to enter into a shared world
of significance; in other words, to learn together. Fell, Russell, and Stewart
(1994) reiterate this critique of instrumentalism and call for manners of living
and knowing consonant with poetic stances:

The reputed unreliability of feelings, combined with a
craving for immediate technological remedies to treat
uncomfortable feelings, have contributed to a profound
devaluation of the lived experience. Yet the extraordinary
clarity and precision by which poetic images enable us to
recognize the subtle nuances of emotion in one another
suggest that it is only in our lived experience—not in our
theories—that we can know the satisfaction which we call
genuine understanding.

Though we prefer the term "interstanding" in lieu of "understanding"
(a distinction developed in endnote 5), Fell, Russell, and Stewart's writing
reminds us of the dynamic interplay between language and experience.

This interplay influences how we engaged with the title of this collection through our experiencing the power of stories. Without citing the quote about the carp, how could we settle on a title that spoke to the dynamic interactions embedded within our histories, bodies, and languages as editors? How could we find words to express what, for us, was never a fixed singular entity, but one that evoked our interstandings across time? The tensions that emerges while trying to find a language for our title are recognized by Fell, Russell, and Stewart (1994) as they identify languaging with structural coupling:

> No matter how satisfying the explanation may be, it
> is not the same as the experience—it cannot substitute
> for the experience or make it appear or disappear. This
> is the limitation inherent in our languaging. For one
> thing it is an aspect of our behavior which is a relational
> domain involving, not only our bodyhood, but its
> surrounding medium as well. Another way of putting
> it is that we know that the word is not the thing—they
> are separate phenomenal domains. However, there is
> a fascination in the western world today with the
> search for a better explanation—in an attempt to
> improve the fit between our explanation and what
> we experience.

We settled on the preposition *through* as a key word in our title to reflect the possibilities announced by structural coupling. This word seeks to express the idea that we are part of the educational experiences we read and write.

Text is not simply information transfer. Stories become the songs that we sing together and the pictures that we envision. The power of language to enhance or diminish wor(l)ds of being is entangled with our engagement through narrative-as-possibility. Storytelling through poetry or other forms of writing reintegrates us with the living world. The "extraordinary clarity" of poetic images described earlier by Fell, Russell, and Stewart (1994) is not a permanent transformation of muddy ponds of the unknown to the mirroring lakes of the known, but a momentary glimpse of clarity, a brief image which flashes up at an instant "when it can be recognized and is never seen again" (Benjamin 1969). Performative languaging allows the reader to participate by contributing breath while reading silently or aloud. It opens the pores and the senses to the momentary present that lives within the sounds and images that emerge. This enables a mutual triggering of emotions between and amongst writer and reader, via text. While engaging with text as a living medium, we would be amiss if we did not include the stories of our collaboration as editors and friends and the ways in which this book evolved.

Collaborative Journeys (Un) Folding...

In the fall of 1996 Warren and Brent were enrolled in a seminar on narrative in their graduate programs at the University of British Columbia (UBC). Every Monday evening after class course participants would go out for dinner at a nearby Chinese restaurant. This became a course ritual. One evening Johnna joined us. She was a fellow student in a new graduate seminar entitled *Enactivism and Education: Interdisciplinary Studies of Cognition, Culture, and Curriculum.* Course instructors were Karen Meyer, now Director of the Center for the Study of Curriculum and Instruction at UBC, and Brent Davis, now on faculty in Education at York University, Toronto, Ontario. Participants in the Enactivism[6] and Education class read and discussed works by Bruner (1996), Lave and Wenger (1991), and Varela, Thompson, and Rosch (1991). We analyzed understandings of knowledge and cognition and their representations in constructivist and socially situated theories of learning and curriculum. The seminar sensitized us to, and left us feeling frustrated with, the pervasiveness of dualisms in contemporary philosophies of education. Our journey through spaces of possibility began unfolding.

In 1997, the Enactivism and Education seminar was offered again. All three of us, along with several other returning students, decided to enroll in the hope of continuing our dialogues and interstandings of enactive thinking. By this time Brent Davis had moved to Toronto, so Karen Meyer led the seminar herself. She embraced two recently published works by Abram (1996) and Capra (1996) as course texts. Whereas a focus of the original seminar had been to introduce participants to the ideas and principles of enactive theory and language, one of the emphases this year was exploring ideas in action—a consideration highlighted by our understandings of enactive theory. As they unfolded, such explorations came to include activities in phenomenological writing, storytelling, drama, poetry, and pastel drawing.

The three of us continued our weekly restaurant gatherings on campus. Each one of us was pursuing doctoral studies in different departments within the Faculty of Education at UBC: Johnna in Curriculum Studies, Brent in Educational Studies into embodied learning,[7] and Warren in Language Education. Our participation in the same graduate class reflected our interests in interdisciplinary inquiry and curriculum and the need to move beyond traditional modes of learning.

We became aware of our individual and collective learning needs and priorities. Although our senses of direction ebbed and flowed and our interstandings were far from complete, we began to apply enactive and ecophilosophical thinking to our developing research projects. Warren concentrated on questions of inquiry and participation in drama facilitation; Brent explored questions around pedagogy and participation in higher education classrooms; and

Johnna focussed on the phenomenon of experiencing in outdoor adventure education environments. What had initially started as academic interests in embodied knowing now connected our ways of living through our personal embodiments as educators, learners, and researcher/writers.

We often felt senses of tension, contradiction and isolation in our roles as doctoral students. So, we began to consider how our engagements with one another might unfold into a more expansive community of co-inquirers.

There are many ways in which embodied learning might be experienced and revitalized at all levels of education. In an era known for its growing consumerism, electronic technologies, and global cultures, a preoccupation with bodymind might be construed as unnecessarily self-serving or self-limiting. We would argue otherwise. Although trends such as corporate sponsorships and technology-based learning cannot be dismissed, neither should they exclude possibilities for bodymind pedagogy and curriculum. We believe that instead of representing knowledge as a commodity or toolbox it is crucial for educators to expose students to authentic forms of learning that reflect the embodied, dynamic, collective and ecological webs of knowing. The depth and rigor of this engagement will enable the emergence of students and teachers "sensitive to the conditions and genuine possibilities of some present situation and...able to act in an open manner" (Varela, Thompson, and Rosch 1991, 123).

We demand no less from ourselves as learners. Before putting together this book we were re-examining our practices as teachers, learners, and inquirers. Brent instructed an undergraduate course on adult education and continues to work part-time as an elementary teacher. Warren taught undergraduate communication courses in teacher education and continues to facilitate drama workshops with teachers and students in Saskatchewan. Johnna taught a science education course to student teachers and conducted participatory research with high school students in outdoor education. She also conducted work with Karen Meyer, investigating children's theories of swinging as an embodied phenomenon. For all three of us, the need to engage and live through interstandings of bodymind becomes evident through the contexts of daily living.

It was out of these backgrounds that the aforementioned conference, *Bodymind: Holistic Explorations of Cognition, Action, and Interaction in Education,* evolved. Like this book, the conference served as a possibility for talking through the practical and theoretical, scientific and poetic, secular and spiritual, interdisciplinary dimensions of its title. In addition to sessional presenters, two keynote speakers, David Abram and David Jardine, were invited to share their views of bodily awareness through education.

All conference presenters were invited to use their sessions as springboards to develop texts that could be submitted for this volume. The processes of reflecting, writing, and reviewing manuscripts unfolded over one year. In some cases the final version of a chapter closely resembles a particular conference session; in others, it is a re-articulated, re-presented and re-crafted piece of writing. Our engaged, embodied experiences as conference organizers and presenters confirmed the value of networking and community-building. We share insights from the Vancouver conference and elaborate on its significance in the next section. This is followed by an explanation of the book's organization and themes.

Re-Experiencing the Bodymind Conference

Up high in the sky,
an Eagle is soaring,
floating on air currents
that
we can only imagine.
(Johnna, March 2000)

The Bodymind Conference was more than an academic event: it was an opportunity for experiencing conversation and community. As organizers, our bodies connected with landscape bodies and those of other participants through language, gesture, and possibility. We were curious as to what was happening elsewhere in bodymind explorations of education. Consequently, we encouraged narrative, poetic, and performative presentations that would embrace interstandings of bodymind.

The conference emerged into an international event with a common interest and interpretation of bodymind from individuals in Europe, Australia, North America, and Mexico. In the spirit of interdisciplinary scholarship, we organized presenters into groups and encouraged individuals to network with one another prior to the conference. We spent time exploring the possibilities while allowing for the emergent nature of this cross-disciplinary collaboration.

Joys as well as frustrations permeated conference planning. As graduate students, we felt a collective weight of responsibility to ensure that the conference would provide a format that would allow for conversation and intimacy, while supporting future and current researchers. We also wanted a location that would encourage inquiry and community—hence our choice of the Botanical Gardens at the University of British Columbia. As the conference began to assume a life of its own, we embraced the emergent conference process.

In retrospect, the conference has been a key milestone in our evolvement as doctoral students. By the time it transpired in May 1999, there were 33 presentations scheduled and 70 attendees. Presentations explored embodied forms of experience, research methodologies along with other forms of inquiry, and ecophilosophical thinking. Conference research and theories challenged us to reinterpret and re-imagine the possibilities for bodymind relationships and interactions.

Because the University of British Columbia is situated on First Nations land, we invited an Elder, Vincent Stogan Sr. (Tsimalano), from the local Musqueam Nation to open and bless the conference. This simple though rich ceremony embodied an awareness as Brent re-imagines below.

> *All of the thoughts that had been racing through my mind were suddenly redirected toward the front of the room where Tsimalano spoke. His words were sincere and at times humorous, but I think they reminded us all of our places as academics in a more-than-human setting. Members of the audience were invited to join hands in preparation for the blessing of the Bodymind Conference.[8] This simple act of bonding set the tone for the conference and inspirited it with new visions of possibility and kinship, shifting my bodily participation.*

As we had anticipated, conversations and networking require time. Many participants addressed this need by walking among pockets of brightly colored flowers, dialoguing with new-found friends, and meditating in quiet spaces with/in the Botanical Gardens between sessions. We arranged for a communal dinner before the end of the conference at the same restaurant where the three of us had met regularly.

Following the dinner, conference participants returned to the Botanical Gardens to end the day with a circle discussion. The circle became another interactional space that allowed individuals to share their impressions of the conference and their thoughts on evolving fields of holistic education. Although the three of us were extremely tired, we also found this discussion revitalizing. Johnna recalls the end of this successful adventure:

> *I became aware of voices all around me....*

> *The frogs and peepers grow louder in my ears, making me laugh and then cry, a wonderful chorus. It is midnight and I am leaving the Botanical Gardens on my bike. The conference has ended! Participants embody what it might be like to learn outside in the beautiful, speaking, breathing world of British Columbia. The cattails stand out in the full moon, tranquilizing me.... Every time I think of something from the conference, tears emerge. Tears of overwhelming joy, accomplishment, success, beauty, praise. I keep recalling words of praise, words*

that mattered, words that were poetry to my ears like the
peepers amongst the cattails. (June 3, 1999)

The success of the conference was due to the efforts, enthusiasm, and risk-taking of many individuals, including our keynote presenters, David Abram and David Jardine. Although we had compelling reasons for inviting two speakers, we did not realize the extent to which they would complement one another. They referred to the increased violence and technological underpinnings of North American schooling, asking us to re-imagine education. Both spoke passionately about how we come to know and interact within the world as sensing, and sentient, human beings.

Prior to the conference, David Abram had instructed a writing workshop on site at the Botanical Gardens. He had encouraged us to revisit and communicate with nature through our bodies, which we did in poetic (image)inings. Workshop participants wrote about their embodied experiences of sitting in the notch of a tree, touching the flowering vegetation, and interacting with pond life.

The Bodymind Conference opened opportunities for re-experiencing past encounters with the more-than-human world, and enabled the possibility of releasing the "budded, earthly intelligence of our words, freeing them to respond to the speech of things themselves" (Abram 1996, 273). The conference interactions brought forth an interplay of fresh, embodied perceptions which we hope continue to unfold through the book. Warren's poetic narrative below, inspired by an autumn walk, shows how we might continuously re-experience such moments through writing, letting language take root, intertwining and enfolding us.

Spider Moving Watch
Whisping Wandering Sun
Web Thread Worldly[9]

We were stopped by a wondrous si(gh)te.

                        Suspended in mid-air a small spider moving
upwards.

                                     up
                                     up
                                     up

              SLOWWW....LY   moving
We move ever closer

                               Shifting our stances
as we see

Grasping the dappled sun as it glistened off a thin silvery thread

Orange egg sac spider moving upwards

Folding thread un-to itself as it climbs

Ravelling and un ravelling

Folding and

Unfolding

Defying gravity

Having spun its silk from a branch high in a spruce

this spi(e)der now retreats

From the road below

Pulling its thread with what seemed incredible strength to return high above human (sp)eyes

To begin again

And we quietly crept on by.

Wondering by its sight.

I can't help thinking of this experience as a metaphor for explorations that began before the conference and were furthered by it. At the conference and afterwards, we were weaving a web to the what *if;*

to that attachment that may or may not be there;
always preparing to re-experience our journeys as we
retrace them, little by little, rediscovering diverging paths

And, at times, just suspended in

mid
a
i
r

Ready for our journey

Anew

Our journeys into new spaces helped us to reconnect with a world that is passionate, animate, and energizing. As conference organizers, we yearned for a spirit of aliveness in education that would echo our connections with the natural world—one full of vibrant, buzzing activity and interactions. How might education unfold, like a prairie thunderstorm, revitalizing, flashing glimpses, and soothing this sensual landscape?

Whether experiencing peepers, moonlit cattails, lightning storms, or body-mind awareness, we all need to journey along the unknown to discover the limits of our capabilities. What we know deep inside emerges into being. Otherwise accomplishment is nothing but an illusion (Gammelgaard 1999, 41). We seek support from visitors from nature, our fellow graduate students and the gardens of possibilities that arise during the conference experience. The mystical call of our footsteps moving forward to explore the potential of our bodily sensations turns slowly toward living life fully. The storying of bodily, earthy places allows us to re-experience shifting phenomena esthetically. While breathing in unascertainable garden worlds, we follow the cairns set down in a journey of experiencing a bodymind conference in the making.

Participants expressed a desire to keep the conference spirit and sense of community alive. This book invites a continuation of this interaction through our inquiries and dialogues of bodymind interpretations/perspectives within/through education. Join us in our struggle to sustain dialoguing, webbing our way through the airy forest, and embracing emerging possibilities

> **(Image)ining communities**
> **Embodying conversations**
> **Unfolding words shifting through pages**

Although chapters in this book vary by topic and style, the authors grappled with the structures and boundaries invoked by the term *bodymind*. Besides attending to notions of embodied knowing, chapters are linked through their explicit educational focus around research, curriculum and pedagogy. Each contributor in this volume combines theory and practice through one or more disciplinary lenses, including teacher education, language studies, religious studies, nursing, as well as case studies in public and higher education.

Chapters are further linked by process; that is, how writers enter into and interact with their writings. In keeping with the dynamic and contingent nature of cognition, contributors were encouraged to strive for a sensuous, dynamic text. For some, this meant experimenting with the fluid and creative elements of language and metaphor. For others, it meant combining concepts and practices from diverse bodymind traditions such as Buddhism and eco-feminism. Still others inspirited their writing by contesting traditional academic boundaries of format and style and risking alternative forms of inquiry and presentation. Risk-taking of this type is important to us. We are still learning how to support and facilitate efforts of this kind within the conventional structures of academic research and publishing. We welcome fresh theories and reformulations of holistic education—not another "how-to" manual to leaf through on a rainy day. Our hope is that the writings in this collection will open possibilities for action and interaction for their readers.

Our references to process as textual interface are meant to open awareness of relationships that emerge through engagement—in reading and writing specifically. These relationships exist within, beyond, and across the pages in this book. In his work on the literary imagination, Dennis Sumara (1996, 1) notes:

> Because all texts are particular forms that are historically, culturally, and politically effected and situated, the experience of engaging with *this* form rather than *that* form means participating in one complex set of relations rather than another. Furthermore, the place of reading matters. All texts are read in relation to the contexts of reading. And so, understanding the act of reading cannot be accomplished without an inquiry into the relations among forms, readers, and overlapping contexts of reading.

Our fascination here is with patterns of discourse and complicity that influence textual accessibility, participation, interpretation, and performance.

Embracing bodymind...

The importance of the reader-writer interaction for us is that it speaks to a cosmology of knowing as enacting "an ongoing bringing forth of a world through the process of living itself" (Maturana and Varela 1992, 11). Authors, like David Abram (1996), have been influenced by the bodymind thinking of French phenomenologist Maurice Merleau-Ponty (1962). His insights into the body as "a lived, experiential structure and the body as the context or milieu of cognitive mechanisms" (Varela, Thompson, and Rosch 1991) suggest a view of bodymind as a coupling between bodily form and structure. The overlay between knowing what and knowing how—both integral to experiencing—connects and distinguishes chapters in this book. As you become familiar with bodymind, we believe the distinction between embodied knowing as content and engaged knowing as process will disappear. They have for us. We now use the terms embodiment, engagement, and experiencing interchangeably, recognizing the possibilities as well as tensions of language when overlaying nouns and verbs.

Even as we strive to incorporate bodymind into our own lives, this book is another textual encounter that offers diverse spaces of engagement for researchers, teachers, and learners. We challenged ourselves to not only talk about an unfolding of bodymind; we also wanted to undertake this in the book's process and layout. Varela, Thompson, and Rosch (1991) consistently emphasize the idea of going beyond an objective/subjective dichotomy and exploring experience through a middle way. Our idea of the middle way is best expressed as a quest-in-practice for enactive approaches that unfold through "knowing in action." Exploring this through textual interplay can be explained through three different lenses that look at cognition (Rangarajan 1993) as we read *The Embodied Mind* (Varela, Thompson, and Rosch 1991), and then applying them to our interactions with a text. Following Varela , Thompson, and Rosch, Rangarajan lists three conceptions of the mind *(cognitivist, emergent, and enactive)* in the historical development of the cognitive sciences. For example, if we look at text through each lens, a cognitivist view is descriptive and disembodied with knowledge and the world being defined objectively and rendered accessible to readers as a description of a real world to which the author provides access. An *emergent* text separates the subjective "I" from the objective "text" with the reader (the subjective "I") reading the text from personal biases and understandings.

Each of the reading/writing styles of *cognitivism* and *emergence* is self-limiting for different reasons. As editors, we are striving for an enactive text that is inter-textual, never static, always moving in a dance between the "I" which is constantly changing, the text and the reader's/audience's world, viewing the text in a process of embodied and interactive reflection, intermingling thoughts of the reader with the process of reading. We are not only reading the text through our own experiences but also alongside our experiences in reading the text and against other texts. This experience in reading the text also relates to the style and form of the text. How do we enable an interactive reading, so we begin reading a text against experience and theory and vice versa in what Salvio (1997, 248) calls an "interpretive event"? This may happen in the middle space where the tension between our narratives and the text enacts possible worlds. We no longer look just for a meaning of the author but become comfortable exploring meaning that emerges through interaction with the text. Understanding and interpretation then are not acts of "an individual conscious mind but enactments, performances" (Schwandt 1999, 455) through which we are open and willing to engage in a conversation, a process of learning.

We are *aspiring* for this type of text. But this will only emerge through exploration and experimentation (in the French sense of the word *expérimenter*: to experience). Not all chapters reflect fully this perspective but we hope our dialogues that precede each section enable you, the reader, to join the conversation and perhaps enable a glimpse of what might be.

We also know that you, the reading audience, and your encompassing land-scapes will be diverse. By landscapes we not only mean the more-than-human world but also the human environments in which we work. Possibility unfold-ing through the reading experience will be equally diverse. Some might use this text as a springboard for further exploration. Others might concentrate on a section or a chapter, reading and rereading to play with our words. Still oth-ers might use a specific chapter as a dwelling or "seeing" place, noting how it affects their educational practices. The folds that will enfold are as endless as the world that is unfolding.

Enfolding With/in the Book Again and Again...

So, how might these concepts be enacted in a text, which after all, contains ordered letters page after page? We considered different possibilities. First, we considered a linear process: the mind, then the body enacting the mind and the mind enacting the body. Or: outlining theory, then its application. But this wouldn't have been true to our focus and beliefs about interconnectedness. We also considered using randomly situated chapters (for example, using alphabetical order) but wanted to explore what kind of complex structure would assist the reader in seeing the web of connections, recognizing our own complicity and participation in the process.

Some other method was needed to enable you, the reader, to fold your experience into text—much like a chiffon cake where a sponge is made and the lighter whipped egg whites are enfolded into it; the fluffed egg white provid-ing lightness, the batter bulk. One depends on the other"...there are no real boundaries here: each is enfolded in and unfolds from the other" (Davis, Sumara, and Kieran 1996, 10).

As editors we became aware of engagements between, and amongst, the different angles of exploration chosen by authors. We faced questions about how to balance different criteria as editors: how to be inclusive, how to facili-tate improvements to writing without telling contributors what to do. We also had to improvise different ways to communicate because we all lived in differ-ent geographies: Brent in Vancouver, British Columbia, Johnna in North Monmouth, Maine, Warren in Regina, Saskatchewan. As editors, we each had different views of what the book should look like, as well as what we should say and how we should say it. Knowing how best to proceed tested the limits of our individual and collective wit, patience, flexibility, and creativity.

This idea-weaving process was not new for us. One of our primary objec-tives for the Bodymind Conference was to put together presentations that spoke to each other. We hoped that, in their interplay, fresh spaces of possibil-ity would open—spaces that allowed for complex themes and issues to feed off each other, resonating with participants. Through exploring possibilities, we came to embrace the chapters in this volume as complex folds upon folds of theory, story and imagination. They all enfold within them aspects of theory and practice; narrative of experience and analysis; and methodology and perception. While reading, chapters in conversations enfold with one another.

Ultimately, we developed four sections which contain chapters that speak to one another and open up, we feel, spaces of possibility.

So we bring you this text in four sections:

1. *Turning Together on Paths of Awareness*
2. *Embodying "Pedagogical Possibilities": Teaching Being, Being Teaching*
3. *Education and Culture: Experiencing Im/possibility*
4. *Ecological Interplay—Humans/Nature in Freefall*

In Section 1 we invite you to explore with us pedagogic practices; in Section 2, embodied awareness; in Section 3, the intertwining of bodies with other bodies and landscapes; and in Section 4, the implications of ecological interplay. We conclude this volume with an afterword by David Abram and David Jardine that unfolds new worlds to explore.

Writing becomes a rhizomatic[10] (Deleuze and Guattari 1987) assembly of demanding, entangled crossroads, passages and galleries complemented by multiple analytic stances…providing a reading that brings different possibilities together. Its recognition of subject is mediated by other versions of that subject, always opening to multiple acknowledgements, displacements or layers, and larger, shifting perspectives. We are your guides in the rhizomatic passages as we pass through the possibilities that emerge. You see our themes through different folds. Writing and reading rhizomatically also means that there is a bit of adventure as we penetrate what is growing and see and feel strange new possibilities. These possibilities are unknown to all of us until the moments when they happen, embracing our unfolding bodyminds.

Interstanding Sitting Reading Writing: Engaging Possibilities

So, given all of the above, what do we want from you, the reader? Engagement, Interstanding, Openness to the spaces that emerge in the reading. What happens to you as a reader in/through these texts?[11]

We ask ourselves, what can be done to enable an environment in-the-reading that encourages or facilitates the occurrence of this experience we have taken to call "interstanding" (see endnote 5)? A book that provides an opportunity for different languaging (which is not the same as saying that we seek agreement with all that is written) may also open possibility and interstanding. Interstanding is in the enfolding of meaning in the interplay among stories told, storyteller and story reader/listener. Interstanding is a shared desire to continue exploring the landscapes of educational bodymind unfolding.

You, the reader, are invited to join us in walking the path of possibility that we are all making through these explorations. Join us in our dialogues between sections; make your own; write yourself into the texts. Let's see what unfolds as we open the door to the rest of our journey into the un/knowing of bodymind...

Notes

1. We use the term "holistic" to refer to dealing with the mystery of the unknown. In this sense, the word derives from *holy* ("where the invisible can appear" [Brook 1968, 42]). It also refers to the "complex ways human bodily subsystems [and those beyond] interact with one another" (Davis, Sumara, and Luce-Kapler 2000, 173) and with the "more-than-human world."

2. An example: while writing this part of the introduction, the editors noted an invitation to a yoga/stress therapy that arrived in the mail: *Rejuvenate! Body Mind & Soul for the Millennium.* The workshop was being put on by an organization called Inward Bound. The combination of the title and the name of the sponsor indicates an orientation to bodymind as an inward journey, whereas we prefer the term to express a rejuvenation as we mindfully interplay inwards/outwards through an arising, unfolding world.

3. A Mobius strip is a one-sided continuous surface, formed by twisting a long narrow rectangular strip of material through 180 degrees and joining the ends. It was named after German mathematician August Ferdinand Mobius (1790-1868), who described this non-Euclidean geometric form.

4. A fractal is a geometric form with similar structure when either reduced or magnified. The input for each fractal form is the output of the previous one. Brent Davis introduced us to this metaphor for writing. In a later article Davis and Sumara (2000, 6) write that such reiterative processes give rise to the property of self-similarity, "meaning that the form might be seen as being assembled of reduced copies of itself." For example, a branch of a "fractal" tree can be broken off and magnified. We can then see a resemblance to the original tree. *Fractals* then leads us to iterative and reiterative forms of writing, where, for example, each section of this book can be akin to the tree branch broken off from the whole book and yet still contain all the elements of the whole.

5. "When depth gives way to surface, under-standing becomes inter-standing. To comprehend is no longer to grasp what lies *beneath* but to glimpse what lies *between*... Interstanding is relational but not dialectical, connective but not synthetic, associative but not unitive. The between of the inter "neither fragments nor totalizes" (Taylor and Saarinen 1994, 8).

6. As editors and scholars, one of our ongoing challenges has been to find and engage with different languages of possibility. This challenge is highlighted by our perceived understandings of "enactivism" versus the "enactive" approach to cognition. Consistent

with our graduate seminar experience, our original preference was to use the language of enactivism as an expression "of a theory of learning and a methodology" (Reid) and to link disparate theories (a University of Denver School of Education website contains many links under the theme of "Enactivism"). We are less comfortable with this term today because it seems to encode in language an ideology that, for us, has become an ongoing and shifting set of relations. In this introduction, the editorial conversations, and our own chapters we use the term enactive to "propose a way of seeing cognition not as a representation of the world 'out there,' but rather as an ongoing bringing forth of a world through the process of living itself" (Maturana and Varela 1992, 11). Our perceptions of this world are mediated in the spaces between our living, breathing bodies and the words we inscribe on paper. Our use of "enactive" acknowledges our individual and collective complicities as writers and as educators to open (invisible and visible) possibilities to engage through/with.

7. Brent has since transferred to the Centre for the Study of Curriculum and Instruction.

8. We were saddened to hear of Vincent's passing in June of this year. Jo-ann Archibald, Director, UBC First Nations House of Learning commemorated Vincent's life in a campus newspaper:

> One of the important teachings that Tsimilano left us is the teaching of "hands back and hands forward." When Tsimilano says a prayer, he asks us to form a circle and join hands. In joining hands he says that we hold our left palm upward to symbolize reaching "back" to receive the good teachings of the Ancestors. These teachings become a part of us and when we hold our right palm downward, we give these teachings to the younger and future generations. In this way the teachings of the Ancestors continue and the circle of human understanding and caring grows stronger. (Archibald 2000, 11)

9. We share a haiku ("play verse") which is meant to be read over and over again, for often with each new reading a new interpretation may be gained. The reader is left to fill in the idea and make their own meaning.

10. As a rootstock, a rhizome extends horizontally with all sorts of branches. Bearing this image in mind, the reader may enter the text at any section—none matters more than the other, and no entrance is more privileged even if it seems an impasse, a tight passage or a siphon. We will be trying only to discover what other points our path connects to. Sometimes you will have to go in reverse to find another passage; sometimes you might stay in one spot and ponder what is right there, or before and above you.

11. We are interested in your additions, suggestions, proposals, reflections, desires for this book. Your comments on sections, chapters, approach, content are welcome. Please join us in our conversation by going to our bodymind website at http://sk.sympatico/ca/stmarys/book.html

References

Abram, David. 1996. *The spell of the sensuous: Perception and language in a more-than-human world.* New York: Pantheon Books.

Archibald, Jo-Ann. 2000. Elder strengthened circle of human understanding: In memoriam. *UBC Reports*, 46 (13), 7 September.

Badiou, Alain 1994. Gilles Deleuze: The fold: Leibnitz and the baroque. In *Gilles Deleuze and the theatre of philosophy*, edited by C.V. Boundas and D. Olkowski. New York: Routledge.

Bateson, Gregory. 1972. *Steps to an ecology of mind.* New York: Ballantine Books.

Bateson, Mary Catherine. 1994. *Peripheral visions: Learning along the way.* New York: Harper Collins.

Benjamin, Walter. 1969. Theses on the philosophy of history. In *Illuminations,* edited by Hannah Arendt, translated by Harry Zohn. New York: Harcourt, Brace and World.

Brook, Peter. 1968. *The empty space.* London: MacGibbon and Kee.

Bruner, Jerome. 1996. *The culture of education.* Cambridge, MA: Harvard University Press.

Capra, Fritjof. 1996. *The web of life: A new scientific understanding of living systems.* New York: Anchor Books.

Cohen, Jack, and Ian Stewart. 1994. *The collapse of chaos: Discovering simplicity in a complex world.* New York: Penguin Books.

Davis, Brent, Dennis J. Sumara, and Thomas E. Kieran. 1996. Cognition, co-emergence, curriculum. *Journal of Curriculum Studies* 28(2): 151-69.

Davis, Brent, and Dennis J. Sumara. 2000. Curriculum forms: On the assumed shapes of knowing and knowledge. *Journal of Curriculum Studies* 32(6): 821-45.

Davis, Brent, Dennis J. Sumara, and Rebecca Luce-Kapler. 2000. *Engaging minds: Learning and teaching in a complex world.* Mahwah, NJ: Lawrence Erlbaum Associates.

Deleuze, Gilles. 1993. *The fold: Leibuiz and the baroque.* Translated by Tom Conley. Minneapolis: University of Minnesota Press.

Deleuze, Gilles, and Felix Guattari. 1988. *A thousand plateaus: Capitalism and schizophrenia.* Translated by Brian Massumi. London: Athlone Press.

Dewey, John. 1929. *Experience and nature.* 2d ed. LaSalle, IL: Open Court.

Fell, Lloyd, David Russell, and Alan Stewart, eds. 1994. *Seized by agreement, swamped by understanding.* Http://www.northnet.com.au/~pfell/book.html

Gammelgaard, Lene. 1999. *Climbing high: A woman's account of surviving the Everest tragedy.* Seattle, WA: Seal Press.

Haskell, Johnna. 2000. *Experiencing freefall: A journey of pedagogical possibilities.* Ph.D. diss., University of British Columbia.

Lave, Jean, and Etienne Wenger. 1991. *Situated learning: Legitimate peripheral participation.* Cambridge: Cambridge University Press.

Maturana, Humberto R., and Francisco J. Varela. 1992. *The tree of knowledge: The biological roots of human understanding.* Revised ed. Boston: Shambhala.

Merleau-Ponty, Maurice. 1962. *Phenomenology of perception.* Translated by Colin Smith. London: Routledge and Kegan Paul.

Morley, David. 1992. *Television, audiences and cultural studies.* New York: Routledge.

Nachmanovitch, Stephen. 1990. *Free play: Improvisation in life and art.* New York: Jeremy P. Tarcher/Putnam.

Rangarajan, Anand. 1993. Review of *The embodied mind,* by The Observer, 10 February, 1. Http://kevin.www.media.mit.edu/people/kevin/Observer_01.html

Reid, David. *Professional background.* Http://ace.acadiau.ca/user/dreid/cv.html#res.

Salvio, Paula. 1997. On keying pedagogy as an interpretive event. In *Action research as a living practice,* edited by Terrance R. Carson and Dennis Sumara. New York: Peter Lang.

Schwandt, Thomas A. 1999. On understanding understanding. *Qualitative Inquiry* 5(4): 451-64.

St. Pierre, Elizabeth. 1997. Circling the text: Nomadic writing practices. *Qualitative Inquiry* 3(4): 403-17.

Sumara. Dennis J. 1996. *Private readings in public: Schooling the literary imagination.* New York: Peter Lang.

Taylor, Mark and Esa Saarinen. 1994. *Imagologies.* New York: Routledge.

University of Colorado at Denver School of Education. *Enactivism.* Http://www.cudenver.edu/~mryder/itc /enactivism.html

Varela, Francisco J., Evan Thompson, and Eleanor Rosch. 1991. *The embodied mind: Cognitive science and human experience.* Cambridge, MA: MIT Press.

SECTION ONE

Turning Together on Paths of Awareness

"The Trail Is Not a Trail"

I drove down the freeway
And turned off at an exit
And went along a highway
Til it came to a sideroad
Til it turned to a dirt road
Full of bumps, and stopped.
Walked up a trail
But the trail got rough
And it faded away—
Out in the open,
Everywhere to go.

— Gary Snyder

Turning Together on Paths of Awareness

Risking Flowing Writing Reading

Warren: The writers in this section talk about learning as unfoldment. New worlds of possibility open paths of unexpected entanglements through teaching and learning. In an ecological, dynamic and flowing view of pedagogy our whole body becomes merged in a sensory interplay between us and worlds we are part of, whether visible or invisible, evident or unsaid; underwater or above ground. Our unfolding path is laid in walking as action and knowing become one. We begin to leave behind structured ways of viewing the world, our ordered texts, as we explore "out in the open." Such an unfolding of possibility involves risk since we don't know what the path is or where it will take us.

Brent: Risk is a fundamental quality of lived experience that allows us to enact teaching and learning. Taking risks means that there is still breath in our bodies, that we are capable of participating in the world and therefore capable of engaging with possibility. The question is not whether pedagogy will catch our bodies in active unfoldments of knowing, but *how* it catches them. The chaos and risk that permeate acts of knowing bring opportunities for reconnecting with the world. The underbelly of risk is revelation, an awareness that in education as in life understanding emerges through relationship. Without engagement there is no interstanding. It is our complicity with other bodies that allows us to enact our relationships and therefore our humanity. Inter-play allows us to connect, to linger in conversation, and to re-imagine worlds beyond our own.

Warren: It's interesting you refer to risk and breath. I am mindful of the fact that when I take a risky step I forget to breathe! Recently I was performing dramatic material at a workshop and the audience pointed out at the end that they noticed I hadn't been breathing at all.

Johnna: *Risk*—a word, yet also full of experiencing for me. I think we risk every day and take for granted the risks. However, this brings up the notion of perception of risk. Driving a car down the road at 60 mph is often perceived as an acceptable "risk" in society. However, when someone dies in an avalanche or while mountain climbing, well, this is considered more risky. Risk involves this tension of what is known, practiced, embodied and yet moves us through our actions into the unknown. When we become familiar and "relaxed" with this risk, we remember to breathe. I think it takes a great embodied awareness to breathe and participate, engage and encounter the unknown. Some people's perceptions of risk can move the body in and out of breath, depending on the day, the level of anxiety and the perceived limits/awareness of the day. This happens especially through a practice of doing. Kayaking, mountaineering, skiing over 40 mph down a hill all require a presence of breath, a breathing in. We continue to want to risk so that we experience this embodied awareness. This is the potential we seek, an activity where experiencing breath revitalizes the body, physically tiring us, and yet inspiring fresh rivers of energy tingling throughout the interstices of our human body and worldly bodies.

Brent: How do we allow ourselves to experience risk in ways that honor the infusion of breath into bodies that are at once animate and engaged? In the course of everyday living many of us have come to associate risk-taking with the loss of breath. Have educators become so afraid of pushing the threshold of possibility that the idea of risk alone is enough to

> stop
>
> us
>
> in our tracks?

Or, is the removal of breath simply another way of moving through the world—one that makes us aware of our bodily limitations and therefore mindful of how we engage with risk? A key question for me is: *How do we prepare ourselves for encounters in education and with/in the life world?*

Johnna: Can we as educators help do this, and if so, how? This is my notion of turning points and freefall pedagogy (Haskell 2000) where I believe we can prepare students for unknown wonder—an encountering with the world. There is no one strategy or pedagogical recipe. Another concept that fits with risk and breath is the notion of fear. Are we willing to venture forth anew in the world, into the unfamiliar, embracing the unexpected adventures awaiting through the "chiasm"[1] (Merleau-Ponty 1962) of possibility?

Brent: I wonder, Johnna, how the human body at this level engages with risk? Do our genes experience a sense of energy and redefinition as they interact with one another? What would happen if, as educators, we began to accept risk as an experience, one that reflects our dynamic constitutions as social and biological beings? I think this might allow us to freely engage with other living bodies without the constraints of the rational-analytic mind. I am reminded of David Abram's (1996) embodied stories of engagement with other animals. Elements of risk in these instances are offset by curiosity, possibility, and kinship. Perhaps we lose breath in some encounters because we start to exchange the breath of the other. If the engagement catches our breath, it is vital and alive. Much better this than a lecture or conversation in which we breathe shallowly and fall asleep from lack of interest.

Warren: I recall one instance where I was mindful of an engagement through breathing...

Watching the Cloud Gate Dance Theatre of Taiwan performing *Requiem* in November 1997 in Richmond, British Columbia...

> One woman on the stage, her arms in the air, a skirt that whirls to the music of Franz Liszt's funeral march, tinny sound as from an old record. She twirls on one foot for what must have seemed like ten minutes. Twirls in one direction.
>
> Sitting in the audience, I am very aware of my body, of my reaction. I stare, I gaze, I cannot breathe as I watch in amazement, transfixed by this...this swirling skirt enveloping this woman turning turning...I am barely breathing in and out...

Brent: (body swaying... arms flowing... breath suspended... turning... swaying, singing) As I dance with your words, Warren, I am reminded of another body-moment, another dance that caught my breath:

> I had been invited by a friend, a music therapist, to a variety show, an evening of song and activity that he had organized for residents of a local nursing home to showcase their talent. Several people at the home, including staff, residents, and their families had been invited to watch the unfolding events.
>
> When I arrived I saw all of these individuals—some in chairs, others in wheelchairs or standing with walkers—assembled in a circle around the performance venue. There was an ambiance of hushed silence that one might expect in more formal settings as if something wonderful was about to happen.
>
> And it did.

Shortly after the show started, my friend invited an elderly resident to the center of the floor while the assembled guests looked on. In her youth the resident had been a ballerina. Although those days had long since passed, her body still remembered how to dance. Very slowly, very gingerly, as the music from Le Cygne (The Swan) by Saint-Saëns played, she moved with her dance partner across the floor, turning, twirling, feeling her way from one space-moment to the next. She was now in her eighties; he in his thirties. But the performance was compelling. The intensity of emotion among members of the audience was so great that it seemed to stifle our breaths, to choke our bodies while holding us in awe.

It was as if we were all performing the dance with those on center stage.

Dancing With/in Unfolding Possibilities

Warren: Unfolding possibilities challenge us to explore how we may bring the reader into dances such as these, but on the page.

Brent: When you ask, "How can we as writer/educators bring readers into the dance of life?" my response is that they are already on the dance floor. In his work on the literary imagination, Sumara (1996, ch. 1) notes how reading is embedded in the complex relations of everyday experience. The very possibility of a reader means that we are already embedded as writers in the lives of others: wondering what to say, how to say it, and how our worlds will be received and woven into conversation.

Warren: And, I, as in the twirling dance performance, am no longer separated from the text, but beside it, "becoming part of the texture of its discourse" (Hall 1998, 90).

Brent: I would say "with/in" it rather than "beside" it.

Johnna: Using a slash opens the interrelationship for not only thinking inside, but also outside. Ted Aoki, in a recent talk on interdisciplinarity in education adapted one of Canadian poet, singer and songwriter Leonard Cohen's (1992) lines to refer to the slash as

a crack to let the light in.

I use the slash as a way to open possibilities, to go beyond what we see and let the light open a crack in the dark of the unknown.

Brent: So, what is needed to dance passionately, even playfully? First, we need to trust our bodies; that is, that the texts we create will invite rather than exclude a sense of relationship. We need confidence to dance grace-fully without tripping or falling out of rhythm. Using peripheral vision, we can notice what is happening around us on the dance floor:

> *What is the larger context that shapes our interactions as*
> *dancers?*
> *As readers and writers?*
> *What will be our frame of reference when the music softens and*
> *the faces of the band members start to fade in the background?*

In this shifting environment of movement, sound, and rhythm, we may feel ourselves

slipping

in

and

out

of our bodies. Only after the dance is over might we remember to look down, wipe a sweaty brow, and lament our sore feet.

These are the hallmarks of an engaging encounter. To experience resonance with other moving bodies in time and space—this is the reward for a satis-fying dance in educational discourse and writing as in the jazz hall and ballroom.

Warren: Then you are talking about this encounter as a dance of possibili-ties. Do you know that the roots of the word conversation (con versare) are "to turn together" (Fell, Russell, and Stewart 1994)? So, every conversation is an improvised encounter...

Brent: I am glad that you refer to improvisation. It speaks to how our bod-ies might turn with other bodies. When we refer to encounters in a domain such as education we are talking about knowing/emerging interactively. The encounter may be textual and involve formal language or it may engage other modes of interaction such as music and non-verbal body lan-guage. I am reminded of a wonderful book on this topic by Mary Catherine Bateson, who talks about "life as an improvisatory art, about the ways we combine familiar and unfamiliar components in response to new situations, following an underlying grammar and an evolving aesthetic" (1990, 3). To be a successful educator we need to improvise along the way. When we enter into conversation we may indeed turn together, but we may also fall apart. Until we know the art and skills of improvisation it is difficult to connect with others in ways that respect the fluid, emergent nature of embodied interaction, "meandering its way toward a destination that is not specific, but that will be commonly known" (Davis 1996, 27).

Johnna: So is improvisation enacting? Dancing among bodies, human, animate and inanimate?

Warren: What kind of dancing? Paula Salvio relates how, unlike those who dance simply to win a ballroom dancing competition by miming other people's steps, the actors in Baz Luhrmann's film *Strictly Ballroom* attend to "motion, synergy and the internal and variant rhythms of consciousness" (1997, 248) in their bodies as well as the bodies of those with whom they live/dance. The meandering between and amongst bodies means that we must move beyond purely intellectual understandings of co-experiencing. Feelings must come into play for

> only when we dance in the flow of emotioning of another
> can we experience understanding. Then we are moving in
> the same stream—cognitively flowing together. Other
> metaphors from physics such as "being on the same wave-
> length" or "getting up to speed" also reflect this idea. (Fell,
> Russell, and Stewart 1994)

Brent: One of the important elements in this conversation about writing-as-dance involves an awareness of knowing and its enactment. Often what is perceived as standard academic writing is a form of representation based on assumptions about the ability of an author to glue words on a page and leave them there for posterity.

Johnna: This is a very important question as Abraham Maslow indicates, "Most difficult of all, however, judging by my own inhibitions, will be gradually opening up our journals to papers written in rhapsodic, poetic or free association style" (1962, 204-5). Peak experiences will best be communicated this way, acknowledging the challenge this poses: "The most astute editors would be needed for the terrible job of separating out the scientifically useful from the great flood of trash that would surely come as soon as this door was opened. All I can suggest is a cautious trying out" (p. 205).

Warren: Yes, as educators, we need to begin to look creatively at the stances we embody when we engage with texts. We need to seek out diverse modes of interaction that extend the written, incorporating verbal communication, body language, and other forms of performance. Can we negotiate this tension between the structure of the dance/text and the need to transcend it, using the "variant meanings of motion, space and time to articulate aspects of our identities" (Salvio 1997, 248) as pedagogues? This requires an enactive understanding of language and knowing.

Johnna: We may first want to ask ourselves how we have come to put language together and come to know and use words in education. Can we understand language or is languaging an interstanding?

>Language
>   is often
>   found in the spaces
>
>   the places   of opportunity
>
>that you refer to earlier with   Abram's encounters with animals.

How do we open ourselves to this language? How do we change the ways we think about reading? Do we read to retain—to repeat—to stimulate, or simply to experience? Do we have these expectations going into reading? How can we as editors and writers pre/pare the reader? Again, I don't think (well, for myself) that I have done this well in this book journey. I get stuck in my conceptions of understanding instead of stepping out from under and into the interstanding of poetics or performative or narrative communicating as art.

Brent: This goes back to my comments about improvisation, which is an embodied orientation in the world—a willingness to dance in unfamiliar ways. There is skill as well as art to a performance; that doesn't mean that it needs to be proprietary. Improvisation can be taught if someone is willing to take time and risk to learn.

Johnna: Improvising or enacting—is risking moving/acting through the space of the unknown?

Warren: Della Pollock (1998), in an essay on performative writing, shares the response of a colleague who argues for conventional forms of writing ("the dull and steadfast forms of the academic article and monograph" [p. 76]), which are more accessible and democratic than the experimental writing "because {traditional writing} could be taught" (p. 76). Her colleague points out that because of this, "anyone could contribute to the formation of social knowledge" (p. 76). Pollock argues that her colleague is thus saying we shouldn't take *risks;* we should embrace mediocrity, shirking *challenge, conflict* and *debate.*

Brent: What are we saying about teaching and learning if there is no risk, no conflict, no struggle? What are we saying about the places and authorities of the teacher versus the places and authorities of the learner? I do not dispute the significance of grammar and style. But students need to learn to write for different purposes and different audiences. Since writing is a reflection of our being, I think it is critical that we begin to

S   T   R   E   T   C   H

our engagements with texts as far as possible, recognizing that in any encounter, the dance between structure and form speaks to certain kinds of relationships and commitments that are important to us in the moment.

Johnna: In education, I think we need a balance and to not stretch writing differently for the sake of it but to engage fully in the experience like painting or

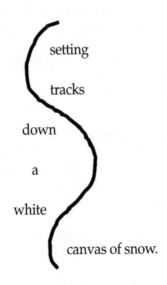

setting

tracks

down

a

white

canvas of snow.

Warren: We are opening up a questioning of the very idea of how and why we write. There is a tension here between form and content that we can play with. Bob Kull, one of the contributors in this book, makes the point that we cannot begin scuba diving without knowing the basics of the skills involved and the dangers one encounters underwater. So, modeling of the skills is required. Bob mentions that the teaching of SCUBA diving skills enables students to be introduced to a new watery world that they can become both part of, and interrelate with. Perhaps experimenting with writing is also a way of opening up other possibilities for awareness. Can performative writing, like diving, enable us to experience the unknown under the waves and render the absent present through evocative languaging?

But if that unknown is beyond language, what, then, is the role of writing?

Johnna: Does it have to have a role? If we have attained some skills with words on the page and I suppose graduated from "school" then can we wander, explore, inquire into the place/spaces of mystery in language, in writing, in experiencing? "It is almost as if by writing [text]...into the world, it exists with words streaming out in long thin cloudy wisps spiraling through the air. I just reach up and touch them as they stream onto the page, flowing, glowing, and knowing what character to write, what action to enact, what thought to evoke" (Haskell 2000, 132).

Warren: Well, this brings us to a big question I have. Do we have to know how to work in a conventional structure, with conventional descriptive writing, before we can venture forth into new worlds of possibilities? A facilitator in Australia, Martin Ringer (1999), writes,

> Once facilitators have a sound grasp of active listening, assertiveness, models of group development, tools for facilitation, they will be in a stronger position to focus on building their capacity to work directly on unconscious, intuitive and systemic aspects of groups. Concurrent focus is fine, but the emergent aspects of groups tend only to fully make sense once the empirical aspects are understood.

This linear approach implies that we cannot improvise or explore out of bounds until we are comfortable within the boundaries of conventional structures. I would disagree. We spend our whole lives living with/in boundaries. The world operates with this dualistic and restrictive system of mind versus body, me versus other, self versus world that the authors in this book are all questioning.

These boundaries that limit possibilities are symbolized in an exercise I do at the beginning of a drama workshop whereby participants are asked to connect

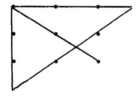

nine dots with four lines without
lifting their pencil off the paper. The
only way this can be done is to go
outside the box formed by the dots.

Brent: In my roles as an educational researcher and elementary teacher, I am beginning to question more deeply what we mean by *structure* and *boundary*. I don't read these as closed systems but rather as constellations of being and possibility arising through the world in particular ways. I don't think that it is possible to exist without boundary or structure.

Whether I become a concert pianist because I have learned the theory and skills of my art or because I have a wonderful ear for music that allows me to write concertos before I have acquired these skills—both orientations speak to different kinds of structure. We need to challenge conventional understandings of structure and see them as dynamic bodies of experience with fluid boundaries. What is more problematic for me is Ringer's use of the word "empirical," which suggests a particularly scientific reading of the world.

Johnna: Are boundaries then skills? Can we exist with/out them or do we just perceive that we must have boundaries and structures? Maybe boundaries are sites of tension or interactions rather than "things we must achieve or acquire."

How does drama, dancing, diving, or mountain climbing unfold new paths of awareness?

Warren: I recently facilitated a group of teachers using some fairly simple drama exercises that led to dramatic and emotional encounters. This is probably what I mean when I talk about this work as "risky business," leaving certainty behind. Though a drama workshop is not the same as diving underwater, it is also not so different. Risks are involved, risks that unexpectedly merge with our emotions and fears.

For example, I would never ever go SCUBA diving. (I think this fear comes from watching the '60s TV program *Sea Hunt* and remembering watching shows with horrible stories of what happens when a diver gets "the bends.") I imagine there are SCUBA divers who would be scared to perform on stage. But I have (and would again) climb mountains and walk across glaciers. I remember getting up at 4 A.M. to climb my first mountain on a climbing course.

Memories of Fear, of Anticipation.

Feelings of Impending Danger.

Questioning Why I Was (Going) Up There.

These are similar feelings that I have had before I begin leading a drama workshop.

Entering into the unknown.

Diving in...

or Climbing Up.

Johnna: We may need to ask, "Is the risk of summiting Mt. Everest worth the yearning to seek our potential?" As the mountain climber Anatoli Boukreev says,

> I would like to believe that the roads we choose depend less on economic problems or political battles or the imperfections of our external world, and more on our internal calling, which compels us to go anew into the mountains, to the heights beyond the clouds, making our way to the summits. The sparkling summits and the fathomless sky above our heads, with their grandeur and mysterious beauty, will always draw humanity, which loves all that is beautiful. This was, is and will be the magnetic strength of the mountains, independent of the worldly, trivial vanities and fusses, beyond which, at times, we cannot see the real, the beautiful and the eternal. (Gammelgaard 1999, 207)

Warren: The same would apply to teaching and learning—and, perhaps our challenges in writing about them.

This is vividly illustrated by the four chapters in this section. All of the authors are working in risky areas, be it in preparing people to dive, or simply in teaching a class. John Ippolito undertook what was for him a simple inquiry, but one where *subjects'* responses to the process of inquiry led to insights about the nature of research and the role of the researcher. Marylin Low and Maria McKay taught ESL and encountered surprising responses from their students. Bob Kull, aware of the delights of the underwater, prepares his students through embodied modeling. My own writing of the drama process illustrates the improvised nature of emerging worlds through drama facilitation.

Recently I began writing about a drama exercise in which I participated over fifteen years ago. It all came back to me. Suddenly, as I was writing, I found myself back in my childhood, in a playground game that had a lot of aggression. The embodied experience of the drama exercise conducted in a safe workshop environment became, through my writing, an embodied memory of me evading capture on the elementary school playground. How could I have known that that would happen through my writing? I only realized this was happening when I felt my sweaty palms on the computer keyboard and my emotional reaction as I wrote (and read) those words.

Johnna: I think most of my narrative writing is feeling this. In poetry it can be as well, as if...words express this intense embodied emotion. Does the reader feel this in the writing? How do we bring this into text?

Warren: One way of conceiving of this laying down a path is in the storying of our experience. As David Abram says, "Stories, like rhymed poems or songs, readily incorporate themselves into our felt experience; the shifts of action echo and resonate our own encounters—in hearing or telling the story we vicariously *live* it, and the travails of its characters embed themselves into our own flesh" (1996, 120).

Johnna: Yes, I just couldn't have said it better. I feel as though I am there not in reflection but in reliving, re-experiencing and feeling the words sound off my tongue—rolling off in sweet cadence and shifts of cadence to a music that only my ears hear. Is my body there or is it here? This reminds me of *The Matrix* (Wachowski 1999), which explores a computer-generated place that people lived in with their minds, a virtual world of perceiving a body but using only the mind. So what really is perception—what we see or the body "sees"?

Warren: The writers in this section interpret their experiences through their stories and, as we read these, we are interpreting our experiences along with them. Hence, as David Loy (1993, 481) says, "Texts never attain self-presence, and that includes the text that constitutes me." He asks us, "What would happen if this claim was extrapolated into claims about the whole universe?" Textuality (literally, "that which is woven, web") thus carries us beyond language. It means that what we write and how we write it move beyond the insights and interpretations of a particular writer towards writing as being nothing less than part of *the interdependent,*

Johnna: you mean, *interplay with/in...*

Warren: web of life

Everywhere we go.

Note

1. "Chiasm is the interaction that occurs in...(for example)...genetic crossing over and that of the chiasma of the optic nerves. Barbara McClintock, a Nobel Prize winner and geneticist working with corn discovered 'jumping genes' where genetic elements actually exchanged places with other chromosomes during cell division. This intermingling of chromatid material during cell division is a rather complex process that biologists are still trying to understand. The interaction among chromosomes is much like interactions during kayaking, breathing, and experiencing" (Haskell 2000, xi).

References

Abram, David. 1996. *The spell of the sensuous: Perception and language in a more-than-human world.* New York: Pantheon Books.

Bateson, Mary Catherine. 1990. *Composing a life.* New York: Plume.

Cohen, Leonard. 1992. Anthem. http://www.leonardcohen.com/anthem.html.

Davis, Brent. 1996. *Teaching mathematics: Toward a sound alternative.* New York: Garland.

Fell, Lloyd, David Russell, and Alan Stewart, eds. 1994. *Seized by agreement, swamped by understanding.* http://www.pnc.com.au/~lfell/book.html.

Gammelgaard, Lene. 1999. *Climbing high: A woman's account of surviving the Everest tragedy.* Seattle, WA: Seal Press.

Hall, John. 1998. Missing persons: Personal pronouns in performance writing. *Performance Research* 3(1): 87-90.

Haskell, Johnna. 2000. Experiencing freefall: A journey of pedagogical possibilities. Ph.D. diss., University of British Columbia.

Loy, David. 1993. Indra's post-modern net. *Philosophy East and West* 43(3): 481-510.

Maslow, Abraham. 1962. *Toward a psychology of being.* Princeton, NJ: D. Van Nostrand.

Merleau-Ponty, Maurice. 1962. *Phenomenology of perception.* Translated by Colin Smith. London: Routledge and Kegan Paul.

Pollock, Della. 1998. Performing writing. In *The ends of performance,* edited by Peggy Phelan and Jill Lane. New York: New York University Press.

Ringer, Martin. 1999. The facile-itation of facilitation? Searching for competencies in group work leadership. *Scisco Conscientia* 2(1): 1-19. http://members.xoom.com/experientia/V2N1.htm.

Salvio, Paula. 1997. On keying pedagogy as an interpretative event. In *Action research as a living practice,* edited by Terrance R. Carson and Dennis Sumara. New York: Peter Lang.

Snyder, Gary. 1986. *Left out in the rain: New poems 1947-1985.* San Francisco: North Point Press.

Sumara, Dennis. 1996. *Private readings in public: Schooling the literary imagination.* New York: Peter Lang.

Wachowski, Andy, and Larry Wachowski, dirs. 1999. *The Matrix.* Los Angeles: Warner Brothers. Film.

Wo/a ndering through a Hall of Mirrors...
A Meander through Drama Facilitation

Warren Linds

WARREN LINDS, a popular theatre facilitator living in Regina, Saskatchewan, Canada, has been working in popular theatre and community education for the past twenty years. He is a doctoral candidate in Language and Literacy Education at the University of British Columbia in Vancouver, British Columbia, Canada, where his research is on the facilitation and development of transformative drama processes through a performative writing and research methodology.

Abstract. In this performative writing I explore the phenomena of my experiences facilitating improvised drama. Through the interplay between enactive conceptions of knowing and bodymind as an integration of feeling thought action, I contemplate my experiences interacting (Dreyfus and Dreyfus 1999) with the living/lived experiences of the participants. This is a process which Varela et al. (1991) have described as "letting go," unlearning the habits of mindlessness, and beginning to pay attention to what I am thinking/ feeling/doing in the moment of (inter)action with others. In this way the sensing, and sensuous, experiences I have as an improvising facilitator may help others learn about the pedagogical possibilities of thinking/doing "educational" facilitation.

Keywords. Drama, Embodied Action, Enactive Learning, Performance, Teaching as Improvisation.

Acknowledgments. I thank my co-supervisors Jan Selman, Department of Drama, University of Alberta and Dr. Carl Leggo, Department of Language and Literacy Education, UBC for their support and encouragement of this performative inquiry. Gratitude also goes to all the participants and facilitators who have shared with me their skills, dreams and challenges through drama workshops and performances. I gratefully acknowledge the receipt of financial support for this work from an Izaak Walton Killam Memorial Predoctoral Fellowship.

Wo/a ndering through a Hall of Mirrors... A Meander through Drama Facilitation[1]

Warren Linds

Wandering Arrivals

> A hall of mirrors, a passage way in which (two things) not only reflect one another and get confused in the multiple reflexivity, but in which reality and illusion often co-mingle. (Brougher 1996, 14)

I have been facilitating workshops based on Theatre of the Oppressed (Boal 1979) for the past fourteen years. Theatre of the Oppressed (TO) is a popular theatre approach which proposes that knowledge emerging aesthetically through a series of theatre exercises and games is already in itself the beginning of a transformation.

At the beginning of every drama workshop there is a space...a space of possibilities. I enter this space initiating action but from that moment forward I (inter) play with others in that space....

It is the opening series of presentations at the Bodymind Conference in Vancouver, British Columbia in May 1999. I decide to begin the session with a series of warm-up (or tuning-up [Johnston 1998, 116]) exercises that will enable the group to begin to find their collective rhythm.

I ask everyone to walk around randomly,
Pay attention to the ways your

feet hit the floor, your
bodies move in the space, your
thoughts, your
> *breathing,*

Become aware of others around you, then
greet them with eyes,
> *face,*
>> *body,*
> *Shake hands,*
>> *Talk to each other,*

As partners for further exercises.

One inter-action flows into another as I sense their readiness to play.

Things are moving (in both senses of the word) but,
What about me?

I begin in a static position, eager to see the activity commence. I—confident, but giving directions in Instructional Mode.... As I guide the group I find myself walking with them in their randomness...paying attention to what they are doing, but also becoming aware of MY body, MY breath, MY place in this space of being and interbeing. I am the sole voice in this room, but this voice is calmly moving alongside the rhythm of the walking around me...a resonating process of entrainment (Nachmanovitch 1990, 97) where my words weave in and around their movements. Yet at the same time, I am aware of time pressures and the need to move on.

I press on letting the movements of the dozen or so people dictate the rhythm of my suggestions. I am consumed by the meandering, and also observing its consumption.

> *Wandering   and   Wondering...*

As improvised dramatic creation Theatre of the Oppressed investigates relationships and embraces and recognizes the tacit and implicit knowledge that emerges in the performance process. This knowing is expressed in the interplay between our lives and the stories of our lives that is opened up by participants through the drama process. In this way drama is an enactive process where "every reflection brings forth a world" (Maturana and Varela 1992, 26).

Inspired by Merleau-Ponty's (1962) concepts of embodied action, an enactive[2] approach means that knowledge does not develop only in minds, but emerges collectively through engagement in joint and shared action. I will explore in this essay the interplay between my learning

enactively,

> where I am part of a particular series of improvised dramatic experiences which are shaped by, and unfold in, the drama workshop environment I work in;

> and through

> > *embodied knowing,*

> where my learning depends upon having a bodymind[3] actively attuned in the world.

(Inter)actively...I will explore the interplay between sensing, and sentient, experiences I have as an improvising living learning facilitator.

Meandering...in the spaces between and amongst these mirrors, experiences will reflect and refract as we encounter them from different perspectives.

Reflecting, Refracting, Responding...Through this I hope we can learn about the pedagogical possibilities of thinking/doing "educational" facilitation.

I lay down the flowing passageways between mirrors; as I uncertainly peek around a corner, I come face to face with my new perceptions. The refracted (from Latin *refractus*, broken up) experiences I have depend on my angle of view. I engage with my (e)motion as I discover through writing/dramatic improvisation...

Improvisation is a process in which experiences arise through focused physical explorations of stories and themes. The heart of improvisation is the free (inter)play of consciousness and action as situations emerge from our body-mind for further exploration. Through facilitation of dramatic exercises by "side-coaching" (providing ideas for focus or concentration) I enable participants to become conscious of their moment-to-moment thoughts, sensations, emotions, actions, feelings and fantasies. They observe where they place their focus, how they react to the context they are part of and examine who they are and how they (inter)act. Because this happens collectively, those other stimuli include other human and non-human parts of the workshop environment.

I am a learner in the workshop environment. Although I am facilitator, I am co-implicated and co-evolving alongside the other participants in the process. I shape the process and the process shapes me in a circular exchange. Facilitating learning becomes a continuous tinkering (Sumara and Davis 1997) with what is going on around me. So as facilitator I must improvise in an *encounter* of spontaneous creativity, which is "extemporaneous, unstructured, unplanned, unrehearsed...in the moment," in the here, "in the now," and "in becoming" (Moreno 1960, 15-16), dealing with always fresh experiences.

As pragmatic inquiry, the practices involved will help me transform my own drama facilitation experience. As I respond to the situations I am working in, I skillfully cope (Dreyfus and Dreyfus 1999) with the living/lived experiences of the participants. This is a process which Varela et al. (1991) have described as "letting go," unlearning the habits of mindlessness, and beginning to pay attention to what I am thinkingfeelingdoing in the moment of (inter)action with others.

Danish physicist Niels Bohr has written, "Whatever I say should not be taken as an assertion but as a question." In the same manner, this inquiry is an effort to raise more questions for me (than I started with), to transform my own practice in doing this and thus enable other practitioners to see the possibilities that emerge from mindful, open-ended reflection on embodied and enactive facilitation/teaching practices.

Mirrors, Mirrors Everywhere...

mirror n. (from Latin *mirari*, to wonder at)

Our senses suffer as a result of the overwhelming stimuli in our world. We start to feel little of what we touch, listen to little of what we hear, see little of what we look at. We adapt to what we need to do at any particular moment but we don't fully use our entire body. Augusto Boal in his Arsenal of Theatre of the Oppressed (1992) has codified a series of awareness exercises in order to rekindle our sensitivity to our senses. The first principle he articulates is that the human being is a unity, an indivisible whole. Ideas, emotions, sensations and actions are interwoven. A bodily movement is a thought and a thought expresses itself through the body. All ideas, all mental images, all emotions reveal themselves through the body.

The second principle is that the five senses are linked. We breathe with our whole body. We sing with our whole body, not just our vocal chords. One example is chess. Good chess players do physical training before a match because they know the whole body thinks, not just the brain. This training enables them to respond intuitively to situations on the chessboard as they come along (Dreyfus and Dreyfus 1999).

Theatre requires us to be in the moment. In order to achieve this, we need to re-sensitize, we need to awaken the memory of our senses, to re-connect with these senses, these muscles and this body. The body begins to speak through sound and movement. The facilitator helps in this process, enabling full participation with all our senses. Journeying through these exercises we begin to see elements of the flow of facilitation through a synaesthesia, a fusion of the senses (Abram 1997) as rhythm and movement sensitizes us to, among others, our eyes and ears.

A series of mirror exercises[4] incorporates one such exploration...

I have started the group in a rhythm of movement, introducing them to feeling their bodies in this space of this room, walking automatically around the room. Then becoming aware of each other in the room, greeting first with the eyes,
then the face,
then the full body, then a warm handshake.

Non-verbal, then verbal conversations, a delicate dance of dialoging.[5]

A flow from body in space through body in social space.
Gradually a community is being formed.

Partners now, mirroring each other's movement of greeting.
One leads, the other follows. Slow movements of rhythmic dance.
I lead, the group follows me. Paying attention to each other.

Then switch. The other leads, the other follows.

I watch them work in slow moving spirals. Some move around the room. Hands mov-

ing rhythmically, bodies moving towards the floor...Up to the ceiling...Yes, they are now caught up in the dance of possibilities.

Now, the critical moment...I cry out, "Unify." No/Every one leads; every/no one follows. Who leads, who follows?

What is the feeling of facilitating/being facilitated by the group? Where is the start/Where is the end? Slow motion rhythms, spiraling one into the other.

> Each partner has the right to do any movement he wants, together with the duty to reproduce movements made by his partner.... The key to the exercise is synchronization and fidelity of reproduction. (Boal 1992, 122)

There is a graceful flow in the room. *Synchronization and fidelity of reproduction.* The tension between the freedom to move and a structure provided by an exercise that begins and ends. I provide suggestions for focus of explorations but ultimately the group is free in its movements. Yet, there are not all curves and sweeps of the arms and legs. One couple finds its own freedom through using jerky motions to create machine-like movement.

In this (inter)play of bodies where actions flow one into the other, a synthesis of senses surfaces.... I as facilitator must become attuned to this intertwining and, at the same time, respond to it as the flow of my energy (e)merges in a fully sensed (inter)action with others.

I follow the group's actions. My voice takes on a rhythm of the mirroring going on in the room. Partners working together in a slow Cadence. I move slowly around the room... Watching...Listening...Participating. The group leads...I follow...I make a suggestion... some follow...others are in their own space of possibility flowing one with the other...

Unveiling the Flow of "Feeling-thought"

Last year I guided a group through a mural-making exercise. One preliminary exercise involved participants speaking only numbers as they walked around the room interacting with each other. Playing with emotion and feeling and communicating through the numbers. A harsh six...A soft o...n...e. Explore which number fits which feeling... Which consonants, which vowels express power, anger...I felt the power of the feeling in the room, sometimes as though I was watching a performance, sometimes feeling a part of everything as I make a suggestion and a ripple of actions and emotions moves through the room as we interplay in a kind of secret complicity between us. I was amazed at the effect and the seriousness and tension in the room. Excited, in fact, but also very aware of feeling fear of the intensity of the work and responsibility for it, too. Where to go with it, what next? And envy I couldn't be "playing" in the midst of it...

I offer suggestions for actions as I guide the group. Not only do these actions bring forth an awareness of feelings in the group, they also bring me into contact with my own senses as the ripples of group action echo back to me. These senses are "translated" into each other, or at least understood in terms of the other senses, as a unity provided by the body (Merleau-Ponty 1962). The visual resonates with the sayable; the light is capable of eliciting a tactile response; hearing can be visualized. Senses combine their effects with each other. Each sense meshes with the other "sensory worlds."

I hear the sounds of the numbers and, simultaneously, see their effect. And, in a split second, I respond intuitively with new suggestions for focus as I swim in the flow of interaction between my instructions and their actions. In those moments I feel a part of the integrated BodyMindSpirit...

What is this idea of BodyMindSpirit? An integration of the senses, including thought as a sense (I think of the expression "making sense of something"). As Levinas (1996, 41) points out,

> to perceive is both to receive and to express, by a sort of pro-lepsis.[6] We know through gestures how to imitate the visible and to coincide kinaesthetically with the gesture seen; in perception our body is also the delegate of being.

This kinaesthetic sense (what Clive Barker [1977, 29] calls *body think*) means that sensing and being sensed do not happen separately; they function and flourish in bodies of interaction, flowing (Csikszentmihalyi 1997) together. Flow is "autoletic," that is, it seems to need no goals or reward. Action and my awareness of it are experienced as one. To flow is its own reward...

Sometimes feeling a part of everything, I watch my suggestions ripple through the room. Actions and emotions intertwine in a kind of secret complicity between us. I hear numbers and at the same time see the feelings/feel the seeing of the numbering...

Wasn't I also playing in the vortex of this flowing interplay?

"And envy I couldn't be 'playing' in the midst of it?"

Feeling left out of the intensity because of my role leading this...being in a rotating center yet not in the spinning, flowing spiral around me.

Flow is movement in which one action blends into another according to an inner logic which seems to need no conscious intervention on our part: we experience it as a unified flowing from one moment to the next, in which our actions and responses become one. There is little distinction between self and others, between stimulus and response, or between past, present and future.

Csikszentmihalyi (1997) sees this type of flow as a common, though by no means inevitable, experience arising when people act with total involvement, whether in play or sport, in the creative experiences in art and literature, or in religious experiences. Within a dramatic process, each interaction presents new challenges, demanding new skills.

My "self," who is ordinarily the broker between my actions and another, simply becomes irrelevant. As facilitator I often find myself in synchronization with my (inter)actions and environment. I usually don't know it when "flowing" but on reflection "in tranquility," I begin to realize in these situations that my skills were perfectly matched to the demands made upon me. But I am not reflecting on these experiences as a detached observer looking for guiding principles. In writing this I am fully engaged in feeling again those "gripping, holistic experiences" (Dreyfus and Dreyfus 1990, 242) that have become the basis for new learning.

Through improvisation we synchronize our bodies. Interacting with our Mirror. Encountering moments of resistance. Pausing…Waiting for our partner to slowly move…Tuning into each other's eyes, bodies…the rhythms of motion in space.

    Synchronization   *Oscillation*

So I continue to dive into those spaces of oscillating interactions between and amongst individual bodyminds…

Last year I was facilitating a guided visualization in a teacher education class in drama in education at the university. I was very nervous at first and it showed in my rhythms and in the words that came out. My words became a list of actions I was asking THEM to do.

It was funny…. I said before we began, we're going to do a visualization. The participants immediately all found a comfortable spot, closed their eyes and were ready for me. But I wasn't ready for them…. I hadn't found a comfortable spot nor closed my eyes.

Aoki (1991, 185-86) asks us to reflect on how enchanted we are with the eye:

> Could it be that the time is right for us to allow sonare [to hear] to dwell juxtaposedly with videre [to see]?…Might we offer ourselves to listen to [the earth's] soundings and resoundings, to the tone of sound, perhaps even to the tone of silence, which some say is the mother of sound?

As I gradually got into the experience, into the flow of words, I could feel my body relax, my eyes close, my directions change from being

closed
    ("breathe through all your muscles," you are in "such and such a place")
to

opened

("you look up and you see...")

and even more pauses and silences. Freeing of my voice, a freeing that was a slowing of the momentum...

I wasn't trying to finish one part of the visualization to move on to another, but now in the moment(s) of my own visualization process...seeing, hearing and feeling the words I am speaking. I speak the words.... I feel the wind as I fly high above a river watching the rocks below.

Afterwards the participants commented I had talked too much for the first half of the process, so that my words were interfering with their processes of exploration. They underlined that they could sense my nervousness and also sense when I was in tune with them, when there was a noticeable relaxation and freeing of my voice, a freeing that was a slowing of the momentum...no longer was I trying to finish one part of the visualization to move on to another, but now in the moment(s) of my own visualization process.

I had had a whole plan that the visualization fit into...I wanted to get to the heart of the plan. This hampered my presence in the process. Only when I let go of the plan and concentrated on the moment was I able to be present with the others.

So, closing my eyes, playing with the words as poetic form and rhythm and leaving behind the questioning judging mind helped...

The ethnographer Unni Wikan's own work in Oman, a place where she found people treasure silence, called her to rethink her ethnographic work:

> I gave into the silence, and suddenly I tuned in to a lot that was happening between people. To experience silence not as a void or an absence but as a space full and pregnant with meaning is difficult for a word-mongering academic. (1992, 470)

Being forced to live with silence, Wikan learned to tune into her momentary connections with the Omani. Embodied knowing occurred through experiential knowing in-action, where there was a momentary, but full, encounter with other worlds, perceptions and experiences. What resulted was a feeling similar to how Ted Aoki (1991, 183-84) reports figure skater Brian Orser knows

> resonance with the surface of the ice, with the music and with the spectators [so-called]...Such a knowing known bodily seems vastly different from rational knowing that knows action only derivatively as application...He is calling for an attunement such that thinking and acting simultaneously inhabit his body.

I think of that similar tension I felt when I started that dramatic exercise, and then tuning my rhythm of side-coaching suggestions, watching and feeling...

So, closing my eyes, playing with the words as poetic form and rhythm and leaving behind the questioning judging mind helped...opening myself in all my senses to the experience I was part of in that room...listening and feeling those resonances between my sensing/sentient body and the others...

Resonance, Re-sounding...Wikan also did research in Bali, in which she says the Balinese don't split feeling from thought but regard it as part of

> one process, keneh, which I translate as "feeling-thought."
> "Can anyone think but with the heart?" they ask rhetorically.
> Thus resonance is a way of reaching for that hither side of
> words, attending to the concerns and intentions from which
> they emanate. (1992, 463)

A Balinese philosopher-teacher told her she must create resonance through "feelingthought" in herself with the people and the problems she sought to understand. Resonance "requires you to apply feeling as well as thought. Indeed, feeling is the more essential, for without feeling we'll remain entangled in illusion" (p. 463).

How is this cultivated? Partly through engagement with the Other, which conveys meanings that reside neither in words nor texts but evolve in an encounter in a constantly moving shared space.

> We need not have the "same" experience to be able to attend in
> the same way. But we must dip into the wellsprings of our-
> selves for something to use as a bridge to others. It does not
> come by an act of will, though will helps. Practical exposure to
> a world of "urgency, necessity" is required. (p. 471)

This engagement does happen in drama workshop facilitation, although at times, I am not aware of it when it occurs. It requires some form of being in an embodied and flowing experience myself as facilitator just as I might have had as a "facilitated participant" in other drama workshop experiences. Thus facilitation becomes an embodied dialogue between and amongst the artist-participants-facilitator.

Sensing/Being Sensed through the Looking Glasses

> In *Fill the Space* the actors must walk around very quickly trying
> to ensure that their own bodies are always more or less equidis-
> tant from everyone else's, and they all spread out over the

whole room. From time to time, the leader yells "Stop!" and everyone must come to a halt—it should be possible to see an empty space in the room. Whenever one sees an empty space, they go and fill it with their body, but they can't stay there, so a moment later it is empty again, except that someone comes to fill it, but they can't stop there either...(Boal 1992, 116)

As an artist I engage in a facilitated process of dramatic creation that is filled with such rapidly evolving uncertainties. As in this exercise, facilitation is a dialogical and social process. Things happen spontaneously as people play and inter-play with each other, finding and filling spaces for dialogue and interaction. We don't know where the spaces will open up. We jump into these uncertainties whenever they appear. This intertwining of subjectivity, context and meaning in facilitating theatre is illustrated in this evocative metaphor:

To draw a carp, Chinese masters warn, it is not enough to know the animal's morphology, study its anatomy or under-stand the physiological functions of its existence. They tell us that it is also necessary to consider the reed against which the carp brushes each morning while seeking its nourishment, the oblong stone behind which it conceals itself, and the rippling of water when it springs toward the surface. These elements should in no way be treated as the fish's environment, the milieu in which it evolves or the natural background against which it can be drawn. They belong to the carp itself...The carp must be apprehended as a certain power to affect and be affected by the world. (Morley 1992, 183)

This metaphor captures nicely the sense of what Varela et al. (1991) call struc-tured coupling in a co-emerging of world and entity. One does not exist with-out the other as organism and environment enfold into each other and unfold from one another in the fundamental circularity that is life itself (Varela et al. 1991).

Similarly, I as the drama facilitator work in/am part of a series of constantly shifting spaces that emerge from the interplay between my suggestions and what the participants do. These spaces are much like an ecotone (Booth 1998), a term used in botany and ecology to designate the transition zone between plant communities such as marshland and better-drained ground. "Tone" is a Greek term that means stress, as in maintaining muscle tone. Ecotones are places where the interplay of resources and nutrients generate rich possibilities for living, of habitat where knowing might emerge. These overlapping places of my experience and those of others are places of complexity and dynamism. In this process,

human intelligence and the given cosmos are engaged in a
co-creative dance, so that what emerges as reality is the fruit of
interaction between a given cosmos and the way Mind[7]
engages with it. We actively participate in the cosmos and it is
through this participation that we meet what is Other.
Participation between sensing body and other bodily beings.
(Heron and Reason 1997)

That sensing body is also being sensed. We need to make "sense" of what this
means for facilitation.

Our bodies are multi-sensory, not only in sensing the world but also in being
sensed by the world. This fundamental gap of being is illustrated by the concept of the double sensation (Merleau-Ponty 1962).

Just think of it. My right hand is touching my left hand, yet the left hand is
also touching the right hand at the same time. Between touching and being
touched, seeing and being seen, there is reversibility. My left hand has the sensations of being both object and subject of the touch as well as the interaction
between the two. At least in the case of the feeling of touch, the subject is
implicated in its objects and its objects are constitutive of the subject. Between
feeling and being felt is a gulf spanned by the indeterminate and reversible
phenomenon of the being touched and of the touching; the ambiguity which
entails each hand is in the position of being both perceiver and perceived.

Other senses also illustrate this. I never hear myself as I hear others. Seeing
entails having a body that is itself capable of being visible. This is the fundamental basis of the mirror exercise I described earlier, where we begin with
one person leading the other, then the other leads the first, then I may give the
direction "unify" and there is no leader and they work together. The mirror
shifts...At that moment of transition to "no/every one leading" is a moment of
movement to unspoken unity. This is the space where interaction flows as the
reversibility is always "just about happening." There is always a slippage, a
transformation as the interacting bodies bring to the world the capacity to turn
the world back onto itself,

> to fold it over itself and the world, introducing that fold in
> which the subject is positioned as a perceiving, perspectiv[e]
> mobility. (Grosz 1994, 102)

The human body thus is both perceived in a world as well as a perceiver in the
world doubling back on itself. With "I" and the "other" perception each is
implicated in and necessary for the existence of the other. They are indelibly
etched one into the other, open to each other, coupled in sensing/sensed bodies and world.

The Flowing Encounters of Facilitation

In the everyday coping activity of a drama process, I as facilitator am not standing back from some independent product and then observing it. We are in a much tighter relationship, as (inter)acting is experienced as a steady flow of skillful activity in response to my own sense of the situation. I continually adapt to the situation in an embodied way. As Merleau-Ponty (1962, 153) puts it,

> whether a system of motor or perceptual powers, our body is not an object for an "I think"; it is a grouping of lived-through meanings which moves towards its equilibrium.

I don't think about what I want to do but, rather, experience the situation and that experience draws my "doing" out. Those experiences build up one upon the other and I draw on them the next time a similar situation occurs. This is a common phenomenon in artistic creation. For example, the process of

> painting is an intimately communicative affair between the painter and (their) painting, a conversation back and forth, the painting telling the painter even as it receives its shape and form. (Schon and Rein 1994, 167)

An artistic process involves a simultaneous process of making (I do) while also reflecting on that intuitive making in the process of developing form (I observe). The resulting form is often the only evidence of the intuitive understandings that occur during the development process. Implied in those interpretations are my judgment and standards as to what has worked or not, and choosing processes for the next stage.

As the potter Ellen Schon (1998) points out,

> I try to push myself to be open to the reflective process in order to be more responsive to what the material/situation is telling me so that I don't impose my tools and ideas on the material in a mismatched way.

This is a description of skillful mindfulness (Varela et al. 1991) or spontaneous coping (Dreyfus and Dreyfus 1999) responding to the needs of a particular situation. Whatever part of the workshop process I'm in, each part of the process informs and is integrated into the other. And other experiences I have had emerge through a reciprocal process, full of surprises and accidents (unintentional results to be noticed and made use of the next time or not). There may be no clear end point to the process. This uncertainty is typical in my work.

Ellen Schon works with clay. A successful form results from an artist such as she being able to "regard the wood or the metal as a living thing with needs and feelings of its own and to let the material direct them as much as they direct it" (Schon 1964, 127).

An example of this is in my facilitating with people as "intelligent clay,"[8] using images as part of drama workshops. Either form of clay is not static. In potter's clay each form is part of a series or family of forms that are different but related. The difference from the potter is, of course, that I am working with thinkingfeelingacting clay where each person's dramatic telling of a story through image changes in terms of emotion, feeling, thought or action, depending on when and how it is told and by whom. I react to these non-verbal, kinesthetic images that I see in front of me.... It speaks to me, I feel something and I respond by asking questions of those inside it or making suggestions for further exploration within that image. Quick and spontaneous transformations occur in these interactions as the invisible is made visible. Time and space, people and relationships all unfold, are condensed, and changed. Memory and imagination become engaged in an interplay as we become engaged in a conversation, an *encounter* of togetherness where we are "communicating with each other in a primary, intuitive manner by speech or gesture...becoming one—*una cum uno*" (Moreno 1960, 15).

Many images are produced and erased and called up again perhaps another day. Participants begin to "remember" these images, their bodies in interaction with each other, the stories and feelings recalled. In the same way, I remember these encounters, but that memory is not in thought; it is embodied memory of all the feelings I had at that moment. These memories call up a set of actions I have had in the past to these varied situations. This is a form of structured method, with certain thematic or physical boundaries—and improvisation— where many things interact and change at once. Structure becomes co-depen-dent with the freedom to experiment...and to venture into places where there is no flow.

In this context, facilitation can be seen as a constant improvisation in which each person becomes a spontaneous actor, writer, audience member, director, and critic. This is in contrast to a master plan, with preordained roles according to some script. Mis-takes, mis-cues, and forgotten lines are part of the play of "per-severing and bringing our desires to fruition" (Nachmanovitch 1990, 12).

Wondering Still...

Relationship is the mirror in which one can see oneself as one is.... [It] can help people to observe, listen, be attentive and alert and to understand one another. (Rahnema 1990, 218)

Our bodies speak from experience if we listen to them. I continue to learn facil-itation through opening up my senses to, and being sensed through, the rela-tionships that emerge in both taking and leading workshops. Such connections are made bodily through experiencing the process itself. We then use what we have lived through to open up possibilities for interpreting and understanding new experiences. We become listeners in the drama experience as we begin to know and understand through intuition and introspection. In this way, by going through similar experiences we might listen better to the experiences of others (Howard 1996).

Using "experiences" rather than words has implications for learning to become an expert facilitator. Dreyfus maintains that the

> teachers of a skill are frequently articulate dispensers of help-
> ful facts, procedures and principles. As such, they may hasten
> the student's progress from novice to advanced beginner to
> competent performer. But if, like expert systems, all they
> know are facts and rules of inference, such teachers cannot
> possibly be successful doers or guides on the way to expertise.
> (Dreyfus and Dreyfus 1986, 201)

How can I move beyond "facts" and "rules of inference" to intuitive action based on common sense, wisdom, and mature judgment? I move within the space/time of my working not as a detached observer but as someone implicated in a spell of involvement in the here and now. In this way, skills aren't something I just turn to, but experience the enactment of drama as the drawing of movements out of me (Dreyfus 1999, 15).

So how can this be applied in learning to know sensing/sensed facilitation? The tools are present in the Theatre of the Oppressed workshop process. There we rediscover our senses through exercises that enable us to feel what we touch (walks, massages, gravity); "see what we look at" (images, the memory and integration of the senses, object games); "listen to what we hear" (sounds, melody, rhythm, breathing internal rhythms)...There are over two hundred exercises of the first three alone in *Games* (Boal 1992).

I have been engaged in facilitation of learning for at least twenty years. Though some of that time didn't involve theatre work, I recognize how a variety of situations to which I responded provided a set of skills. These situations as seen from the same perspective as facilitator, each requiring different tactical decisions, enabled me to adapt what has worked in the past.

In the continuing development of my own expertise in this work, this will mean not to develop new exercises, but to enhance and accentuate in situated practice these aspects that are already present in the exercises. It will mean me continuing to experience these exercises from constantly shifting perspectives as I explore the hall of mirrors. At one point I am facilitator. At another point a participant. Just as in the Hall of Mirrors I turn a corner and see myself at another angle, experiencing the spontaneous surprise of recognition in an embodied way, shifting in the flowing process of interplay between other human mirrors. For example,

In May 1997 I was part of a workshop in Seattle, Washington, with Augusto Boal. I was there as participant, engaged in the activities, but part of my mind was evaluating where I might take these exercises and adaptations I might make. This "reflective" stance as participant enabled me to notice things that were happening to me.

We engaged in an exercise called Brown's Blank Character. My partner was to become a "blank character" and I was to choose an oppressor, someone in my experience who had power over me and become that person. She would create her "oppressed" character in reacting to me.

But I tried an experiment. I didn't have a clear idea of who my "oppressor" was so I watched her reaction to the little I did know and we fed off each other as I watched her and she watched me. A conversation was created in a flow from just using the eyes, then the whole face, then the entire body (with more time we could have gradually used different parts of the body), then the body in space, then dialogue with gibberish, rhythm and sound, then dialogue with words, sentences of improvisation.

What happened for me was that my oppressor was vague at first. This enabled me to construct that oppressor from the gradual building up of gestural, then physical, then verbal dialogue. I saw the reaction to my oppressor in my blank character opposite me and the oppressor/oppressed emerged in dialogue with me. She was no longer a blank from the first instance she act or re-acted to me. Engaged in a "dance of understanding" (Fell, Russell, and Stewart 1994), we emerged in a dance of becoming characters.

Such relationships are not based on cause and effect....

> *We moved through passages and spaces in the Hall of Mirrors that resonated, reflected and refracted off each other in an unspoken unity of expressive interaction.*

...They are open to the possibilities where being, knowing, and acting come forth in dramatic reflection allatonce (Sumara and Davis 1997).

> *The visual, the aural, the unknowable, the unspeakable emerged in moments of creative spontaneity.*

I was fully there in Brown's Blank Character, experiencing the moments of spontaneous (inter)action in the same moments with the facilitator and with my fellow participant. Through this wandering process, set off by a facilitator's suggestions, our evolving characters co-emerged. My learning through facilitation comes through such active participation as facilitator/participant. When that happens in a drama process as participant or as facilitator I find myself interwoven with/in the situation, absorbed in, and encompassed by, embodied interplay.

*A complex series of improvised interactions in a Hall of Mirrors
spirals into Being Doing Knowing myself as (becoming
sensing/being sensed) facilitator.*

Notes

1. "Facilitate" is a dissatisfying word to describe what I do: "to assist the progress of" (Hanks 1979, 521). But this word is one among many to describe my role (for example, Johnston [1998] outlines five tasks and seven different role models for this work). I find the word problematic as the roots of the word is the Latin *facili* "easy" while some of the work in fact involves making things more difficult for participants through the challenging work. So I use the term provisionally as I improvise through the complex interactions with others in my inquiry.

2. "The world that is enacted is inseparable from how we act in it" (Varela et al. 1991, 140).

3. I use the term bodymind or BodyMindSpirit to indicate the integration of feeling and thought that emerges from/within experiential knowing by our "sensous and sentient" (Abram 1997, 45) body. Our awareness of this knowing exists only in the interactions it has with the world.

4. "Theatre games by nature resist copyrighting. Whoever originates a particular exercise is likely to be echoing an earlier one, which itself may well be rooted in a children's game or folkloric ritual" (Johnston 1998, xiv). So it is difficult to source the ultimate beginnings of many of these drama exercises. Many are very old and only have recently been written down in books. Others are (re)invented as they are modified in action.

5. "The roots of 'conversation,' *con versare,* mean 'turn together'" (Fell, Russell, and Stewart 1994).

6. By this he means that one action anticipates its own response.

7. In an email communication with me Peter Reason (1997) clarified their use of Mind rather than BodyMind: "With regard to embodiment I think our perspective on this is embedded in the notion of experiential knowing, by which we mean the *full* encounter with otherness (emphasis added)."

8. Intelligent clay is a sculpted person who fills the shape s/he is in with feelings and thoughts that come from the interplay between the physical shape and the bodymindspirit. Thoughts and words emerge from an interaction of the individual's awareness of the static body in the image and the world around that image.

References

Abram, David. 1997. *The spell of the sensuous: Perception and language in a more-than-human world.* New York: Vintage Books.

Aoki, Ted. 1991. Sonare and vidare: Questioning the primacy of the eye in curriculum talk. In *Reflections from the heart of educational inquiry: Understanding curriculum and teaching through the arts,* edited by George Willis and William Schubert. Albany, NY: State University of New York Press.

Barker, Clive. 1977. *Theatre games.* London: Eyre Methuen.

Boal, Augusto. 1979. *Theatre of the oppressed.* London: Pluto Press.

Boal, Augusto. 1992. *Games for actors and non-actors.* Translated by Adrian Jackson. New York: Routledge.

Booth, Philip. 1998. Email to author, 23 January.

Brougher, Kerry. 1996. Hall of mirrors. In *Art and film since 1945: Hall of mirrors,* edited by Russell Ferguson. Los Angeles: Museum of Contemporary Art.

Csikszentmihalyi, Milhaly. 1997. *Finding flow in everyday life.* New York: Basic Books.

Dreyfus, Hubert. 1999. How neuro-science supports Merleau-Ponty's account of learning. Paper prepared for the Network For Non-scholastic Learning Conference, 4-8 June, by Sonderborg, Jutland, Denmark.

Dreyfus, Hubert L., and Stuart E. Dreyfus. 1986. *Mind over machine: The power of human intuition and expertise in the era of the computer.* New York: Free Press.

Dreyfus, Hubert L., and Stuart E. Dreyfus. 1990. What is morality? A phenomenological account of the development of ethical expertise. In *Universalism versus communitarianism,* edited by D. Rasmussen. Cambridge, MA: MIT Press.

Dreyfus, Hubert L., and Stuart E. Dreyfus. 1999. The challenge of Merleau-Ponty's phenomenology of embodiment for cognitive science. In *Perspectives on embodiment: The intersections of nature and culture,* edited by Gail Weiss and Honi Fern Haber. New York: Routledge.

Fell, Lloyd, David Russell, and Alan Stewart, eds. 1994. *Seized by agreement, swamped by understanding.* Http://www.pnc.com.au/~lfell/book.html.

Grosz, Elizabeth. 1994. *Volatile bodies: Toward a corporeal feminism.* Bloomington: Indiana University Press.

Hanks, Patrick, ed. 1979. *Collins dictionary of the English language.* London: Collins.

Heron, John, and Peter Reason. 1997. A participatory inquiry paradigm. *Qualitative Inquiry* 3(3): 274-94.

Howard, Peggy. 1996. Interpreting the evaluation experience through embodiment, conversation and anecdote. *Qualitative Studies in Education* 9(2): 167-80.

Johnston, Chris. 1998. *House of games: Making theatre from everyday life.* New York: Routledge.

Levinas, Emmanuel. 1996. Meaning and sense. In *Emmanuel Levinas: Basic Philosophical writings,* edited by Adriaan T. Peperzan et al. Bloomington: Indiana University Press.

Maturana, Humberto R., and Francisco J. Varela. 1992. *The tree of knowledge: The biological roots of human understanding.* Boston: Shambhala.

Merleau-Ponty, Maurice. 1962. *Phenomenology of perception.* Translated by Colin Smith. London: Routledge and Kegan Paul.

Moreno, Jacob L. 1960. The principle of encounter. In *The sociometry reader,* edited by J.L. Moreno et al. Glencoe: Free Press.

Morley, David. 1992. *Television, audiences and cultural studies.* New York: Routledge.

Nachmanovitch, Stephen. 1990. *Free play: The power of improvisation in life and the arts.* New York: Putnam.

Rahnema, Majid. 1990. Participatory action research: The "last temptation of saint" development. *Alternatives* 15: 199-226.

Reason, Peter. 1997. Email to author, 28 October.

Schon, Donald. 1964. *Invention and the evolution of ideas.* New York: Associated Books.

Schon, Donald, and Martin Rein. 1994. *Frame reflection: Toward the resolution of intractable policy controversies.* New York: Basic Books.

Schon, Ellen. 1998. Online Conference on Donald Schon's *Reflective Practitioners.* ACTLIST response, 27 March. Email: ACTLIST@lists.singnet.com.sg

Sumara, Dennis, and Brent Davis. 1997. Cognition, complexity, and teacher education. *Harvard Educational Review* 67(1): 105-25.

Wikan, Unni. 1992. beyond the word: the power of resonance. *American Ethnologist* 19(3): 460-82.

Varela, Francisco J., Evan Thompson, and Eleanor Rosch. 1991. *The embodied mind: Cognitive science and human experience.* Cambridge, MA: MIT Press.

A Scuba Class
Holistic Teaching/Learning through Lived Experience...
or
how I dove into the sea and surfaced in academia

Frank Bob Kull

BOB KULL is a Ph.D. candidate at the University of British Columbia. He considers himself a 53-year-old jack-of-all-trades; one of those trades was teaching scuba diving in the Caribbean for several years. He also writes short stories and performs as a storyteller. For his Ph.D. research he will retreat into wilderness solitude for twelve months and document the shifts of consciousness he experiences. Bob may be contacted at kull@interchange.ubc.ca

Abstract. In this chapter I invite you to join me in a scuba class and then experience your own dive through imagery and rhythm. I hope you enjoy the journey. I also examine some important elements of diving instruction and then bring them from the sea into the classroom. Because I write primarily as a storyteller, the style of this chapter is unusual. I not only talk about the importance of modeling, but directly model holistic teaching/learning. The insights I present do not reflect a formal theoretical orientation, but come from my own experience as a scuba instructor in the Caribbean. How I taught and how I think about how I taught emerged from what I learned while teaching.

Keywords. Direct Experience, Emotional Engagement, Fear, Modeling, Mysterious Unknown, Physical Touch, Scuba

Author's Note. Thank you to Johnna Haskell and Patti Kuchinsky for engaging with me so fully in the dance of writing this chapter.

A Scuba Class
Holistic Teaching/Learning through Lived Experience...
or
how I dove into the sea and surfaced in academia

Frank Bob Kull

In Haiti they say it was a meteor long ago that made the hole in the earth now filled by the sea. However it came to be, there is, not far from shore, a sheer, marine wall that drops 3000 feet into the abyss. My student and I were diving down the face of this wall. After a time among the corals, sponges, and grouper, she touched my arm and pointed...out toward empty water. The question of safety hung between us, but again she pointed. We left the storied rock and swam into the unknown. Fingertips just touching, we glided weightlessly engaged through fluid space. A hundred feet above, the surface shimmered faintly; looking back, our visions' far reach found the vague shapes of other divers against the dreamlike mass of the wall beyond; below, a half mile of phantomed mystery buoyed and beckoned to us. The skills I'd modeled in class were now hers, and we were free to explore/create a world together.

> In this attempt I cannot lay any claim to being an authority, especially as intelligent and well-meaning men of all times have dealt with educational problems and have certainly repeatedly expressed their views clearly about these matters. From what source shall I, as a partial layman in the realm of pedagogy, derive courage to expound opinions with no foundations except personal experience and personal conviction? If it were really a scientific matter, one would probably be tempted to silence by such considerations.
> Albert Einstein (1954, 59)

At a recent conference I modeled and discussed a holistic style of teaching/learning exemplified by scuba instruction. It grounds itself in the actual lived experience of the individual teacher rather than reflecting an adopted theory. The conference itself was intended to embody enactive education. For me it was successful; we did bring forth a new world together. In this book we have been encouraged to continue the process and integrate our original presentations into a broader understanding that has emerged for us from the conference. Writing this chapter has been an exciting adventure, a journey of exploration. I have been stimulated to experience the world in a new way—

to reflect on my personal scuba teaching practice and interpret it in a larger context. The topic has stretched beyond an originally narrow focus on scuba instruction and now includes not only the engagement between student and teacher in the realm of the sea, but also their teleportation from sea to classroom, a sometimes bumpy ride. I briefly touch on the encounter of teacher with academy, which involves traditional, citation-based writing and the validation of knowledge. But most importantly, I invite you to dive with me into the present moment of our lives.

This chapter is unusual for an academic publication. It contains few citations referring to theory. Instead, it is grounded almost entirely in my own lived experience. This is my truth in the domain of pedagogy. I have little knowledge of formal educational theory; it is not my academic field. The insights I present here arise from the actual practice of teaching scuba diving in the Caribbean. To cite authority that had no apparent influence on my teaching style (of course, embedded as I am in western culture I have undoubtedly been indirectly influenced by theory) would be misleading. The authors I do cite were not the source of my practice or insights, but rather provide an essential link from the personal to the collective.

I write as a storyteller and include specific details of the diving class I created and taught as the source of my ideas about teaching. The actual content of the class is important and relevant. With trepidation I dive into (sometimes murky) academic water and point to David Abram's 1997 book, *Spell of the Sensuous*, as support for embracing the actual. He shows that each Native American Apache teaching story unfolds in a specific physical location that contributes to the operative potency of the tales. While they may carry a universal message, they are not abstract. In the same way, the story I tell in this chapter derives its meaning and power from the actual situation in which it is rooted. Given this perspective, it would feel unnatural to cite theory and leave out the actual content of the class. This would be "talking about" modeling and lived experience instead of actually modeling both and inviting you, the reader, to join me in the journey.

In the world of immediate experience, each situation is unique and can be clustered with other unique instances only by abstracting out the common elements and ignoring the rest (Maslow 1966). But this can be a serious problem in modern education; the reliance on universal curricula and methodology violently disregards the actual, unique humans involved in the learning process. We need to celebrate diversity in teaching, in learning to teach, and in writing about both. Sitting on the dry land of tradition rather than diving right into the uncertain process of change prevents us from transforming our practice and our lives.

I am not suggesting that theory is invalid or useless. I studied scuba theory, yes (Graver 1978), but I learned to teach scuba diving first by watching and then by doing. Dynamic teaching/learning is, at bottom, not about theory or facts, not about the transfer of information, but rather about inviting students to engage deeply with the teacher so that together they directly experience the world in a new way.

Engage is a lovely word, both in its sound and in the connection it implies. I use it frequently but not esoterically. Emphasizing it may seem strange because we often don't examine our student/teacher relationships. We take for granted the efficacy of our accustomed modes of communication. This chapter is all about engagement, and the full meaning I attribute to the word will emerge as we go along.

The relationship between modeling and the invitation to engage is rich, interesting, and complimentary. In an open-ended interaction with another person, we begin by modeling behavior and wait for a response. If we feel that response has no coherence with our action, there is little opportunity for engagement unless we take the other's behavior as our model and respond to it.

In teaching/learning there are usually interactive constraints guided by the objectives the teacher has in mind. So modeling/response is more directional until the student masters essential skills. If the skills are vital to the success of further engagement (as in scuba diving), the need for precise modeling/imitation becomes very important. The barrier to engagement is not the process of modeling/imitation, but the lack of willingness by both teacher and student to be physically, emotionally, and cognitively present in the encounter. As teachers we can demonstrate this willingness to engage by responding to the student's desires and actions, and even more importantly by openly examining and discussing our objectives for the interaction. But it is important to remember that modeling/imitation of skills is neither the beginning nor the end of teaching/learning. We start by sharing a vision we hope will inspire and then together we reach toward freedom, responsibility, and the unknown.

I begin by modeling a diving class and hope you'll jump in and swim along without worrying too much at first about our destination. Don't wait for me to reassure you that I know where we are by pointing to imagined references along the way. As Krishnamurti (1929) tells us, "Truth is a pathless land." Trust me to get us where we're going, and trust yourself to see what might be useful to you along the way.

Experience

Hi, welcome to diving class. I'm glad you are here. Diving is absolutely wonderful! You'll love it. Well, I love it, and think you will too. It's very easy. You just use a mask so you can see, a regulator so you can breathe, and a pair of fins to help you move through the water. Then you relax and discover a whole new world. Diving will change you and change the way you see the world. This class isn't just about teaching new skills. The skills you learn are important only because they will allow you to come with me and experience the underwater world directly for yourselves. This is your own personal journey.

You might feel a bit nervous. That's natural since this is new for you. But diving is very safe. You will be glad to know there is an excellent survival rate among my students. I usually manage to bring back fully 90% of those who go into the ocean with me. If I lose any more than that, my reputation suffers and repeat business falls off. So your chances of getting through this alive are very good. Just relax and let's have fun together.

The first thing you need to learn is how to put on the mask efficiently. At each step, please watch closely while I demonstrate. Don't do it with me; just watch. Then, when I ask you to, do the exact same thing. There are different ways to put your mask on, but I will show you the way that works best for me. Do it my way first. When you feel comfortable doing it my way, you can experiment until you find what works best for you. Okay? (Since you, the reader, are not actually with me in the water, if you wish to participate fully in this process you will need to visualize what I am saying. Once you have a clear image, try it for yourself.)

First, wet your hair and push it back off your forehead. If hair gets between the mask and your skin, it will prevent a seal and allow water to leak in. Hang the mask from your fingers by its strap. No, don't do it with me. Just watch. Your hand is in front of you, palm downward, fingers curled with the mask dangling from their tips. The nosepiece of the mask is toward you. Splendid. Now grasp the hard rim of the mask with your other hand and place it against your face. Once the mask is in place—not before—pull the strap gently to the back of your head. Feel to be sure there are no twists in the strap. Again, grasp the hard rim of the mask, but with both hands, pull it one centimeter away from your face, move it around a bit and re-seat it against your skin. This will insure that the flexible silicon skirt is not folded under. To check for a complete seal, suck in through your nose; your eyeballs should pop out. Okay, now you do it. Did it work smoothly and easily? Good.

With the scuba regulator in place use only your mouth to inhale and exhale. You will notice it is pretty hard to talk while using a regulator, especially when under water. So we must switch to hand signals. I will show you only two right now. The first is the OK signal. Make a circle with thumb and forefinger and hold the other three fingers straight up. When I give you this signal, I am asking if you are okay. If you are, return the signal to me. Don't nod, or smile, or anything else. Return the OK signal to me. If I hold up my palm toward you, immediately stop what you are doing and focus on your breathing.

This brings us to the most important part of the class, so pay close attention here. I want to talk about panic and breathing. The one thing you absolutely do not get to do while diving is panic. Panic can kill you. Not the ocean, not sharks, not equipment failure—your own panic. Panic is not fear. Fear is a natural part of our emotional experience and can be worked with. Panic is the uncontrolled attempt to escape from fear. Panic is always accompanied by rapid breathing. If at any time you notice you are beginning to breathe more rapidly, immediately stop whatever you are doing no matter what and consciously slow down your breathing; nothing is more important. You cannot directly neutralize your fear, but you can control your breathing. Your body, mind, and emotions are integrated, and by controlling your breathing, you can indirectly influence your thoughts and your emotions. So pay attention to your breathing and keep it slow and steady.

When we are under water I will help you remain calm and confident. I absolutely promise I will let nothing harmful happen to you while you are with me. Stay physically close so I can touch you and you will be able to clearly see my eyes. During class and then while diving together we will remain in close physical, mental, and emotional contact. Ready? Let's go down under the water now.

I have presented this short segment of a diving class to demonstrate several things I think are important in many domains of education. I will explore these elements below, but first, since I strongly feel direct, personal experience is of primary importance in all situations, I want to invite you out for a dive. This way you'll have a taste of what it's like beneath the sea, and I'll get to share the magic of the underwater world with you.

Diving into the Wild Sea

It's difficult to believe, walking along the beach, looking out at an expanse of flat, empty water, just how much delicate life and beauty there is beneath the surface. It's also difficult to describe, but I'll try. Sometimes on a very special dive, this is how the ocean seems to me. It might appear very different to you, and that's part of the wonder.

Imagine you are in the Caribbean and about to go scuba diving for the first time. It's ten o'clock in the morning and a warm sun is scattering some clouds in the eastern sky. As it climbs higher, the sun hardens the edges of the palm fronds along the beach and penetrates more deeply into the water below you. From the cliff where you're standing, you look out over the bay and wonder, again, what is hidden down there waiting to be discovered. You feel excitement and, perhaps, just a small tingle of fear. That's okay. It lets you know you're alive, and this is your first dive into the wild ocean. Your thoughts start to run amok. Oh no! Maybe something will chase me down and eat me! Maybe I'll drown! After all, I'm not a great swimmer. Help!!! *Then you tell yourself*, Wait now. Take it easy. Relax and take some slow, deep breaths. Ahh, that's better.

Just then your guide calls you all to gather round and says, "I know I have assured you that sharks are not a problem, and usually that's true. However, if we should see a shark, it's important to know how to act." You think to yourself, Now he tells us—after we've paid. The guide continues, "The main thing is don't panic and start thrashing around in the water. If you do, the shark may get nervous, and the last thing we want is a nervous shark near us. Stay calm. Form a circle, shoulder-to-shoulder, facing outward so that no matter where the shark comes from, it will have to face someone. Hold hands. This is vital because it prevents gaps in the circle. If there are gaps, the shark can get inside the circle and the most important thing is to prevent the shark from getting into the middle of the circle. The reason this is so important is that I am going to be inside the circle and I'm terrified of sharks."

Relaxed now from the laughter, you look around at the others in your group, a collection of people of all shapes and sizes, ranging in age from thirteen to seventy. You wonder how they will do on the dive. They probably feel nervous too, but like you, they will be fine.

Below you the sea is a rumpled blue sheet, and scattered here and there under the surface are dark patches, the reefs. That's where you're headed, out to the reefs. From up here you can tell the water is clear, and your excitement grows when you see fish swimming around down there.

Hey, you think, this is great; let's go. Wait; slow down a bit. Pay attention to what you are doing, and talk it over with your buddy. You're both in this together. Plan where you'll go into the water and where you'll come out again. Look for landmarks that will guide you to the reef and then back to the beach. Are there any currents that could cause problems? Scuba diving is so exciting, and the underwater world such an incredible place, that it's easy to forget to take care of yourself. Don't let that happen. Always remain mindful of where you are and what you are doing.

You climb down to the beach, wade into the water and put on the gear. Everything seems okay and your buddy is ready, so you head out to the reef.

kick kick kick

> your thoughts keep rhythm with the fins.

kick...kick kick

> water's nice and clear.

kick kick

> buddy still with you.

kick kick...kick kick

> check direction using ripples in the sand.

kick

> not much to see out here, only sandy bottom.

kick...kick kick kick kick kick

> this is sure a long way out—wonder if I missed the reef.

kick

> *what's that???*

And suddenly there you are. The reef spreads out before you and you realize there really is magic here under the sea. Then you are gone, lost in another world, a world filled with light and wonder.

Lifting up from the white sand bottom, strange, angular shapes of elkhorn and staghorn coral fling their jagged branches in all directions. Scattered in between are the rounded domes of star and brain coral—a contrast and a balance. If you slow down and look closely, go closer—careful—you can see intricate, geometric patterns of form and texture that repeat endlessly smaller and smaller and smaller, forever.

Look, there's a sea urchin covered with needle-sharp spines. The spines are blue-black, but deep inside the body is glowing orange-red. Can you see it just sitting there minding its own business? Or perhaps it's aware of you watching it. Who knows what goes on in a sea urchin's mind? You realize that although you will be injured if you accidentally kick it, it is not trying to get you. It means you no harm. You relax and notice that your fear has faded, and you begin to take care to not damage anything rather than to worry that you will be hurt.

Seeing the urchin reminds you to watch for critters, and yes, there they are. Brilliant fish, flashes of color really, dart in and out of the reef. And as you watch them disappear here and reappear there, you realize the reef is riddled with hidden passages. You wonder what it's like to be a fish and travel freely through that maze of dark and light. Other fish catch your eye as they hang motionless in open water. It never ends—so much beauty, beauty everywhere.

Hey, there's a lobster. It's crouched in a cave like some bizarre creature from outer space that's astonished to find itself here. It doesn't seem to like the look of you though, and as you move in for a closer look, it snaps its tail and is gone.

You wish you knew the name of something. But no, wait; don't break the spell. You can learn the names later. Now all that matters is the direct experience of shape and color and movement.

And again it's movement that snares your eye, the graceful, waving sweep of sea fans and soft corals. Back and forth, their hypnotic rhythm carries you deeper inside. As you float without effort, you can feel your body hook into the motion of the sea. Its rhythms become your rhythms. You sense that the moon, which causes the ebb and flow of the tides, affects your blood in secret ways. Your tears are nearly the same as the water in which you float, and you can't tell where your joy ends and the light that flickers all around you begins.

It comes to you that the world is not a collection of objects and you are not a separate thing. Rather, it is an interwoven tapestry of wonder and you are part of it. For the first time in a long time you feel peaceful and really at home. You feel renewed within, and you know that this is why you are here.

Examining the Experience

When I began to teach diving I did so as apprentice to a master. I learned the basics by imitating Felipe Scheker, a certified PADI scuba instructor in Puerto Plata, Dominican Republic, then developed my own style during the actual practice of teaching. Only later did I abstract out what I thought were the important elements involved.

The key thing I learned is the importance of full physical, cognitive, and emotional engagement between teacher and student. For me, teaching is less about transferring information or learning skills than it is about inviting another person into a relationship and into a new way of being and behaving. The primary intent is not to describe, but to create the opportunity for and catalyze direct experience. In diving instruction I invited students to join me in an unknown world, and only secondarily transferred the skills that would allow them to make the journey. This experience changed them and me, and in this change, the whole world changed. Lee Gass, a science professor at UBC who recently won Canada's 3M teaching award, told me, "If we want to be effective teachers, we must believe and be willing that the encounter will change our lives."

Maturana and Varela (1987) claim that information transfer is not the function of language. Languaging is the means by which we coordinate our consensual behavior. We live in a Multiverse rather than a Universe—endless potential domains of experience. When we engage together we become coupled and co-emerge ontogenetically along a goalless epigenetic pathway, creating new worlds together as we go. Einstein (1954, 60) addressed the process of transforming our living in the context of academia:

> Sometimes one sees in the school simply the instrument for
> transferring a certain maximum quantity of knowledge to the
> growing generation. But that is not right. Knowledge is dead;
> the school, however, serves the living. It should develop in
> the young individuals those qualities and capabilities which
> are of value for the welfare of the commonwealth. But that
> does not mean that individuality should be destroyed and the
> individual become a mere tool of the community, like a bee or
> an ant.

Working as a diving instructor was a good way to learn to teach for several reasons. First, there was a lot at stake. From my perspective, my livelihood depended on success. If students did not develop new behaviors, come to trust me, and have fun in the process, they would not go diving and I wouldn't get paid. From their perspective, survival was on the line. So we all tended to be very present and deeply engaged. It is easy to dismiss this danger aspect of scuba instruction as irrelevant to academic education, but that would be a mistake. In all education our survival is always at stake, if not physically, then certainly intellectually, emotionally, and spiritually. Whitehead (1929, 11) wrote:

> Students are alive, and the purpose of education is to
> stimulate and guide their self-development. It follows as a
> corollary from this premise, that the teachers also should be
> alive with living thoughts.

In teaching diving I had the opportunity to see clearly what worked and so to change what did not. Behavioral feedback from my students was always present. It was immediately visible to me when they got hung up in the flow of our interaction. From their body language (once I became sensitive to it), emotional tone—especially the shift between confidence and fear—was also evident. Because in diving panic can kill, awareness of and immediate response to emotional distress was imperative. More accurately, through conscious, emotional engagement, I could influence the students' emotions through physical touch and eye contact as well as with verbal language when above the surface.

Sensing the emotional tone of students through the feelings their posture and behavior trigger in our own bodies is also important in the classroom. David Abram (1997) passionately encourages us to know and respond to the world through this mode of intuitive, irrational apprehension. Since the physical expression of emotion tends to be common across individuals and cultures

(Ornstein 1991), we can listen to our students this way too...but only if we are alive to our own bodies and to the sensations that arise in us.

This points to the importance of physical touch. Because so much of the scuba process was underwater and nonverbal, I came to recognize that physical contact is fundamentally important to the flow of communication. Full human engagement is also vital in the academic setting. If emotion and, even more strictly, vibrant physicality are discouraged in the classroom, then the channel of acceptable interaction is narrowed to focus almost exclusively on cognition. But how much teaching/learning can happen if teacher and students are only minimally present and partially engaged with each other? To paraphrase Woody Allen: Teaching is easy, 80 percent of it is just showing up. (Just showing up...really being present to ourselves and our students—ahh, now that's the hard part.) Yet sometimes the criteria for appropriate classroom behavior still seems to require bodies and emotions to be immobilized or even absent. If the student, as a sensuous human animal, is not touched in any real way there is little possibility for transformation of either student or teacher.

Alison Pryer (this volume) explores the attempted exclusion of Eros from the classroom. She claims this is impossible because Eros will always slip in through the cracks in the hearts of both students and teachers. Daydreaming, spontaneous outbreaks of exuberance, love of student for teacher—erotic life thus invades the deadening structures of meaningless discipline. Wonderful! Pryer celebrates the indomitable, wet, juiciness of life. It is not only more joyful, but also more practical to not deny the inevitable, but to openly encourage the direct experience of erotic aliveness within academia. When we do, students no longer desire to escape the casket of dead facts and second-hand experience that often encases the classroom. The discipline required to gain important skills ceases to be an odious burden and is a path we can follow in our personal exploration of the unknown.

Here the question of fear arises. When we touch the unknown there is fear as well as excitement. If we wish education to come alive, it will help to welcome fear and our full range of emotions into the proceedings. We are emotional beings and just because we deny our emotions does not mean they go away:

> Meanwhile the practically real world for each one of us, the
> effective world of the individual, is the compound world;
> the physical facts and emotional values in indistinguishable
> combination. Withdraw or pervert either factor of this complex
> resultant, and the kind of experience we call pathological ensues.
> (James 1958, 129)

By opening a space in which our emotions are embraced, we begin to transform fear into excitement and expectation. One powerful way to do this is through physiology (Robbins 1986). Touch, eye contact, relaxed body language, and rhythmic breathing exercises are all important elements in the process of comforting and encouraging students to feel and transform their own fears.

Since many of us are loath to admit and address our fear directly, another powerful way to build trust and defuse fear is through humor. Humor creates a context within which we can acknowledge our fear, become aware that we are not alone in our experience, and relax our physical and psychological tension. Humor can transform fear into excitement. This is what the 1998 film Patch Adams, starring Robin Williams, is all about.

During the years I taught diving, I began to realize how important precise modeling and exact imitation can be. When inviting students to experience this strange, underwater world, I wanted them to feel comfortable and glad to be there. By clearly demonstrating important skills and insisting on close imitation, I encouraged them and minimized their discomfort.

When students step into the uncertainty of the unknown, the difference between excited confidence and fear is tenuous. If their first experience is positive, confidence grows and they quickly move into a positive feedback situation. If, on the other hand, their first attempt fails and results in discomfort, the natural reaction is to draw back into the safety of the known. Then the instructor must not only demonstrate how to accomplish the task successfully, but must also work to rebuild trust and confidence. Because of this, I learned to insist on behavior that would increase the likelihood of success from the outset, which necessarily limited the students' freedom of action at first. Then, since our goal was their own direct experience, as soon as they demonstrated behavioral competence, students were encouraged to explore this new world for themselves.

If curriculum and criteria of success are mandated from a central authority, teacher and students can get stuck with preconceived notions of the right way to do something that are inappropriate to them and their particular environment. This is a real danger to the health of the people involved. But it is as serious a mistake to neglect specific, detailed modeling as it is to demand that students remain anchored to those models. The heart of the process is a commitment to encourage direct, personal experience and exploration of the world by everyone involved.

In diving class it was clear that direct experience was the goal and acquiring physical skills the means. How relevant is this style of scuba instruction to the academic setting? In teaching physics, for example, what is being learned? Classically, perhaps a collection of facts and formulas. But I think what we really wish to do is introduce students into the domain of physics and catalyze a change in the way they see the world. We wish to share those skills with students that will allow them to experience and explore the world as physicists.

When we do this, the whole process becomes dynamic and alive. The teacher embodies and invites the students to join the community of physicists. To do this, the teacher himself must in some way belong to that community. Kuhn (1962) describes the process of socializing students into a particular paradigm. It is a process in which the teacher models the appropriate behavior, attitudes, and worldview and slowly the students come to embody the paradigm in themselves. Einstein (1954, 57) says it bluntly: "The only rational way of educating is to be an example—if one can't help it, a warning example."

It is, however, important to not solidify any particular paradigm of science or education. While useful, each is ontologically empty and so available to change. In the September 1999 issue of Patterns (p. 4), Humberto Maturana and Heinz von Foerster exchanged these words:

> Humberto Maturana: Because education will not be so much about the knowledge of the words, but about what is happening in the relationship between the teacher and students. If it is so that the world arises in the interplay of our living together, then which way do we live together so that the world that arises is the one that we want to live in?

> Heinz von Foerster: The main shift for the teacher is that he or she doesn't enter the class saying I know everything. I have to tell you what I know and you have to learn what I know. Instead s/he enters saying I know nothing. Let's find out what's going on. An invitation to search, to create, to participate in a game that constructs the universe in which they all want to live.

Yes, we enact a world together with our students, and finally, on the deepest level we each know nothing at all for sure. Yet as teachers we have a responsibility to bring to our encounter the skills that, in our own lived experience, have worked for us before—always remembering that it may be our attachment to those skills that holds in place a world we wish to change. It is here, I think, that students touch our arm and point us out toward unknown waters, and if we have the courage, we go with them.

Conclusion

When we plunge with our students into the mystery of the unknown, are we discovering or constructing what we see? The question seems moot to me and of little interest. More important is our wonder in the adventure. I have argued that modeling skills is important but not an end in itself; nor is it a beginning. Everywhere along our teaching/learning journey the unknown calls to us if we pause to listen. Once I had learned to teach diving the way my teacher taught, and began to develop my own style, the major changes reflected a different attitude toward the sea. For him, the underwater world was a resource to be used as the arena for a dive. His charismatic relationship with his students was the focus of attention. But I came to the sea as a lover and felt her as my source. To share this deep belonging with my students I led them gently, pausing to listen and wait for their hearts to soften and hear her call.

When we dive into holistic teaching/learning, we are each called to honor our own experience, whatever it is. In remembering to be present in our own lives, we become available to engage more fully with our students. If we have lived predominately in the academic community, and developed our attitudes, knowledge, and ideas in that context, it is important and useful to publish and credit specific sources as contributing to our ideas. However, for those of us who have lived most of our lives beyond the academy, much of what we offer is "street knowledge," ways of behaving we've seen modeled and then developed for ourselves through trial and error—through practice. Individuals who embody the vision, energy, and courage needed to catalyze change in our schools are sometimes disqualified out of hand. Yet they may lack the required publications precisely because their ideas and knowledge have come primarily from their direct engagement with the practical world, rather than through the exchange of writing. Both paths are valid and valuable.

Is this book an enactive endeavor? Is there an open, non-coercive space where authors, editors, and readers dance together and bring forth a publication that is alive? In the context of peer-review approval this can be difficult to achieve. The relationship of power inherent to submission and acceptance may potentially turn the dance into a march. If you feel yourself falling into alignment, perhaps we have failed.

I often reach out through storytelling. In some sense, all stories are teaching stories and this one is no different. It is grounded in particular places and times—rooted in the actual. It begins with a diving class, dives into the ocean, and emerges from academia. When speaking as a storyteller, I resist the urge to moralize and analyze. The story arises in its own space and each listener is welcomed and offered the freedom to move into it and be touched in her own way. This is my desire here, too. I claim no authority to validate what I model—other than it has worked for me. I hope you enjoyed our encounter.

> Education is an admirable thing. But it is well to remember from time to time that nothing that is worth knowing can be taught...Thought is wonderful, but adventure is more wonderful still. (Wilde 1997, 111)

I began this chapter with a story, and I'd like to end with another one that reminds me of things that seem to matter.

In 30 feet of clear, Caribbean water, I was leading one student down the anchor rope from the boat and tensely watching the other I'd just taken to the bottom. Stiff posture, jerky arm movements, and rapid bursts of air bubbles exploding from the regulator told me he was slipping into panic. I felt his fear in my own body, and without conscious thought, signaled the woman by my side to wait and dove for the bottom. I grabbed his tank strap, pulled him close, and stared fiercely into his unfocused eyes. His surging terror of the unknown broke against his concrete fear of my anger. I signed, "Are you okay?" and he nodded vaguely. Again I demanded with my gesture the response he had been taught. Finally he remembered and signed OK in return. The adrenaline rush ebbed from my body as he came into engagement with me. I held his arm to reassure that he was safe and looked up to my other student still holding firm and easy to her anchor line. We signed OK and I signaled them both to check their air supply, which grounded our thinking in the practical. A large, pale-purple jellyfish drifted near the woman. I felt delight in her gaze and waited until she looked our way, then beckoned her down. Her lyric glide through the water sang of her comfort in her body and the sea. Together we explored the reef. My link with each of them was unique. She stayed engaged, but was entranced with the beauty around us. He and I remained physically/emotionally close; his attention focused on himself in relationship with me. But finally, he, too, reached out to touch the life around us. And so we became triads of wonder: student, teacher, and mysterious unknown.

References

Abram, D. 1997. *Spell of the sensuous*. New York: Vintage.

Einstein, A. 1954. *Ideas and opinions*. New York: Bonanza Books.

Graver, D. 1978. *PADI diver manual*. Santa Ana, CA: PADI.

James, W. 1958. *The varieties of religious experience: The Gifford lectures, 1901-1902*. New York: New American Library.

Krishnamurti, J. 1929. Truth is a pathless land. Speech delivered at Annual Order of the Star in the East Camp, 2 August, in Ommen, Holland. http://www.kfa.org/gfxindex.html.

Kuhn, T.S. 1962. *Structure of scientific revolutions*. Chicago: University of Chicago Press.

Maslow, A.H. 1966. *Psychology of science*. New York: Harper and Row.

Maturana, H.H. and F.J. Varela. 1987. *The tree of knowledge: The biological roots of human understanding*. Boston: Shambhala.

Maturana, H.H. and H. von Foerster. 1999. Conversation in *Patterns: ASCD Systems Thinking and Chaos Theory Network Newsletter* (September) Soquel, CA.

Ornstein, R. 1991. *Evolution of consciousness*. New York: Prentice Hall.

Robbins, A. 1986. *Unlimited power*. New York: Ballantine Books.

Shadyac, Tom (Director). *Patch Adams*. Film starring Robin Williams based on *Gesundheit: Good health is a laughing matter* by Doherty Adams.

Whitehead, A.N. 1929. *The aims of education*. New York: Macmillan.

Wilde, O. 1997. *The critic as artist*. Act 1. Gilbert. Cork, Ireland: CELT, University College. http://imbolc.ucc.ie/cgi-bin/uncgi/patrefs.

Co-emerging
in the Second Language
Research Process

John Ippolito

JOHN IPPOLITO is a Ph.D. candidate at York University in the Faculty
of Education's graduate program in Language, Culture and Teaching. His
academic interests include the relationship between language and thought,
issues of methodology and representation in qualitative research, and
second language studies. Most recently, he has extended his work to a focus
on language and ethics. He has a professional background in teaching
English as a second language.

Abstract. What are the implications for educational research of suggesting that
research participants and researcher are not distinct entities to the research
process? Drawing on Varela, Thompson, and Rosch's (1991) concept of
embodied action and Abram's (1996) notion of perceptual and linguistic
reciprocity, I share my thoughts on carrying out a second language research
study. The study sets out to investigate second language acquisition in the
context of a particular ESL (English as a Second Language) conversation
activity, but turns into an extended reflection on the co-emergent quality of
perspective and language. The tension between the conceptual and data-
driven demands of an experimental research tradition on the one hand and the
researcher's own lived, embodied experience of carrying out the research, on
the other, proves to be the catalyst that unexpectedly derails the ostensible
research agenda.

Keywords. Qualitative Research, Methodology, ESL, Lived Experience,
Embodied Action, Perspective, Reciprocity, Representation, Co-emergence

Co-emerging
in the Second Language
Research Process
What It Means to Research What It's Like

John Ippolito

John: So generally you think I should be giving some very general directions.

Magda: Very, very general.

John: Very general.

Magda: You know, like, just, just (laughs) five percent.

John: Okay. I like that. About five percent direction. I gave you about one percent direction. (Magda laughs)

Magda: Yah, I didn't really know what you wanted me to say.

The research study from which this excerpt is drawn began as a data-based ethnographic empirical inquiry into second language acquisition. Specifically, it set out to assess the pedagogical value of an exercise for improving the conversational skills of community college ESL (English as a Second Language) students. However, as the excerpt suggests, it turned rather decidedly into a learning experience for the researcher. This paper traces that learning experience. It reflects on the evolution of my relationship to the study and to the research participants, that is, from an investigative concern with *what it's like* to take part in a second language conversation exercise—as one of the research participants put it, to my own personal concern with *what it means* to be in research that co-emerges between researcher and research participants.

My ostensible interest was with a conversation exercise in which community college ESL (English as a Second Language) and TESL (Teachers of English as a Second Language) students shared thoughts on topics as diverse as acculturation, tourism, and divorce. Rather than serving as a "source of data," however, the research participants' reflections on these informal conversations became important for me in other, quite unexpected, ways. This is to say they became important to me as the thoughts of interesting people who were sharing the research with me and, I should add, enriching my experience of it. In hindsight, this should hardly have been surprising since the research participants embodied an intriguing diversity of perspectives: Some were bilingual students educated in Canada; some were educated abroad and had come to the college as mature students or visa students from places as far removed as Somalia, Korea, and Poland; some were in their late teens and some had families with two or three children. It should also have come as no surprise that a second language experimental research methodology, which is typically concerned with gathering research data from which to extrapolate strategies for second language pedagogy, would "miss the mark" as far as a meaningful appreciation of my interaction with the research participants. Having been an instructor at the college before returning to do graduate work in education, it now seems strange that I should have imagined the rapport I once enjoyed with students would have to somehow be put on hold for my new persona as "researcher." Perhaps this speaks to the weight of an experimental research methodology in the field of second language acquisition, or to my own worries about the research producing worthwhile findings, or to both. Whichever is the case, it is clear that research conducted within an experimental tradition casts the researcher in the role of "discoverer." Simply put, he or she is expected to "discover" something that is already "out there," waiting to be uncovered.

The Study: Data Collection or Felt Kinship?

I used a two-stage approach in an effort to gain a multi-layered experience of the conversation exercise. I first videotaped the conversations of five ESL/TESL groups and then audiotaped a discussion of the videotape with each of the research participants individually. Since the focus of the research was the perspective of the research participants on the videotaped conversation, my contributions to the audiotaped discussion were limited to points of clarification or elaboration. The videotaping was done in one of three private screening rooms in the college. Several of the participants mentioned that they felt more at ease in these rooms than the usually noisy cafeterias and coffee shops where they normally met. With respect to the presence of a camera and the knowledge that they were being taped, most of the participants said that they did not feel particularly anxious in the presence of a camera. Some mentioned that they had forgotten about the camera after ten or fifteen minutes. This was gratifying to me, since even at this early stage in the research when my concern was ostensibly with collecting data, I felt a kinship with the research participants through my efforts to make them comfortable and this, I should stress, had nothing to do with collecting data.

Notwithstanding the unmistakable pull of a felt kinship, data collection continued to be a central preoccupation, perhaps a vestige of the experimental research methodology with which I felt increasingly at odds. My interpretation of this methodology led me to minimize my part in the videotaping sessions. After conducting a pilot videotaping session with colleagues several weeks before my taping at the college, I reasoned that if I sat in on the conversations, I would have to define a role for myself. If I could not do that, there was no reason for me to be there. In fact, my presence might have become an added source of anxiety for the participants. All this considered, I decided to set up the equipment, let the participants know I would be back in an hour, and leave. At the time, it did not occur to me to ask them if I could attend the conversations as a colleague or friend who was interested in what they had to say.

Once again, my sense of how to most effectively collect data determined the schedule for the following stages of the research. My audiotaped discussions of the videotaped conversations took place from one to three weeks after taping and, rather than previewing the videotapes as I had originally intended, my initial screening of them was with individual participants. This change in plan was in response to the suggestion that I would be more receptive to the participants' perspective on the videotaped conversations if I had not had the opportunity to view and then reflect on those conversations. Once again, it did not occur to me that I might have been able to more fully appreciate the research participants' perspective on the videotaped conversation if I had considered them beforehand and acclimatized myself to potential points of difficulty for the participant.

However misguided my sense of research methodology, I cannot help but think that it was being tempered by a felt kinship with the research participants. After all, a relationship with each of the participants and myself was now taking shape as we became more familiar with each other. For instance, at each of the sessions, the audiotaping began before the videotape playback. During this interval, I invited the participant to comment on anything related to the particular conversation we were going to be viewing, the conversation activity in general, or the research of which they were a part. Then, in preparation for viewing, I explained to the participant that I wanted them to talk about their experience of the original conversation or their experience as they viewed the video. For instance, part of my introduction for one of the participants, Sean, went as follows:

> *John: So what do I want you to talk about? I want you to talk about any thoughts or feelings that you have to the conversation or the video. Anything that you think is important, that you want to talk about, is what I want to hear.*
> *Sean: So, you don't ask anything to me?*
> *John: It's up to you. Whatever you want to talk about—I'm looking for your perspective on this conversation.*
> *Sean: Yah.*

I then demonstrated the operation of the pause function and gave the participant the remote control, pointing out that they were at complete liberty to pause the tape at any time and comment on any aspect of the conversation. I also encouraged the participant to talk over the videotape even at those points where they were not inclined to pause it. I might account for these gestures as attempts to address the power imbalance that invariably exists in favor of the researcher, but the question that would still remain is "why?" Why would I take it upon myself to encourage a relaxed and conversational discussion, and why was it so important to let the participant take the lead in the discussion? A more disciplined researcher would argue that this facilitated the collection of data, but I am firmly convinced that it had more to do with my felt kinship to the research participants and less to do with collecting data. The discussion of the videotape was an effort to get the participant's perspective on the conversation, but the motivation for that effort, and the means by which it was carried out, was not a *fait accompli* in favor of the priorities of data collection.

As I made my way through the individual discussions with the research participants, it became clear that the participants were being taken by surprise by the fact that my instructions were so open-ended. It seems that my lack of expectations was difficult for them to understand. I recognized that this was making their task somewhat more difficult, but my notion of research methodology made me reluctant to influence the direction of the conversation by suggesting a focus at the outset of the discussion. As a compromise, I decided to keep my instructions open-ended at the beginning of the conversation and to ask the participants for their reactions to these instructions at the very end of the conversation. In this way, I thought I could prevent myself from unduly influencing the direction of the conversations and at the same time gain some sense of the impact of this strategy on the participants. Perhaps this was one of the compromises between collecting data and feeling kinship. As it turned out, this compromise became crucial. It pulled me into the research by both sensitizing me to the potential unease my methodology might be causing the participants and encouraging me to let the methodology evolve in response to what the participants were saying. Magda's thoughts were invaluable:

> *Magda: You know, you said to me at the beginning, "Say something wherever you want to say anything." I didn't really know what you meant, what you expected from me. If you said, "Say something about participation," then I would have a point of view, you know?*
>
> *John: I know what you're saying.*
>
> *Magda: So maybe next time you should tell people in a general way what you really expect.*
>
> *John: So you think I should be telling them content or form or something.*
>
> *Magda: Something like that, so they have the point to hook up to, you know? Because actually I didn't know if—because always if I'm doing something, I'm thinking that I'm doing it wrong, you know? And even if I talk about this, I thought maybe it's not what you expect from me, you know? So maybe you can give some clear...*
>
> *John: So I should be clearer about my expectations.*
>
> *Magda: Yah, but not clear like you give them exact questions...because if you give people questions, they are not creative.*
>
> *John: That's what I'm afraid of.*
>
> *Magda: That's why I'm saying just give, like a general, just like one point so they can take, so they can look at that point. I mean, not really just that one question, but in general they have the main idea...*
>
> *John: So generally you think I should be giving some very general directions.*
>
> *Magda: Very, very general.*

John: Very general.

Magda: You know, like, just, just (laughs) five percent.

John: Okay. I like that. About five percent direction. I gave you about one percent direction. (Magda laughs)

Magda: Yah, I didn't really know what you wanted me to say.

These post-discussion conversations about the participants' reactions to my research methods prodded my methodological orientation to the research. I felt like I was beginning to share the experience of the research with the participants, moving away from the position of self-isolated researcher documenting research participant perspectives and toward a co-perspective,a far more liveable and meaningful shared viewing of the videotaped conversations. Initially, I thought I would be best able to listen to the participants if I stepped back from the discussions so as not to influence their perspective. However, this did not turn out to be the case: It was impossible for me to listen to those voices without being closer to the participants, without being more involved in the discussion sessions. As a researcher, I could not bracket myself from the research. My methodological decision to remain a passive observer who was, nonetheless, listening with a purpose prevented me from fully listening to the participants. In this sense, "passive" cannot mean "inactive," since listening is activity and engagement. This point is consonant with the enactivist claim that "perception consists in perceptually guided action" (Varela, Thompson, and Rosch 1991, 173). Similarly, in the case of listening, it could be said that "listening consists in listening guided action," listening that selects and reaches out to what it listens to. As such, I was selecting and reaching out to what I wanted to listen to for the purposes of the research, even if those purposes were not specifically defined. The movement I am describing in my relation to the participants and to the research can be seen as the movement from a passive but controlling listening toward "a very active, vigilant, absorbing passivity, which is not related to being in charge of one's subjectivity: Rather, it involves letting go of the idea of being-separate-and-in-charge altogether" (Heshusius 1994, 18). I imagine this as a felt kinship that attunes the researcher to the research participants. I learned that at a very basic level I was being shaped by the research participants and research activity at least as much as I had thought I would be shaping them. The research moved me toward a place where, as Harré and Gillett explain, "it no longer makes sense to talk of observers and subjects at all. There are only coparticipants in the project of making sense of the world and our experience of it" (1994, 21). I also learned that this struggle with the identity and place of "researcher" raises fundamental questions about the notion of *perspective*. If, as a researcher, I cannot move closer to understanding the perspective of individual research participants by isolating them from the influence of my thoughts and questions, what, then, does it mean to understand a research participant's perspective? Is all this to suggest perspective is implicitly plural, completing itself in that which is perceived and, in turn, influencing the perception?

An Embodied and Reciprocal Linguistic Experience

My response to the place and perspective of researcher begins with a consideration of the conceptual basis for an experimental research methodology. This protocol set the tone for much of the research agenda, yet "missed the mark" as far as moving me toward a meaningful appreciation of my interaction with the research participants. This failure has its roots in the experimentally informed view that language can be isolated and studied as if there were a clear border between the language researcher and the speaker being researched.

One way to situate this belief is against Descartes's distinction between *res cogitans* and *res extensa*, the thinking being and the material being. As Descartes expresses it in *Meditations on First Philosophy*, "It is certain that I am really distinct from my body [and everything else outside of my thinking being] and can exist without it" (Cottingham 1996, 54). When the nature of being is shaped by a distinction between our thinking selves and that which we think about, it becomes possible to characterize mind as an inner faculty whose primary function is to represent the external world. So-called "representative theories" do just that; that is, they propose a correspondence between aspects of the external world and our efforts to make those aspects comprehensible. For example, in a representative theory of perception, objects in the external world correspond to mental representations of those objects; in a representative theory of meaning, particular objects in the external environment correspond to particular words as symbolic representations. A representative theory of meaning is premised on the distinction between thinking being and material being and impacts views of research and language. In the case of research, it is echoed in the distinction between researcher and research participants and in the case of language, it is perhaps nowhere more entrenched than in a generativist perspective wherein, as Chomsky puts it, "Behavior and its products...[are] of interest insofar as they provide evidence for what really concerns us, the inner mechanisms of mind and the ways they form and manipulate representations, and use them in executing actions and interpreting experience" (1997, 17). Chomsky's account of language is quintessentially Cartesian in that inner, *thinking being* is held to be "manipulating representations" of outer, *material being*. One extension of this notion is that just as the manipulator of linguistic representations is separate from the object of linguistic representations, so too are interlocutors completely separate, with speaker and listener sharing nothing more than a representation at various stages of manipulation. I should add that the object of those representations, the so-called "external" world, is also fully removed from either interlocutor.

A research methodology appropriate for looking at the lived experience of language needs to address, at a very basic level, the relationship between researcher and research participants and the relationship between language and cognition. In the case of research, the question that needs to be addressed is whether the distinction between researcher and research participants is transparent or whether it is, in fact, part of a more complex, blurred dynamic; in the case of language the question that needs to be addressed is whether language is solely a tool for representing the contents of external worlds to inner minds or whether, in fact, it has some other than representational function. I recognized that these twin concerns around research and language were central to my concern with *what it means* to be in research that co-emerges between researcher and research participants. In addressing these issues, I drew on the concept of *embodied action* (Varela, Thompson, and Rosch 1991, 172) and the notion of *perceptual and linguistic reciprocity* (Abram 1996, 90). I begin with *embodied action*.

In laying the groundwork for a re-characterization of the gulf between inner mind and outer world, Varela, Thompson and Rosch's (1991) notion of *embodied action* treads a middle ground between the Cartesian extremes of realism and idealism. As the authors express it, "These two extremes both take representation as their central notion: in the first case representation is used to recover what is outer; in the second case it is used to project what is inner" (1991, 172). The value of *embodied action* for my reconsideration of the researcher/research participants distinction is that, at a very basic level, it challenges the presumed distance between thinking being and material being. As a consequence, it also contests representation as a means of coming to understand experience. Within the framework of *embodied action*, "sensory and motor processes, perception and action, are fundamentally inseparable in lived cognition" (1991, 172-73). For my purposes, this suggests that my perception of the research participants is inseparable from the conduct of the research. In other words, what I see is inseparable from what I do just as, conversely, what I do is inseparable from what I see. The point here is that my interaction with the research participants, as part of what I do, is inseparable from my unfolding and evolving perspective on the research. Once again, the converse would suggest that the research participants' interactions with me are inseparable from how they view the research. Simply put, we, researcher and research participants, are inextricably tied to one another. In coming to understand the research experience in this way, I am compelled to recognize what the authors call the *mutual specification* of what, within a Cartesian framework, would be seen as the impact of "outer world" on "inner me" and "inner me" on "outer world."

Having said this, I am not suggesting *embodied action* be construed as a patchwork of realist (outer world) and idealist (inner me) proclivities. It is, rather, a real alternative in that it pushes an understanding of the research experience away from either extreme or, for that matter, an oscillation of extremes. In other words, in understanding the research experience, I am pushed into a position where I am already conceding the impossibility or, perhaps more to the point, undesirability of imagining research activity which exists prior to my experience of it or the research participants and, at the other extreme, conceptualizing an autonomous researcher without regard to his manifestation in the research among research participants.

The relevance of *embodied action* for my efforts to think outside an experimental research framework became particularly clear for me through the authors' related notion of *codependent arising*, the idea that a subject, its object and the relation between them cannot exist independently of each other (Varela, Thompson, and Rosch 1991, 221). The authors express it in this way: "How can we talk about the seer of a sight who is not seeing its sight? Conversely how can we speak of a sight that is not being seen by its seer? Nor does it make any sense to say that there is an independently existing seeing going on somewhere without any seer and without any sight being seen" (1991, 222). What this suggests in the case of research is that it makes no sense to talk of a researcher without a research participant in the absence of a research activity. It makes far more sense—quite literally to be in tune with the senses—to understand all three entities, that is, researcher, research participants, and research activity, as inextricably bound up in the same lived dynamic. The possibilities for research premised on the inseparability of researcher and research participants in the research process, which I extrapolated from the related notions of *embodied action* and *codependent arising*, lend themselves to Abram's other-than-representational notion of language, which he develops in relation to the idea of *perceptual and linguistic reciprocity* (1996, 90).

For Abram, the ability of written language to speak from a page is attributable to the same process by which our senses "perceive" the world. I use "perceive" advisedly here since Abram is not suggesting that perception involves the recovery of an external reality, but rather that the act of perception is inseparable from that which is perceived, just as for Varela, Thompson and Rosch (1991) perceiving a world is inseparable from being and acting in that world. Abram reiterates this active participation in the world or, perhaps more accurately, active participation *of* the world by drawing on the work of Merleau-Ponty in proposing that perception is "inherently participatory... perception always involves, at its most intimate level, the experience of an active interplay, or coupling, between the perceiving body and that which it perceives" (1996, 56). Abram argues that this propensity of the senses to couple with the "object," or perhaps more to the point, the propensity of the senses to couple with the "other half of perception," was transferred from the natural world to the printed page through the mediation of written script. He further suggests that this bodily, physical basis of language has, for the most part, been silenced by a view of language as a system of abstract representations. Abram's reading of language as representation gives a clear outline of the position against which he is reacting. "Language, in this view, is rather like a *code*; it is a way of *representing* actual things and events in the perceived world, but it has no internal, nonarbitrary connections to that world, and hence is readily separable from it" (1996, 77). This view reiterates the Cartesian separation of thinking and material being. Language, as a code, partakes of the disembodied quality of thinking being while *the perceived world*, as an entity separable from and represented by language, assumes the qualities of an external, independently existing material being.

Abram's notion of *reciprocity* extracts language from representation, from a dualistic framework of inner mind and outer world. He does this by suggesting that language, like perception, begins and ends in the actually existing world. This is wholly intelligible within Abram's view that perception and language are not the self-contained activities of organisms but rather the very relationship between organism and ecology. Drawing once again on Merleau-Ponty, Abram writes, "Perception...is precisely this reciprocity, the ongoing interchange between my body and the entities that surround it. It is a sort of silent conversation that I carry on with things, a continuous dialogue that unfolds far below my verbal awareness—and often, even, *independent* of my verbal awareness" (1996, 52-53). My research orientation took its cue from this challenge to representational models of language and placed a pronounced emphasis on language as part of a simultaneous coming into being of research participants, researcher and research activity. Taking my "other-than-representational" cue from these two notions, *embodied action* and *perceptual and linguistic reciprocity*, I came to see that the research participants and I were not distinct parties to the process. Our interaction in language had significance beyond its representational contents in that the interaction constitutes one of the dimensions by which we were completing ourselves in each other or, to use the term from Varela, Thompson and Rosch (1991), *mutually specifying* each other.

The term I came to use to describe this radical reciprocity is co-emergence.[1] When cognition is seen as a process of co-emergence of researcher and research participant, speaker and hearer, knowledge becomes more than objectifiable matter and knowledge creation becomes more than an experimentally informed research approach. For instance, since cognition is a relationship of mutual specification, the nature and quality of the relationship between researcher, research participants and research setting becomes paramount. Further, when language is thought about in other than representational terms, as something for which speaker and hearer are both responsible—since the spoken is completing itself in the listening just as the listening is completing itself in the spoken—language becomes an act of co-emergence. It retains its ability to refer to things, as it does in a representational framework, but the vocalizing of a word or sound becomes itself a co-emergent act involving speaker, listener and setting.

Productively Derailed

My study originally set out on the terms of an experimental research inquiry, tacitly taking the Cartesian separation of thinking and material being as a *fait accompli*. However, representative theories of perception and meaning, whose ground of possibility lies within this Cartesian separation, induced an ominous echo of disembodiedness that had little resonance with the research experience. My attempt to isolate researcher and research participants, on the one hand, and the concept of language from the sensuously experienced lives of interlocutors, on the other hand, impeded, rather than facilitated, the research. I was denying the research participants and myself a fuller sense of both the ostensible focus of study, the conversation activity, and the connection between the co-participants in the research. The tension between the conceptual and data-driven demands of an experimental research tradition and my own lived, embodied experience of carrying out the research study proved to be the catalyst that fruitfully derailed the original research plan. A study that set out to investigate second language acquisition in the context of a particular conversation activity turned into an extended reflection on the co-emergent quality of perspective and language. I would not be so presumptuous as to claim that I now know what it means to be in research that co-emerges between researcher and research participants. Nonetheless, I will say that a meaningful understanding and experience of second language acquisition lies in the direction of a co-emergent reality for which no one entity is ever solely responsible.

Note

1. It has since come to my attention that the term *co-emergence* is also used by Davis and Sumara (1997) in their discussion of complexity theory and action research in education. For an intriguing discussion of action research as a *mutually specified* relationship, see their chapter "Enlarging the space of the possible: Complexity, complicity, and action-research practices."

References

Abram, D. 1996. *The spell of the sensuous: Perception and language in a more-than-human-world.* New York: Pantheon.

Chomsky, N. 1997. Language and cognition. In *The future of the cognitive revolution,* edited by D. Johnson and C. Erneling. New York: Oxford University Press.

Cottingham, J., ed. and trans. 1996. *Descartes: Meditations on first philosophy (with selections from the objections and replies).* Glasgow: Cambridge University Press.

Davis, B., and D. Sumara. 1997. Enlarging the space of the possible: Complexity, complicity, and action research practices. In *Action research as a living practice,* edited by T. Carson and D. Sumara. New York: Peter Lang.

Harré, R., and G. Gillett. 1994. *The discursive mind*. Thousand Oaks, CA: Sage.
Heshusius, L. 1994, April. Freeing ourselves from objectivity: Managing subjectivity or turning toward a participatory mode of consciousness? *Educational Researcher* 23(3): 15-22.
Varela, F., E. Thompson, and E. Rosch. 1991. *The embodied mind: Cognitive science and human experience*. Cambridge, MA: MIT Press.

When the Wind Blows,
the Barrel Maker Gets Busy

Marylin Low and Maria McKay

MARIA MCKAY teaches young adults from Japan at an international college in North Vancouver, BC, Canada, and, in this chapter, writes of her co-teaching experience with her co-author, Marylin Low. Currently Director of Academic Programs, Maria has opportunities, in/out/be-side the classroom, to work/walk with students, struggling with and engaging in "genuine" pedagogic conversations. As a master's student, she finds herself wandering and wondering midst (inter)relational sites of difficulty with-in spaces and places of translation and hybridity.

MARYLIN LOW teaches young adults from Japan at an international college in North Vancouver, BC, Canada, and in this chapter writes of her co-teaching experiences with her co-author, Maria McKay. After completing doctoral work that questioned assessment practices of language and (its dis)content(s), Marylin continues to write into the double folds of the "inter" of international pedagogical praxis—as/in im/possible sites of hybridity, translation, and difference as tensioned sites of an Aokian "living pedagogy."

Abstract. We are reminded of the interconnectedness of seemingly random events—in our case, of unexpected conversations enmeshed in the day-to-day living of a second language classroom that disrupt our often taken-for-granted stances of the way things are. That is, our conversations with students are sometimes experienced as disassociated and resistant. Yet, when traced, are often found to be rooted in complex interconnections. Unforeseen conversations awaken in us relationships that are sustained by our inquisitiveness and yet infused with risk. We enter "genuine" conversations already begun—with students, with each other—textured by the winds of unexpected moments from the classroom and write authentically, not of "ourselves" or of our "stories," but of felt pedagogic relationships with students.

Keywords. Disruptions, Living Pedagogy, Co-Teaching, International Students, To (Be) Educate(d), To (Be) Mark(ed), Generativity and Danger

When the Wind Blows, the Barrel Maker Gets Busy

Marylin Low and Maria McKay

When the wind blows, dust rises and settles in peoples' eyes, rendering some blind. It was once tradition in Japan for blind people to take up a musical instrument like the shamisen (a three-stringed Japanese banjo). Because shamisens are best made from cat skins, the more people want them, the fewer cats there are. With fewer cats, there are more mice to nibble away at barrels. Thus the barrel maker has to get busy making more.

Source unknown

In scripting the title, taken from an age-old Japanese proverb, we are reminded of the interconnectedness of seemingly random events—in our case, of unexpected disruptions[1] in conversations enmeshed in the day-to-day living of co-teaching in a second language classroom that disturb our taken-for-granted stances of the way things are. That is, we sometimes sense resistance in our conversations with students. Yet, when traced, those resistances are often found to be rooted in complicated and unforeseen interrelations. We are reminded of the post-secondary student from Japan who became unsettled with our desire to include students in curricular decision-making. In further conversations with him, we explored his resistance and traced it to his elementary school experiences in Japan. His pronouncement of the inappropriateness of this approach for college students took us by surprise. He was seeking an expert/novice relationship with his teachers. This disturbed our taken-for-granted stance of inclusion. As the conversation continued, the three of us struggled to remain open to the paradoxical stances that embodied us and, together, we began listening to each other midst the difficulties of living relations.

Being caught in the spell of the mundane broken with life, how do we speak of difficult pedagogic experiences? For us, these experiences are akin to ecological journeys that take us into entangled webs of living pedagogy (Aoki 2000), into ambiguously vibrant spaces of generativity and danger. Unanticipated conversations awaken in us relationships that are sustained by our inquisitiveness and yet infused with risk. We enter conversations already begun— with students, with each other—textured by the winds of unexpected

> *Humans are tuned for relationship. The eyes, the skin, the tongue, ears, and nostrils — all are gates where our body receives the nourishment of otherness.*
> David Abram (1996, p. ix)

moments from the classroom, and write authentically[2], not of "ourselves" or of our "stories," but of felt pedagogic relationships invoked midst "the nourishment of otherness."

We resist reading life in the classroom as a "thing" that can be captured and understood outside of its ecological connections. Instead, we read the classroom hermeneutically, interpreting instances of life in "a space surprised by difference"[3] while heeding David Smith's (1999, 27) warning that our "interpretations could lead [us] into trouble with 'authorities'."

Troubled Terrains of Mysterious Interconnections

For some, interpretations may be troubled by those fluctuating, mysterious interconnections of in/visible events—troubled in that it seems the work is not done until the flux, the chaos, is arrested, under control, becomes known. Yet, we are reminded of "certain invisible aspects of the visible environment, certain unseen regions whose very hiddenness somehow enables or makes possible the open visibility" (Abram 1996, 212) of the whole. In the classroom, we are aware of the things that surround us, even when we do not always have them in view. They are not concealed from us, nor are we disallowed access to them. A turn or a few steps to the right or left may quickly make visible the unseen. We have become masters of the ocular, of "seeing" only the external elements, of freezing the flux of our environment, of giving import to the visible, the known.

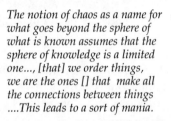

> The notion of chaos as a name for what goes beyond the sphere of what is known assumes that the sphere of knowledge is a limited one..., [that] we order things, we are the ones [] that make all the connections between things ....This leads to a sort of mania.
>
> Jardine (1998, p. 119)

Yet, while we are aware of that which is temporarily hidden, we have begun to ponder the mysteries of that which seems to refuse our gaze: the obscure webs of interconnectedness that embody our work with students. We read the writing of students in our class and wonder about the unsaid. We have come to realize the absences present in their words are integral aspects of the writing that "falls outside of the sphere of knowing." Absences, often relegated to insignificance, are returned to significance through our conversations with students. It is the mysterious, unscripted relations that ground us, connect us to under-the-ground[4], keep us in the humus, in humility with each other.

> The notion of mystery entails that we are connected to and dependent upon what falls outside of the sphere of knowing. Our actions must become delicate and careful and attentive to what crackles beyond the boundaries that our knowledge has set.
>
> Jardine (1998, p.119)

Is absence a taken-for-granted so familiar that many have become blind to it, no longer concerned by it? Our conversations with students often travel under-the-ground, exploring the humus of our lives lived together. There is danger in the journeys underground; mis-connections and detours are re/routed and entangled in un/marked paths, darkened alleys, endless mazes. In inviting students to question their experiences in our classroom, we sometimes found ourselves wounded by their disinterest in what we thought were well-planned activities. Consumed by our own assumptions of what was "good" for them, we had neglected a pedagogical listening with them. In learning to be open, we and the students traversed troubled terrains, often laying the path as we entered into conversations already begun. Sometimes we faltered in the slipperiness of ambiguity and uncertainty. Often we were halted in the unexpectedness of the response. Always, we were determined to keep the conversations going, even when it seemed there was no way out.

To (Be) Educate(d)

We understand the process of education to be ecological—not linear—in its openness to dynamic opportunities and disturbing tensions incited by the constant interplay of relations between learners and teachers, between educating and being educated. Our experience has taught us that the positions of learner and teacher are not polar, but rather con/divergent, wherein the interplay is not predictable or ever finalized; we toil with the difficulties and possibilities inherent in learning and knowing together. In this heavy work, education is not a sterile passing back and forth of self-contained units of the "said." Instead, for us education is realized in the humus of human interaction—sites of mis/dis/re-connecting inter- actions between the said and the unsaid. Hence, an "emerging uniqueness" is invoked. "Unique" because we cannot anticipate or duplicate (inter)personal dialogue. "Emerging" because it is spontaneous to that moment of interaction; co

> [O]ur most profound challenges lie in dealing creatively with the relation between our rationalized conceptual systems and the systems and the emerging uniqueness of life as it presents itself in the lives of our students.... Good teaching requires getting to know one's students personally, uniquely, individually, so that a genuine conversation can exist between you, and knowledge is mediated in a way that has a human soul.
>
> Smith (1999, pp. 8-9)

(-e)merging because what is invoked are fragile and fragmented moments of togetherness as we struggle to understand/be understood. And so we converge, we meet as teachers/ learners and learners/teachers and experience (un)common, (un)stable grounding. What is so often visible in our work is the expected role relationship of teacher and learner. Yet, our encounters with these international students have become more than this; within unexpected dynamic and precarious moments of telling and tearing, "genuine conversations" are invoked. It is the students' conversations with us—(e)merging and (con)verging with tensions—that challenge us to educate and be educated midst the unexpected, and to dwell there with them with our experience and our humanity. We write of two such instances with students: one from an email and another from a conversation.

Instance one

After a class on social justice that involved questions of personal power—a class that seemed difficult for students—we were disrupted by an unexpected message from a student. In that class, the students had been asked to explore the power relations in an incident reported in the news and to offer creative and unusual ideas that had the potential to alter those power relationships in the story. The pedagogical task was based on a particular model that explored five types of power and was used to show how focusing on one type of power rather than another could alter the possible outcome of the event. Two days later, a message arrived from a student who had been unusually silent yet seemingly engaged in class activities that day. Now his silence erupted on the screen.

> I have some questions about last class.
> I didn't understand the purpose of the activity.
> We should find creative and unusual ideas.
> Why should the ideas be creative and unusual?
> Why should we change the situation that one person
> ha[s] more power to another situation that the other
> ha[s] more power? Thank you. Kotaro

Surprised by difference, we began to explore our own unquestioned assumptions of the value of creative and unusual ideas, and of power shifts. Caught up in attempts to impose what had become common sense views, his query offered us a certain humility. We, as teachers, were being questioned on the very work for which we had been educated. Our knowledge, our plans, our valuing of "creative and unusual ideas" were usurped by Kotaro. His words cracked the world we had constructed, broke the spell of the mundane—a plan of our best intentions became actions lived through a sense of betrayal experienced by Kotaro. It had become a dangerous territory; we were complicit in burdening our world on another.

Listening to Kotaro's questions, we sensed an unwillingness to participate with the dominant voice of the classroom—ours. Initially reading his questions as critique, we momentarily thought of how we could re-order his world, infuse our logic on what was given to us. Yet, the mystery of his resistance called on us to reconsider our potential ruinous acts of domination. Instead, we entered a conversation "delicately and carefully and attentively," opening to the wounds and wisdom of the living pedagogic moment. Responding to Kotaro, we began to de-center ourselves in the "sting of ecological insight,"[5] realizing that he was not there for us, but there with us, being in the world in his own way, living with us in shared relations of uncertainty and curiosity that emerged from under-the-ground. In the convergence of our humility, we traced Kotaro's refusal to become a single voice with us. In his reply— his reading of things otherwise— we began to realize that the

> Somehow mutually caught up in a living, vital relationship in which each of us needs the other to be what we are. We need each other, not just as raw, inert material upon which our forms can be forced, but as an alternate voice which puts into perspective my own en-forming activity, resists it, suggests alternatives, shows that my knowledge is not equal to the world but is just a posibility living among and sustained by others I have not constructed, and occasionally outright refuses such bestowals of meaning.
> Jardine (1998, p. 121)

strange tensions we initially felt in Kotaro's questions were more about our need for order and authority. As we listened to his words, wary of the troubled tensions imbued in contradictions, a sense of mutuality opened up to (un)known interconnections we shared. His knowledge fell outside of the world we had constructed through the classroom activity that day. Our actions could have been damaging. Instead, by careful attunement to the potential wounds of a quest(ion), the three of us educated, and were educated by, each other.

Instance two

Kai seemed uninterested in working with other students to learn, not initiating and even eluding participation in dialogue opportunities with a partner or small group. Our experience suggested that this must be a lack of confidence, a "problem to be solved" through creating a safe classroom environment, with cooperative learning tasks and opportunities to talk about meaningful content in various groupings of students. Kai was shy and so we watched for growth in comfort levels. During a dialogue of evaluating presentations in a small group, we stumbled on a discovery:

> T: Are you comfortable with other students in the class
> (more, less, or the same than last term)?
> K: Less comfortable...
> T: (with eyebrows raised and head cocked to the left)
> Can you learn from others?
> K: (reluctant affirmative nod)
> T: Can they learn from you?
> K: I will not share.

Such a small phrase softly penetrated: "I will not share," revealing a hard protective shell, not to be broken, and yet, this phrase cracked our perceptive teacher shell, understandings and expectations layered through time and "knowing and living" in the classroom. Cultural assumptions about how Asian students will(ingly) work in groups were shattered by that determined, independent whisper. How often the unspoken voices had been filtered out as we selectively heard and assigned meaning and intention. Our monotonous stereotypes polished the kernels of our knowing, hardening and burnishing the visible until sharp words cracked the outer layer to reveal the once invisible, the complex, tough and tender strands beneath the surface. Once uncovered, these tend(e)rils of insight, feeling and wondering were exposed to the elements of self-knowing and other-knowing. Expectations of the learning process seemed deeply embedded in culture and experience, resistant to being moved and changed.

> T: How will you learn?
> K: By myself.
> T: Can you learn from others?
> K: I prefer to work alone.
> T: Can I learn from you?
> K: No, you are the teacher.

What followed was an exploration of the idea of the student being a teaching-learner and the teacher being a learning-teacher, there being more than linearity or reciprocity but rather a symbiotic relationship; one could not *be* without the other and each did not have a singular or solitary role. Cooperative learning-teaching is not doing a task together without conflict but is rather struggling together through a dynamic process.

To (Be) Mark(ed)

Writing marks. Marks impress. Impressions remain. Brent Davis (1996) contends that marking entails (en)grave(ing) acts on the body. We had not understood evaluation in this way. Our shift from a technical rationality of marking to an embodied one helped us to realize that to mark another is to mark oneself. Opened to the possibility that assessment could be experienced as

> A hint of what evaluation 'is really about' might be gleaned from a review of the terms associated with evaluative practices, such as 'marking', 'scoring,' and 'grading.' While their metaphoric origins have been largely forgotten in the modernist quest for objectivity, we would do well to recall that... one's marking, scoring, and grading of a learner involves a certain violence as one leaves 'impressions' on that person's body. Evaluation involves a marking for life.
>
> Davis (1996, p. 245)

embodied pedagogical moments, we invited students into our conversations of their evaluation, conversations that soon became sites of regular and unexpected disruptions for us, rich with life's unforeseen ambiguities and risky in coming to know our practices may have endangered those to whom we had been entrusted. We share two such instances in which the marks marked us.

Instance one

In our classroom, we invited students to respond to "being marked." One student wrote autobiographically of her *invisible* self in resistance—in a desire to be *dis*connected—to a mark.

> N: To tell the truth, I disagree [with] this grade. Before my presentation, I prepared questions...However, I forgot to write questions on [a] presentation plan sheet. Also, it was very hard for me to write my idea because I thought I would repeat my idea. As a result, I decided I ha[d] to write the most important things, and then I practice[d] doing [the] presentation many time[s]. It will be hard for other people to understand...my [invisible] effort, but I want you to know my effort.

The invisible disrupted our commonplace knowing of judging the *other*. Noriko opened us to the invisible, a presence that was absent, unmarked. The unmarked marked us. Woven into the presented fabric were the webs of *effort* she brought to bear in her work that we had not attended to. Visibly obscure, we were not attuned to the presence—the breath—of her effort. Instead, those necessary but seemingly unremarkable winds quickly became sterile and empty as we dutifully attended to her progress in consuming ever-increasing knowledge and skills. Her breath disrupted and exposed unrecognized formations of the winds that blow. We are now becoming more sensitized to the wind as "a thick and richly textured presence, filled with invisible...influences" (Abram 1996, 27). But, how *do* you mark the invisible? How does it mark us? Noriko's comment served to remind us of the enfolding wind, of being immersed in influences both present and absent, of connections that are integral to and call for a "re-marking," a re-conceptualizing of marking.

In response to her response, we began "re-reading" her present(ation) to us—her gift, her way of marking without leaving marks—re-membering that texts interweave ever incomplete and untold stories. We were reminded that what is made visible is only partial. The disruption stirred in us the importance of remaining open to the possibility of re-reading marks, hers and ours. Through our conversations with students, assessment has become an embodied practice, guided by an etymological return to its Latin stem, *assidere*, meaning *to sit beside*. Together, in the "felt matrix of [our] breaths" (Abram 1996, 26) the invisible becomes more visible, knowing that behind the inadequateness of words, obscure and "unintended kinships are born" (Jardine 1994, xxxii).

Instance two

What marks mark our students? How are they marked? In the following instance, Yasu's comment disrupted our expectations of a student's typical desire for "high" marks, disconnecting what we thought was a given. In our desire to be fair to all students, we had decided to give Yasu a lower mark because of what was missing—absent—but had been requested in the instructions of the assignment. As part of our embodied assessment practices, we invited all students to respond to the mark we gave in erasable ink. Yasu's comments were unexpected; a positive response to an unremarkable mark came from a motivated student. Entering into a conversation with him helped us to understand the undefined interconnectedness of a satisfaction that marked him average. The questions in italics are what we wrote as part of the evaluative feedback we gave for this assignment.

> Yasu: *Why do you include Japanese?* Answer: If when I forgot some vocabulary, I can check, and I can [put] in other words. *What about questions prepared for discussion?* Honestly I forgot to make some questions. I made some questions on the spot but I should [have] made question[s] before the class. I am satisfied with the results of [the] presentation but I think it isn't important for me to get good result[s]. I think "Could I get a lot of knowledge? or Could it be [a] worthwhile presentation for me?" I think I could be these two things. I am glad to be evaluated [for] my presentation.

A mark that normalizes, that makes possible to qualify, to classify and to punish or reward, neglects the interrelations of the subject marked. Marks seemed not to mark Yasu; instead his "mark" was the worthiness and interrelated implications of "get[ting] a lot of knowledge."

Were we blind to the absences present in his performance? What we marked was the presence of a performance, a presence that we had predetermined to establish what was important. We had forgotten, neglected, the absences-the unsaid values of the other. They hadn't concerned us, we had become numbed by routine, we were no longer grounded. We judged the present and marked him average-a label we impressed upon his body, a mark he had learned to dis/place with a value of his own. His re-marking marked us. We realized we had become blinded to the holistic act of the assignment and had chosen to attend to what we had designated important. In our conversation, Yasu had disrupted our blindness and brought us back to the importance of being with students in acts of judgment. Only through conversations with students could we begin to understand the holistic landscapes of what it means for students to do assignments and be marked. A lack of attunement to the under-the-ground in the mark given to Yasu marked us. Through our relationship with him, he had helped us to come to know ourselves.

Walking on Walking, Under Foot Earth Turns. (Snyder 1996, 9)

Repeatedly in the past, we have worked to avoid troubled terrains of the unexplained, invisible connections experienced in the classroom. We had not (at)tended to the earth "under foot" and the marks that we leave impressed on each other. Instead, leaving our impressions, our marks were expected signs of order and authority. The possibility of our acts being ruinous emerged in the unexpected conversations with students, calling us into difficult tensions and unexplored interweavings of our worlds together. Dwelling with students in the detours, traversing the frayed and fragmented entanglements of life, we entered the risk and richness of the unknown—educating, and being educated by, each other.

We have found ourselves at times urging reticent students to stand in that place of resistance with us. Sometimes students have willingly stood in that place waiting for us to join them, but we did not. These students had the courage to enter a genuine conversation with us—a conversation in which we were not the center of attention, a conversation in which we could begin to see the other in ourselves.

Courage

Is not   the
                towering
              oak that sees
            storms come
                 and
                 go;
               it is   O   S
    the fragile blossom that   p   n
                                  in the snow.

(Based on Alice Swaim quote.)

With courage, we reposition ourselves in the richness of pedagon (Smith 1999) and its nexus of complex and uncertain interconnections—those disturbing classroom conversations that disrupt the fragility of the pedagogical moment. The "sting of ecological insight" given to us by students was an invitation to become open to the mutuality of our lived experiences; they have taught us well. As we listen to the wisdom of the proverb, *when the wind blows the barrel makers get busy,* we are reminded of the deeply entangled and delicate interdependencies of our lives together in the classroom. Pondering education as an ecological site teeming with its inherent difficulties, dangers, and risks, we open nervously to genuine conversations with students.

Notes

1. Janet Miller (1997) claims that disruptions "constitute the lived practice of our research" wherein "no two days in the classroom are the same and no one theory holds together the disruptions" (p. 199).

2. David Jardine credits Charles Taylor for a thoughtful "distinction between two different senses of 'authenticity' in discourse: there is a fundamental difference between feeling a deep and profound connection to what I am writing about and writing *about myself.* Writing 'authentically' need not necessitate that I am the topic. This is a central mistake of much work in 'teacher narrative'." Jardine, 1994, p. 4.

3. In support of Deborah Britzman's comments on research, Patti Lather (1999, p. 5.) argues for research as a disruptive space, a space to be "wounded by thought", a "performance of practices of not-knowing".

4. David Abram (1996, p. 213) extends this notion of "the absence of the under-the-ground" in *The spell of the sensuous.*

5. The sting of ecological insight that David Jardine (1998) speaks of is his coming to know that the "pine and spruce trees, and this snow and the Chinook winds... are not there for [us]... that they have an agenda and an integrity of their own and they are not waiting for [us] to make sense of them or to graciously bestow them with order" (p. 120).

References

Abram, D. 1996. *The spell of the sensuous.* New York: Random House.
Aoki, T.T. *Locating living pedagogy in teacher "research:" Five metonymic moments.* Invited paper presented at the Teacher Research Conference, April 2000. Baton Rouge, LA.
Davis, B. 1996. *Teaching mathematics.* New York: Garland.
Jardine, D. 1994. *Speaking with a boneless tongue.* Bragg Creek: Makyo Press.
Smith, D. 1999. *Pedagon.* New York: Peter Lang.
Snyder, G. 1996. *Mountains and rivers without end.* Washington: Counterpoint.
Swaim, Alice Mackenzie. Courage. http://www.cyber-nation.com/ victory/quotations/authors/quotes_swaim_alicemackenzie.html.

Embodying "Pedagogical Possibilities": Teaching Being, Being Teaching

There is an undecidability to teaching.
The good teacher is one who gives
what s/he doesn't have;
the future as undecidable,
possibility as indeterminable.

—Elizabeth Ellsworth

Embodying "Pedagogical Possibilities¹": Teaching Being, Being Teaching

Embodying the Flesh of the Wor(l)d

Brent: In our roles as editors, writers, and inquirers, we have played with perceptions of holistic thinking and education, stretching and shaping them through our bodies. This section intertwines *bodymind* with the languages of *embodiment*. Heesoon Bai draws on Buddhist thought to emphasize the importance of direct sensory experience as a means of reclaiming our connections with the environment. Genét Kozik-Rosabal discusses embodiment in terms of personal dispositions and transformative learning as they relate to teacher education. Alison Pryer reminds us of the carnal, erotic nature of classroom embodiments. Ronald Burr and Sherry Hartman suggest that teaching and learning embody theory and practice. They recount their journeys as instructors in higher education, seeking to bridge individual and disciplinary bodies of knowing.

These languages of embodiment differ according to the thinking, experiences, and research orientations of their authors. The languages are never fixed, but always unfolding, always seeking to catch the ephemeral and possible worlds that emerge through bodies of teaching and educational inquiry. Heesoon Bai suggests that we should treat words as "guests" rather than substituting them for direct sensory experience. I wonder how we can learn to be mindful of the relationships that we embody as teachers and learners *through language?*

Johnna: In my dissertation (Haskell 2000) I have explored mindfulness, which I refer to as *embodied awareness*. This "way of being" allows us to inquire, experience, know, and be with the world. Embodied awareness is the flesh of the world. We cannot contain it but only help bring it forth through our interactions with other bodies, human and non-human.

Brent: There is a detailed description of Merleau-Ponty's understandings of the "Flesh" in David Abram's work, *The Spell of the Sensuous:*

> Merleau-Ponty was striving for a new way of speaking that
> would express this consanguinity of the human animal and
> the world it inhabits. Here [in *The Visible and the Invisible*]
> he writes less about "the body" (which in his earlier work
> had signified primarily the *human* body) and begins to

write instead of the collective "Flesh," which signifies both *our* flesh and "the flesh of the world." ...The Flesh is the mysterious tissue or matrix that underlies and gives rise to both the perceiver and the perceived as interdependent aspects of its own spontaneous activity. (1996, 66)

This shift from the human to more-than-human body prompts us as educators to be mindful of

word   thought   gesture

possibility

a   c   t   i   o   n

stices

inter

sections

webs

we call

relationship.

Our bodily relationships are distinctive as Dreyfus and Dreyfus, borrowing from Merleau-Ponty, recognize:

[They are] not up for interpretation and, since perception depends on the body, neither is the perceptual world. On this account, embodiment refers to the actual shape and innate capacities of the human body—that it has arms and legs, a certain size, and certain abilities. (1999, 103)

The ability to distinguish our body from those of others is a form of mindful awareness. Abram (1996, 68) says, "We can perceive things at all only because we ourselves are entirely a part of the sensible world that we perceive! We might as well say that we are organs of this world, flesh of its flesh, and that the world is perceiving itself *through* us."

Enacting Transformative Pedagogies

Brent: In the introduction to this volume we referred to structural coupling, the notion that living systems come together, reorganize, and bring forth new worlds. I am interested in how this concept might be overlaid with understandings of embodiment as a transformative phenomenon. In other words, how might the worlds we embody through structural coupling facilitate transformative processes in the classroom? Varela, Thompson, and Rosch (1991, xv) introduce their work "with the conviction that the new sciences of mind need to enlarge their horizon to encompass both lived human experience and the possibilities for transformation inherent in human experience." My primary concern is not how we might facilitate transformation in an instrumentalist sense, but rather how we might be mindful of the ways in which transformation is integral to embodied pedagogy; that is, how our bodies change as we enact teaching and learning.

Warren: Often we have taken the notion of transformational pedagogy to involve simply changing minds—changing ideas. It may be concerned with issues of societal change at an ideological or structural level. In this context there is an overlap with critical pedagogy.

By far the most well-known transformational pedagogue was Paulo Freire. Freire wrote in one of his last books, *Pedagogy of the Heart* (1997), about relational experience on the level of existence and of interactions, the level of living. He adds that there is a fundamental element in interaction, which takes on greater complexity in relationship. He is referring to curiosity, which he defines as "some sort of openness to comprehending what is in the orbit of the challenged being's sensibility" (p. 94). This is a disposition that is often ignored in teacher education and is linked to desire. As Freire says, "it is this desire, always alive, of feeling, living, realizing what lies in the realm of one's 'visions of depth'" (p. 94). This curiosity, this desire to see what's around the corner, means we are always ready to question. Without questioning of what is, there is no *possibility* of knowing what might be.

Adding elements of embodiment moves us towards a holistic approach; our idea of consciousness moves us from something exclusively rational and in the mind, and broadens it to include feelings, emotions, desires and our bodies. Transformation begins through our embodied interactions with/in the world.

Johnna: Yes, our breathing bodies full of potential, possibility, embodying a flesh alive with "transformation" as we slough off the epidermis of cells—much like a snake casting its experiences behind a rock or a lobster precariously waiting for its shell to harden. Maybe we are like the lobster staying protected in our classrooms waiting for our shells to harden to the watery world.

Warren: Funny you mention lobsters. I just read an article on them at our local fresh fish shop on the Canadian prairie (which sells live lobsters brought in from the East Coast—amazing!). My understanding from reading this is that lobsters don't just wait for their shells to harden but eat certain things that contain the calcium necessary for this process. Thus, hardening as transformation is not a waiting, but a continuous process that involves enacting and interacting with the world.

Brent: One of my goals as an educator is for learners to experience transformation as a nurturing, generative process—a journey of risks and explorations, but one that ultimately strengthens pedagogic senses of wonder and relationship. Many people experience change as unsettling, but if we are not changing, we are not learning. A crucial issue for me is how we embody unstable changes as vital processes of everyday living.

Warren: Varela, Thompson, and Rosch have a nice way of putting this:

> The results of the path of mindful, open-ended learning are profoundly transformative. Instead of being embodied...out of struggle, habit, and sense of self, the goal is to become embodied out of compassion for the world. (1991, 251-52)

Mindful, open-ended learning means we need to be present in our actions. I think of it in terms of my facilitation of drama workshops. I write down an agenda that I refer to if I need to but often I am caught up in the interplays of doing drama with students or teachers, responding to what I see, feel, and sense. If I start thinking about what I want to accomplish, the magic is lost. But when it works it is like floating on a flowing stream, responding to the currents of interaction.

Brent: To be "with body," then, is to immerse ourselves in the phenomenon before us, allowing it to spill through our being. We do not abstract ourselves out of a situation in order to *understand* how we are changing. Rather, we allow ourselves to become part of the change, to attune ourselves with other encompassing bodies.

Johnna: Yes, we have to stop grasping experience. I don't think we "reflect on" experience but we re-experience our socio-historical coupling as worldly bodies. Experience is never the same and cannot be replicated exactly. Like a river or waterfall, our bodies arise not by the same water molecules passing over rocks, but by their constant flow and exchanges with one another. As experiencing is never truly *dis*embodied, perception arises through embodied awareness, not going away but boiling forth through moments of (inter)action.

Embodying Awareness

Brent: One summer several years ago I enrolled in a science education course for student teachers. It focused on embodied approaches to teaching science. It seemed at the time that I had to relearn how to *be* with my body. I have had this feeling before in music and drama classes and more recently, when exploring the use of manipulatives as an embodied form of mathematical instruction. In each instance I have experienced my body learning differently. I have had to let go of habits and experiences from the past that have served to undermine my felt senses of bodily awareness and participation. I have also had to risk new ways of embodied being as I re-attune myself with my encompassing environment; that is, to be mindful of my adult body here-and-now—not as a being that performs learning but one that is performing through learning.

How do both of you think classrooms and teachers can/should support embodied pedagogies?

Warren: The best way to approach learning embodied and mindful practices is to engage in those practices that could be inherently mindful. Ronald Burr and Sherry Hartman illustrate one set of activities used in higher education. Genét Kozik-Rosabal illustrates another. It would be a contradiction in terms to talk about "teaching" mindfulness. It has to be something that co-emerges in the interplay between teacher and student. Finding ways for this to happen is the big challenge. Drama has the potential to do this, as it is successful if engaged through mindful practice.

Brent: Do some activities facilitate mindful awareness better than others? Or, is it possible to be mindful in any situation? When the three of us started learning about embodied and enactive approaches to learning in Karen's course, we studied *Situated Learning: Legitimate Peripheral Participation* (Lave and Wenger 1991). At the time there was a great deal of discussion among educators about "authentic" learning in socially situated contexts of practice. The term *authentic* was identified with notions of apprenticeship, modeling, and expertise. That discussions of this type were and continue to be so popular stems in part from a feeling that what happens in formal education does not constitute authentic practice. When I asked if some activities are better suited to mindful awareness, I was ruminating on this body of literature.

Johnna: Recently, after hearing David Blades, a science educator from the University of Alberta, speak at the University of British Columbia, I asked him what he meant by authentic experience. He replied with a story from one of his biking trips to and from the university where he teaches. One day, he stopped when a wolf was in the middle of his path. Would most of us continue biking without "seeing" the wolf, or choose to interact and communicate with this fleshy body?

Brent: I once encountered a coyote while jogging on a local path in Stanley Park. My senses were alerted to this animal trotting down the trail ahead of me. I felt waves of curiosity and fear in the pit of my stomach. How had this body come to be with my body? What was it thinking?

> Walking in a forest, we peer into its green and shadowed depths, listening to the silence of the leaves, tasting the cool and fragrant air...we may suddenly feel that the trees are looking at us— we feel ourselves exposed, watched, observed from all sides. (Abram 1996, 68)

Was Coyote watching me with the same animated curiosity that sustained my gaze? This animal continued its light canter and then disappeared into the forest as quickly as it had made itself known.

Have we become so preoccupied with our own bodies that we have forgotten the art of pedagogical watchfulness and wondering? Of looking and loving? The observation by David Blades reminds me of something about watchfulness[2] that I recently read by June Aoki and Ted Aoki: she referred me to the work of Ted Aoki, where I discovered the following quote: "Authentic teaching is watchfulness, a mindful watching flowing from the heeding of the call in the pedagogical situation that the good teacher hears. Indeed, teachers are more than they do; they belong to that which is beyond their doing; they are the teaching"[3] (1990, 16). Watchfulness permeates our bodies as teachers with those of our learners. One of the reasons schooling may be perceived as inauthentic is because we have overlooked the importance of watchfulness as a pedagogical orientation for staying connected with others. Watchfulness is an embodied phenomenon that affords different ways of relating to our encompassing environments.

I wonder how different senses of place allow us to stay mindful of our connections with a more-than-human world?

Embodying Placefulness

Johnna: Outdoor adventure education opens opportunities for interactions among bodies, for risk-taking, and for preparing students to make choices, set goals, and push their limits. Do classrooms support this type of learning? Some do. We also have to take time to let this arise. This involves patience. Sometimes this learning can not be expressed in the moment and may take years of re-experiencing before we come to an awareness of our intuitive embodiments.

Warren: I have been working with a group of special needs students who have a lot of energy. Enclosed by the four walls of the classroom I sensed that they want to break out and play. We moved the drama workshop out of the regular classroom and desks and rows into a neighbouring lunch-room where we created a circle so we could share and see each other. I know it is not enough, but even this slight change means a change in their relations with each other. In the late winter of the Canadian prairies it wouldn't be possible to work outside. Perhaps in the spring when the flowers bloom and blossom we might try something outdoors. But we are faced with the constraints of the landscape as well as its potential. There is a need for these students to express themselves orally and to be heard. Working outdoors with its wind and sounds of cars on the nearby highway makes it difficult.

I think there are ways to bring the outdoors into school. I don't mean bringing plants and animals and other more-than-human beings inside as is often done. I mean bringing in the idea of getting to really know our landscape, including manufactured things: stones now cement, or trees now desks. That would include finding new ways of being in these human-constructed environments. That is why my work concentrates on opening our senses.

Johnna: How do we embody our experience of the outside with/in human-constructed environments? Are you saying that in order to learn we need to separate ourselves from the car noises or other classroom noises? Even in cities many are creating gardens of opportunity with waterfalls and sensuous landscapes. We experienced this in the Botanical Gardens at the Bodymind Conference.

Warren: No, we need to become re-attuned to our senses, to listen to what we hear, to see what we look at. A few years ago I chatted with a theatre colleague about how we might incorporate the landscape as a character in our theatre processes rather than using landscape as simply a backdrop or the content message of the play. We thought people would try and under-stand how a rock might feel or talk or move...there are lots of possibilities here. One is a wonderful activity called *The Council of All Beings* (Seed, Macy, and Fleming 1988), which begins to address this. I used it once inside a Drama in Education class for elementary teachers. Students played different life forms, attempting to interstand them through visualization, making a mask, embodying the way they moved, spoke and thought. I remember one student in particular who played Granite, who spoke in a low, measured tone, very solid. He had lots of insightful things to say as granite. Students were affected by this activity. I now see how this type of performative inquiry (Fels, 1999) can be extended into the outdoors.

Brent: I too am interested in engaging learning with the classroom as an animate life form. In recent years I have encouraged students to participate in a variety of interactive phenomenological writing, drawing, and drama activities in order to understand the ways in which architectural landscapes engage us as humans. Learning to be mindful of the environment is essential if we are to communicate with one another as sentient beings.

Developing this type of rapport requires an appreciation for the ways in which space influences our lives, as it is an important consideration when we think about how bodies emerge through the world. Typically, we associate space with emptiness or with containment. As a teacher, I am sometimes frustrated with the limitations of working with 29 physical bodies in a small box we call the classroom. One of my challenges is to re-visualize space in such a way that it becomes part of the conversation I am trying to facilitate with the environment—to allow it to become part of my perceptual foreground rather than staying inactive in the background. The disruption of commonly accepted figure/ground relationships is one way that I have found to stay mindful.[4]

Johnna: I taught a three-week course outside in the woods at the University of British Columbia. Teachers practiced using their bodies to demonstrate chemical reactions, vector forces, centripetal force, and many ecological relationships. One activity that was rather fun was when we all had certain cards for water, food, and other items. We were some type of animal that might be predator or prey to another. I was a cougar with a bright red shirt on that day, making it hard to blend in with the environment. Later humans were introduced. When someone was tagged, that person lost a card. When all the cards were gone you died and were out of the interaction (game). These "embodiments" facilitated new connections and brought out different attitudes and choices for each human and animal body.

Embodying Pedagogy as Choreography

Brent: Thinking through teaching as an embodied phenomenon is much like thinking through the dynamics of choreography. If you were teaching a course on embodied knowing to student teachers, how would you help them put their knowledge of this choreography into action?

Warren: One cannot teach embodied knowing. One must "do the dance." By *dance*, I mean "the sensed patterning of the motional narrative," a narrative that is "abstract, the dynamic ebb and flow of motion set in and existing through space and time" (Blumenfeld-Jones 1995, 398). Form is both internal and external (Stinson 1995). So, one must be involved in it both on the inside and the outside in order to realize what it feels like. That is the biggest contradiction in graduate education. Many courses are *about* something rather than endeavoring to teach through *doing.*

Johnna: I think that we have responsibilities as teachers/learners to prepare and push ourselves into uncomfortable places. Time in the outdoors helps us embody our education. Sometimes we need to find a voice for questioning aloud those professors recognized in higher education. My professors welcomed this disruption and encouraged me to meander down unknown paths. I think that the tension professors/teachers play with on the belay rope while their students are climbing life's rocks is delicate. If teachers hold on too tightly, students' bodies can only move in certain ways, which might hold the body too close to the rock for their movement. Maybe students need to be further away to move upward. A choreographed interaction can open opportunities for some students to dance up the rock and for others to dwell for a moment in the struggles, while still wanting to climb.

Warren: Of course, choreography is more than designing dances for others. It requires an embodied understanding of the bodies of the dancers, the landscape of the dance space, and many other media such as lighting, sound, and time. There are also different kinds of choreographies, depending on the dance.

Brent: We have returned to dance once again—a focus in our first conversation. We seem to have come full circle, caught in the hermeneutic iterations of our own languages and embodiments.

Warren: I am currently working on "training" teachers in the improvisational arts of drama facilitation. Recently, I taught a class for a friend who observed me in action. He told me that it was like watching good jazz...he followed the line of the "music;" he knew the underlying structure that was part of the form of the theatre process, and he could see where I had made choices to follow one thread or move on to another.

So in answer to your question...

I would say there are many aspects required to enable an embodied knowing of teaching and learning. This would involve working at many levels of experience—observation, participation, reflective writing of mindful practice, as well as engaging in the teaching process itself.

Johnna: Evolving aspects transfiguring visibly, yet "pregnant with the invisible" (Merleau-Ponty 1968), unknown, and unexpected—what a wonderful pedagogy of embodied awareness and possibility.

Notes

1. "Pedagogical possibilities" is taken from the title of Johnna's doctoral dissertation (Haskell 2000).

2. For this insight, I thank Nancy Everett, who was a vice-principal at my school for several years, and who pointed out the work of the Aokis. The topic of watchfulness came up with one of my conversations with Nancy during the 1999-2000 academic year.

3. This quotation is rephrased slightly in another work by Ted Aoki: "Authentic teaching is watchfulness, a mindful watching overflowing from the good in the situation that the good teacher sees. In this sense, good teachers are more than they do; they are the teaching" (Aoki 1992, 26).

4. Brent Davis introduced me to the significance of figure/ground relationships in my Enactivism and Education seminar at the University of British Columbia. The figure is that which we highlight in our field of perception at any given time; the ground is that which has dissolved around the figure. One understanding of this relationship is reflected in the interplay between positive and negative space in art. Pictures used in psychological testing also manifest this relationship (e.g., the young woman and old woman within the same face). In our desire to "understand" the world we often forget that the picture before us is a reflection of our own participation in the world. Merleau-Ponty (1962, 3-4) also talks about the figure/ground relationship in his analysis of perception. For further information about figure/ground perception, see Davis, Sumara, and Luce-Kapler (2000, 14, 23-25).

References

Abram, David. 1996. *The spell of the sensuous: Perception and language in a more-than-human world.* New York: Pantheon Books.
Aoki, June, and Ted Aoki. 1990. Silent voices of teaching. In *Voices of teaching: Vol. 1,* edited by T. Aoki and M. Shamsher. Vancouver: British Columbia Teachers' Federation Program for Quality Teaching.
Aoki, Ted. 1992. Layered voices of teaching: The uncannily correct and the elusively true. In *Understanding curriculum as phenomenological and deconstructed text,* edited by W.F. Pinar and W.M. Reynolds. New York: Teachers College Press.
Blumenfeld-Jones, Donald 1995. Dance as a mode of research representation. *Qualitative inquiry* 1(4): 391-401.

Davis, Brent, Dennis Sumara, and Rebecca Luce-Kapler. 2000. Engaging minds: Learning and teaching in a complex world. Mahwah, NJ: Lawrence Erlbaum Associates.

Dreyfus, Hubert L., and Stuart E. Dreyfus. 1999. The challenge of Merleau-Ponty's phenomenology of embodiment for cognitive science. In Perspectives on embodiment: The intersections of nature and culture, edited by G. Weiss and H.F. Haber. New York: Routledge.

Ellsworth, Elizabeth. 1997. Teaching positions: Difference, pedagogy, and the power of address. New York: Teachers College Press.

Fels, Lynn. 1999. In the wind clothers dance on a line. Performative inquiry: A research methodology. Ph.D. diss., University of British Columbia.

Freire, Paulo. 1997. Pedagogy of the heart. Translated by D. Macedo and A. Oliveira. New York: Continuum.

Haskell, Johnna. 2000. Experiencing freefall: A journey of pedagogical possibilities. Ph.D. diss., University of British Columbia.

Lave, Jean, and Etienne Wenger. 1991. Situated learning: Legitimate peripheral participation. Cambridge, MA: Cambridge University Press.

Merleau-Ponty, Maurice. 1962. Phenomenology of perception. Translated by Colin Smith. London: Routledge and Kegan Paul.

Merleau-Ponty, Maurice. [1964] 1968. The visible and the invisible, followed by working notes. Translated by Alphonso Lingis. Evanston, IL: Northwestern University Press.

Seed, John, Joanna Macy, and Pat Fleming 1988. Thinking like a mountain: Towards a council of all beings. Gabriola Island, BC: New Society Publishers.

Stinson, Susan W. 1995. Body of knowledge. Educational Theory 45(1): 43-54.

Varela, Francisco J., Evan Thompson, and Eleanor Rosch. 1991. The embodied mind: Cognitive science and human experience. Cambridge, MA: MIT Press.

Beyond the Educated Mind:
Towards a Pedagogy of Mindfulness

Heesoon Bai

HEESOON BAI, a longtime student of Buddhism, teaches and researches in Philosophy of Education, with a specialization in Moral Philosophy and Education. Currently, she is an assistant professor in the Faculty of Education at Simon Fraser University, Burnaby, B.C., Canada.

Abstract. Faced with increasing social and environmental disintegration worldwide, and moreover, a seeming inability to respond adequately to the exigency, I reprove the intellectualist bias and resulting disembodiment in our educational practice. I argue that this bias contributes to the problem at two levels: lack of intrinsic valuing of the world and inability to translate knowledge into action. I then propose the practice of mindfulness as a tool with which we can recover our ability to value the world intrinsically and to embody knowledge.

Keywords. (Dis)embodiment, Mindfulness, Interbeing, Environment, Earth, Perception, Non-Conceptual Awareness

Beyond the Educated Mind:
Towards a Pedagogy of Mindfulness

Heesoon Bai

Whenever I quiet the persistent chatter of words within my head, I find this silent or wordless dance always already going on—this improvised duet between my animal body and the fluid, breathing landscape that it inhabits.—David Abram

Consider David Korten's (1995) diagnosis that social and environmental disintegration now affects "nearly every country of the world—as revealed by a rise in poverty, unemployment, inequity, violent crime, failing families, and environmental degradation" (p. 11). By all accounts, humanity is facing a crisis, and this is widely acknowledged by the public.[1] Yet, what is most disturbing is our inability to act on this knowledge. Havel (1998, 56) states: "[E]ven though we are aware of these dangers, we do almost nothing to avert them. It's fascinating to me how preoccupied people are today with catastrophic prognoses…but how very little account we take of these threats in our everyday activities."

The translation of knowledge into action is what education is for and what pedagogy is about.[2] Thus, our inability to take appropriate action for the crisis we face calls our practice of education into question. The starting point of this discussion is the following question: What factors in our education contribute to the problem? I find a clue to my question in Whitehead's notion of "inert ideas." Received inert ideas, like inert gas, do not interact with you as a whole being, affecting your perceptions and feelings; hence, they do not move you to action.

But what kinds of ideas are inert? Whitehead's explanation is most illuminating. Inert ideas are unutilized ideas and by utilization, Whitehead (1929,) means "relating [ideas] to that stream, compounded of *sense perceptions, feelings,* hopes, desires, and of mental activities adjusting thought to thought, which forms our life" (emphasis mine). In short, inert ideas are disembodied ideas: ideas that are not worked into one's whole being with senses and feelings. Consequently, they are incapable of compelling us to action.[3]

Whitehead notes that inert ideas are a perennial problem in education. The objective here is both to account for the entrenchment of the problem and to point towards the direction for solving it. I base my explanation and strategy in the Buddhist theory of mind and the practice of "mindfulness." The key insight that Buddhism provides is this: our linguistic-conceptual mind is inherently disembodying in that it replaces percepts with concepts.[4] When this happens, our ability to experience reality directly as a perceiving and feeling being is compromised by the excessive (and obsessive) engagement with concepts. This, briefly, is disembodiment.

The pedagogical recommendation that results from my above analysis is twofold: first, help students become aware of the mind's tendency toward disembodiment; second, provide them with opportunities and tools to work at embodiment by recovering percepts and restoring them to the center stage of consciousness. Borrowing the Buddhist term, I shall call such pedagogy the "pedagogy of mindfulness."[5] I will argue that this pedagogy is fit to address not only the pedagogical problem of translating knowledge into action, but also the more substantive task of healing human alienation from the world.

What is Disembodiment?

The claim that we (speaking generally) suffer from disembodiment is bound to raise puzzled looks in people. Don't we all have bodies? Yes, I reply, but "having" a body is not a sufficient, though a necessary, condition for the experience of being a fully sensing and perceiving body. Consider the following examples as illustrations of what I mean by disembodiment.

Suppose that on one glorious autumn day, you and your friend, whom you have not seen for some time, meet at the parking lot of a nearby national park and set out on a walk through the woods. You have looked forward to this escape from the city and a full immersion into Nature. Not having seen each other for a while, though, naturally you want to catch up on events, and so you start chatting. You then become so engrossed in talking that for the entire walk of two hours you barely notice all that meets your senses. You have auto-piloted through the trail but you have not experienced fully all the sights, sounds, smells, and the feel of the woods available to you on this particular walk. Thus, as far as the nature walk is concerned, that walk has been a disembodied experience. It is as though your body and its senses were not fully present in the experience.

The next example comes from the legendary Nobel-laureate physicist, Richard Feynman (1985). Feynman was in Brazil at one time, teaching physics to a group of students who were training to be physics teachers. He discovered that the students were incredibly good at memorizing everything from the physics textbook and could regurgitate their knowledge during exams with near one hundred percent accuracy. But he also discovered, to his dismay, that the students understood little from this memorization. They could not describe and explain the described physical phenomena in the terms of possible or actual experience:

> After a lot of investigation, I finally figured out that the students had memorized everything, but they didn't know what anything meant. When they heard "light that is reflected from a medium with an index," they didn't know that it meant a material *such as water*. They didn't know that the "direction of the light" is the direction in which you *see* something when you're looking at it, and so on. (p. 192)

Besides illustrating the meaning of disembodiment, the above examples suggest what typically causes disembodiment: failing to ground ideas, concepts, and thoughts in sense perception. This happens easily because when we are preoccupied with the activities of the conceptual mind, such as thinking, reading, talking, or any other symbolic manipulation, we lose "sight of" or "touch with" the dimension of the sensuous. Of course, this does not mean that we stop perceiving. Rather, it means that our sensory awareness moves into the mode of semi-consciousness or even unconsciousness. Consider the times you have auto-piloted safely through busy traffic to your home all the while being heavily preoccupied with something. People speak of unconscious or subconscious body memories and body intelligence.[6] For sure, we can only be thankful for this feature of ourselves. But it is not entirely a positive one.

Moral Implications of Disembodiment

Disembodiment poses a serious concern for the way it affects our being-in-the-world. Our primary connection with this physical world is through our body and its senses. This should be no surprise. The body and its senses have co-evolved with the material, physical world.[7] What our senses "tell" us constitutes our primary understanding of the world. This basically is the foundational tenet of empiricism.[8] But what is usually absent in the empiricist thesis is the mention of the affective dimension of the bodily-sensorial understanding. This dimension is the home of the "carnal, sensorial empathy" (Abram 1996, 69) that connects the being of the human self with the being of other material entities, or taken in totality, the earth or biosphere. To experience another physical being in the mode of direct and sensuous perception is to realize the primordial bond between oneself and that being, which disposes one to value it intrinsically.

What is this primordial bond like? I find a particularly lucid articulation of this bond in Frederick Franck's (1973) description of what he calls seeing/drawing meditation. Drawing for Franck is the Zen way of seeing: seeing that overcomes the usual "looking at" that efficiently labels and judges things for an instrumentalist purpose. When Franck sees/draws, through his sustained and undivided attention to the object before him he "enter[s] into direct contact with [the object's] life process, with Life itself" (p. 7). What is revealed to Franck through his drawing/seeing is the "sheer miracle" of Being. He states: "The Zen of seeing is a way from half-sleep to full awakening. Suddenly there is the miracle of being really alive with all the senses functioning...How wondrously strange and miraculous: I see! I see a lettuce! I see you!" (p. 28).

When this primordial bonding with the material world is interfered with by the hyperactivity of the linguistic-conceptual mind, the result is our emotional alienation from the material world. We "look at" the world as a foreign entity, an object categorically separate from us, the subject. Alienation brings about the loss of receptivity and sensitivity to that from which we are alienated. This loss is sensorially experienced as absence of or diminished hearing, seeing, smelling, and feeling. The forest from which I am alienated does not "speak" to me, does not address me, does not embrace me: I do not "hear" the ancient chorus of the cedar trees; I do not "feel" the embrace of the gathering darkness; I "see" no glory of life manifest in the blueness of the sky shimmering between the red and gold autumn leaves. Thomas Berry (1996), an ecotheologian, diagnoses this loss of perception and sensation as a form of "autism" and attributes our insensitivity to nature as due to it:

> The thousandfold voices of the natural world suddenly became
> inaudible to the human. The mountains and rivers and the wind
> and the sea all became mute insofar as humans were concerned.
> The forests were no longer the abode of an infinite number of
> spirit presences but were simply so many board feet of lumber
> to be "harvested" as objects to be used for human benefit.
> Animals were no longer the companions of humans in the
> single community of existence. (p. 410)

The danger of this sort of autism is far more serious than our pale appreciation
of the world. What is at stake is moral harm. Evernden (1985) in his discussion
about our perceptions of the natural world paints a chilling description of the
ways in which lab animals are maimed during vivisection. He tells us about
the practice of severing the lab animals' vocal cords so that the experimenters
wouldn't hear the cries and can carry on with the vivisection without being
disturbed (p. 16). When we cannot see, hear, and feel the other, it is all too easy
to impose our own desire and design on it, oblivious to or disregarding the
possibility of harm to the other.

The kind of autism that Berry speaks of is the result of our particular epistemic
commitment that reality is seen as construed and constructed according to our
conceptualization.[9] Reality is what you make of it, so to speak. The moral
implication that follows is the denial of inherent value to those entities which
we may recognize as existing but with which we have no perceptual and emotional involvement. That is, all the beings that constitute the reality do not exist
for themselves but exist for our needs and wants. Hence, they have only instrumental value. They are not subjects unto themselves but objects for us. Note
that beings are "objects" because we have objectified them in the first place.
Furthermore, if we objectify the world, then it is at our disposal. The world
becomes a source of materials to realize our projects and a waste sink to
receive the by-products of our excessive construction and consumption.

Consider land. As most people seem to see it, land exists for the sake of human
use. Its value lies in its usefulness to humans. Hence, it only has instrumental
value to us.[10] No intrinsic valuing here. The kind of exploitative and damaging
practices we inflict upon the earth's surface, with resulting rampant ecocide,
are the logical consequence of our exclusively instrumentalist perceptions and
practices. We have largely lost the sense of the sacredness of the earth, of its
intrinsic value. We have lost it because we have forgotten our fundamental
grounding in the senses. Percepts come to be absorbed into concepts, losing
their centrality in our consciousness.

Thus, education dedicated to the goal of reversing the social and ecological
degradation has to start with learning to value the world intrinsically. What
this means to me is bringing back the senses to the center stage of consciousness so that we may take up residence in it rather than in the abstract linguistic-conceptual mode. This does not mean that we must banish words, ideas,
concepts, and thinking. It is just that they will be our guests, rather than our
master: they are invited to play with us but not dictate and control us. Names
and other linguistic devices are convenient and effective in terms of social
coordination, just as money exchange is convenient compared to bartering. But

we must not focus only on the gain, forgetting the loss. Language has gifted us a convenient means of *communication* but it can rob us of the opportunities of *communion*, which is the sensuously grounded being-to-being connection.[11]

Zen masters have warned us of the danger of reification, using the parable of a finger pointing at the moon: Don't look at the finger; look at the moon that the finger is pointing to. Our language, like the finger, points to the possibility of sensuous experience beyond itself. If language is used with the understanding that it only points to rather than represents reality, we would avoid the trap of reification and its resulting disembodiment. But if language is used without this understanding, it only serves to alienate us from the possibility of sensuous experience. And to carry on with the above metaphor, the reason why we are prone to looking no farther than the pointing finger is because the sky is so completely filled with pointing fingers that you cannot see the sky. To be more literal, one's field of sensuous awareness is so filled with a constant torrent of mind-chatter and external stimuli in the form of words and images that it is difficult to gain a clear view of it. But difficulty is not impossibility. There are ways to control mind-chatter.

Mindfulness

According to Buddhist psychology, the mind's "job" is to convert percepts into concepts (Kalupahana 1987).[12] To put it another way, mind superimposes concepts on percepts, thereby concealing the latter from our ordinary introspection.[13] And this operation is automatic and ceaseless. How do we interrupt the ceaseless and relentless activity of the conceptualizing mind? The Buddhist response is first and foremost to become aware of the automation of conceptualization. That which is automatic is "invisible" to us, and we cannot change what is invisible.

What we call intellect is largely the operations of the linguistic-conceptual categories that we have received and internalized through our membership in linguistic-cultural communities—hence the ceaselessness and automation. Consider how readily we identify and name familiar objects: cup, disk, flower, and so on. It takes a fraction of a second of pattern recognition to name these everyday objects. But when this happens, pattern-recognition-naming preempts a sensuous contact and engagement with the "object." The result is a missed opportunity to experience being-to-being connectedness to the "object."

The Buddhist "mindfulness practice" (*satipatthana*), popularly known in the West as "meditation," is a way to recover the non-conceptual awareness. Its technique is simple and clear enough. You direct your "bare attention" to the moment-by-moment arising and passing of perception, sensation, emotion, thought, and so on. But mindfulness is difficult to practice because of the ceaseless activity of the mind. It has routinely been observed by beginning students of the mindfulness practices that the hardest challenge is to become disengaged from the constant chatter of the mind (Gunaratana 1991). Thoughts come so thick and fast that one gets swept into the torrent and carried away. Before one realizes it, one has abandoned the calm physical awareness of breathing and drifted into mind-chatter, endlessly thinking of what happened, could or should have happened, will happen, or will be made to happen, and so on. This constant thinking in the form of mind-chatter is not peculiar to meditators but is the usual mode for most people in their waking hours and even in their sleep.

As anyone who has tried to suppress mind-chatter knows, no amount of will power will accomplish the suppression. But, the point is not so much getting rid of thinking as recovering the underlying foundational field of non-discursive awareness. In other words, the problem is with the hyperactivity of thinking that conceals the non-discursive, embodied awareness. Thus, the meditator's primary task is to calm the hyperactive mind.

The contemporary meditation master in the tradition of Tibetan Buddhism, Soygal Rinpoche (1993 74), explains of meditation: "The secret is not to 'think' about thoughts, but to allow them to flow through the mind, while keeping your mind free of afterthoughts." When thoughts are allowed to arise and pass away freely, which is made possible when we do not cling to them and identify with them, then we can catch glimpses of the spacious awareness between and around the thoughts. In other words, catching the glimpse of, and moving into, the gaps between arising thoughts affords us the best way to establish ourselves in the practice of meditation. Again to quote Soygal Rinpoche "So the work of meditation is to allow thoughts to slow down, to make that gap become more and more apparent" (p. 75).

The standard technique for not getting ensnared into the thought-stream is anchoring the attention to the moment-to-moment arising of sensations. Sensations of breathing are especially helpful as an anchorage because breathing is constant and rhythmic, as well as calming. Still, it is only with much perseverance and effort, comparable to learning to play a musical instrument or mastering any other rigorous art, that one gradually trains one's attention and learns to dwell in the wordless and thoughtless space of sensuous awareness. As a well-established resident of this space, we can then welcome the guests who come to visit in the form of concepts and words. The guests come and go, however frequently, but we stay home in our non-discursive awareness.

Attaining mindfulness is an achievement that impacts our relationship to the world. For through mindfulness we sense the "interbeing" (Nhat Hanh 1993) or co-emergence of all beings.[14] One realizes, not just conceptually, but in one's senses, that one is not separate from the world, that one *is* the world as its one local expression.

Educational Implementation of Mindfulness

Education is foremost an act of disciplining. While learning may take place naturally every moment, even without our conscious effort, education is an intentional act of disciplining the mind-body-heart to be in alignment with certain ideals we set up before us. Thus the heart of education is praxis, or what Whitehead (1929, 4) called "utilization." Education for embodiment is about disciplining ourselves to see rather than look at; to hear rather than listen; to feel rather than react; and so on. For example, in Zen practice, we undertake walking meditation, eating meditation, listening meditation, feeling meditation, and so on. In these meditations, we unlearn the habitual auto-piloting of the senses and relearn to center our attention on the senses themselves.

To walk in the usual way is just to get from point A to point B. Walking is merely a means of transportation, a slow and cumbersome one for many people who prefer driving. In walking meditation, we return to the experience of walking itself, which is marvelous beyond description. We feel our body interact intricately, moment by moment, with the ground, the air, the trees, the sky, and all that embraces the body. Likewise with eating meditation. We return to the experience of eating itself. We are fully mindful, through the senses, of eating. With our eyes and, later, with our mouth, we meditate on the gift of life. What more intimate moments of communion can there be than in the act of eating? The miracle of "interbeing" between ourselves and the Plant and Animal Kingdoms is enacted in every mealtime.

In the next two sections, I will consider two specific applications of mindfulness to education: Environmental Education and Civic Education. Challenged by the global crisis of social and environmental disintegration, we need to make environmental education and civic education as central to schooling as the core academic subjects. How can the pedagogy of mindfulness help?

Mindfulness for Environmental Education

There are many ways to address environmental education: consumer education, recycling programs, reforestation projects, and so on. While all of them have something vitally useful to contribute, the kind that I think would make a difference at the foundational level is one that teaches people to perceive the natural world as a sacred order in which they participate as friends and lovers of life. Turning us around from entrenched instrumentalism and orienting us instead towards intrinsic valuing of the world: this is what environmental education can do. How do we teach ourselves to value intrinsically? Through the senses! To quote Abram (1996, 69):

> It may be that the new "environmental ethic"…will come into
> existence not primarily through the logical elucidation of new
> philosophical principles and legislative strictures, but through
> a renewed attentiveness to this perceptual dimension that
> underlies all our logics, through a rejuvenation of our carnal,
> sensorial empathy with the living land that sustains us.

Environmental education in the manner of Abram above is an aesthetic education in the sense that we learn to see, hear, smell, and feel the world in such a way as to value it intrinsically.

One who finds that "[d]awn and sunset are once again transforming experiences as are all the sights and sounds and scents and tastes and the feel of the natural world about us, the surging sea, the sound of the wind, the brooding forests" (Berry 1996, 411) would not have the desire, with respect to Nature, for domination, manipulation, and exploitation. If I perceive myself as "one-bodied" with this enchanted world, feel it in my own nervous system, love it in my own heart, and wish to look after it and defend it like my own body, I will be least motivated to do things that harm it, however "useful" and "profitable" such practices may be.

Thus, the most potent form of environmental education is one that occasions in the students experiences of profound interconnectedness or "interbeing" and its attendant love of life. Suppose we take our students to a nearby forest on a warm summer day fragrant with sweet pine and cedar. We sit ourselves down in the cool shade under some pine trees. Calming our mind-hearts, we breathe slowly and deeply, paying full attention to every detail of breathing. This is mindfulness practice. We notice the sweet pine-scented air entering the lungs, invigorating us, and then leaving our lungs; we picture a similar process taking place in the trees. As we breathe in and out, we visualize the trees and human beings exchanging breaths.[15] After breathing thus for a while, how does the forest appear to us? Do we feel the intimate being-to-being, body-to-body connectedness with the forest and all its inhabitants? We can think of a whole array of practices we can adopt to occasion the experience of interconnectedness in any physical environment.

Now, I do not wish to give an impression that in the kind of experiential environmental education that I recommend, we have no use for ideas and theories. As I explained in connection with the Zen parable of the pointing finger, so long as we understand that ideas are the pointers and that the reason for ideas is to get ourselves oriented towards experience, we can in fact make safe use of these pointers. Thus, we can introduce our students to all kinds of up-to-date scientific theories and science ideas, but with a clear understanding of their use as a pointer that orients us towards possibilities of experience. Education for embodiment is not anti-intellectual or anti-cognitivist.

Mindfulness for Civic Education

For the most part, humanity lived deeply rooted in its ancestral history and place. But this has changed drastically since the "Great Transformation"— Modern Industrialization. "Never before," notes Rasmussen (1999), "have so many humans attempted to exist without any sense of multi-generational abiding in a meaningful, historical locale" (p. 26). Communities are eroding everywhere. Families are breaking up. Extended families are disappearing. More and more people abandon their ancestral land and flock to cities only to become wage-laborers and participate in the commodification of labor.[16] Everywhere the monoculture of market consumerism seems to be colonizing the world. American TV channels seed the planet with the same images and messages for the Good Life: "The dream of corporate marketers is a globalized consumer culture united around brand-name loyalties that will allow a company to sell its products with the same advertising copy in Bangkok as in Paris or New York" (Korten 1995, 153). What an utter perversion of the idea of interconnectedness!

Rare is a school mission statement that does not mention economic progress.[17] In fact, I have not seen one. In the current context of economic discourse, economic progress means competitiveness in the global market economy feeding on the monoculture of consumer capitalism. Thus, to partake successfully in economic progress means becoming vigorous consumers whose life profiles may include urban dwelling; upward mobility; youthful looks; high income; fancy cars; spacious homes; overseas vacations; lots of flying and driving around; a limitless amount of prepackaged and disposable products; over-consumption of a high-fat, high-calorie, meat-based diet; fashion-conscious clothing; and so on. In short, successful participation in economic progress implies ecologically and socially unsustainable lifestyles. Civic education dedicated to the vision of a more equitable and cooperative world would change this.

Civic education is not for teaching the young to memorize all kinds of information about who, what, where, when, and why from our country's past and present. It has a far more important role than this: to teach the young the value of roots, neighborhood, community-building, local history and local initiative, conservation of resources, protection of land, frugality, diversity, and all manner of manual work put to the service of caring for our local environment and community (Orr 1994).

But such education cannot be accomplished without cultivating in the young a profound love for the local habitat and community in the first place. Since there is no such thing as love from a distance, the first step in the cultivation of love is physically taking ourselves to where we want love to take root—to our neighborhood fields, forests, streams, mountains, ocean; to the streets, farms, kitchens, community centers, hospitals, day cares, wilderness rehabilitation centers, prisons, and so on in our vicinity. The usual sightseeing and field trips that act as a diversion to an overwhelmingly indoor pedagogy are not what I have in mind. In such trips, students and teacher are like tourists, mostly just sightseeing, disconnected from the people and the places they see. But in the civic education based in interbeing, we go out to these places precisely to overcome our disconnection and to stretch and enlarge our boundaries of self and self-interest. There, we *surround* each person and each thing we encounter with our mindful awareness, feeling our sense of interbeing grow, and learning to share ourselves and what we have with each other. We would genuinely feel for our neighbors. We could not bear to have homeless fellows. We would feel hurt if they were without food and shelter.

While the usual notion of citizenship concerns knowing one's rights and obligations and participating in public debates and voting, from the perspective of the pedagogy of mindfulness, citizenship is primarily about realizing the interbeing of oneself with all the members of small and large civic and biotic communities. Out of this realization, we would be disposed to practice conservation, build communities, recycle, and in general care about and care for places and people.

Concluding Remark

Words and concepts, though handy and lovely in their own right, can never substitute for direct sensuous experience, which can generate in us the sense of interbeing and show the oneness of the perceiver with the perceived. To be, says Thich Nhat Hanh (1991, 96), is to "inter-be." The experience of interbeing is the direct source of empathy, compassion, love and care. Here, I shall quote Franck (1973) one last time for his insight that the realization of interbeing is the source of love and compassion:

> Zen experience is…a direct seeing into what I am in reality. It is the healing of the alienation (in French "aliéné" means "mad") that hides my true identity—which happens on its deepest level to be my identity with all that is born and will die. This insight into my real condition is the wisdom that is inseparable from compassion. (p. 14)

I outlined in this paper a solution to globally spreading social and environmental disintegration. This disintegration is human-induced and thus reflects "a prior disorder in the thought, perception, imagination" (Orr 1994, 2). I argued that this disorder is the result of our increasing disconnectedness from Nature and humanity. I further argued that excessive linguistic and conceptual activity interferes with our experiencing a deep being-to-being interconnectedness with the world. If my analysis is correct, then the greatest contribution education can make is to help us all to recover our non-discursive, sensuous connection to the physical world and all its inhabitants. I have termed the art of such teaching "the pedagogy of mindfulness." There is much to explore and develop in this pedagogy, but I must leave that task for another time.

Notes

1. I have used two sources (Harrison 1996; Starke 1999) for a comprehensive update on the state of the world.

2. Education is a normative enterprise. By this, I mean that education is norm-setting and prescriptive, and therefore aims at transforming students to the ideal of life, society, and humanity we hold up to them. Hence, education does not function simply as a purveyor of existing knowledge and information, although such is often the impression, calculated or unwitting, given to the public these days. (This impression is irresponsible because hiding behind the seeming neutrality of knowledge, the education establishment evades the responsibility of debating and justifying the implicit ideals it puts before the students.) Now, distinguishing education from indoctrination and conditioning, successful education is one that enables students to utilize the knowledge made available to them so as to effect a desired change in their own self-formation and conduct. How well we as educators can do this task of enabling is the question of pedagogy—the art of teaching.

3. Action tends to follow from perception and feeling. Recognition of this fact has had a salutary effect on our moral theorizing: it has shown us that as moral educators, our primary site of work is our students' moral perception and emotion rather than their moral reasoning. See works by Murdoch (1970), Blum (1994), Nussbaum (1990).

4. By "percepts" I mean the immediate (read: unmediated) objects of sense perceptions. By "concepts" I mean abstract objects of the intellect. According to the Buddhist

analysis, mind *(mano)* as an intellectual faculty performs the special function of assisting "in bringing back the impressions produced by other sense faculties and, as such, constitutes a form of 'reflection'" (Kalupahana 1987, 30). Thus, concepts are "generally considered substitutes for percepts" (p. 30).

5. Establishing "awareness" or "mindfulness" (*satipatthana* in Pali: "sati" means "awareness" or "mindfulness," and "patthana" means getting established extensively) is the cornerstone of the Buddhist practice. This practice is also known as *vipassana* or insight meditation. Goenka (1998, 5) defines "sati" as "the witnessing of every reality pertaining to mind and body within the framework of the body." Here, a particular emphasis is on "within the framework of the body," which is the hallmark of the Buddhist meditation. Essentially, what the meditator does is pay full attention to the arising and passing away of *vedana* (sensations, feelings) in each moment exactly as they come up. Space does not permit an explication of the practice here, but the main point I wish to convey is that the mindfulness practice is all about freeing ourselves from the tenacious grip of the abstract, disembodying conceptual mind (intellect) and recovering the embodied awareness. More on this later.

6. Much of our memory involving the movement of our body is unconscious. For example, when I type, my fingers "know" where the correct keys are without my having to look; certain familiar telephone numbers, I cannot recall too well, but I am able to dial them accurately once my fingers are on the number pad. One of the most dramatic instances, albeit pathological, of body memory is what neurologists call a "phantom": patients who have lost limbs or other body parts retain a persistent image or memory of these missing parts, even for years. See Sacks (1985) for many intriguing accounts.

7. This understanding forms the fundamental basis of the current cognitivist theory of enactivism. One of the chief proponents of this theory, Varela, states:"[O]rganism and environment enfold into each other and unfold from one another in the fundamental circularity which is life itself" (Varela, Thompson and Rosch 1991, 217).

8. The best-known *school* of empiricism is that of the British empiricists of the seventeenth century: Locke, Berkeley, and Hume. However, empiricism as an epistemological/ontological *orientation* has been with us from the beginning (consider Aristotle) and is still very alive in such contemporary schools as pragmatism and phenomenology, whose influence is massively felt in education. For instance, consider Dewey's educational philosophy and the central role that experience plays in it.

9. This constructivist thesis (that reality is what we construct) goes hand-in-hand with the fundamental tenet of Linguistic Philosophy that all our perceptions are conceptually mediated; that is, mediated by language. In the latter's understanding, seeing is always "seeing-as" (e.g., Wittgenstein 1976; Hanson 1958). While I agree that much of our ordinary perception is in fact conceptually mediated, I reject the implication that there cannot be unmediated perception. More on this later in the discussion of the Buddhist mindfulness practice.

10. Let us not forget that the conversion of land into economic property was a historical invention. Before the "commercialization of the soil" took place in modern Europe, people had a different conception and attitude towards land. See Polanyi (1957).

11. Think of the difference between communication and communion in this way: Suppose I describe to you, who have never tasted an apple, what an apple tastes *like*. I have given you information that might give you some idea about the taste of an apple. I have communicated to you. But, if I gave you an apple and had you taste it for yourself,

then you and I can have an experience of communion with respect to the taste of an apple.

12. In the view of Buddhist psychology and epistemology, the conceptualizing mind is counted as one of the sense organs, along with eyes, ears, and so on. In other words, unlike in the modern Western tradition, Buddhism does not equate the conceptualizing mind with consciousness or awareness. See Kalupahana (1987).

13. Venerable Gunaratana explains percepts in the following way: "When you become first aware of something, there is a fleeting instant of pure awareness just before you conceptualize the thing, before you identify it" (Gunaratana, 1991, pp. 149-150).

14. The Buddhist term for this concept of inherent interconnectedness of all beings and their phenomena (in fact, in the Buddhist ontology, there are no "beings"—only phenomena) is *pattica-samuppada*, meaning "dependent origination." The original formulation of this notion is as follows: "When this is, that is…This arising, that arises…When this is not, that is not…This ceasing, that ceases" (Walpola 1959, 53). See Macy (1991) for a lengthy treatment of Dependent Origination from the perspective of contemporary Systems Theory.

15. The reader may ask: "Isn't visualization a form of conceptualization?" Yes, it is. "Are we not trying to discourage conceptualization because of its disembodying tendency?" Yes, but the point of this discouragement is strategic: to recover the non-discursive awareness. When this recovery is made (permanently or temporarily) and we dwell in the space of non-discursive awareness (even if temporarily), then one can use conceptualization for specific purposes, such as, in the present example, enhancing our awareness of how we are intrinsically and vitally interconnected with the forest.

16. See Polanyi (1957) for an extended historical treatment of how Europeans became displaced people, having become disembedded from the land, which coincided with land becoming commodified. Individuals severed from their embodied connections with the land have become floating social atoms, ready to become "human rentals," that is, wage-laborers.

17. Here is a local example: "The purpose of the British Columbia school system is to enable learners to develop to their individual potential and to acquire the knowledge, skills, and attitudes needed to contribute to a healthy society and prosperous and sustainable economy" (Cochrane 1992, 2).

References

Abram, D. 1996. *The spell of the sensuous*. New York: Pantheon.

Berry, T. 1996. Into the future. In *This sacred earth*, edited by R.S. Gottlieb. London: Routledge.

Blum, L. 1994. *Moral perception and particularity*. Cambridge, MA: Cambridge University Press.

Cochrane, D.B. 1992. The stances of provincial ministries of education towards values/moral education in Canadian schools. *Journal of Moral Education* 21(2), 125-38.

Evernden, N. 1985. *The natural alien*. 2d ed. Toronto: University of Toronto Press.

Feynman, R.P. 1985. *"Surely you're joking, Mr. Feynman!"* New York: Bantam Books.

Franck, F. 1973. *The Zen of seeing: Seeing/drawing as meditation*. New York: Vintage.

Goenka, S.N. 1998. *Stipatthana sutta discourses.* Seattle: Vipassana Research Publications.

Gunaratana, H. 1991. *Mindfulness in plain English.* Boston: Wisdom Publication.

Hanson, N.R. 1958. *Patterns of discovery.* Cambridge, MA: Cambridge University Press.

Harrison, P., Ed. 1996. *Caring for the future: Making the next decades provide a life worth living* (Report of the Independent Commission on population and quality of life). Oxford: Oxford University Press.

Havel, V. 1998. The divine revolution. *Utne Reader* 98(88): 56-57.

Kalupahana, D. 1987. *The principles of Buddhist psychology.* Albany: State University of New York Press.

Korten, D. 1995. *When corporations rule the world.* San Francisco: Kumarin Press.

Macy, J. 1991. *Mutual causality in Buddhism and general systems theory: The Dharma of natural systems.* Albany: State University of New York Press.

Murdoch, I. 1970. *The sovereignty of good.* London: Routledge and Kegan Paul.

Nhat Hanh, T. 1991. *Peace is every step: The path of mindfulness in everyday life.* New York: Bantam Books.

Nhat Hanh, T. 1993. *Interbeing.* Berkeley, CA: Parallax Press.

Nussbaum, M.C. 1990. *Love's knowledge: Essays on philosophy and literature.* New York: Oxford University Press.

Orr, D. 1994. *Earth in mind: On education, environment, and the human prospect.* Washington, D.C.: Island Press.

Polanyi, K. 1957. *The great transformation.* Boston: Beacon Press.

Rasmussen, D. 1999. *The Queen wishes her red children to learn the cunning of the white man.* Master's thesis, Simon Fraser University.

Sacks, O. 1985. *The man who mistook his wife for a hat and other clincal tales.* New York: Harper and Row.

Sogyal R. 1993. *The Tibetan book of living and dying.* San Francisco: Harper Collins.

Starke, L. ed. 1999. *State of the world* (Worldwatch Institute report on progress toward a sustainable society). New York: Norton.

Varela, F.J., E. Thompson, and E. Rosch. 1991. *The embodied mind: Cognitive science and human experience.* Cambridge, MA: MIT Press.

Walpola, R. 1959. *What the Buddha taught.* New York: Grove Weidenfeld.

Whitehead, A.N. 1929. *The aims of education and other essays.* London: The Free Press.

Wittgenstein, L. 1976. *Philosophical investigation.* G.E.M. Anscombe. Translated by Oxford: Basil Blackwell.

How Do They Learn to Be Whole?
A Strategy for Helping
Preservice Teachers Develop Dispositions

Genét Simone Kozik-Rosabal

GENÉT SIMONE KOZIK-ROSABAL lives at the foot of the Rocky Mountains in Boulder, Colorado, where she is pursuing a doctorate in Education. The mountains are in her bones, and so is being a teacher and a teacher educator. Genét obtained her Bachelor of Arts degree in 1984 from Western Washington University in Bellingham, Washington, in the field of Secondary English Education, and then moved to Alaska to teach in a Native Alaskan village, and then in Juneau. The inner calling to pursue higher education led Genét to the University of Minnesota at Mankato, where she obtained a Master's Degree in Women's Studies in 1994. Always looking for ways to connect social and political issues with teacher education, Genét found herself in the Department of Educational Foundations, where she had the good fortune to work with Dr. Renée Hersrud and Dr. Dottie Scholtz, two extraordinary women who served as mentors to Genét in the truest sense of the word. It was also in Mankato where Genét learned of the exercise described in this chapter.

Abstract. Teacher education typically occurs in institutions of higher learning that intellectualize experience and pay primary attention to developing content knowledge and developing effective teaching strategies. Lost in the wake of theory and methods courses is a crucial aspect of teacher education: the development of teaching "dispositions." Dispositions—or what this author defines as the beliefs, attitudes, and affective aspects of teaching that provide for authentic learning—are usually taken for granted in teacher education. Preservice teachers are expected to already embody certain dispositions, like curiosity, patience, and respect for others, or they are supposed to magically acquire them somehow before finishing their degree. This author maintains that good teaching dispositions must be intentionally identified and developed in order for the other two thirds of teacher preparation—knowledge and skills—to mature. All three aspects of teacher preparation are needed for people to become effective instructors in today's diverse communities and schools. In this essay preservice teachers demonstrate how the Personal Process Transformation Exercise helped them to negotiate this much neglected territory.

Keywords. Teacher Education, Dispositions, Holistic Teaching, Transformation

Acknowledgments. I would like to express my gratitude to the hundreds of students who had faith in me and in themselves to venture forth on the elusive and challenging road of personal transformation. I am deeply grateful to my friend, Jennifer Woodhull, for providing the excerpts from Deepak Chopra's work, and for introducing me to Candace Pert's remarkable scientific discoveries on emotions. Jennifer's extraordinary ability to take complex information and simplify it for the common layperson, making it possible for me to incorporate these important points. Also, I want to thank Gina Kozik-Rosabal for her wonderful support over the years, and guidance on early versions of this manuscript.

How Do They Learn to Be Whole?
A Strategy for Helping
Preservice Teachers Develop Dispositions

Genét Simone Kozik-Rosabal

"I was really enthusiastic about this project when it was assigned, because it is rare that one is given school work that relates significantly to everyday life." (Maya, student) [1]

"I am really glad you gave us the opportunity to work on this. School doesn't always address our soul, which is one of the most important things there is to learn about, especially as a teacher." (Brie, student)

American society demands a lot of teachers. Teachers are expected to be knowledgeable in their content areas and skillful in their classrooms. They must be able to assist at a moment's notice the tremendously diverse population of our nation's children, whose learning styles and aptitudes range from severely neglected to wonderfully gifted. As such, teacher education programs are continually focusing, changing, and refocusing goals and requirements for teacher training and certification.

In my experiences as a teacher and a teacher educator in Washington, Alaska, Minnesota, and now in Colorado, I have found that most programs revolve around three themes: knowledge, skills, and dispositions.[2] These themes may be called different things in different schools, but they are essentially the same across America's teacher education programs. Open any university's guidebook for teacher education, and you will see these standards laid out. Knowledge, of course, has to do with the content or subject matter to be learned in any given field, such as math or science, language arts or music. Skills training concerns things like classroom management, and the organizational and administrative aspects of teaching. Prospective teachers are trained in these areas through their methods courses and practicum experiences.

While it is possible to identify and evaluate what a teacher should know and be skillful at doing, figuring out how a teacher should *be* requires a different focus and effort. This "being," or what I am referring to as the "disposition" of a teacher, is harder to quantify and evaluate than knowledge or skill. In the Merriam Webster dictionary, dispositions are defined as our moods, temperament, and tendencies to act in particular ways in certain situations and under specific conditions. Teachers are expected to embody moods that are consistent and fair; temperaments that are caring, firm, and supportive; and tendencies toward being flexible and respectful, among others. They must have a good sense of themselves, and be able to adapt to changing circumstances with a modicum of consistency and ethical behavior. They must, as William Ayers asserts, negotiate within the realms of "pain and conflict," "uncertainty and ambiguity," and sometimes have "more judgement, energy, and intensity than seems humanly impossible" (1993, 5).

Current research on teacher education, certification, and accreditation heartily supports the development of these qualities. The general consensus of teachers and researchers is that teachers must be able to communicate effectively with students and colleagues (Ball and Rundquist 1992; Heaton and Lampert 1992; Wineburg and Grossman 1998); care for themselves and others in meaningful ways (Noddings 1992; Shor 1992); and work effectively with diverse groups of children (Delpit 1995; Liston and Zeichner 1996; Zeichner and Melnick 1995).

The National Council for Accreditation of Teacher Education (NCATE), which rates teacher education programs on these same qualities, specifically highlights the need for teachers to have a "professional conscience," which NCATE defines as a "commitment to inquiry, knowledge, competence, caring, and social justice."[3]

It is wonderful to see these dispositional "promotions," but how do teacher educators proceed with teaching and developing those qualities in their students? For instance, how will preservice teachers develop an ability to care about others who may not be, to them, likable? How can they value students from diverse backgrounds, or be prepared to build a community in their classroom, when their students come from families with a plethora of potentially conflicting values, beliefs, and agendas around education? More importantly, how can teacher educators—within the confines of an institution that intellectualizes experience—help future teachers *embody* these dispositions that relate to emotions and feelings, not initially to thoughts?

Before sharing one approach I have used over the years for negotiating this process, we first need to take a look at some underlying ideas regarding dispositions and their development. First, there is the notion that dispositions arise from more than our thoughts: they are aspects of our true being. Second, we need to stretch our current beliefs on reflective practice—a term that is widely used in teacher education—and explore the importance of awareness practices that can guide us further in our quest to understanding thoughts, feelings, emotions, and behavior. That discussion will bring us to the edge of new scientific inquiry that is changing the way we think and work with the human mind. Finally, the process and results of the Personal Process Transformation Exercise will be shared as proof that awareness practices, even in higher education, are a powerful means for helping preservice teachers develop the dispositions they want and need to be effective teachers in the twenty-first century.

Dispositions: Embodying Versus Thinking

Dispositions cannot be attained by merely reading about them, reflecting on them, and then wishing with all our might that the ones we want to have will just magically become part of who we are. They must somehow be "embodied" or rather authentically drawn into or out of our human being. Working on our dispositions requires intention, will, risk-taking, awareness, and the ability to change course when things are not working out.

It is one thing, for example, to require that students in teacher education programs model the disposition of respect for others. It's something else to move those students to a place of actually *feeling* respect—embodying respect—and not merely trying to act on a thought, such as, "Oh, I'm supposed to be respectful of this child, even though she does not appear to respect me or this school." Sooner or later, that teacher's true feelings of anger, frustration, embarrassment, distrust, or what-have-you will emerge, and the possibility of building a community in their classroom will likely remain elusive.

The dispositions that researchers and accrediting institutions want all teachers to have must, therefore, be addressed in such a way that invites more than a nod to politically correct rhetoric or a reflective journal entry after a long day. I have found over the years that most students read about and discuss social issues, like racism and heterosexism, but they don't know what to do with that information; they do not know how to make sense of it in their lives. In the past I have asked students to reflect on what they've learned, but the journals they submit are filled with reactionary thoughts of remorse and guilt, or justification for the way things are. Reflective practices, therefore, are not enough to help students wrestle with new information and realize how it is impacting their lives.

There is a distinct difference between reflecting on something—which is a common practice in teacher education—and being aware of feelings, thoughts, and physical responses to those events as they are happening. While I am an advocate of reflective practice, I believe that it is only capable of reaching the cerebral, intellectual, or reasoning levels of our understanding. Reflective practices do not appear to be enough for helping students wrestle with new information and how it is impacting their lives.

Not reflection, but the practice of awareness of the present moment, brings people to a deeper level of personal growth that allows work on dispositions to occur (Chödrön 1991; Kabat-Zinn 1994; Lama Surya Das 1997). Reflection can help our investigation into thoughts, feelings, and behaviors, but it cannot always bring us to the point of true discovery and understanding, because when we reflect on an event our minds are working with old information (Krishnamurti 1969). We tend to misconstrue the facts, ignore uncomfortable feelings, or judge ourselves harshly for things we did or didn't do.

In most cases, meditation is a powerful tool in developing awareness. However, students may have a difficult time trusting in it, because it smacks of religious practice. This point, I believe, can be addressed by understanding that meditation in its simplest form is the practice of becoming aware of one's emotions, thoughts, and feelings at any point in time; it is merely the practice of paying attention to our minds, which is different from most religions where we are asked to pay attention to someone else's mind. Lama Surya Das (1997 260) notes, "Awareness is the common denominator of all sentient beings... Demystified and divested of religious and cultural trappings, meditation basically means the intentional cultivation of mindful awareness and pure attention—an alert, wakeful presence of mind." Other practitioners, like Dawn Groves (1993, 9), concur that meditation is a "nondenominational practice."[4]

Awareness, therefore, is what preservice teachers need in their programs, and they need an awareness that will go beyond intellectual-level discussions of what teachers do or don't do that makes them good teachers. The dispositions required for effective, authentic teaching need to be embodied; they need to be lived through as well as reflected upon. To "embody" means to "give body to a spirit." It means to organically incorporate or embrace something we might not be able to readily see or measure. We already embody a host of dispositions, some of which are conducive to teaching and some of which are not. What I am suggesting is taking deliberate and intentional steps on our personal paths toward embodiment that will lead us to a place beyond intellectualizing experience, a place where we have accessed the fundamental reservoirs of our being.

Much research must still be done in this area, but in recent years there has been increased attention within medical, scientific, and mainstream circles about the "mind-body connection." Typical Western thought positions the mind as separate from the body and emotions, where it can apply reasoning to help us live through life's tribulations, successes, and joys. New discoveries and scientific proof about the human body, however, are illuminating the fact that our bodies *are* minds, not merely receptacles for them.

> About 20 years ago, it was discovered that our thoughts and our feelings have physical substrate to them. When you think a thought, you make a molecule...thoughts, feelings, emotions, and desires translate into a flux of neuropeptides in the brain... What science is discovering is that we have a thinking body. Every cell in our body thinks. Every cell in our body is actually a mind. Every cell has its own desires and it communicates with every other cell. The new word is not mind and body connection, we have a body-mind simultaneously everywhere. So when you say, "I have a sad heart," then you literally have a sad heart. (Chopra 1991).

Recent research by Dr. Candace Pert (1997), a professor in the Department of Physiology and Biophysics at Georgetown University Medical Center, supports this conviction. Dr. Pert contends that our emotions don't come from our thoughts, but rather from the cellular level in our bodies. The cells in our muscles, tissue, blood, and bones have receptors (molecules on the surface of the cells) identical to those in the brain's limbic (emotional) system. All constantly receive information simultaneously. The limbic system then transfers that information to our frontal cortex, where we become conscious of it. It is only at this point that we begin to form ideas about what we are feeling. So, the experience itself occurs at a preconscious, physiological level.[5]

A discussion of cells, receptors, and limbic systems, is beyond the scope and intention of this essay, but suffice to say that with these new advances in medicine and our growing understanding of the dynamics of the human body, it becomes very important for teacher educators to start thinking beyond what dispositions teachers should have to *how* teachers can identify, develop, and embody them.

To begin this process requires a willingness to first identify and examine barriers in our personal lives that keep us from developing dispositions we'd like to pursue. For example, it will be very difficult, if not impossible, for a prospective teacher to develop compassion for homeless children when he or she harbors the classist belief that if people just tried harder, they'd have a home and a job. That teacher's resentment will likely stand in the way of developing true compassion and understanding for the children's plight. Becoming aware of that initial boot-strap belief is the starting place for identifying whether or not working on the disposition of compassion is, indeed, the place to begin.

The practice of awareness requires tapping into the unconscious (Vaughan and Walsh 1998). As stated above, traditional Western thought nudges us to regard "tapping into the unconscious" as a mental exercise. But "discovering one's unconscious is, precisely, *not* an intellectual act, but an affective experience, which can hardly be put into words, if at all" (Fromm 1998 100). Fromm's thinking is consistent with Pert's (1997) conviction that emotions occur at a preconscious, physiological level. Developing dispositions, therefore, requires the full engagement and awareness of thoughts, emotions, and physical responses to the world in order to make stronger connections between who we are and how we teach. Parker Palmer (1998, 13) calls this "teaching with integrity" when our preconscious, conscious, and physical entities are completely aligned.

There is very little in teacher education literature to suggest how teachers, preservice or otherwise, might develop the dispositions they need or want to have. This situation is further exacerbated by the reality that genuine development of dispositions is a voluntary act. We cannot inherently force people to change who they are. I could encourage a student teacher, for example, to treat her students more equitably; I could even grade her on her efforts. However, unless that student teacher agreed to be genuinely equitable and opened up to the possibility of *embodying* equitability, there's no telling what would happen when I left the room. Working on dispositions is a very personal process and it has to develop from the desires of each individual.

This belief in embodiment and in the necessity to pay attention to and nurture the mind, body, and spirit of humans is referred to as "holistic education" (R. Miller 1993). Teaching effective teacher dispositions can *only* be accomplished through this approach, because it is the only way by which preservice teachers can gain self-knowledge and become the kinds of teachers they talk about having loved their whole lives. Parker Palmer says, "We teach who we are" (1998 2), and the teachers my students love the most are the ones who respected them, listened to them, cared about them, and treated them honestly.

The Personal Process Transformation Exercise

We return to the question, "How can teacher educators, within the confines of an institution created for intellectual pursuits, help prospective teachers learn about and come to embody dispositions which are difficult to define, much less see or evaluate?"

What we need is an awareness practice that invites preservice teachers to first understand who they are, and then willingly work to develop dispositions that will help them become better at teaching and relating to others. Several years ago, I was introduced to such a practice. Initially referred to as the Personal Process Evaluation, it was used in human development courses for preservice teachers at a midwestern university. After several years of using this exercise in teacher education courses, my students wanted to change the name so it more closely reflected its impact on their lives. Rather than being an "evaluation" of who they were, students argued that it was actually a tool for personal transformation. Hence, they dubbed it the Personal Process Transformation Exercise, a detailed description of which can be found in the Appendix. In short, the exercise includes six steps:

- identifying a teaching disposition to develop
- setting a goal for developing it
- mapping the process of growth
- establishing a check-in system
- confirming outside support
- celebrating efforts.

Typically, the teaching dispositions students pursue include things like, "I want to improve my self esteem," "I want to exercise better judgement," or "I want to improve my interactions with people by being more open to cultures that are different from my own." Whatever students choose as a goal is valid, as long as they identify it as a disposition that will enhance their teaching and learning. It has to be something they identify for themselves, thus alleviating the dilemma of not trying to force change, but letting it grow out of each individual on a voluntary basis.

At first, I offered the exercise as an optional assignment. I did not believe it was right for me to require personal growth for passing a course. The students who tried it were not graded, but they received written and verbal encouragement from me. However, the results of those few students' efforts were so remarkable, and their feedback to me so strong about "the need for everyone in teacher education to do this exercise," that I began to make it a regular part of my courses. I have used it in classes on human and learning development, evaluation and assessment, and in courses dealing with the foundational aspects of education, such as history, politics, and social issues. It does not matter which content area we cover; my students always say that it is a timely and worthwhile assignment.

Although I still do not believe in assigning a grade for disposition development, I do ask students to assess their own efforts, while I concentrate on the mechanics of their written report: Was their plan clear? Did they provide specific examples of experiences? I am always open to students' suggestions for evaluation, and we work together to modify that aspect of the exercise.

In spite of slight modifications over the years, the essence of this exercise holds its integrity, and the results are absolutely stunning. What happens for students—sometimes for the first time in their lives—is a voluntary, personal realization of their teaching spirit. Students begin to realize and understand the fundamental reasons for their beliefs and actions, which places them in a position for personal transformation free from outside forces. In other words, they find a way to work on their teaching dispositions, just like all of the accrediting agencies want them to.

The power of the exercise is that the learning is in the process, not necessarily in the accomplishment of a goal. While most students do meet their goals to a certain extent, it is the process of finding out who they are that makes the assignment so worthwhile for them. For example, one first-year teacher education student, Brian, remarked, "My combination of both being a very sensitive person and also having a very difficult time forgiving and forgetting made me the perfect 'grudge-holder.'" Brian became aware of this aspect of his personality, and he worried that it would damage his relationships with students in the future. This awareness helped him find ways to transcend his grudge-holding. Instead of beating himself up for a character "flaw," Brian began to identify moments when this attitude—this disposition of grudge-holding—arose. Watching that process, in itself, helped Brian shift his disposition into a less judgmental one, opening up opportunities to grow. At the end of the semester, Brian ended his paper with, "This was a very successful assignment for me and because of it I can truly say that I have become a better person."

The learning of a new skill is always invigorating, especially when the skill is focused on identifying a relatively hidden aspect of one's personality, and experiencing what it means to take tangible steps toward developing it in positive ways. This is an extremely important point. Students have been schooled for many years to rely on the teacher to tell them what they need to know, and even how they should feel about themselves. John Taylor Gatto (1992) calls these dynamics "Intellectual Dependency" and "Emotional Dependency."

Students continue this process in college. Who among us, as college professors, hasn't had students asking repeatedly, "What do you want? How many pages should that paper be? How do you want me to write it?" They rarely receive direction or support for figuring out why they are even asking those kinds of questions, or why they do the things they do, or react to certain situations in particular ways. The Personal Process Transformation Exercise shows them in an intimate way not only that they are in charge of their own learning and actions, but also how that learning and those actions unfold in the course of their daily lives. As human beings about to step into the teaching role, the realization that they can set a goal, monitor their progress, and persist when the going gets tough can be a powerful experience. Said one student named Ellery, "I feel as though I have taken on a life-long challenge to monitor the controlling tendencies that I have recently become aware of. Having recognized this myself and regulating my own behavior is something that I did not previously know I could do. I now feel that I can take on any issue I have with myself and tackle it head-on. I know that I will not necessarily see immediate results but over time my awareness is sure to pay off."

Confidence is definitely a common outcome for students. They write about improving their self-esteem and handling difficult situations with more tenacity and less guilt for revealing their opinions and beliefs. One student, Dana, wrote, "It is almost as if a huge burden has been lifted, because I am more willing to let my opinions be heard instead of keeping them inside."

Another student named Ben decided that improving his self-esteem was exactly what he wanted to do. Rather than experiencing an improved sense of self as a by-product of another goal, he wanted to focus on building relationships with others not only to learn about them, but also to build up his confidence when meeting new people. At the end of the semester, he wrote,

> I feel much more confident expressing myself...This assignment
> provided me with concrete means to explore these issues within

my life. Even though all of my goals weren't fulfilled, I still learned much about who my friends are, how to build a new friendship, and how to leave an uncomfortable situation.

Another example of building confidence and self-esteem came from a young woman who was struggling to "come out" as a lesbian. "Sarah" was tired of hiding her sexual orientation, but she was also fearful about what might happen if she revealed it. We had spoken in class about the overt and covert discrimination gay teachers often face, and this worried her a great deal. Her goal began as "learning to question anti-gay slurs and jokes," but ended up as something much more profound:

> Overall, I decided to include [as a goal] coming out as a lesbian, because it was something I wanted to work on and it was intricately tied to the other goals. I found that throughout the semester, my self-worth has dramatically improved, although I feel increasingly alienated from mainstream society. Because of this assignment, I have grown enormously in my feeling of self-worth...This assignment helped me gain a better understanding of myself and address areas of my life that had been seemingly "dirty secrets" before...It has been one of the most personally rewarding assignments ever given to me in school.

This is a wonderful example of one of the aspects that the Personal Process Transformation Exercise invites students to do: change their minds. Some students started working toward one goal, but as they became more aware of their thoughts and feelings, they realized that the original goal was really a symptom of something much deeper in their body and their unconscious mind. In Sarah's case, wanting to stop gay jokes was merely the first step in her process of living openly as a lesbian.

As an "out" lesbian myself, I can attest to the magnitude of Sarah's transformation. In spite of all of the positive information entering mainstream society that people who are gay, lesbian, bisexual, or transgendered can be healthy, inspirational human beings, myths of them as pedophiles, drug addicts, and emotionally and physically sick individuals prevail. For a person entering the teaching profession, the weight of these lies keeps them closeted for many years and saps the glorious energy and passion for teaching they could instead direct toward their work. I have known wonderful teachers, gay, lesbian, and bisexual, who have gotten ulcers, had nervous breakdowns, and experienced all kinds of stress-related illnesses, which they believe were the direct result of living two lives: one public and one private. In light of the extreme difficulty of being a teacher who is gay in the United States, I admire Sarah's willingness to face her fears.

Given the hundreds of students who have attended my classes and worked with me on teacher dispositions, I have found that the best role I can play is "coach." I try to help students identify a meaningful goal, show them how to devise a method for measuring their progress toward reaching it, and follow up with questions when they get stuck. It's an advisory role, in which I challenge them to keep at it, to change course if needed, and to give themselves credit for their efforts. The results point directly toward students' success developing teacher dispositions on their own terms in spite of the difficulties that surface. Maya found that she didn't like to make mistakes and, consequently, she had a hard time allowing others to do the same. Her awareness of this trend in her life helped her shift her stance and relax a little, a step that she recognized was critical to her teaching. She wrote,

> I realize that it is very important as a teacher to allow students the space to make mistakes...Also, it is important that people not feel restricted in their behavior because of me...This aspect of my personality is something I have struggled with for my entire life, and I was really ready to work on it. Although I am sure that there is a lot more work to be done, I feel a sense of accomplishment.

Another student, Sky, made a direct connection between his goal and the school-based practicum that was another requirement for the course:

> My goal was to be more accepting of my mistakes...By giving myself the emotional space to learn from my mistakes, I improved my whole outlook. I became less reserved and a little more outgoing in my school practicum. I tried to connect with some students who seemed uninterested in getting help from the student teacher. Some of my efforts were successful; others failed. Overall, I was less critical of myself in a variety of ways...This process has helped me to realize that mistakes are a good chance to learn and improve.

Finally, the Personal Process Transformation Exercise brings students to a deeper understanding of what was discussed earlier in this article about the body-mind connection, something that most people would agree is difficult to find and nurture in higher education. Through the experience, students start to realize how their thoughts and emotions manifest themselves bodily, for better or worse. Deepak Chopra wrote, "I think the first major breakthrough in medicine, if that's what we're going to call it, is that *the mind has escaped the confines of the brain. It's not confined to the brain, it's everywhere in our body*" (1991, emphasis added). An awareness of this "body-mind simultaneously everywhere" can help teachers approach difficult situations with more intelligent responses, as opposed to knee-jerk reactions based on habitual patterns.

In his book, *Awakening the Buddha Within*, Lama Surya Das (1997, 306) says, "Tensions, fear, and stress don't come from outside. These are internal weather conditions we ourselves produce." I want to recognize that not everything that happens to us is a product of our own doing; there also exist external forces, sometimes out of our control, which influence our lives. However, holistic educators argue that you cannot be an effective teacher unless you are aware of these internal dynamics (Miller, P., 1994; Miller, R., 1993; Palmer 1993; Steiner 1927, 1934).

Sally, one of the many students who experienced and began to understand this connection, summed it up well. She wrote:

> I have always had a terrible problem with stress, and as a result I consistently take on fifteen tasks and everyone else's problems, leaving little time to pay attention to what's important to me. Comparatively, this project did wonders for me. I was sleeping better, my appetite started to come back a bit, and I had fewer physical problems...This project gave me a chance to regroup. Each of us needs to recognize what we are about, and what we are here for...If we do not have a firm understanding of ourselves, we can only approach our lives feeling lost and driven by unfulfilling obligations and expectations.

After several weeks of paying close attention to her way of being in the world, Sally began to recognize that mental choices ("taking on fifteen tasks and everyone else's problems") were in fact affecting her physical well-being. Her body and mind were already inherently connected, but the new-found awareness of that connection was helping her make conscious decisions to alleviate the stress in her life. Once Sally realized how her former disposition was making her sick, she naturally shifted from being a frazzled caretaker to a more confident, centered, healthy individual. As such, Sally's relationships with children and adults improved remarkably.

After several years of working with students on their Personal Process Transformation, I firmly believe that it is a worthwhile exercise. While I worried at first about forcing it on students, they have assured me that what I was really doing was giving them permission to try something they wanted to do, but didn't know how to do. Ellery wrote, "By integrating this [assignment] into your courses, you are allowing your students the opportunity to work on themselves." Another student, Mary, said, "Overall, this process has been an exciting one for me...It has been wonderful, because it has given me results I might not have otherwise seen. I leave this class with a new idea about who I am and who I want to be." Julie commented, "This assignment helped me to examine the trouble areas in my life. It also gave me a chance to set goals for things I never would have otherwise."

You may be asking, "Does everyone succeed in accomplishing their goals?" As with any lesson, the answer is, "No." Some students are just not interested in it at this point in their lives; others are so overwhelmed by school, home, and work that they just give up. I encourage these students to try anyway, and I model for them another desirable teacher disposition: *flexibility*. My willingness to help them tailor the assignment to fit their needs shows them how to do the same thing for themselves, and then in the future with their own students. As stated before, we can gently and actively coax changes in dispositions, but we cannot force them.

In one situation, I had a student named Tom who really needed this support. He wrote,

> I failed to achieve the goals I set out for myself...As the semester progressed, I became *less* likely to introduce myself to new people. I also began to use drugs more at social gatherings and during my free time...This is not to say that this assignment was a failure. On the contrary, it was an irrefutable success. Keeping a journal of my drug use forced me to recognize that I have a serious drug abuse problem. In March, I gave up using illegal drugs...I have started to grow...

Conclusion

Parker Palmer notes, "good teaching requires self-knowledge, [which is] a secret hidden in plain sight" (1998, 3). Teachers, however, need to learn *how* to develop self-knowledge, and then how to guide their students in that process. As teacher educators, we cannot simply expect our students to embody dispositions like caring, respect, or social justice if all we ask them to do is read articles and write papers, and then cross our fingers that "common sense," as we see it, will transfer into their lives. We need to find ways that will not only convince preservice teachers of the importance of this work, but also have them *experience the process and be aware of it as it is happening.* In other words, we need to bring them to a place where they can actually start to embody dispositions which—until now—have either been "hidden in plain sight," or seemingly impossible to reach.

Above an office door at the university where I work hangs a bumper sticker from the Ghandi Institute for Non-Violence, something left there from a previous graduate student. It says, "We must be the change we wish to see." For a long time, I have been searching for ways to teach my students how to "be the change they wish to see." With the Personal Process Transformation Exercise, these words are starting to become a reality.

Notes

1. Students whose work appears in this chapter gave written permission to use their own words. They chose to use their real names or provided pseudonyms.

2. The terms "knowledge," "skills," and "dispositions" come from the *Student Handbook for Undergraduate Students Pursuing Careers in Education* at Mankato State University, in Mankato, Minnesota (now called the University of Minnesota at Mankato). The term "skills" has been replaced by "performances," but the essence of that category remains. Students in teacher education are expected to meet "Standards of Effective Practice" established by the State of Minnesota in the areas of Subject Matter; Student Learning; Diverse Learners; Instructional Strategies; Learning Environment; Communication; Planning Instruction; Assessment; Reflection and Professional Development; and Collaboration, Ethics, and Relationships. Within each of these areas, the College of Education helps students learn the necessary content knowledge, the skills (or performances) required for teaching, and the dispositions needed for effective instruction. Most teacher education programs have this kind of framework. For example:

Diverse Learners:

Knowledge. The teacher understands how students' learning is influenced by individual experiences, talents, and prior learning, as well as language, culture, family, and community values.

Performances. The teacher uses teaching approaches that are sensitive to the multiple experiences of learners and that address different learning and performance modes.

Dispositions. The teacher appreciates and values human diversity, shows respect for students' varied talents and perspectives, and is committed to the pursuit of "individually configured excellence."

3. A complete listing and detailed explanation of the NCATE Standards can be obtained from their website, http://ncate.org.

4. In addition, there is growing proof that requiring mediation practice in teacher education can have positive results. Students at the Ontario Institute for Studies in Education are starting to demand it. For further information, see J. Miller (1994a), and visit the website for OISE at http://www. oise.utoronto.ca.

5. I am indebted to my friend and colleague, Jennifer Woodhull, for providing the excerpts from Deepak Chopra's work, and for introducing me to Candace Pert's remarkable scientific discoveries on emotions. Jennifer's extraordinary ability to take complex information and explain it simply to the common layperson make it possible for me to incorporate these important points.

References

Ayers, W. 1993. *To teach: The journey of a teacher.* New York: Teachers College Press.
Ball, D., and S. Rundquist, (1992). Collaboration as a context for joining teacher learning with learning about teaching. In edited by D.K. Cohen, M.W. McLaughlin, and J.E. Talbert. *Teaching for understanding: Challenges for policy and practice,* San Francisco: Jossey-Bass.

Chödrön, P. 1991. *The wisdom of no escape and the path of lovingkindness.* Boston: Shambhala.

Chopra, D. 1991. What is the true nature of reality? The basics of quantum healing. Speech delivered at the Seattle Center, 18 May. Originally appeared in vol. 1, no. 21 of *The Sovereign Scribe*, P.O. Box 350, McKenna, WA 98558. http://www.ascension-research.org/reality.html

Delpit, L. 1995. *Other people's children: Cultural conflict in the classroom.* New York: The New Press.

Fromm, E. 1998. Psychoanalysis and the art of knowing. In H. Palmer (Ed.), *Inner knowing: Conscientiousness, creativity, insight, intuition,* New York: Jeremy P. Tarcher/Putnam.

Gatto, J.T. 1992. *Dumbing us down: The hidden curriculum of compulsory schooling.* Philadelphia: New Society Publishers.

Groves, D. 1993. *Meditation for busy people: 60 seconds to serenity.* Novato, CA: New World Library.

Heaton, R., & M. Lampert. (1992). Learning to hear voices: Inventing a new pedagogy of teacher education. In edited by D.K. Cohen, M.W. McLaughlin, and J.E. Talbert. *Teaching for understanding: Challenges for policy and practice,* San Francisco: Jossey-Bass Publishers.

Kabat-Zinn, J. 1994. *Wherever you go, there you are: Mindfulness meditation in everyday life.* New York: Hyperion.

Krishnamurti, J. 1969) *Freedom from the known.* New York: Harper and Row.

Lama Surya Das. 1997. *Awakening the Buddha within: Tibetan wisdom for the western world.* New York: Broadway Books.

Liston, D., and K. Zeichner. 1996. *Culture and teaching.* Mawah, NJ: Lawrence Erlbaum.

Miller, J. P. 1994a. *The contemplative practitioner: Meditation in education and the professions.* Westport, CT: Bergin and Garvey.

Miller, J. P. 1994b. Contemplative practice in higher education: An experiment in teacher development. *Journal of Humanistic Psychology* 34(4): 53-69.

Miller, R. 1993. We need a holistic teacher training program. In edited by Carol Flake. *Holistic education: Principles, perspectives, and practices,* Brandon, VT: Holistic Education Press.

Noddings, N. 1992. *The challenge to care in schools: An alternative approach to education.* New York: Teachers College Press.

Palmer, P. 1993. *To know as we are known: Education as a spiritual journey.* San Francisco: HarperCollins.

Palmer, P. 1998. *The courage to teach: Exploring the inner landscape of a teacher's life.* San Francisco: Jossey-Bass.

Pert, C. 1997. *Molecules of emotion: Why you feel the way you feel.* New York: Scribner.

Shor, I. 1992. *Empowering education: Critical teaching for social change.* Chicago: University of Chicago Press.

Steiner, R. 1927. *The education of the child.* London: Rudolf Steiner Publishing.

Steiner, R. 1934. *Paths of experience.* London: Rudolf Steiner Publishing.

Vaughan, F., and R. Walsh. 1998. Technology of transcendence. In edited by H. Palmer. *Inner knowing: Conscientiousness, creativity, insight, intuition,* New York: Jeremy P. Tarcher/Putnam.

Wineburg, S. and P. Grossman. (998. Creating a community of learners among high school teachers. *Phi Delta Kappan* (January) 350-53.

Zeichner, K., and S. Melnick. 1995, February. *The role of community field experiences in preparing teachers for cultural diversity.* A paper presented at the annual meeting of the American Association of Colleges for Teacher Education, Washington, D.C.

Appendix
Personal Process Transformation Exercise

Purpose: To develop a teaching disposition you deem important to your effectiveness as a teacher; to encourage the development of awareness, self-reflection and evaluation of your personal style of interaction with others.

Steps:

First: Complete the sentences below (these comments are seen only by you). Respond by thinking about your general patterns of behavior: [Note to the reader: I recommend reading these items out loud to others, and giving them a few minutes to write on each one (as opposed to sending them home to write on their own).]

    1. I would characterize my interpersonal strengths as...

    2. I am less likely to clearly express my thoughts and feelings when...I think this happens because I...

    3. I am less likely to be assertive when...

    4. I tend to respond to conflict by...I think this happens because I...

    5. I am less likely to value and support differences in people (from myself) with respect to race, class, sexual orientation, ability, or gender (pick one, or choose another) when...I think this happens because I...

    6. I am less likely to actively listen to someone when...I think this happens because I ...

    7. I will take risks with others only when...

    8. I am less likely to support my own self-esteem in circumstances where... I think this happens because I...

    9. When I am faced with a less than effective interpersonal situation, I may attack, dominate the conversation, withdraw, or become defensive (pick one, or choose one of your own). This usually happens because I...

Second: Take fifteen minutes to review what you've written. Choose ONE item to work on this semester, and write out your goal in one sentence. Examples: "I want to handle conflict in more productive ways." "I want to stop withdrawing whenever there's tension in the room." "I want to reach out and be more comfortable meeting people who are different from me."

Third: You cannot force changes in your life to make this goal a reality. Instead, simply take note of times during your day when you become aware of this aspect of your life as it unfolds. For example, if you want to "handle conflict in more productive ways," pay attention to what happens to you—emotionally, physically, cognitively—when conflict occurs, and write about that experience as soon as you can. Do you face any internal resistance? Write about that, too. Consider possible, tangible steps you could take to improve the situation next time. The first step is being aware of what is happening; the second step is acknowledging solutions that naturally occur to you with regard to those situations. Remember, there are no right or wrong answers to what you learn or what happens.

Fourth: Identify a way to systematically track your experiences on a daily or weekly basis. Keep your tracking system simple, yet detailed enough so that you can reflect later in writing what happened.

Fifth: Devise a support system. Ask a trustworthy individual to be a sounding board for you. This person needs to be someone who will support your efforts, not a person who will tell you what to do.

Sixth: Devise a reward system for your efforts.

This kind of personal work is never done. However, in the space of one semester, you can see and feel significant changes that will lead to larger changes over your lifetime.

* * * * *

(I also share this encouragement with my students along the way):

RELAX—Just practice being mindful of the present moment.

TRY TO BE OBJECTIVE AND SEE THE BIG PICTURE—As you pay attention to your thoughts and feelings, keep in mind the entire situation.

BE COMPASSIONATE WITH YOURSELF—Support your efforts, and don't judge yourself when things don't go as planned. You are not "failing," but rather growing aware of the "signposts" for how to proceed. Every experience is just that: an experience.

BE OPEN TO CHANGE—As you learn new things about yourself, be open to the likelihood that your goal may change.

Bodymind Learning:
Interdisciplinary Conversations on Campus

Ronald L. Burr and Sherry L. Hartman

RONALD L. BURR, Ph.D., University of California Santa Barbara, Comparative Philosophy, has been on the professorial staff in the Mississippi University System for more than twenty years. He conducts courses in Asian Philosophy, 20th Century Western Philosophy, and others in the history of philosophy. He has been a Fulbright Scholar/Lecturer in Southeast Asia on the topic of Applied Ethics, which has also been the focus of his recent publications. He is also an organizational development consultant to profit and nonprofit organizations. He travels extensively as an educational director on international social service projects, most recently in Mongolia and Northern Ireland.

SHERRY L. HARTMAN, Dr.P.H., R.N. received her doctoral education at Tulane University, New Orleans, in Health Systems Administration. Following several years in nursing practice, she has been teaching at the University of Southern Mississippi, College of Nursing, in the community health and administration majors for ten years. She also teaches theory development in the doctoral program. Recent grant work and papers have related to health promotion and risk reduction in adolescent populations. She also has extensive international experience, having worked with students and nursing faculty in India, Nepal, and Thailand.

Abstract. This chapter will describe the teamwork between two university educators that served as an opportunity for exploring bodymind forms of classroom practice. Such exploration unfolded in relation to two courses, Holistic Nursing and Contemplative Theories and Practices, that emphasized mindfulness meditation and tai chi. We describe the underlying rationale and development of these as well as class activities and methods of evaluation. Our goal is not only to identify critical elements of bodymind practice, but to reflect on the value of interdisciplinary teamwork as a framework for higher education instruction.

Keywords. Tai Chi, Mindfulness, Meditation, Holistic Health, Wellness, Contemplative Practices, Contemplation, Experiential Education, Interdisciplinary

Acknowledgments. The authors want to thank the reviewers and editors of this volume, especially our University of British Columbia editor, Brent Hocking, for their many helpful comments, without which this chapter would have been much less. Any mistakes that remain are of course ours.

Bodymind Learning:
Interdisciplinary Conversations on Campus[1]

Ronald L. Burr and Sherry L. Hartman

Sherry and Ron: As we reflect on the beginning of our collaboration, it seems quite a coincidence that a professor of nursing and a professor of philosophy/religion would have both decided to integrate bodymind components into their programs in the same year. Ron, a member of the graduate and undergraduate faculty in Philosophy and Religion, University of Southern Mississippi, was dissatisfied that his upper division undergraduate and master's level course in religious experience was all reading and discussion about an author's or guest speaker's experience. It seemed odd to him and his students alike that the course included no practice of the sort that reportedly led so many of the authors or speakers to their enhanced bodymind learning. As a result, he instituted a course entitled "Contemplative Theories and Practices." Sherry, a member of the College of Nursing, was teaching in a health care tradition mainly informed by a bio-medical approach to curing disease. A recently growing narrative tradition from scholars in nursing has indicated an increasing belief in the need also to attend to the role of mind and/or spirit in creating and maintaining wellness.

In this essay we will discuss the shifts in thinking that prompted a re-evaluation of our classroom practices and the need for bodymind learning involving tai chi and Buddhist meditation. By *bodymind learning,* we mean an experience of learning from our bodies and spirits as well as our intellectual minds, and learning more about relationships of body, mind, and spirit. We highlight the teamwork that found both of us integrating and incorporating language and understanding from the other's discipline into a broader rationale for bodymind awareness in the classroom. Integral to this teamwork was the role played by Ron in enhancing bodymind learning experiences for the nursing students. We will provide a description of our courses along with outcomes reported by students before reflecting on the value of our interdisciplinary collaboration as educators.

History of Our Courses and Collaboration

Ron: At the time our collaboration began, I had over twenty years of experience practicing both meditation and tai chi. I taught courses in tai chi for the university tai chi club, and occasionally gave private sessions on meditation at the request of students and community members. I had meditation training in the Zen tradition in Japan, and also had a stint in a mindfulness meditation center in Myanmar. I had studied and taught several styles of tai chi, including the Chen family style. The Chen family style, "old frame," is now widely thought to be the oldest form of tai chi. Although some exercises drawn on to form tai chi were partially utilized in earlier, undated Shaolin Temple practices, the sequence of moving "postures" used today dates back only from the late eighteenth century in the Chen Village, China. Later styles of tai chi are developments of the Chen style.

About the time Sherry's holistic nursing course was in the planning stages, my department, Philosophy and Religion, instituted at my request a course entitled "Contemplative Theories and Practices." I had taught a similar course for years under the title of "Religious Experience."[1] Students in that earlier course were intellectually stimulated by both their readings and the guest speakers who regularly recounted their own peak experiences and how they were cultivated. However, many of the students expressed dissatisfaction with the lack of instruction in practical methods and with no part of the grading system being connected with those methods. I had also been on the lookout for some inspiration and legitimacy for including some activities in this course to develop bodily and spiritual awareness in a way that integrated intellectualized theories. I wanted to supplement the traditional, exclusively intellectual approach of philosophy and religious studies courses.

The University of Southern Mississippi, being located in a conservative area of the southern U.S., was, and still is, a context unwelcoming to nontraditional religious experimentation in a publicly supported institution. Local residents are overwhelmingly oriented toward religion as a weekly or biweekly church presentation of Christian doctrine. In those presentations faith and service heavily overshadow any spiritual exploration, and usually prohibit any exploration outside their denomination, let alone outside their religious tradition.

The opportunity for a change of content for my course and its title came about as a result of a grant application to the American Council of Learned Societies (ACLS) to support founding courses on the subject of contemplative practices.[2] In addition to funding the development of courses and teaching materials that "explore contemplative practices," the fellowship also has the stated goal of supporting the study of contemplation as "a method to develop concentration, to deepen understanding, and to cultivate awareness." Applying for this grant provided the requisite legitimacy for the course.

I applied for the fellowship with the goal of supporting the integration of more contemplative practices into university classrooms, at least to offset the overwhelming amount of exclusively theoretical methodologies being utilized in American universities. The course named "Religious Experience" was changed to "Contemplative Theories and Practices" to suit the title of the grant and my interest in better serving the students' previously mentioned interests in practical instruction. The addition of the word "theories" into the title was meant to reflect a middle path between the almost exclusively theoretical course being taught and the new one that would include practices. The course proposed in my grant application was for one period, of a two period per week class, to be devoted to readings on contemplation, the other day to be a day of practice, not necessarily related to the subject of the readings that week. In practice the course was more integrated than just described, especially since some guest speakers were invited to suggest readings in advance of their visit, and then conduct practices related to those readings upon arrival.

Because of my background, the principle contemplative methods taught in the course were sitting in mindfulness meditation, meditation in a yogic reclining posture, and tai chi upright moving meditations. The rationale for the combination was that bodymind integration would most likely occur if practiced in, as Buddhists say, "the three postures" of sitting, standing, and lying down.[4] I selected mindfulness meditation because of its religious neutrality. It has no religious subject as a focus of concentration. Its outcomes may be interpreted variously, however, depending on any religious beliefs an individual practitioner may hold.[5]

Students were taught the first eight "routines" in the Chen family essential tai chi form, a series of choreographed moves reminiscent of martial tactics, but performed exquisitely slowly in order to integrate imagery and intent with well-executed movement. This integration is designed both to enhance the learning and execution of the movement, as well as to heighten the ability of the practitioner to act out mental and spiritual ideals in movement. As one becomes more adept at intentionally integrating thought and will with action, one's bodymind becomes more energetic and powerful.

Sherry: Prior to turning to nursing education, I practiced clinical nursing for many years. From hands-on clinical practice focused on treating the ill, my further education in public health led to working in health promotion and disease prevention. Education and training of clients and other practitioners in a variety of areas became one of my major modes of practice. In developing skill in training I learned the importance and usefulness of experiential, activity-based training methods. Among many techniques developed to incorporate experience into training sessions, my first step toward fostering mind-body connection was the technique of guided imagery. The simplest form, one among many I have learned since then, included guiding someone through a process of systematic muscle relaxation, followed by giving them suggestions they could use to create images supportive of their own self-development goals. About ten years ago I entered academia and began to transfer the techniques I had used in training into the academic classroom.

Through the years I had also from time to time been introduced to various levels of intense practice in meditation methods from Asia—principally from

Indian and Japanese Buddhism. Training in the U.S. involved instruction in the method of zazen (Zen sitting) along with receiving a koan—a cryptic, enigmatic historical saying, from Japanese or Chinese Buddhism. When focused on, a koan is meant inevitably to foil the intellectual mind so that the heart-mind (we might say spirit) can emerge. I had been doing short daily meditation in this way for some years when my most intense practice, and most intense challenge, was presented. It was two weeks in a Buddhist meditation center doing continuous meditation, eight hours a day, with occasional breaks for instruction in mindfulness meditation. These experimentations were occurring at roughly the same time I began teaching graduate courses in nursing theory and research. I discovered that the sort of Asian bodymind views with which I had been experimenting had achieved slight but important notoriety as having an influence on, or at least a similarity to, developing nursing worldviews.

During my career as a nurse-educator, the traditional Western medical model of health care—based on a biological germ theory of disease and a Cartesian view of persons as separate mind and body—had fallen under critique from a number of sources (Allen and Hall 1988; Watson 1999). Teaching nursing theory led me into nursing discussions about the sources of nursing knowledge and, more specifically, about the view of knowledge as rooted in intuitions. In an effort to remain true to holistic worldviews (for those in their care) nursing researchers have explored definitions of science and persons that depart from the corresponding definitions informing medical theory and practice (Watson 1999; Kim 2000). Along with theoretical work in differentiating nursing, other efforts have been to "refocus," "re-emphasize" and thus to "rediscover" holistic nursing approaches in practice. Inspired by these critiques that highlighted the limitations of the bio-medical model, and seeing resources and methods that were indicating an expanded model of healing and health, I decided to pull these critiques, resources, and methods together in an exploration of the possibilities for a new course. Hopefully, it would be a strong counter force to the limitations of the bio-medical model.

For nurse scholars it might seem redundant to offer a course in holistic care to nurses, because nursing has historically differentiated itself from the bio-medical reductionism of medical practice by claiming to practice nursing care with a holistic approach to persons. However, both nurse scholars and practitioners agree on the seduction of nursing by the rational scientific model. This model focuses on diseased parts of the body and biological abnormalities rather than a holistic approach. A holistic approach recognizes that there are interacting mental, emotional, social, spiritual, and environmental influences on the health of "whole humans." As nursing has "progressed" as a discipline it has had to struggle with reconciling its holistic ideal with the methods of medicine—its de facto role model in many ways.

The majority of my students were practicing nurses returning for further education and advanced degrees. Many of these nurses wished to practice nursing in holistic ways that contrast with the one-dimensional focus on the (diseased) body alone as in traditional medicine. The textbooks I examined in holistic nursing[6] indicated that in holistic nursing care courses, the holistic ideals of nursing are reclaimed and reinforced. These courses also have often included an update on the current alternative/complementary health practices being accessed by clients. Such course development constitutes an expansion of the repertoire available and accepted by nurses for working with clients. Reading about this repertoire has become more of a common practice among nursing students. However, for this course I wanted to do more than just present a cognitive understanding of the theory underlying much of the alternative approaches to healing, which connect body and mind and/or spirit. I believed that nurses needed to develop the abilities to implement integrated bodymind strategies, both for themselves and for clients. I obviously needed to provide classroom means for personal experience of degrees of this integration.

As I turned to Ron for assistance, the real benefits of interdisciplinary collaboration began to flourish. Starting from our own points of strength, each of us sought to find the theoretical, experiential (and applied, in the case of nursing) connections between our respective fields. We both came to a fuller understanding of how to link the body, spirit, and mind. For me, nursing could be learned by drawing on spiritual practice. For Ron, tai chi began to be more than a moving meditative spiritual practice and connections began to grow regarding the bodymind practices as a health practice. In a parallel to the integration we both sought in our respective classrooms, our teamwork began to harmonize and produce the rationale for introducing Buddhist meditation and tai chi into a nursing course.

Rationale for Meditation and Tai Chi in Holistic Health Care

Sherry: Central to supporting holistic practices in nursing is the need to hold a view of people as whole entities, persons or human beings. Many nursing theories conceptualize people in this way. I came to believe that Martha Rogers' (1990) "science of unitary human beings" would be useful in this course. Her view of human beings has been compared with the sort of Asian practices I mentioned above, and that are believed to inform many of the holistic approaches integrated into health care. Some have concluded that Rogers' worldview holds areas of similarity to that of some Buddhist concepts (Hanchett 1992). In the early '70s, Rogers, introduced into nursing the concept that the fundamental unit of the living system was an energy field, coextensive with the environmental field (Rogers 1970). For Rogers, the human energy field and the environmental fields were infinite and integral with continuously changing patterning. They were different only in the pattern, such that there were two integral fields of dynamic unity.

The Buddha expressed our present condition as "that which is arisen dependent upon" (Kalupahana 1997). "In very brief form, dependent arising...indicates the interrelatedness of things in the universe. Things arise dependent on causes and conditions; they gain their identities in relation to other things. Nothing stands alone, autonomous, and isolated, but instead exists only in a web of interconnectedness" (Napper 1992, 3). According to dependent arising, phenomena and their functions are recognizable by ordinary persons. For Rogers, manifestations of field patterning require recognition of the behaviors of the individual. Integrality, the continuous mutual human and environmental field process, demands recognition of the interconnected web of reality.

The above insights helped to clarify the implications of nursing education methods that promote viewing persons as integrated parts and encourage nursing practices that address all of the human dimensions. Such beliefs and practices are what make holism the contrast to a one-dimensional biological focus on persons. For nurses to grasp the idea of connectedness, I thought that the contemplative methods of Buddhism would be useful, perhaps even central, to a view of persons consistent with Rogers' nursing theory.

Ron: The theoretical background of tai chi is useful for religion and health care practitioners alike. Both tai chi and traditional Chinese health practices rely on philosophical Taoism (Daoism) for much of their theoretical understanding. These traditionalists hold that the indescribable tao manifests in two aspects, yin and yang, each unthinkable without the other. Power or energy either flows actively (yang) through bodymind or else is inactive (yin) (Wolf, Coogler, and Xu 1998; Jacobson et al. 1997). The more open the flow the greater is thought to be the power, energy, and health. As acupuncture is believed to help open up energy flow, tai chi is thought to activate power and energy throughout the bodymind. An advantage of tai chi for classrooms and for health practitioners is that it is noninvasive and is initiated from the bodymind of the practitioners.

In an endeavor to bring relevance to the nurses I would be teaching, I began to appreciate and integrate the language of another discipline into my understanding. I sought to fathom the full impact and opportunities available for nurses who sufficiently learn about tai chi. Fortunately, I could draw on the recent proliferation of research about tai chi and its relationship to bodymind integration.[7] Much of this recent research emphasis regarding tai chi is in the area of geriatrics. This is not surprising, given that tai chi is most often associated with an aging population in China, its country of origin. It is also opportune, in light of soon-to-be-expected inordinate growth of this population relative to other age groups in North America. However, not all recent research about tai chi addresses just this geriatric population. While noting the benefits of tai chi for older adults, Schaller (1996, 17) also notes: 1) Physical inactivity is a leading cause of morbidity and mortality; 2) Nurses are frequently in the position to recommend and encourage exercise and physical activity for all clients.

What sort of physical functioning could be expected to be improved and maintained with tai chi? Briefly, in comparison to control groups, tai chi practice improved balance, kinesthetic sense, and strength (Jacobson et al. 1997), decreased body fat and increased oxygen uptake and trunk flexibility (Lan, Lai, and Wong 1996), increased muscle strength in knee extension and flexion (Lan et al. 1998), delayed onset of falls and decreased fear of falling in the elderly (Wolf et al. 1997), improved average velocity of sway (Shih 1997), relieved osteoarthritis through strengthening of joint muscles, increased range of motion, and flexibility (Lumsden, Baccala, and Martire 1998), and improved eyes-open balance (Schaller 1996).

The nurses I was to teach could add to the above that tai chi has been recognized to be a pleasant, social activity, and that given this factor, it is easier to promote adherence to practice than with many less bodymind-oriented activities (Ross and Presswalla 1998). Lan, Lai, and Wong (1996, 614), referring to exercise such as tai chi, recognized the role the mental aspect has in encouraging good physical health when they claimed, "Elderly people prefer mind-body exercise with low velocity that is easy to learn and convenient to practice." Belief that exercise is easy and convenient augments the practice.

Description of Mindfulness Meditation Practice and Tai Chi Practice

Sherry: The actual practice of mindfulness meditation is deceptively simple. Directions are given simply to narrow attention to (focus on) some bodily function such as breathing. This puts the mind and body immediately into harmony or tandem. A simple device is to count one's in-breaths up to ten and then start over. Another is mentally to say "in" on in breaths and "out" on out breaths. If distractions arise, as soon as they are noticed, they are noted with a label—e.g., "feeling, feeling..." for as long as they last, then focus returns to "the practice."[8] For the course, the technique of guided imagery for progressive relaxation preceded the meditation to help ease the students into the practice.

Ron: Chen family-style tai chi masters say that body is moved by, or follows, chi—energy or power flowing from a location near a body's center of gravity below the navel and centered from front to back (Lumsden, Baccala, and Martire 1998, 87). They further maintain that chi is moved by, or follows, intention of mind. Movement takes place most efficiently when mind is calm, body is relaxed, and chi is "gathered," that is, allowed to grow in amplitude as judged by increased energy and power. Consistent with the theoretical background of tai chi, chi is cultivated both while still and in activity. Still intention and body are practiced mainly in standing meditation while attending to breath, as in mindfulness meditation, or focusing on repetition of a single word such as "peace."[9]

Tai chi activity is still conceived as occurring in various combinations of yin and yang. Into a quieted mind an intention may be introduced to move in relaxed, circular, and bi-directional ways. Circles are most easily seen in movements of the waist, arms, and hands—although areas of the solar plexus may be noticed by adepts to be moving in circles as well. Often adepts will express higher value on the "inner" movement rather than "external" manifestation. Intention is said to direct change from the waist, twisting and turning out to extremities—like a silkworm spinning and reeling silk out of a cocoon. Arms sometimes moving in different directions simultaneously foster a sense of integration consistent with theories about left and right brain cooperation.

By means of an introductory exercise, practitioners can get a sense of how their intentions direct energy-filled activity throughout their bodies. They are instructed to feel the desired intention-directed energy in an arm, in contrast to the same arm while completely tensed, or completely relaxed. The "tai chi arm" is sensed both as being stronger while at the same time using less effort. Once this sense-memory is in place, beginners immediately are able to practice slow, circular, weight-shifting movements, in the same intentional, relaxed, energy-filled way. With the addition of "reversing" their breathing— abdominal muscles in rather than out on in-breaths, out rather than in on out-breaths—beginners can immediately get a sense of sinking into a straight-backed stance. There is but one thing left for a neophyte to remember: that as one sinks, the knees move out a bit into the strength of an arch, rather than being allowed to weakly collapse inward.

Our Classes

The question might arise in a reader's mind about what happens in our classes. What might an observer who walked into one of our classrooms actually see?

Ron: We usually have a theory day and a practice day. If you walked in on a theory day, you would see me walking around the room looking at students' answers to study questions I passed out the class period before about the reading for the day. Later you would see teams developing a consensus answer to a question for which each of them had written preparation. Here is a sample question from the class as I last conducted it: Describe the breathing instructions given by the archery master in *Zen in the Art of Archery,* and compare them with your own breathing in tai chi practice. With a question like this the aim is for class participants to discuss more than what the text says. They also discuss each other's applications of what they read. A second aim is to see to it that theory and practice are not too neatly divided.

If you walked in on an activity day, at the beginning of class you might see one of the participants sweeping the floor with a broom borrowed from the janitor. No, this is not a Zen practice. After the floor is cleaned up the participants lay blankets or mats down on the floor, so they can lie flat on their backs in the yoga posture called "the death pose." I explain that this is a quick way to learn to feel deep relaxation, but that it is not recommended for meditation, because it readily leads to sleep. As soon as they are so relaxed they might sleep, I suggest that they sit up in cross-legged meditation. I recommend elevating the hips with a pillow, as Zen practitioners do. If this is unduly uncomfortable, sitting up straight on the front of a chair seat is fine. We might sit for ten minutes and then do a standing meditation for another five minutes in preparation for tai chi moving meditation. I either show a videotape that demonstrates the movements we will be practicing that day, or demonstrate them myself, or both. We practice each of the movements several times together. I watch them perform the movement, and suggest changes. We stand in meditation for another five minutes, and then sit in chairs for the remaining time reviewing our experiences of the day, as well as taking questions and comments.

Sherry: Our nursing course has so far been offered as a forty-hour, one-week intensive course that is quite different in format from the students' other nursing courses. Because of the limited number of days, the students get an immediate introduction to mindfulness meditation on the first morning. On the first day, following a get-acquainted activity to foster group interaction and sharing, Ron teaches the meditation practice. For the nursing course, the progressive relaxation through guided imagery precedes ten minutes of meditation. The time is short because very few students have ever done such practice. On subsequent mornings of the weeklong class students volunteer to conduct the progressive relaxation prior to the meditation, which increases a few minutes each morning. The carpeted room is made conducive to quiet and calm with meditative music while the students sit in a comfortable position on floor cushions or in a chair if they prefer.

Throughout the rest of the course, practitioners of various complementary therapies (i.e., yoga, biofeedback, herbals, therapeutic touch, massage, Chinese medicine, acupuncture, etc.) speak on the principles, often holistic, underlying their therapies and demonstrate it with as many of the class members participating as possible. They have group discussion of their reactions and experiences. Ron introduces tai chi as a form of moving meditation with special health benefits on the second or third day. The students learn a few movements that can be integrated into their morning meditation.

Following the week of classroom meetings, students continue for two months with assignments that they complete on their own. Very many of the students continue incorporating meditation or relaxation techniques into this extended period.

Reflections on Practice

Sherry: Students in both the nursing and the religion classes evaluated their "practice" (for course purposes) by keeping a journal. At best, some comments regarding integration resulted. For example, one nursing student wrote after the third day's meditation,

> I felt better able to relax and got into the relaxation and remained super aware of around me [sic]. It doesn't make me feel tired

when I am done. I feel more in control of myself and my
emotions. I feel more centered. My mind isn't racing and I'm
not worried about anything. It is easier for me to prioritize and
limit myself to one thing at a time. I'm feeling serene. I'm
comfortable in my skin.[10]

And another observed,

I used to think meditation was going to a quiet place and
separating yourself from others. I learned today that this is not
true. Instead of withdrawing from others, you include yourself
with everything that surrounds you. Feelings of peacefulness,
relaxation, openness, and awareness were some of the things I
experienced during this remarkable time.

In most cases students reported more relaxation, concentration, and energy.
Some said their practice became a renewing break from long hours of studying.

Ron: One Religious Studies student wrote,

Now when I start to feel stiff and sleepy from studying, I go
outside and do the form. Then I have the energy to study
longer than I did before. Relaxing and energizing my body
with intentional practice, is not two things, but one. I feel the
effects in a way I would formerly have said was mentally and
physically. Now I don't know where the difference lies, and it
is of no concern.

In "Contemplative Theories and Practices" class, 20 percent of the class evaluation was on attendance and participation, the rationale being that one has to
be present and alert to practice. An exam over the readings and guest presentations was worth 30 percent. Up to 25 percent was awarded for keeping a
diary of classroom practice and one contemplative project outside of class.
During the three-hour final exam period, I observed each student's seated
posture and the tai chi form and awarded up to 25 percent for the quality of
the performance.

Sherry: Evaluation in the Holistic Nursing course is based on learning contracts
written by each student and negotiated with the instructor. During the week of
class time the students complete self-administered holistic health assessments
that are used as a basis for part of a contract for work that extends two months
following the class time hours. Students are given guidelines for C level, B level
and A level requirements and they then develop individual learning objectives
for the level they select. They include in the contract the criteria for the evidence
of their successful completion of their objectives. Personal health objectives and
an in-depth exploration of at least one complementary/alternative therapy are
included. Many of the students incorporate continuing their meditation or tai
chi and keeping a daily journal on their experience as part of their contracts.

Reflections on Classroom Experiences

Ron: So, Sherry, what have you learned by doing this class? Do you think the students enjoyed the innovation? Would you do it again the same way? Is it a valuable, even essential part of nursing education for you?

Sherry: This class can be counted among some of the best teaching experiences I have had in education. The students' engagement and receptivity has been immense. Many notebook comments from the first day reflect an initial surprise and even discomfort with strange new practices, but these rapidly disappear. I believe it provides a way to help them make desired connections with patients that they sometimes don't have the understanding to carry out. It is immensely helpful to the students because it focuses on their awareness of themselves as whole persons first and then allows for them to see how this can affect and help their caring practice. Interaction and exposure to someone from another discipline with quite different expertise allows them to expand their ideas and repertoire of what is possible and useful in creating health, not just curing disease. The only part of the course I would change is the time frame. The contact hours are concentrated into one week and the development of bodymind sensitivities would be even greater, I believe, with a longer time frame. Reports from those who elect to continue the meditation into the extended period confirm this.

What are your reflections on your class, Ron? Do you think some practical exercises that religious practitioners really use are a valuable component of education for philosophy and religion students? Will large numbers of students ever do this? Any disappointments, or changes you think need to be made?

Ron: I think it is a very limited group of students who will ever self-select themselves into this optional course. Those who do seem genuinely grateful to have a learning experience that is unavailable anywhere else in our university—except in your nursing course. I am particularly pleased that one student learned tai chi well enough that he could substitute for me in responding to calls to teach tai chi.

I liked being student-directed in the choice of readings, and believe continued flexibility in text choice is a must as a response to student interest. However, next time I will be more prepared with practice-related options from the world's great traditions. Of course, I remain open to students' suggestions for readings from less orthodox sources. The class was also student-directed or student-led in another important way. Unlike the control an instructor has who gives a short lecture and leaves plenty of time for questions, I never knew how much tai chi I would be able to teach in a class period, because the students determined how quickly they would be able to learn skill-based instructions. If I were teaching tai chi outside of the university and the students were frustrated with the pace, they just wouldn't come back. Here, my ability to provide skill-building experiences at a pace deserving of a university grade, while at the same time not garnering complaints about an obvious educational experiment in the southern U.S., put quite a bit of pressure on me. I wanted the course to reflect well on my department and also to meet the goal of broadening students' educational experience beyond the traditional cognitive, theoretical, just-listen-memorize-and-give-back-on-the-test variety. Having gotten through the maiden voyage without drowning, I think I will be able to relax and enjoy the journey more next time.

Final Thoughts

Ron and Sherry: In North America, unlike traditional Asia, we seem to have lost a sense of bodymind awareness in activity as being important for mental/physical health of the whole person. Some ways to reclaim that sense have been reported here. Traditional Asian practices of meditation and tai chi may seem natural to religious studies disciplines, just as promoting health may seem natural to a discipline like nursing. However, taking Asian practices, as well as notions of whole person health, outside of normal disciplinary lines can result in theories and practices that complement and enrich one another.

We chose mindfulness meditation and the moving meditation of tai chi as the vehicles to help students discover the integration and connectedness of two human dimensions. There are other dimensions in addition to mind and body. Indeed, the spiritual dimension is another that we and others have recognized as also a part of the human totality. We can only speculate on how much the bodymind techniques of mindfulness and tai chi meditation address this or other dimensions of the human. We believe the more human dimensions integrated in the classroom, the closer we come to meeting the challenges of education.

Notes

1. This course was largely theoretical in orientation, which led to a bit of a paradox. The figures read about in the course were more on the non-theoretical, non-dogmatic side of the great religious traditions, sometimes bordering, as in the case of Zen, on the iconoclastic. Some Zen Buddhists have tended to devalue icons, theory, scriptures, and the like, in favor of one-on-one instruction leading to the authentication of Buddhist ideals in a practitioner's own experience. While studying figures like St. John of the Cross, Siddharta, Ramana Maharshi, Lin-chi, and Rumi, we discovered that in comparison to their personal experience, the words we were reading were paradoxically reported by them to be a distant second in importance to their religious lives. Guest speakers with first-hand experience were also invited to speak in order to connect the course with more personal accounts of religious experience. Again, they made clear that the words they used paled in importance when compared with the results of their practices.

2. The American Council of Learned Societies (ACLS) is the same agency that administers Fulbright grants. The purpose and description of "Contemplative Practice Fellowships" may be found on the ACLS web site, <http://www.acls.org>.

3. Traditional Buddhist teachings place great value on the ability to be calm and peaceful, with mind unperturbed, in what they consider the only three possible physical positions.

4. For example, one may view Robert Thurman's Buddhist interpretation of the outcome of his own mindfulness meditation in Chapter 2, "Searching for the Self," of his book *Inner Revolution*.

5. The total nursing course content was developed in cooperation with another nursing faculty member, with co-author Hartman responsible for developing the bodymind practices component. Those interested in more information on content are referred to the *Journal of Holistic Nursing* and *Holistic Nursing Practice*, as well as the latest edition of the text *Holistic Nursing*.

6. "Over the years, the emphasis in TC [tai chi] became far more focused on body environment and mind-body interactions than as a martial art" (Wolf et al. 1998, 886).

7. Co-author Ronald Burr was given these instructions from the Ven. Upandita during a meditation retreat in Myanmar (Burma).

8. Co-author Ronald Burr has practiced tai chi for more than twenty years. For the last three years he has been studying with Yang Yang, a master of the Chen family-style. The instructions included in this paragraph and the following are drawn from those studies, although any mistakes in interpretion are solely the responsibility of the author.

9. These quotes are shared with the permission of the students.

References

Allen, J.D., and B.A. Hall. 1988. Challenging the focus on technology: A critique of the medical model in a changing health care system. *Advances in Nursing Science* 10(3): 22-34.

Hanchett, E. 1992. Concepts from Eastern philosophy and Rogers' science of unitary human beings. *Nursing Science Quarterly* 5(4): 164-170.

Jacobson, B.H., H. Chen, C. Cashel, and L. Guerrero. 1997. The effect of t'ai chi chuan training on balance, kinesthetic sense, and strength. *Perceptual and Motor Skills* 84: 27-33.

Kalupahana, D. 1997. Buddha: The founder of a tradition of peace. Paper presented at the Conference of the Inter-Religious Federation for World Peace, 27 November, Washington, D.C.

Kim, H. S. 2000. The nature of theoretical thinking in nursing. New York: Springer Publishing Company.

Lan, C., J. Lai, and M. Wong. 1996. Cardiorespiratory function, flexibility, and body composition among geriatric tai chi chuan practitioners. *Arch Phys Med Rehabil* 77: 612-16.

Lan, C., J. Lai, S. Chen, and M. Wong. 1998. 12-month t'ai chi training in the elderly: Its effect on health fitness. *Medicine & Science in Sports & Exercise, the Official Journal of the American College of Sports Medicine* 30: 345-50.

Lumsden, D.B., A. Baccala, and J. Martire. 1998. T'ai chi for osteoarthritis: An introduction for primary care physicians. *Geriatrics* 53(2): 84-88.

Napper, E. 1992. *Dependent arising and emptiness: A Tibetan Buddhist interpretation of Madhyamika philosophy emphasizing the compatibility of emptiness and conventional phenomena.* Boston: Wisdom.

Rogers, M. 1970. *An introduction to the theoretical basis of nursing.* Philadelphia: Davis.

Rogers, M. 1990. Nursing: Science of unitary, irreducible, human beings: Update 1990. In *Visions of Rogers' science based nursing,* edited by E.A. Barrett. New York: National League for Nursing.

Ross, C., and J.L. Presswalla. 1998. The therapeutic effects of tai chi for the elderly. *Journal of Gerontological Nursing* (February): 45-47.

Schaller, K.J. 1996. Tai chi chih: An exercise option for older adults. *Journal of Gerontological Nursing* 22(10): 12-17.

Shih, J. 1997. Basic Beijing twenty-four forms of tai chi exercise and average velocity of sway. *Perceptual and Motor Skills* 84: 287-90.

Thurman, R. 1998. *Inner revolution: Life, liberty, and the pursuit of real happiness.* New York: Riverhead.

Watson, J. 1999. *Postmodern nursing and beyond.* London: Churchill Livingstone.

Wolf, S.L., H.X. Barnhart, G.L. Ellison, and C.E. Coogler. 1997. The effect of tai chi quan and computerized balance training on postural stability in older subjects. *Physical Therapy* 77(4): 371-81.

Wolf, S.L., C. Coogler, and T. Xu. 1998. Exploring the basis for tai chi chuan as a therapeutic exercise approach. *Arch Phys Med Rehab* 78: 886-92.

Breaking Hearts:
Towards an Erotics of Pedagogy

Alison Pryer

ALISON PRYER was born in London, England. She taught for several years in Germany and Japan, and is now a doctoral student at the University of British Columbia in Vancouver.

Abstract. Teaching and learning are erotic acts. The processes of teaching and learning involve the ecstatic abandonment of self to the Other, the continual losing and finding of self in the Other, the intimate, sensual coupling of self with the world. It is eros, catalyzed by the bittersweet yearnings of ever-unfulfilled desire, that moves each of us to seek union with the Other. Pedagogy is a special kind of erotic encounter, a deliberate wounding of the student by the teacher that is mortifying and revivifying, humiliating and life-giving.

Keywords. Eros, Love, Pedagogy, Teaching, Learning, Education

Acknowledgments. The author gratefully acknowledges the receipt of financial support for this work from a Social Sciences and Humanities Research Council of Canada Doctoral Fellowship and an Izaak Walton Killam Memorial Predoctoral Fellowship.

Breaking Hearts:
Towards an Erotics of Pedagogy

Alison Pryer

I will bring you happy flowers from the mountains, bluebells,
dark hazels and rustic baskets of kisses.
I want
to do with you what spring does with the cherry trees.
(Neruda [1924] 1993, 55)

Pederasty is undoubtedly a useful paradigm for classic Western
pedagogy. A greater man penetrates a lesser man with
knowledge....The student is an innocent, empty receptacle, lacking
in his own desires, having desires "introduced" into him by the teacher.
(Gallop, cited by Simon 1992, 70)

Who does not remember the first time they fell in love? I was four years old when first stricken. Her name was Miss Britton.

My family lived in a Victorian tenement building behind the old Coliseum Theatre, which was then home of the English National Opera and Sadler's Wells Ballet Company. On summer days, the dancers would throw the stage doors open and we would watch them practice in their black tights and leotards, sweating in the stifling heat. Sometimes, if we were lucky, we would see the prima ballerina practice. While listening to my mother's old ballet records at home, I dreamed of my debut in the corps de ballet. My mother, knowing how much I yearned to become a ballerina, enrolled me in ballet school.

Before each weekly lesson the littlest ballet students would gather in the cramped changing room. We hurriedly changed into our uniforms: pale blue leotards and pink socks and pumps. Mothers pulled their daughters' hair back into tight knots secured with hairpins, black hairnets, and regulation pale blue hair bands. Many of us needed help crisscrossing and tying the silky, pink ribbons on our pumps. With only a few moments to spare, we rushed into the practice room, rubbed our feet in the chalk box and stood in first position while Miss Britton, the teacher, and Miss Grace, the pianist, entered. We curtseyed and said "Good Afternoon" to each of the ladies in turn. Then we began all the floor exercises, the barre exercises, the music theory, and finally, the dancing. Miss Britton watched each of us and would command: Head up! Tummies and bottoms in! Point those toes! Gentle fingers!

Ten very small bodies were disciplined for one hour. I never minded this discipline. I loved it. Most of all, I loved Miss Britton. The attraction was physical. She had a lithe and supple body, milky-white skin, and blond hair that never fell out of its chignon, even when she leapt right across the room, stirring up the still air so that it caressed our faces. I marveled at the ripple of her thigh muscles when she jumped up high. I lived for her smiling praise and the twinkle in her blue eyes when I had done well. I felt a jealous stab in the chest when she complimented another pupil. Miss Britton embodied a whole world, the world of ballet made flesh. This was the world of which I dreamed when I fell asleep on hot, sticky London nights, listening to the wafts of ballet music that drifted in through my open bedroom window. My love of Miss Britton, and my desire for her body was the expression of my desire to enter the world of ballet, to become a part of that world. At four years of age, I discovered that learning was all about passion and desire, all about love. The ballet studio is long gone—demolished by developers. But whenever I return to London and pass by the place where it once stood, the pangs of unbearable desire return, and I can feel panes of warm afternoon sun streaming onto my body through tall studio windows. What remains to me now is the strong presence of eros.

Eros, like passion and desire, is ineffable and intangible. It is a feeling of "impossible conceptual definition, but also strong experiential presence," and what constitutes the erotic varies socio-economically, socio-politically, and socio-historically (Savigliano 1995, 136). It is eros that creates the desire to unite with others, whether through "affectionate attachments and friendships of the Platonic sort, maternal and paternal love, kin tie and social bonding with work mates or with a community of identity" (Ferguson 1989, 78). Eros is the energy that creates and maintains the strong human bonds required for people to survive individually and collectively. Clearly, gender, race, class, ethnicity, age, as well as one's physical embodiment are all tightly interwoven with notions of love. Ferguson (1989, 62) believes that, in western cultures, sexual and social energies (what I call eros) have been "socially defined, focused and organized" in such a way as to create and perpetuate a system of male dominance over females, as well as other forms of dominance. Paradoxically, we may experience the flow of sexual and social energies as desirable, pleasurable, sensuous, and connecting, even while they promote social and psychic violence (Martusewicz 1997).

But eros is not only that which creates and maintains systems of collective human bonding. My understanding of "eros" is informed by Schroeder's (1998) work. She writes:

> Eros, in the broad sense, is not confined to the erotics of sexuality, but is that which infuses life into all our partnerships and inter-
> actions. Eros is in the partnership of ourselves and creation,
> between one person and another, between colleagues, students,
> friends, lovers, and ultimately in relation to our own selves. Eros
> is the life force. (p. 13)

Eros, the life force, is the vital coupling and uncoupling and re-coupling of the self with environment, an intercourse that gives rise to the reproduction and evolution of both self and environment (Maturana and Varela 1987). We can feel the life force in the rhythmic rising and falling, heaving and rippling of oceans and grasses, kelp forests and sand dunes, winds and rivers. This same force pulsates within our own human bodies, as we too are part of this continuous flow of life. Our bodies form "one organic/perceptual circuit" with the world (Leder 1990, 160). The flow of energy along this circuit is eros.

This erotic flow "cannot be felt secondhand" (Lorde 1984, 59). Still, writers and thinkers have tried to capture the intriguing magic of eros in their nets of words. Like butterfly hunters, they stalk their prey knowing all the while that by the time they have caught their creature and pinned it to a collector's board, it will surely be dead. I too am hunting eros. To guide my way, I summon the multiple voices of others who have gone before me in their search for the heart of eros...

"All of life is eros, an erotic encounter," says Schroeder (1998, 168). "My life and the world's life are deeply intertwined...The world and I reciprocate one another," writes Abram (1996, 33). "Intimacy is the secret law of life and the universe," whispers O'Donohue (1997, xvii). Eroticism is first and foremost "a thirst for otherness," declares Paz (Schroeder, 1998, 122). Eros, firstborn child of the Goddess Chaos, is a central figure in the ancient worship of "sexuality as a primary life-force," notes Walker (1983, 283). Griffin (1995, 42) gently reminds us that the erotic is of the earth: We eat of the earth, we take shelter in the earth, our bodies respond with sleep, blood, semen to the rhythms of the material universe.

Eros is a communal gift, a heaping of happy flowers, bluebells, and dark hazels, that is passed around when one meets another, when I meet you, when spring meets the cherry trees. Eros is an opening and receiving, an attunement to the unique gifts of the other that releases swells of joy, passion, and desire in the body. Eros is an endless becoming, a perpetual birthing. Eros is fecundity, awakening, change, growth, a wet flow of creative energy.

How can I define eros? I can't. Eros is impossible to pin down! It is always in movement, always in relation, always in/complete: becoming, birthing, flowing, breathing, awakening, changing, growing, opening, releasing, receiving, giving, yearning, heaping, intertwining, responding, reciprocating, encountering, coupling, uncoupling, re-coupling. Living. Being. "All you can say of it is that it is, and it is, and it is. No beginning, no end. All middle." (Le Guin, cited by Houtekamer et al. 1998, 143). It is a chaotic flux, an entropic process, polysemous, defying the tyranny of conclusions.

Eros never stops, is never sated. It continually tempts the hungry monster of desire—that monster living within each of us—with tiny morsels of fullness.

"Have you ever desired another because you believed the other could fill you, could fill the empty, lonely, dark places in your heart and imagination and spirit and mind?" asks Leggo (1996, 236). Yes. What happens to the boys and girls and men and women who meet the monster of desire? Theirs is a story about "the nagging recognition of lack and absence and separateness, a story about the unending desire for wholeness and fulfillment and completeness," warns Leggo (1996, 236). Forsooth:

> We spend our lives seeking the Other that will complement us
> and make us whole again as we believe we were once whole. Of
> course, the wholeness never existed, and hence our desire for the
> complementary Other will never be satisfied. Desire is always
> frustrating and frustrated, always fruitful and freewheeling,
> frequently foolish, but fulsome, too. (Leggo 1996, 236)

With experience, we may come to understand that desire is always frustrated and frustrating, and knowing this, we may try to resist the heavy sweetness of its intoxication.

The dance of eros is strange. We find ourselves pushing towards the Other and then pulling away, desiring and fearing, yearning while foreseeing danger. These feelings of tension and ambivalence are present in a poem by Jacopone da Todi (Harvey 1996, 195), a medieval Christian mystic, who meditates on his love of God.

> Love, I flee from You, afraid to give You my heart: I see that you
> make me one with You, I cease to be me and can no longer
> find myself.

Eros creates intimacy between you and me, dissolving the boundaries between us, creating a "transparent self" (Schoeman, cited by Grumet 1988, 165), or transparent selves. This transparency of self allows a "fluidity in friendship, in love, in spiritual communion" (Grumet 1988, 165-166). It is warm, open, and receptive to the other. Yet, the awareness of my own transparency may also be unsettling and disorienting: "[Y]ou make me one with You,/I cease to be me ..." I am no longer as I was, I am no longer myself, I am something else, someone else, I am a reflection of you, I am you, I am a stranger to myself, I am living somewhere between "me" and "you."

We become porous, membranous, wounded when we open to and are opened by eros. We enter and are entered by eros. We must "break form to be transformed" (Schroeder 1998, 91). We are broken by eros.

> My heart is broken,
> open.
> (Ingram, cited by Jardine 1992, vii)

The erotic encounter causes a break in the heart, forcing an opening in the psyche. This opening, even if only a tiny crack, becomes the entry to spiritual growth.

> The agony of lovers
> burns with the fire of passion.
> Lovers leave traces of where they've been.
> The wailing of broken hearts
> is the doorway to God.
> (Rumi, cited by Chopra 1998, 17)

The erotic is a paradox of pleasure and pain. Eros is a gift of happy flowers and the face of death.

Pedagogy is a special kind of erotic encounter, a meeting of teacher and student. The student may find joy in learning something new purely for its own sake. She or he may find pleasure in fulfilling his/her desire to become more knowledgeable or skillful or powerful or competent. She or he may also enjoy successfully meeting the expectations of teachers, parents, and community, thus becoming a part of that wider community. But sometimes teacher and student know all the steps of the erotic, pedagogical dance by heart, finding comfort and safety in its predictable order. Then the pedagogical process degenerates into mere routine. Too much comfort and safety and predictability are anaesthetizing: You cannot sleepwalk through the pedagogical experience. The pedagogical dance is a wild and chaotic process, a struggle that is sometimes joyful, sometimes painful.

Simon (1992) calls the agony of pedagogy "disorganization." Pedagogy, he says, is "a practice within which one acts with the intent of provoking experience that will simultaneously organize and disorganize a variety of understandings of our natural and social world" (p. 56). When students step into this space of pedagogical chaos, they risk the "destruction of their ability to return to a safer, more certain place" (p. 71). Like the shaman taking an apprentice on a magical journey of initiation, the teacher "breaks" the student, bringing the student into the death space in order to give new life.

The erotics of pedagogy—its joy and pleasure, as well as its chaos and agony—is truly grotesque, in the Bakhtinian sense of the word. It is a process of wounding that is mortifying and revivifying, humiliating and life-giving. According to Bakhtin (Morris 1994, 205), the grotesque is characterized by "degradation, that is the lowering of all that is high, spiritual, ideal, abstract; it is a transfer to the material level, to the sphere of earth and body in their indissoluble unity." Pedagogy ruptures the student's everyday understandings, permitting teacher/other knowledge to enter the student. The student merges with that knowledge, becoming, embodying, living out that knowledge in her everyday life. Eros is precisely this process of "natality" which we call education (Jardine 1990).

Contemporary western educational practices are both "enabling and con-straining" (Simon 1992, 56). It is the constraining aspects of the power relations within technical-rational schooling practices that Jane Gallop (Simon 1992, 70) likens to "pederasty," an act of violent imposition. Griffin (1995, 136-137) describes this violent process of coming to know within the technical- rational system of education—what she calls the "scientific" knowledge system—with a startling clarity of perception:

> Here there is no easy posture of receiving. No casual meeting.
> No subtlety or free play. No sultry slow descent to an erotic
> knowledge by which, just as one takes in knowledge, one is
> entered by the known, capsized, transformed. Rather the motion
> is all swift, driven, edged by anxiety, aimed like a weapon is
> aimed, aggressive, conquering. Because dominating every effort
> to know in this terrain is an unmistakable atmosphere of terror.

Griffin continues:

> Because to know is an erotic act, one is made vulnerable to
> what has been before unknown; all knowledge enters the self
> as the force of change. Yet the Western self, ordered as it is
> around dominion, does not want to submit.

Griffin portrays the process of teaching and learning within the technical-rational educational paradigm as a battle to the end.

Like anyone who has been through a public school system, I know this kind of warfare well. One of my clearest memories of elementary school is of the time when we were being taught how to multiply big numbers, numbers like 24 x 953 and 589 x 7102. I was always a diligent student. I knew the steps of the pedagogical routine by heart. But these big numbers were a complete mystery to me, even after Mrs. Lawrence's hour-long explanations. Mrs. Lawrence would scratch chalk marks across the blackboard furiously, until her fat breasts and tummy were covered with chalk dust and her hair was disheveled. Finally, exhausted by her efforts, she would snap, yelling and throwing bits of chalk at me. Still, I had no idea where to begin with an impossible sum like 3871 x 6468. And, anyway, why would I ever want to multiply 3871 by 6468? After being warned twice that I would be punished if my math lessons and my math homework were not completed successfully, Mrs. Lawrence decided enough was enough.

She ordered me to the front of the class, reached into her desk drawer and pulled out the coiled, leather strap. The whole class was watching, breathless: the strap was usually reserved for bad boys. I knew what I had to do. I had already seen lots of boys being belted. First, wait until the teacher has finished reprimanding you. Then hold out your hands steadily. Wait for the sharp stings of the lashes. Do not flinch or move your hands. Apologize to the teacher. With eyes lowered, return to your seat. Somehow, I managed to get through the ordeal, although I was quaking inside. My eyes watered, but I did not let any tears fall.

Of course, after receiving the lashes from the strap, I was still unable to do Mrs. Lawrence's math homework. I told myself "I can't do math, I can't do math" thereby rendering myself virtually unteachable. This mantra—"I can't do math"—stuck with me all through high school. To this day I still do all my counting on my fingers.

Even the best-intentioned teacher may engage in pedagogical warfare of one kind or another. Simon (1992) bravely confesses that as a pusher of liberatory pedagogical practice he has "designs" on his own students. The promise of the lustful lover is also the seductive promise of the teacher:

> I want
> to do with you what spring does with the cherry trees.
> (Neruda [1924] 1993, 55)

I want to bring light to your life, to open you, make you grow. I want to change you. Simon (1992, 71) wonders what alternative there might be to "an eros, which expresses love through the negation of the lived grounds of the other." Is there such an alternative? Are the processes of teaching and learning so fraught with the tensions of teacher and student desires that conflict and change are inevitable?

Indeed, they are. Teaching, learning, and knowing are all erotic acts. Eros is always in movement, always in relation, always in/complete. Eros is a chaotic flux, an entropic process catalyzed by desire. Desire can never be met, filled, satisfied or placated, and is therefore experienced as a lack (Leggo 1996). This is no bad thing in itself. Leggo writes that the "ongoing experience of lack is a reason for celebration" (p. 240).

> Lack refers to the hole in the heart that desires filling. This sense
> of lack drives me to love others, to want to be with others…
> Desire from a personal sense of lack can be liberating,
> strengthening, encouraging. (p. 240)

But does our desire, our innate sense of lack, necessarily drive us to negate the "lived grounds of the other" (Simon 1992, 71) in a violent and coercive way? Leggo (1996, 240) does not think so:

> Lack defined institutionally suggests that people must be
> programmed, filled, activated…prepared for roles, but a
> poetic sense of lack suggests experimentation, risk-taking,
> mistake-making, trying on different masks or subject positions.

Clearly, our collective, socio-cultural understandings of terms such as "desire," "lack," and "eros" affect greatly the nature of our pedagogical theories and our daily educational practices.

Sadly, there is a pervasive fear and mistrust of the erotic among western educators and curriculum theorists. According to Audre Lorde (1984, 54) the erotic is often misnamed or confused with the pornographic. She writes that our culture has turned the erotic into

> the confused, the trivial, the psychotic, the plasticized sensation.
> For this reason, we have often turned away from the exploration
> and consideration of the erotic as a source of power and information,
> confusing it with its opposite, the pornographic...[P]ornography is a
> direct denial of the power of the erotic.

Lorde believes that the erotic has been denigrated precisely because it is so empowering, because it is a source of creative energy. Eros is power is knowledge.

Schooling is deeply concerned with the disciplining of the body because we experience the erotic flow of desire—ours and others'—within, on, through our bodies. Discursive practices are accomplished "not only through language, but through bodies, through ways of moving, dressing and talking, and through ingrained bodily dispositions or habits" (Kamler 1997, 373). Thus, the body is a site of daily struggle for power and meaning.

Luckily, no matter how harsh, disciplined, efficient, and rational a system of schooling might be, it is impossible to colonize every moment, every body, every daydream, and every corner of every classroom. Eros flows into these wild spaces just as water flows into the earth after a long drought. As a schoolgirl, I was a "dreamer." That is what it said on my report card in Mrs. Lawrence's barely legible scrawl: Alison is a daydreamer. I would stare out of the classroom window, way into the distance, to the place right on the other side of the village where the wind roared through two-hundred-year-old beech trees and the crows flew in swirling formations, as if they were black iron filings being pulled this way and that by an invisible magnet. My mind ran free, like the wind in the sky, unhindered by what was happening in the classroom. Dreaming was my way of withdrawing to a space of inner freedom. By giving the crows and the treetops my full, loving attention I entered into a place where eros flowed freely. Much later, as a teacher, I rediscovered the wildness of children. I now understand that technical-rational systems of schooling are never watertight. Wild eros flows into the cracks in the system, and the cracks are everywhere, in the hearts of all teachers and students.

Teaching and learning are erotic acts. The processes of teaching and learning involve the ecstatic abandonment of self to the Other, the continual losing and finding of self in the Other, the intimate, sensual engagement of self with the world. It is eros, catalyzed by the bittersweet yearnings of ever-unfulfilled desire, that moves each of us to seek union with the Other. This vital, erotic coupling of self with environment, giving rise to the reproduction and evolution of both self and environment, is educational in the broadest sense of that word. Clearly, an understanding of eros is crucial to the development of an ecological, non-dualistic ethic of embodiment and holistic educational theory and practice.

By uncovering, musing on, and recounting our own experiences of eros— stories of passion and yearning, pain and loss, betrayal and forgiveness, as well as the blank indifference that is the death of love—we may begin to understand the role of eros in teaching and learning. Yet, strangely, in remembering and retelling stories of eros, we simultaneously unravel and recreate its mystery. Eros is an elusive butterfly. We try to grasp it, and it flutters effortlessly through our fingers.

References

Abram, D. 1996. *The spell of the sensuous: Perception and language in a more-than-human world.* New York: Vintage.

Chopra, D., ed. 1998. *The love poems of Rumi.* Translated by D. Chopra and F. Kia. New York: Harmony.

Ferguson, A. 1989. *Blood at the root: Motherhood, sexuality and male dominance.* London: Pandora.

Griffin, S. 1995. *The eros of everyday life: Essays on ecology, gender and society.* New York: Doubleday.

Grumet, M. 1988. *Bitter milk: Women and teaching.* Amherst, MA: University of Massachusetts Press.

Harvey, A., ed. 1996. *The essential mystics: Selections from the world's great wisdom traditions.* San Francisco: Harper.

Houtekamer, T., C. Chambers, R. Yamagishi, and E. Striker. 1998. Exploring sacred relations: Collaborative writing as action research. In *Action research as a living practice,* edited by T. Carson and D. Sumara. New York: Peter Lang.

Jardine, D. 1990. "To dwell with a boundless heart": On the integrated curriculum and the recovery of the earth. *Journal of Curriculum and Supervision* 5(2): 107-119.

Jardine, D. 1992. *Speaking with a boneless tongue.* Bragg Creek, Alberta: Makyo.

Kamler, B. 1997. Text as body, body as text. *Discourse: Studies in the Cultural Politics of Education* 18(3): 369-387.

Leder, D. 1990. *The absent body.* Chicago: University of Chicago Press.

Leggo, C. 1996. Dancing with desire: A meditation on psychoanalysis, politics, and pedagogy. *Teachers and Teaching: Theory and Practice* 2(2): 233-242.

Lorde, A. 1984. *Sister outsider.* Freedom, CA: Crossing.

Maturana, H., and F. Varela. 1987. *The tree of knowledge.* Boston: Shambhala.

Martusewicz, R. 1997. Say me to me: Desire and education. In *Learning desire: Perspectives on pedagogy, culture and the unsaid,* edited by S. Todd. New York: Routledge.

Morris, P., ed. 1994. *The Bakhtin reader: Selected writings of Bakhtin, Medvedev and Voloshinov.* London: Routledge.

Neruda, P. [1969] 1993. *Twenty love poems and a song of despair.* Translated by W. S. Merwin. San Francisco: Chronicle. Originally published 1924.

O'Donohue, J. 1997. *Anam cara: A book of Celtic wisdom.* New York: Cliff Street.

Savigliano, M. 1995. Tango and the postmodern uses of passion. In *Cruising the performative: Interventions into the representation of ethnicity, nationality, and sexuality,* edited by S. Case, P. Brett, and S. Foster. Bloomington, IN: Indiana University Press.

Schroeder, C. 1998. *A poetics of embodiment: Cultivating an erotics of the everyday.* Ph.D. diss., Simon Fraser University.

Simon, R. 1992. *Teaching against the grain: Texts for a pedagogy of possibility.* New York: Bergin and Garvey.

Walker, B. 1983. *The woman's encyclopedia of myths and secrets.* San Francisco: Harper.

Education and Culture: Experiencing Im/possibility

Learning, remembering, talking, imagining:
all of them are made possible
by participating in a culture.

—Jerome Bruner

Education and Culture:
Experiencing Im/possibility

Re-schooling Bodymind

Brent: In our previous conversation we looked at enactive approaches to education. We focused on teaching and learning as fluid, emergent processes. One way to make sense of their fluidity, we suggested, was through an "embodied awareness" or *mindfulness* as a pedagogic orientation. In the place of prescriptive and instrumentalist approaches to instruction, we discussed a view of the body that led us to mindful pedagogy as choreography.

In this third section a group of contributors asks us to step back and take a global view of curriculum and instruction as cultural and human artifacts. Like Jerome Bruner, the writers remind us that what happens in classrooms cannot be viewed without reference to larger social, cultural, and political phenomena:

> What we resolve to do in school only makes sense when
> considered in the broader context of what the society intends to
> accomplish through its educational investment in the young.
> How one conceives of education, we have finally come to
> recognize, is a function of how one conceives of the culture and
> its aims, professed and otherwise. (1996, ix-x)

Authors in this third section of the book highlight assumptions, values, and beliefs that enable, exclude, and disrupt embodied learning in formal education.

Pille Bunnell and Kathleen Forsythe reflect on the biology of cognition as it relates to our manner of living through language in socially mediated contexts. Their commitment to a pedagogy of compassion is echoed in the work of Darlene Rigo. She analyzes the devaluation of the body in relation to the abstraction of the natural world in family and school cultures. Sonia MacPherson discusses this devaluation as abjection, identifying her experiences as a student in a sixth grade science class with larger cultural forces that have served to exclude women and nature from prevailing discourses about science as cultural capital. Jim Overboe describes his experiences of embodied wisdom and their interconnectedness to education. Such spaces remind us that relationships are not *things* but dynamic moments of interaction that allow us to live, to language experience, and to unfold into being.

Johnna: We have been talking about embodied ways of knowing. What would it mean to *disembody* or separate what is connected? I suppose we can perceive and practice disembodiment. It takes a risk to challenge the perception of sepa-

rate bodyminds. We need opportunities and activities that nurture and revitalize the body.

Do pedagogical practices disembody human relationships through our knowing, doing, and being? We walk down many paths in life through years of
schooling. Do we ever ask where they lead? Do we ever question how we
might walk, jog or meander? Maybe this is what we as educators must ponder:
how our interrelationships and perceptions bring forth the worlds we experience. I think this is what these authors ask us to do.

Brent: Yes, and I think a particular emphasis is how our perceptions and actions
as individuals are weavings in a larger cultural mosaic. Our beliefs and behaviors reflect and are reflected by this mosaic. Education is never value-free nor
disengaged from the contexts in which it is practiced. Discussions about
embodiment and bodymind relationships are themselves culturally mediated.
Like any text or discourse, they privilege some forms of knowing above others.
As educators, we need to be mindful of the values, motivations, and goals we
ascribe to pedagogy and curriculum within particular contexts and cultures.

Johnna: We may want to ask ourselves how words on the page privilege forms
of knowing. Do the emerging words we evoke in the process of writing/dia-
loguing come forth through engagement or embodiment of experiencing
forms? Who or what places the privilege or hierarchy or level of worth on
these words—the reader or the writer? I do agree that we embody awareness
of values and pedagogical possibilities with each enaction, dialogue, or writing. Can we, in writing a book or through teaching and learning, disembody
our experience of education and culture? We can change the language of how
we talk about knowing, doing, and being through an enactive approach to
education, opening the bodymind.

Warren: I would say that these chapters' critical approaches to education and
schooling fill a gap in the literature, linking embodiment to the socio-cultural
aspects of educational pedagogy. Learning is a process in which people's own
situations leave traces not just in their minds but also in their muscles and
skeletons as well. Peter McLaren (1995) terms this *enfleshment* where unequal
relations of power are manifested through our bodies and embedded in our
experiences.

Brian Fay (1987) has argued that one of the limitations of many critical theories
is their failure to take into account the role of the body. He calls for, among other
things, a new theory of the body, its inherited dispositions, and somatic (embodied) knowledge and outlines the direct and indirect forms of somatic learning.

As Fay says, direct somatic learning has no symbolic meaning as elements of a
culture "are transmitted to its newest members without passing through the
medium of the mind" (p. 148). For example, he outlines how the particular

way in which schools structure time and space controls the bodies and bodily motions of their members:

> Most obvious is the arrangement of rooms and hallways; they form an orderly grid which determines the movements of people throughout the building...architecture and interior design shape the bodily responses of teachers and pupils alike. The same is the case with the schedules which organize the school day, where power is enforced through the ringing of bells. (p. 147)

Thus, as these chapters so aptly point out, the shaping of students' bodies is not done solely through an acquisition of a set of beliefs; it also involves how bodies shape and are shaped by their educational environments, a topic from our previous conversation.

Johnna: How is culture different from knowing? Is the verb *to shape* an image that brings in the notion of power and privilege? Alternatively, do we want to think of shaping as interaction and, much like spring coils, the opening to possibility in springing forth potential? If one thinks about the shaping of a sculpture—then we are talking about the interaction with that experiencing form which emerges through this educational opportunity. When we "disembody" the experiencing form (the student) through objectifying learning and ways of knowing, then the tension of interaction may close educational opportunities.

Warren: But we also need to be aware of how, indirectly, pedagogy is always an embodied practice. Ironically it often perpetuates a dualistic form of education that disembodies teachers and learners. This indirect somatic learning is the creation of bodily attitudes in the learning of ideas. Becoming a member of a particular culture means embodying a certain sort of body. For example, soldiers are trained to march in lockstep, and this lockstep march creates a certain form of embodied power (and fear).

Schools of Opportunity

Brent: Over the last few years there has been increased emphasis on the body across various disciplines and schools of thought, including those associated with critical social and culturalist philosophies. Although the writings in this section are critically reflective, I think their form of critique is different from some critical thories such as those associated with the Frankfurt School of thought. I would argue that these chapters do attend to the body in ways that bring forth new meaning to the body. The interconnections they establish among science, culture, and ethics disrupt and reframe questions about social responsibility, inclusiveness, and textual authority. These intertextualities allow us to experience the spiritual and moral dimensions of particular cultures as well as their articulated forms of expression in public schooling and higher education.

Johnna: I wonder what experiencing forms are the same; what theories open the opportunities or possibilities that I think you are referring to, Brent? Do embodied pedagogies open opportunities for freedom?

Warren: Perhaps just the opening up of our embodied knowing enables the possibility of freedom. To Varela, Thompson, and Rosch (1991) freedom is not the same as living in the everyday world conditioned by ignorance and confusion. It is living and acting in the everyday world with realization. Freedom does not mean escaping from the world; it means transforming our way of being, our embodiment, through the living world itself. Becoming free, the authors say, is a progressive process through which one becomes

> sensitive to the conditions and genuine possibilities of some
> present situation and ... be able to act in an open manner that is
> not conditioned by grasping and egoistic volitions. (Varela,
> Thompson, and Rosch 1991, 123)

Notice here that they mention *conditions*. Such conditions include how institutions of education currently operate.

Brent: I am glad that you refer to freedom, since it has served as a central motivation of much critical theory. The writings in this section allude to the emergent nature of freedom in ways that are consistent with the thinking of Varela and other enactive thinkers. Pille and Kathleen refer to the circumstances that facilitate or constrain our ability to live responsibly and in freedom. The citation you just provided, Warren, emphasizes that freedom is never outside of our cultural embodiments, but always *unfolding* through them. This means that freedom is never without structure or tension. It is how we interact in the midst of tension that will allow us to be free or not. Is this how you understand a pedagogy of freedom?

Warren: Much like a rubber band can be stretched, so can the tensions we live with/in the educational system. A pedagogy of freedom would be one that stretches our bodymind to explore im/possibility. To do that we have to become aware of where this stretching is possible and where its impossibility would mean frustration. To do this would involve embodied action, not just pensive analysis. I remember the story of a women's co-operative in a Caribbean country that eventually had supportive development policies. But this women's co-operative had been operating for years beforehand despite a lack of government support, or active government discouragement of their work. I met one of this successful co-op's leaders during the time that there was a supportive government and asked her how it had become so successful. She replied that they simply operated "as if" they had governmental support. It is this "as if" that points to the idea of possibility, of exploring spaces of potential.

Brent: The general topic of freedom for me embraces the particular freedom to be loved and respected. I find it painful to read through the chapters in this section and be reminded of the ways in which the cultures of education have often conserved and even promoted ways of living that are less than compassionate. One of the comments I heard at Johnna's recent doctoral defense was that education often hurts people. How can we address issues of cultural violence and a lack of freedom in some educational practices within the context of this book?

Johnna: According to the Oxford dictionary, compassion would be "a sympathetic pity or concern for sufferings or misfortunes of others" (Pearsall 1999, 290). How do we embody an educational pedagogy that breathes with possibility? Even hurt can open paths of possibility, yet these paths pull on the strings of potential for that student. The paths we open for dancing through education are delicate webs we balance through interaction.

Experiencing Im/possibility

Warren: Normally a book would set out the problem in education, beginning with a section like this one we are introducing. But in organizing the book, we decided it was more important to set the tone of "possibility" and the need for a transformative notion of the body before bringing the reader into contact with experiences of im/possibility.

Johnna: Experiencing im/possibility—what does this mean? I like the opening you give to this word, Warren, of im/possibility. Can there ever be an im/possibility or is our experience of such encounters an opening to possibility? We can perceive this as unlikely or impossible. However, we embody possibility through that interaction. Hurt, freedom, compassion, otherness, and nature are all words filled with possibility depending on how we choose to perceive, interpret or dialogue with them. We can dialogue with dichotomies or we can open up to the interstices of experiencing—a kind of capacity for enacting potential.

Warren: Exactly! Just writing the word as im/possibility has created an opening for further dialogue and interaction. The meaning is in the form of dialogue that emerges. But we shy away from such difficult languaging and ambiguity in formal education.

Brent: For me, one of the central areas of importance when we talk about education as a liberating practice is the freedom to honor diversity in the classroom. The contributions in this section suggest a particularly poor record in this area as far as formal education is concerned. For every word of possibility in this book, are there others of *im*possibility?

Warren: Yes, there are. While facilitating transformative drama in high schools, I try to enable students to explore in a safe place (on stage) the possibilities of changing situations that are oppressive. As this happens, a community of trust, support and respect also emerges. But, as one teacher pointed out to me when I interviewed him about his use of this process, even playing in these safe spaces means enabling students to have a sort of power that schools are not comfortable with. So there is always a tension. I think this tension could better be stated as im/possibility. As we have mentioned earlier the forward slash creates an opening, providing an option for possibility and a space where that would occur.

Therefore this idea that there is a space where there may be possibility is important. Saying "possibility" means that "impossibility" is also perceivable!

I am reminded of a form of political analysis for action I have used called *Naming the Moment* (Barndt 1989). It attempts to undertake an examination of the balance of social forces in a given moment that helps groups to take action to resolve a particular issue. One important part of the process is an outlining of "possibilities" and "constraints" to achieve particular objectives. It is in the free space between these two aspects where possibility arises. We look within the possibilities for constraints and within the constraints for possibility. Now, this process is a very analytical tool that often doesn't include the body. But I feel the concept of "free space" can also be applied to ideas of embodied pedagogy. Without stating it explicitly, this is what several authors in this section have done: Sonia within science education, Jim within the enterprise of higher education, and Darlene within early childhood education have all tried to expand the space in education. Pille and Kathleen propose a specific program through which this might also happen.

Johnna: My work involves pedagogies that embody awareness with/in education. Through different experiences, particularly those involving the outdoors, classrooms open opportunities for initiating and revitalizing a living world. Thus we experience the im/possibility that Warren challenges us to think about. Are there limitations to our practice and perceptions, or is there an infinity of potential which we may need to embrace in the unfolding of educational systems?

Warren: A limitation of any theory is its isolation from our practices. An emphasis on possibility does open things up, but even possibility is still embedded in our day-to-day existence. How do we move beyond a dualistic approach—that of possibility and impossibility, to an idea of im/possibility where the forward slash invokes a space of interaction between the two? How do we critique without being stuck in the "what is" rather than in the "what could or might be?" How do we begin to "play" in the space of what might be, rather than be stuck in the emotional anger of what is? This is a tension in this book, particularly in this section.

Brent: We must remember that the classrooms in which we live are themselves connected to larger spheres of influence, and seek out ways to change education at these levels as well.

Warren: I wouldn't say "connected"...or "levels" or use the idea of larger or smaller, but that classrooms are part of a web of relations. I think you mean that the classroom is part of the system of education, and opening up possibility in classrooms will change other parts of the system as long as we are mindful of how this may happen.

Johnna: How may classrooms, cultures, and education unfold possibility? Living in relationship amongst human bodies and landscape bodies opens us to experiencing possibilities. However, at times we may need to step outside our boxes of familiarity to embrace interactive moments. How do we breathe vitality into education? Is it a matter of disciplining bodies to a compassionate way of being? Do we ask our students to do things that they are not ready for and kill their enthusiasm for science or math?

A tension exists within the ecotones of educational possibility. A rich classroom, much like an intertidal zone, can be washed over daily with the flood of waters breathing with nourishment and fresh possibility, unfolding bodily interactions, perceptions, and im/possibility.

References

Barndt, Deborah. 1989. *Naming the moment: Political analysis for action.* Illustrated by Carlos Freire. Toronto: Jesuit Center for Social Faith and Justice.
Bruner, Jerome. 1996. *The culture of education.* Cambridge, MA: Harvard University Press.
Fay, Brian. 1987. *Critical social science.* Ithaca: Cornell University Press.
McLaren, Peter. 1995. *Critical pedagogy and predatory culture: Oppositional politics in a postmodern era.* New York: Routledge.
Pearsall, Judy, ed. 1999. *The concise Oxford dictionary.* 10th ed. New York: Oxford University Press.
Varela, Francisco J., Evan Thompson, and Eleanor Rosch. 1991. *The embodied mind: Cognitive science and human experience.* Cambridge, MA: MIT Press.

The Chain of Hearts:
Practical Biology for Intelligent Behavior

Pille Bunnell and Kathleen Forsythe

PILLE BUNNELL is a systems ecologist and knowledge architect with several decades experience in environmental consulting with governments and institutions on a worldwide basis. She has developed over 60 programs on simulation modeling, ecology, and environmental concerns for technical, public information, and educational applications. Her current focus is the articulation of the biology of cognition through technical papers, multimedia, and stories, and its instantiation in educational and environmental projects.

KATHLEEN FORSYTHE is a poet and knowledge architect with many years experience in all levels of education. Her work in the epistemology of the imagination and the biology of love has contributed to the concept of natural learning. Her pioneering work in the development of satellite-based telecommunications networks and in the use of widespread computer networks preceded the evolution of today's Internet. She inspires a passion for learning through her articulate and poetic use of language.

Abstract. In this essay we describe some aspects of an experiential course on the biology of cognition, with an emphasis on the relational behaviors implicit in the biology of love. The course, called the Chain of Hearts, is being developed in collaboration with Dr. Humberto Maturana and is based on his work in neurobiology, the nature of the living, language and evolution. A key feature is an endeavor to have participants experience that the only emotion that expands intelligence is love, and that the only conversations that do this without end happen in love. Intelligent living is extended when we live in the emotion of love, that is, in acceptance of the legitimacy of the other and ourselves in coexistence, and it is restricted or diminished when we live in fear, competition and ambition. If we, as parents, teachers and caregivers, are not aware of this, we are blind with respect to what happens with our children, and we deny them through creating situations that diminish their intelligent living. The quality of our existence depends on the quality of our interactions. Intelligence arises in relationship.

Keywords. Intelligence, Biology of Love, Emotioning, Languaging, Co-Inspiration

Note. Some of the material in this paper has been drawn from "The Chain of Hearts," an unpublished manuscript written by Humberto Maturana, Pille Bunnell and Kathleen Forsythe. The authors maintain the right to publish this manuscript in full.

The Chain of Hearts:
Practical Biology for Intelligent Behavior

Pille Bunnell and Kathleen Forsythe

I had a dream. A group of North American children came to me and showed me the state of their hearts. It was a horrific vision that overwhelmed my senses, and tears ran down my cheeks even as I lay dreaming. Just as the hunger, hopelessness and anguish of famine on other continents have overwhelmed me, the children showed me that there was an equal poverty of the soul besetting the children of the lands of plenty. They told me that when they dream, they try to build a daisy-chain of hearts to hold the ones who need help the most...they asked me to help them ... to bring the chain of hearts into the world, so each child will know that he or she is legitimate just as they are.

The dream occurred in 1986. It was powerful enough to have me change my career and my life and to follow a path that, through many circuitous routes, brings me to where I am today and to the inspiration of a child called Hope who lives in all of us and in our future and compels us today to pay attention to what has heart and meaning so that she may survive and the chain of hearts may continue.

The vision of Hope motivates our work, and the image from my dream, of children linked in love, gives this educational initiative its name.
Kathleen Forsythe

The Context

It is the spring of 1999 and another massacre of children by children has just taken place, this time in Littleton, Colorado[1]...the worst in a series of incidents of children killing children in the United States, in Canada, in Britain...

What kind of human beings do we want our children to become?

How can we guide our children along the path of their becoming human beings who respect themselves and other people? The conceptual grounding that addresses this basic question is the biology of love.

Such incidents of child-precipitated violence, reported in the national news and sensed as a growing public concern, point to a pathological dysfunction in the development of the children involved. We believe that such dysfunction is systematically conserved, from generation to generation, by children living individual adult-child interactions that are based, not in love and respect, but in coercion, violence, tyranny and aggression—whether in the home or in our institutions. Much of this has become accepted implicitly as "the norm" in a society steeped in media violence and caught in the belief that competition and aggression are the laws of nature (Bunnell 2000).

We do not have to continue in this. We as humans do have freedom through reflection. We can reflect on two questions...

1) *What kind of human beings do we want our children to become?*
2) *What kind of human community do we want our children to generate through their living?*

As we reflect on these questions, we literally change what we are and how we live. How we live determines what we become. It is our manner of living, not the genome, which is the basis of evolutionary change (Maturana and Mpodozis 2000). Consequently, the concerns that we are now facing are far from trivial. How we address them will determine the kind of species we will become, and, indeed, the species we are presently in the process of becoming (Bunnell 1997). The human species is currently classified as *Homo sapiens sapiens*, the doubly wise hominid. Perhaps this very designation is somewhat arrogant, and indeed we think that the name *Homo sapiens arrogans* or *Homo sapiens agressans* (Sonntag and Bunnell 1996) would better describe much of our current manner of living.

However, even though we have been living in a culture that promotes competition, with success and domination for the winners, over the last few thousand years, our long history of two million years in the evolution of humanness has left us with a configuration that has not yet been lost. We remain a species that feels well when living in a loving manner. Whenever we are faced with a choice between love and not love, there is that in us which responds to love.

Perhaps we still have it within us to remain, or become again, *Homo sapiens amans*, the loving human. It is this fundamental biological configuration that we speak to in the development of the experiential course described below. We can act on the premise that we are still loving beings. We can act in trust that all our various cultural configurations have not yet changed our basic biology as the loving animal.

Only if parents and teachers respect themselves is it possible for them to respect their children and students and not deny them in their recursive interactions with them.

Only when the parents and the teachers accept themselves is it possible for them to accept both their children and their students and not deny them in a recursive devaluation of their being.

Only if parents and teachers respect and accept themselves is it possible for them to trust, respect and accept their children and students, and correct what they do and not deny them as they do so, inviting them to reflection in the openness of awareness.

But for that to happen, most teachers and parents must be reeducated in the biology of love, so that they recover self-love, self-trust and self-acceptance, in the awareness that they themselves and the children have all that they need for education to be a joyful, spiritual, intellectual and aesthetically wonderful manner of living in which children can become happy and socially responsible human beings.

That is a big task, no doubt, but as we attempt it, let us be aware that there is a particular practice that can help us: let us not correct the being of the child, only his or her doings, inviting him or her to reflect and act in awareness of what he or she does, in self-respect and not in obedience. (Maturana and Nisis 1995)

The dream of the chain of hearts inspired us to begin the work of introducing the biology of cognition and the biology of love to parents and educators in North America. We are seeking to work in co-inspiration with others who wish to restore humanness as the basic tenet of the education of children and young people. It is only in learning to understand ourselves as a loving species that we can truly understand and love the biosphere enough to make the changes necessary for our survival (Bunnell and Sonntag 2000). It is only when we educate for humanness that we can generate a society in which all children can live lives of dignity and worth.

Conceptual Basis

We are inspired by the work of Dr. Humberto Maturana, a Chilean biologist who has developed the biology of cognition[2] through neurological research and the consideration of its implications. The biology of cognition explains in neurological, evolutionary, and developmental terms how all living things bring their two domains of existence, the physiological and the behavioral, into congruence. Cognition is not synonymous with "thinking" as we usually understand it. However, since we humans live in a languaging niche, part of human cognition does entail conscious thought. The biology of love, which is the focus of our work, is a dimension of the biology of cognition.

Given the growing incidence of violence among children and young people, and the crises of intergenerational patterns of abuse, it is indeed hopeful that Dr. Maturana's work shows us a basic therapy for restoring love as a grounding emotion. His work points to a method of intervention that can take us to the origins of our humanity by evoking consensual relationships characterized by tenderness, caring and intimacy. He and his colleagues (Maturana and Nisis 1999) have found that such relationships are so fundamental in our biological dynamics that once initiated they become self-sustaining.

Dr. Maturana's experimental work in the biology of vision (Lettvin et al. 1959; Maturana, Uribe, and Frenk 1968) and perception is considered seminal.[3] His explanation of the nature of the living system, of autopoeisis, developed over thirty years ago, has provided a profound and systemic definition of the dynamics of living (Maturana 1970, 1980). Over the decades he has expanded this work into the biology of cognition, into the neurological and ontological and evolutionary basis of emotioning, languaging and intelligence (see Whitaker 1999 for overview, bibliography and tutorial).

The body of work that underlies this essay is unusual as it is set in a constitutive ontology[4] rather than the transcendental ontology that is taken as underlying truth in current cultures. Given the focus and scope of this essay, we can only note that the biology of cognition shows how it is that we, as living beings, constitutively live in an ontology that arises through our living. It thus explains how all sciences, as well as other ways of knowing such as aboriginal wisdom, are valid. These different ways of knowing represent different manners of living grounded in human cognition. It will, however, be evident here and there throughout this essay that what we present arises in a different way of seeing than common in current western cultures, and thus may require a little more thought than what may at first appear. Words, for example, are intentionally used in unique ways to evoke concepts not normally present in English; for example the verb "emotioning" is invented to show that emotions happen as a dynamic flow authored by a living being. The impetus for the Chain of Hearts course is to evoke a fundamental understanding of the biological basis of love and its implications to education, without requiring the participants to know the ontological grounds.

Love as a biological dynamic

When we think of love, we usually think of it as a sentiment, or a feeling, or a thing that happens to us, or as something we may give or receive. In biological terms love is a relational dynamic.[5] All the emotions that we distinguish in our living refer to particular relational dynamics. This does not mean that emotions do not have anything to do with the bodyhood. Different emotions have different ways of bringing the bodyhood and the medium into a coherent flow. Thus an emotion corresponds to a complex anatomical and physiological configuration so that we may say that we are literally different beings, with different bodyhoods, as we live different emotions. As we, through language, have the capacity to "step outside of ourselves" and comment on our condition, we transform the various sensations associated with the different bodyhoods into emotions that we claim to "have."

Each set of relational dynamics creates, in its happening, a domain of living that can be characterized by the actions that are possible in that domain. For example, if one is angry, one cannot sincerely kiss. Consequently, we can tell the emotion by observing the behavior. We usually know that someone is angry by noticing how he or she acting. We can abstract what is common in all the behavior that can take place in any particular relational domain, or emotion. For example, love is the domain of those relational behaviors through which the other arises as a legitimate other in coexistence with oneself. The "other" applies not only to another living being, but also to oneself, or one's circumstances. Without the requirement for any transcendent validation of the "other," the living system is able to sense without prejudice or distortion.

Thus, the biological dynamic that is connoted by love is a domain of living in which there are no distortions of the systemic coherence being lived. Living in love constitutes well-being, as one lives in a fluid dynamic congruence with one's circumstances, whatever they are. In the absence of love an organism lives the continuous breakdown of those systemic coherences. In us humans this happens as we live in various other relational dynamics and the concomitant configurations of bodyhood—namely the emotions of mistrust, expectation, fear, uncertainty, envy, ambition or competition. Such manners of living lead to changes in anatomical and physiological processes, towards a dynamic configuration of internal relations that compensate the lost systemic coherences (Maturana and Nisis 2000). Such compensations may appear in ways that, in the extreme, we refer to as pathologies that manifest in various manners, including violence.

As compensation takes place, the proper bodily configuration for the relational dynamic of love does not easily arise spontaneously, but may be evoked by the configuration of the medium; that is, through being engaged by another being which generates the appropriate relational space. Usually we call such behavior "friendship," whatever formal relation (peer, parent, teacher) this happens in. When we intentionally behave in such a manner as to restore systemic coherence for another, we usually call it "therapy," and use various activities as the carrier for the relational space of love.

Love and the evolution of human intelligence

Dr. Maturana and his colleague Dr. Verden-Zöller have identified the fundamental role that emotion plays in human development. They show that our capacity for relational behavior, as well as the development of language, arise in the close relationship between the child and the adults who care for and nurture the child, be they parents or teachers. Indeed, they present a most compelling explanation of the origin of the human species, of language and intelligence, through the unique expansion of infant care and extended childhood that occurred as our ancestors lived in small groups characterized by trust and love (Maturana and Verden-Zöller n.d.).

This is how our ancestors lived, and preferred to live, and in conserving this preference, it expanded to become the basis of humanness. The result was the constitution of a system of lineages whose evolutionary history was centered on love as the basic emotion in community relations, as opposed to aggression or competition, as has happened with other primates like chimpanzees. We have evolved as a loving animal; this is what characterizes us. And the five to six million years of this evolution has brought with it all our other attributes—in particular, our bodies, our expanded intelligence, our languaging, and eventually our technologies.

In us humans language and intelligence expanded together. Language arose as a manner of extending our capacity for the consensual behavior that we conserved through being a loving animal. Intelligence arose as a manner of expanding the capacity for languaging. Intelligence and languaging grew as a circular progression that supported our ancestral manner of living. We now show this inheritance in our bodyhood, and we retain this dynamic in our development. Even now human intelligence manifests and expands in conversation. It is the quality of our conversational interactions that gives rise to the behaviors that we call intelligent.

Intelligence is something very basic. It happens in all living systems. Intelligence has to do with the ability to participate appropriately in changing behavior and changing relations. In this sense, intelligence, like emotion, does not take place in the brain, although intelligence does require a central nervous system to be experienced. We will refer to the capacity to flow in an appropriate manner as "plasticity." Intelligence is a basic phenomenon that has to do with the plasticity for participation in changing relations.

We distinguish intelligence in another when we notice such plasticity. When we say a person is intelligent, we refer to the plastic flow in whatever relationship the person is participating in, including relationships in various conceptual domains. Accordingly, intelligence is not primarily the capacity to solve problems; rather it is the capacity to participate in the generation, expansion and operation of consensual domains—domains of coordinations of behaviors and emotions through living together.

Our ability to live intelligently depends upon the circumstances of our lives and whether these circumstances have supported us to live in sufficient self-respect to be able to act in a fluid dynamic congruence with our circumstances. In other words, our ability to live intelligently is deeply influenced by the emotions we have lived in the circumstances of our lives. However, we all have the bodyhood (including our nervous system) that enables intelligent development—this is our evolutionary inheritance.

The Biology of Love and Teaching

How do we bring the conceptual understanding of the biology of cognition to people who are not specialists in cognition? How do we shift our behaviors and our institutions such that basic humanness, as understood in this view, is restored? We believe this can be accomplished through evoking understanding that happens in the dynamics of experience. In the view of human evolution presented above, at one time we acted in the biology of love without conscious concern. From where we now are, we cannot return to that state without conscious understanding. What this entails is experiencing our own basic biological competence while observing how it is that we actually live in consensuality with each other. We are changed as we both experience and see the role emotions play in the development of our cognitive processes. We, as parents and teachers, can thus comprehend how the quality of our interactions with children enables their development as caring, self-respecting and responsible humans.

As Dr. Maturana (1997) says in his paper "Morals and Ethics in Education":

> To educate in the biology of love is basically simple, we just have to be in the biology of love. We have to be with the children under our charge in education as we are with our friends, accepting them in their legitimacy even if we do not agree with them. All that our friends do is legitimate even when we object to their doings or are in serious discrepancy with them in that respect. In friendship discrepancies or disagreements are opportunities for reflections in expanding conversations, not occasions for mutual denial. This is why we can talk about everything with our friends. In friendships there are no demands, indeed when a demand appears, the friendship comes to an end. Finally, there is total mutual trust and openness for collaboration in friendship because we are with our friends and do things with them out of pleasure, not from obligation. Friendship is a word in our culture that, most of the time without our awareness, connotes the biology of love.

The Initiative in Chile

In collaboration with Dr. Sima Nisis, and supported by UNESCO, Dr. Maturana developed a course for teachers, documented in the Spanish book *Formacion Humana y Capacitacion—Becoming Human & Training* (Maturana and Nisis 1995). It consists of a series of short experiential workshops that lead teachers to their own understanding of the emotional basis of our humanity in the biology of love. These workshops are currently offered as a series of evenings over a six-month period. Teachers who complete the course are credited and receive an increase in pay.

At the beginning of the course many teachers are bewildered by what the biology of cognition appears to say, for it is very different from what they have learned as "truth." From the perspective of what they have learned, the exercises may not initially appear to make sense. They cannot see that what they have learned does make good sense from a new perspective. They cannot see it yet, as they are trapped by what they have already learned. The new perspective is thus introduced in a delicate matter, in a way that does not require the participants to deny that which they have learned. What happens, usually after a few sessions, is that an opening is created for an expansion of looking wherein existing knowledge is not denied, but incorporated in a more fluid way that enables a different way of living.

One of the teachers who participated in the course tells this story (Maturana and Vogl 1999):

> *I teach in an impoverished area where I have a class of 12-15 year olds. These students are generally very restless and unruly, moving about all the time, making me uncomfortable. I realized that if I could be uncomfortable, so could the students. So I said to them, "I do not like to be where I do not like to be, so I imagine you also do not like to be where you do not like to be. Now I see that you move around so much that you must not like to be where you are seated. Please sit anywhere that you wish." So the students moved around, and sat here and there, and after a while they had each found a spot and were ready to attend to my class.*
>
> *Shortly after this, the Inspector came, opened the door, and found the students sitting all over the place. He asked what was going on. The students all looked at me, so I told him we were doing an experiment. The Inspector said that was OK for today, but tomorrow everybody had to be seated in their proper places. So the students asked me what were we going to do now? I answered, "Well, we must be intelligent. We must invent a way that satisfies the Inspector and allows us to do what we do. So let's talk about it."*

After a while we decided that we would work in groups, so I told them to arrange themselves in groups and sit wherever they wished. After a bit of moving around, everybody was settled and ready to work again. When the Inspector returned the next day, he asked, "Now what is happening?" and the students answered, "We're having teamwork, Sir!" He answered, "Oh well, then!" and walked away.

I saw how this experience created a whole new atmosphere such that the relationships changed, and we had a universe where the students felt free to talk. The essential thing was that I was able to listen to their emotions. Students have to be free. If you listen to their emotions, they are free. If you do not listen, they are not free."

In the Chilean schools the teachers reported that once they began, the response of the students served to conserve[6] and expand the teacher's competence and pleasure and thus the change became self-sustaining.

As a child grows in a human community he or she becomes a human being of the kind proper to the community in which he or she grows. (Maturana and Nisis 1995)

The Initiative in Canada

We have developed a course called The Chain of Hearts, which re-introduces children, parents and teachers to the simple experience of becoming human. The Chain of Hearts (Maturana, Bunnell, and Forsythe 1999) extends and expands the South American work, with a focus on the North American culture and educational system. In it, we have re-contextualized and expanded what we consider to be seminal work in the biology of cognition for the North American culture.

In our experience, as well, we have found that neither reason nor emotion is adequate in itself. The course works through an interlacing of experiences within a context of explanations that enables the participants to begin navigating their daily lives based on the understanding.

We have found that if one emphasizes reason, then argument results, and people begin to live in a tyranny of competitive argument. On the other hand, if one focuses entirely on emotion, then a personal tyranny results wherein emotion becomes the determining factor in one's living. Thus, focusing primarily on either reason or emotion results in distortions of living. Only the continuous interplay of these two aspects of cognition can result in a way of living, and of being with others, through which understanding, and eventually, wisdom can arise.

Consequently each workshop in the Chain of Hearts begins with a very short presentation of about fifteen or twenty minutes. This is followed by a series of exercises. After each exercise the participants talk about their experiences and the insights they had. This conversation is conducted in a manner that results in the experience of co-inspiration; that is, each person has his or her own insights, inspired by the reflections of the other participants. The presenter becomes one of the group who may expand and enrich the understanding by providing further anecdotes or an enlargement of any area in the conceptual domain. Thus we integrate reason and the flow of emotions in the course itself in a manner that models what we intend to convey.

The whole set of workshops consists of twenty units, organized in groups of four. The first four comprise what we consider the minimum foundation from which people may begin to expand the understanding on their own.

Intelligence:
A Topic in the Chain of Hearts

In this section we present some of the content that is relevant to the topic of intelligence. In the Chain of Hearts the information presented below is covered in several units.

We claim, as do Maturana and Nisis (1995, 2000), that love is the only emotion that expands intelligence. Maturana (1980) develops the conceptual grounding for this in the biology of cognition, as the following sections, drawn from The Chain of Hearts (Maturana, Bunnell, and Forsythe 1999) seek to explain this claim.

We are equally intelligent

From a biological point of view we humans are all equally intelligent. Our languaging brain is enormously plastic.[7] It is this plasticity that allows us to generate endless recursions in language, which lead to new domains of living, without any end. The fundamental neuronal plasticity needed for living in language is so gigantic that we are fundamentally equally intelligent.

Of course, there are individual variations in realizing this fundamental plasticity according to whether we have had some malnutrition in our development, or brain damage or disease, or whether we have lived a life that has put us in situations of constraint, despair, or rejection. However, the initial constitution of all human children is essentially equal in the domain of intelligence.

What many of the various measures of "intelligence," such as the IQ, do is to measure the degree of cultural inclusion of a person, and not his or her capacity to participate in a plasticity of consensual behavior.

Love expands intelligence

Emotions modulate the operation of intelligence as a concrete aspect of everyday life. Thus envy, fear, ambition, and competition restrict intelligent behavior, because they narrow our attention and our vision (in all our senses). These emotions prevent us from seeing the other, or from seeing the circumstances in which we find ourselves. This we know in everyday life; we show this when we say, "he is blinded by ambition" or "she is frozen with fear." If you consider your experiences, you will likely see, as we claim, that the only emotion that broadens our vision is love. In love we accept ourselves and the circumstances in which we live, thus expanding the possibility for intelligent behavior. In this sense, love is visionary.

When, through criticism of their being, we undermine the respect for themselves that boys and girls naturally enjoy, we restrict their intelligent operation. Living in continuous control of children's behavior, because we do not really trust them, has the same restrictive effect on their intelligence. This is also the case with continuous devaluation of children's behavior and continuous demands for their obedience or compliance.

We restrict the intelligence of others, particularly our children, and ourselves with our own blindness, vanities, and insecurities when we live in mistrust, ambition, competition, or fear.

Evoking intelligent behavior

Since we exist in relationship, and our intelligence arises in relationship, the nature of the relationship affects the emergence of intelligent behavior. It is not just a matter of unpleasant or stressful emotions masking our "real" intelligence in an interaction. An interaction that does not encourage and evoke the plastic flow of our behavior actually limits our intelligence. Students become intelligent in the interaction with the teacher. The same is true of parenting.

One of the greatest deliverances of intelligent behavior in all those around us is accepting the intelligence of the others. It blossoms forth. In a culture where some have to be less intelligent than others (grading, competition, etc.) this fundamental acceptance is often missing. Our ability to live intelligently depends upon the circumstances of our life and whether these circumstances have supported us to live in sufficient self-respect to be able to act responsibly in an experience of freedom.

Intelligent living is broadened when we live in mutual respect, and it is restricted or diminished when we live in fear, competition and ambition. If we, as parents, teachers and caregivers, are not aware of this, we are blind with respect to what happens with our children, and we deny them in creating situations that diminish their intelligent living.

Understanding through experience

The notions addressed in the above text are understood through participation in several exercises that lead up to the unit that explicitly deals with intelligence. Most of the exercises are designed to allow the participants to sense the relational domains generated in contrasting manners of doing the same thing, and from both sides of a conversation. For example, one exercise that distinguishes the correction of a person's being from the correction of what they are doing is played by partners who trade off being the instructor and the student (or the parent and child). Another exercise is designed to show how performance in a situation in which someone is being evaluated is altered by the emotion of the instructor who is performing the evaluation. Yet another exercise is designed to reveal that the flow of a conversation, whatever the content, is entirely different if the instructor/teacher/conversant assumes that the other is intelligent, and that what they have to say is meaningful in the domain in which they speak it, than if the instructor assumes that the other is inadequate or stupid.

It is not easy to describe an experience such that it is lived as an experience, rather than read as an explanation. The following excerpt from a novel (Bunnell n.d.) describes one of the exercises from the Chain of Hearts in a manner intended to evoke the experience in a reader. In the novel a mentor (Elder) is assisting a young woman (Linda, speaking in first person) to prepare for college exams, and during a break he proposes a game. Elder holds his hand up in a loose fist and asks Linda:

> *"What do I have in my hand?"*
>
> *"Nothing. Air."*
>
> *"Imagine something. Anything."*
>
> *"A cow!"*
>
> *"Ohhh! You saw the tail sticking out!"*
>
> *Somehow he made it seem as if there really had been a miniature cow in his hand! He held up his hand again.*
>
> *"What do I have in my hand?"*
>
> *"Ummm...a train!"*
>
> *"Ohhh, you heard the clickety clack!"*
> *And there I was, hearing the train, and I couldn't help but laugh. And again.*
>
> *"What do I have in my hand?"*

"*A cookie!*"

"*Ohhh, you could smell it!*"

I could.

"*How do you do that? How does it become so real?*"

"*Try it.*"

So I held up my fist, loosely curled around nothing, and asked Elder:

"*What do I have in my hand?*"

"*A mouse!*"

Immediately I imagined a mouse, wiggling around inside my hand, squeaking as if it wanted out.

"*Ohhh, you could hear it squeaking!*"

Linda and Elder talk about how the game works, then Elder comments:

"*I showed it to you because it is something that you will find useful throughout your life.*"

"*OK.*"

"*When the other person tells you what you have in your hand, you have to invent a clue that makes him (or her) right. That's the important part. You are listening to him or her with the intent of making the statement valid.*"

"*Yes...*"

I didn't see how this would be useful.

"*The same applies to any statement made by another person. People don't make nonsensical statements, unless they are just playing, and then you would know. But when they say something that doesn't seem to make sense to you, the trick is to find the domain, to find the particular way of seeing the world in which what the person says does make sense. That's the only way you can listen to them. Otherwise you are just listening to yourself.*"

"*I see...Elder, is that what you do all the time? Is that why it's so comfortable to be with you?*"

Teaching Intelligence

On reflection we can see that the teaching of intelligence, like teaching wisdom (Maturana and Bunnell 1997, 1998), is not something that can be done as a manipulation of students in any form. There is no information, no data, no procedure that will result in intelligent students. But this does not at all mean that a teacher cannot create a context and behave in a manner such that intelligence arises. This is why it often happens in a school that one teacher is considered "lucky to get all the smart students." The students become smart according to the emotioning of the teacher. Teachers can indeed open a path for their students such that their own living, for the rest of their lives, will become a self-enhancing expansion of awareness in all the dimensions that manifest as wisdom. Teachers no more need to "teach" children this than parents need to "teach" their babies to talk. But teachers do need to do something analogous to what parents do that enables their children to discover their existence as humans, and to begin the recursive consensual coordinations which manifest as language.

To evoke intelligence, teachers must live with their students that which they wish the students to learn. Students learn the teacher, not the topic, and if the topic is part of the teacher, they learn it. Thus, too, students learn the manner of living that leads to ever expanding intelligence. In this sense the most important thing a teacher can do is to expand his or her own living and awareness, and to accept his or her own adequacy and legitimacy. Out of this all the rest will flow, without effort or strain. To teach intelligence, a teacher needs only to play with the students in the fullness of the knowledge and understanding that pertain to the domains that are being taught. Teachers have always known this; we have but offered you some of the biological explanation of how this happens.

Conclusion

The Chain of Hearts is still in the process of development. The first group of students who attended the course in the spring of 1999 in Vancouver had this to say:

> *"For me it's the experiences that bring it to life. From doing them I recognize patterns in my own life. And doing them with a partner I can feel it, and this makes it easier to carry it into the everyday. The experience is the most important part."*
> *"The explanations are explanations as gifts, not explanations as ego."*
>
> *"It is wonderful to carry the experiences and understanding out into the week. And because we do it on a regular basis, I can live it. I have been trying it out with my two roommates who are arguing with each other, and it really works. With what I now understand I am able to change everything, and really put it into practice."*

"The theory behind this course is great. I have been reading about and taking workshops in several different things to do with the human condition—spiritual and other. For me this is like a new horizontal doctrine. Kind of like a contemporary Taoism or Confucianism, something suitable for this time. The current situation has never been seen before. All the other practices were developed for a uniform culture, one ethnic background, or one ideology. The old thinking does not work in the current situation. Now there is no single culture, so it is very important to have something that crosses all of them, that has to do with our basic humanness. That is what this is about."

In our current culture we learn to think that we are only good if we are better, intelligent only if we are more intelligent than the others. But this is a big trap. We are equally good, and equally intelligent, and we do not need to pat ourselves on the back for our great intelligence and care, or for our wisdom. We can take pleasure in this, and recognize that it is no little thing to rise as legitimate, loving, intelligent, and even wise beings out of a culture that makes this difficult. And if we do so, we may indeed become again *Homo sapiens amans*. And as we do that, there are enormous implications to the way we live together with each other and with the rest of the biosphere.

Our experiences in developing and teaching the biology of love, as a practical aspect of the biology of cognition, encourage us that it is possible to restore to our educational systems the fundaments of our humanity and with this, the love and hope with which we adults, whether teachers or parents, wish to gift our children through the quality of our living with each other.

> *How we live with our children is how they become.*

Notes

1. On April 20, 1999, two teenage students at Columbine High School in Littleton, Colorado, walked into the school, opened gunfire, and killed twelve students and a teacher before taking their own lives. This event shook the nation, particularly as it was followed by other episodes of child violence in schools throughout North America.

2. The biology of cognition explains in neurological, evolutionary, and developmental terms how all living things bring their two domains of existence, the physiological and the behavioral, into congruence. Cognition is not synonymous with "thinking" as we usually understand it. However, since we humans live in a languaging niche, part of human cognition does entail conscious thought. The biology of cognition comprises an extensive body of work; for the fundaments please refer to Maturana 1980.

3. There are hundreds of references to this work in Biological Abstracts, and several lineages of research and practice derive from it.

4. Ontology has to do with the nature of being. A transcendental ontology assumes a singular reality that transcends whatever we humans may do, which we may attempt to discover or discern. Based in this premise we create various systems wherein some people have a privileged access to "truth," and where people attempt to convince each other of the validity of their particular version. Constitutive ontologies are based on lineages of experiences in various non-reducible but intersecting domains; consequently they allow multiple objective "realities." Cohesion between such realities is attained through interobjectivity. What is particularly relevant to this essay is that both adequacy and responsibility arise naturally in a constitutive ontology, but are systematically eroded in a transcendental ontology. For further reading, including an explanation of why a transcendental ontology cannot be biologically supported, see Maturana 1988.

5. The term "relational dynamic" refers to a particular flow of behaviors that connect a living system with its medium. For many living beings, including ourselves, the relevant aspects of its medium are predominantly other living beings; hence the relational dynamic usually pertains to a particular individual or group behaving in a particular configuration, or emotion.

6. Conserve: to maintain constant during a process of change (Webster's Collegiate Dictionary, 10th ed. 1994). We choose conserve rather than preserve, which has a similar meaning, as the latter has a connotation of stasis or of proprietary access (as in a game preserve).

7. Plastic: capable of adapting to various conditions (Webster's Collegiate Dictionary, 10th ed. 1994). We use "plastic" in referring to intelligence as the ability to participate appropriately in changing behavior and changing relations.

References

Bunnell, P. 1997. An invitation concerning human speciation. Keynote address at Biology, Language, Cognition and Society—International Symposium on Autopoiesis, Belo Horizonte, Brazil.

Bunnell, P. 2000. Attributing nature with justifications. *Systems Research and Behavioral Science*. Vol 17 No 5 (Behavioral Science Vol 45.5), pp. 469-480.

Bunnell, P. n.d. *As ever: A novel in the observer cosmology.* Forthcoming.

Bunnell, P., and N. Sonntag. 2000. Becoming a sustainable species. *Reflections, The Society for Organizational Learning Journal on Knowledge, Learning and Change* 1(4): 66-71.

Lettvin, J.T., H.R. Maturana, W.S. McCulloch, and W.H. Pitts. 1959. What the frog's eyes tell the frog's brain? *Proceedings of the I.R.E.* 47(11): 1940-1951.

Maturana, H.R. 1970. Biology of cognition. BCL Report 9.0. Biological Computer Laboratory. Department of Electrical Engineering, University of Illinois.

Maturana, H.R. 1980. Biology of cognition. In *Autopoiesis and cognition: The realization of the living*, by H.R. Maturana and F.J. Varela. Boston: D. Riedel Publishing.

Maturana, H.R. 1988. Reality: The search for objectivity or the quest for a compelling argument. *Irish Journal of Psychology* 9(1): 25-82.

Maturana, H.R 1997. Biological foundations of morals and ethics in education. Unpublished paper.

Maturana, H.R. and B. Vogl. 1999, September. Teacher education: A priority, and reflections on teaching dynamics and the biology of cognition. *Patterns*, ASCD Systems Thinking and Chaos Theory Network Newsletter.

Maturana, H.R., G. Uribe, and S. Frenk. 1968. A biological theory of relativistic colour coding in the primate retina. *Arch. Biol. Med. Exp.* 1: 1-30.

Maturana, H.R. and G. Verden-Zöller. n.d. *The origin of humanness in the biology of intimacy.* Hampton Press, forthcoming.

Maturana, H.R. and J. Mpodozis. 2000. Origin of Species by Means of Natural Drift. *Revista Chilena de Historia Natural.* Vol 73, 261-310.

Maturana, H.R. and P. Bunnell. 1997. What is wisdom and how is it learned. Proceedings of the North American Association for Environmental Educators Conference, Vancouver, British Columbia.

Maturana, H.R. and P. Bunnell. 1998, February. What is wisdom? *Patterns,* ASCD Systems Thinking and Chaos Theory Network Newsletter.

Maturana, H.R., P. Bunnell, and K. Forsythe. 1999. The chain of hearts: An introduction to the biology of love. Unpublished manuscript.

Maturana, H.R. and S. Nisis. 1995. *Formacion humana y capacitacion.* UNICEF: Chile and Dolmen Publications.

Maturana, H.R. and S. Nisis. 1999. *Transformatción en la convivencia.* Santiago: Dolmen Publications.

Maturana, H.R. and S. Nisis. 2000. Biology of Love: What to Do? Proceedings of the Seventh International Conference on Cognitive Education, June 1999, University of Calgary.

Sonntag N. and P. Bunnell. 1997. Environmental management systems. Proceedings of the Earth Council Conference, Rio+5: From Agenda to Action, Rio de Janeiro, March.

Whitaker, R. 1999. Observer web: http://www.informatik.umu.se/~rhiwt/AT.html (includes Archives, Tutorial, Study Plan, and Encyclopaedia Autopoietica).

Creating a Space for
Embodied Wisdom Through Teaching

James Overboe

JAMES OVERBOE is a doctoral candidate in the Sociology Department at the University of British Columbia. His background as an instructor of brain-injured adults informs his pedagogical interests. His current research examines how the embodied wisdom of disabled people is affected by the concepts of space, time, and aesthetics which privilege a non-disabled embodiment.

Abstract. This chapter asserts that integration into education privileges logic over unrecognized and embodied wisdom (Hennessy 1993; Oliver 1996). My work is organized in two parts: an introductory section illustrating how the embodied wisdom of disabled students is negated and a follow-up section linking the validation of embodied wisdom to shifts in pedagogic thinking, practices, and priorities. This validation, I contend, enriches the education process for all students. I end my chapter by examining the risks involved in acknowledging and valuing embodied wisdom. I employ autobiographical accounts throughout my work to ground my theoretical position. While my analysis is informed by my experience of disability, I feel my observations can apply to other marginalized embodied wisdoms.

Keywords. Wisdom, Embodiment, Disability, Integration, Student, Teacher, Autobiography

Acknowledgments. I would like to acknowledge the financial support of the Peter Wall Institute's project, *Narratives of Disease, Disability, and Trauma*, in the preparation of this chapter. Also, I would like to acknowledge the support and guidance of Johnna Haskell, Brent Hocking, and Warren Linds.

Creating a Space for
Embodied Wisdom Through Teaching

James Overboe

How Desire and Risk Can Create a Space for
Embodied Wisdom in Education

The organization of this paper into two parts corresponds with my experience as a student and my experience as a teacher. I employ autobiographical anecdotes as a means of grounding my theoretical critique in my "lived experience" as a student and a teacher whose spasticity and lack of body control are the opposites of the professional comportment typified by the corporeality of the white, nondisabled, heterosexual male (Young 1990).

More often than not, people of differing races, genders, sexualities, and abilities who are successful within educational institutions are socialized to incorporate the embodiments, sensibilities, and characteristics of this white masculine prototype that has been invoked as the personification of rationality and logic. Because I learn and teach through my body, one that cannot conform to this non-disabled prototype, I often find my embodied wisdom is subsumed under the pedagogical dominance of rationality and logic. Yet in my own life I have found my experience of embodied wisdom enriches my education both as a teacher and pupil. However, I maintain that embodied wisdom should complement logic and rationality, not subsume them.

While this chapter specifically concentrates on my embodied wisdom as someone with cerebral palsy, I believe the notion of embodied wisdom can apply to the corporeality of other people who are not white, heterosexual, non-disabled males. It is the "interactive moment" (Shotter 1997) between varying individual notions of embodied wisdom that will enrich the classroom. Throughout this chapter I illustrate the struggles I endure in my attempts to validate my own embodied wisdom and that of others. The resistance within the teaching profession in educational institutions to embodied wisdom often jeopardizes my progress as a student and my status as a teacher.

The Disavowing of Wisdom Derived from
a Student's Disabled Embodiment

I began my education in a "crippled children's school" because I was deemed not normal. The concept of normality began during modernity. Davis (1997, 10) places the origination of the "idea of the norm" over the period 1840-1860. In 1835 statistician Adolphe Quetelet developed the concept of the "average man" that became the benchmark for normality (Davis 1997, 11). With the rise of normality the school became an institution of disciplinary techniques, which are implemented to improve knowledge and skills (Foucault 1984, 209).

I was not normal but the abject other. The act of abjecting allows for one to make sense of something or someone that is paradoxically meaningless yet disturbing (Kristeva 1982, 2). Kristeva (1982, 4) argues that abjection is not the lack of either health or cleanliness but the disruption of identity, system, and order. At the age of six I was tested to determine my suitability as a candidate for integration into the mainstream education system from a crippled children's school. In short, I was being tested to determine if I could be orderly and fit within a system and if I had the capability of moving beyond abjection to some semblance of normality.

At an early age I realized that my mind worked differently than others in that my intelligence stemmed from my body with its spasms and sensibility of cerebral palsy. Upon being selected for inclusion into mainstream schooling I was amazed that others who were intelligent and also experienced embodied wisdom were not chosen. As I underwent testing, I realized that I must keep my way of thinking to myself unless I wanted to become the abject other again. I understood that I must relate my process of thinking and my subsequent answers to the logical and rational pedagogy of the non-disabled world with its restrictive normality. As I went through the testing procedure, I found that my spasms travel a circuitous route and contribute to my discovering the correct answers. These circuitous routes, emanating from different areas of my body, establish an embodied wisdom.

At this point I would like to try and explain what is meant by embodied wisdom, as it manifests itself in my experience of cerebral palsy. Embodied wisdom derives from my spasms that circulate throughout my body, including my brain. My spasms are like dolphins skimming near the surface of the ocean or like depth charges plummeting to the deepest part of my being and exploding. They cannot be completely controlled or contained. At other times my spasms are feather-like as they move throughout my body.

I do not want to leave the impression that my spasms move in an orderly or predictable fashion. On the contrary, these differing types of spasms interact and are often intertwined. Yet, each type of spasm can be both intermittent and consistent. The interaction of differing spasms with their varying sensations causes me to meander down various paths. It is not a matter of me directing these spasms in order to find wisdom. Rather, it is a case of my spasms circulating through my body and causing me to investigate differing routes. These investigations interact with my education and impact how I process information. Intuitively, I am frightened to allow others to view my spasms or explain my subsequent embodied wisdom to them.

Perhaps it was not simply a matter of my intuition. I had been segregated from the regular school system because my body was considered inferior and therefore my intelligence was suspect too. Consequently, I was chosen because of my ability to conform to the regular education system. As I watched other non-disabled children complete their lessons I noted that they employed a linear rational method that matched their controlled corporeality.

Of course, I could not be sure that other students also were shifting their thinking to adapt to the rational thinking of the education system. But for me there was and still are physical consequences for me to adapt to a rational logical way of thinking. For example, when I attempt to do simple mathematics or statistical evaluations I suffer from seizures which manifest as blinding flashes in front of my eyes accompanied by pain in my head. It feels to me as if my spasms are struggling to break free from the shackles of logical and rational thinking. To this day I have never been able to unlock the secret of how to do either algebra or statistical analysis.

It is difficult for me to explain what the path I meander down or up might be like. The trouble is that the paths are never the same. Consequently, to explain my spasms in hindsight would do a disservice to the spontaneity of their movement. Moreover, such an explanation to some extent suggests that I have the ability to step back and observe my spasms, whereas more often than not I am too busy interacting with my spasms to analyze them.

Even at a young age I was perplexed because if "normal" people were superior to me, then why could they not understand disabled people's "inferior" way of thinking? Put another way, why did I have to demonstrate that I was capable of discerning their method of understanding the world? This method of integration has little to do with helping disabled students reach their maximum potential and more to do with maintaining the social construction of normality.

My experience of integration is not an isolated incident. The educational system accepted without question the principle that normality was a given and any deviation from it was a tragedy to rectify if possible. The goal of this form of integration was commonality over diversity through assimilation.

Susan Lonsdale (1990, 93) writes, "Most children with disabilities, however, attended (and still do) special schools, where they are not only segregated from the majority, but socialized into a lesser, minority status." Those of us who attain a university degree are overachievers, sometimes with overly high expectations for ourselves (Lonsdale 1990, 94). In their interviews Leicester and Lovell (1997, 113) found that many disabled adults felt that "Special Education is a kind of apartheid and encourages the ignorant and hurtful attitudes which they have encountered in mainstream society."

One's ability to succeed in mainstream education lessens one's exposure to ignorant and hurtful attitudes. Oliver (1996) and Wendell (1996) both argue that to a certain extent academic success for disabled individuals validates and legitimizes an educational system that excludes most disabled people. From public school to university I have been able to obtain substantial cultural capital by tacitly agreeing with others that logical rationality is the basis of my success rather than my disabled sensibility.

My experience illustrates the belief "that the voice of the other has not been granted an adequate hearing, and this because the other has either been silenced or forced to speak according to the restrictive dictates of dominant discourses including the human sciences" (Huspek 1997, 11-12). In order to maintain my status I have had to disavow and silence the embodied wisdom stemming from my cerebral palsy and instead interpret it in terms that uphold the discourses of normality.

Thus, integration with its notion of normality preaches the tolerance and acceptance of special needs children (Oliver 1996, 88-89). The problem is that the provider of this tolerance may revoke the tolerance or acceptance if the student does not comply or if the accommodation is deemed too expensive.

Emily Eaton, who experiences cerebral palsy, was denied access to a regular school because accommodations for her were deemed too expensive. Her parents have sued for the right for her to continue to attend an "ordinary school." In her decision, appeal court Judge Arbour observed that in a segregated class Emily "would have fewer opportunities to learn how other children work and how they live. And they will not learn that she can live with them and they with her" (Claridge 1995, A2). Moreover, Judge Arbour argued that "forced exclusion is hardly ever considered an advantage. Indeed, as a society, we use it as a form of punishment" (1995, A2).

The Privileging of the Written Word
and the Myth of Accommodation

Throughout my university life there has been an assumption that if any accommodation concerning my disability is granted then either I have an advantage or equality has been reached. I hope to dispel this myth. Applying accommodations is not a simple process because pedagogical discourses that underpin our educational system continue to privilege an able-bodied sensibility over a disabled sensibility. The following anecdote illustrates the problems with applying accommodations for disabled students. During my master's degree a compulsory sociology course required students to submit a weekly three-page single-spaced summary of articles. Due to my cerebral palsy the writing of these assignments was prohibitive for me. I asked for and received permission to audiotape my reports.

For this course both the instructor and weekly guest lecturers graded weekly written assignments. Before tape-recording my assignments I felt I might be at a disadvantage because I had been trained in a written tradition rather than an oral tradition. Moreover, professors are indoctrinated in an educational system that disseminates information through a visually oriented medium of instruction (mainly textbooks) and testing (where success is measured through written essays and examinations). Keith Hoskins (1990, 46) contends that "written examination and arithmetical marks appear to develop, and then predominate, from around 1800." With the exception of those with visual impairments, professors have become accustomed to analyzing an essay visually, not aurally, because of a pedagogy that privileges the written word. For example, professors can refer back to previous pages to decide if a logical argument has been sustained. The oral tape requires rewinding and re-listening to the tape, which many of the guest professors found irritating. Moreover, the written academic text is supposed to be objective and flat, without emotion. No matter how hard I tried, the inflection of my voice betrayed the passion I felt for my views.

As the course progressed and as I became more comfortable with taping, my marks improved. Similarly, as the course instructor developed an "ear" for my oral reports my marks improved with him. However, with the lecturers I found an interesting pattern. Although those professors who concentrated on content and not pedagogical structure had difficulty in marking my aural tapes, their assigned grades and comments demonstrated that they understood my argument. On the other hand, the professors who gave me lower marks pointed to my deficiency in style and my lack of academic rigor. When I inquired about the sociological argument I had conveyed, they would or could not comment.

Consequently, most instructors had difficulty when they evaluated my tape-recorded short essays. The instructors and I both had to adjust to an audio-oriented medium. My lower marks reflected our adjustments to working with audio-taped essays. In spite of the lower marks, the conservation of my energy was a priority for me. Later in the year, while taking a different course, I switched from the audio tapes back to written assignments, which meant an increase in my energy consumption.

Frequently, the decision to accept or not accept an accommodation for my disability remains a choice between inconveniences. Still it is better to have a choice than to not have one. Throughout my life accommodations for my disability have not given me an advantage—often they just lessen the magnitude of the barriers I have to overcome. Thus, the superficial implementation of accommodation without considering the need for a required shift in pedagogical thinking can be harmful for all concerned, especially the disabled student.

The Facile Acceptance of Different Embodiments at Universities

Hennessy (1993, 11) maintains that the superficial acceptance of plurality within universities is a method of crisis control. Rather than examining the political and economic powers that exclude different cultures and peoples, the difference in cultures is celebrated. By honoring cultural difference, institutions such as the university are able to deflect criticism of their systemic, exclusionary practices.

Agreeing with Hennessy (1993), Erevelles (1996) argues that within the articulations of a plurality of difference "the assumption is that if only society learns to value difference and accept the fact that all difference has a role to play within this social system, all will be well" (Erevelles 1996, 522-23). Best and Kellner (1991, 213) along with Erevelles (1996, 522-23) warn that the politics of identity/difference can be orchestrated to marginalize people by redefining it as a harmless politics of style that leaves relations of domination unaltered and unchallenged.

Similarly, members of a minority group are often pressured by others who have a stereotypical view of the way a minority member should act or how he or she should look. I feel pressure from others to convey what they deem an appropriate stereotypical image of a disabled person. Writing about the issue of stereotyping, Code (1995, 76) comments, "Stereotyping cannot be contested or erased by personal refusals to comply. On the contrary, there is a peculiar elasticity to stereotypical roles and options, which produces the result that their occupant is damned either way."

The following anecdotes illustrate Code's (1995) point. While completing my master's degree, I was confronted by a colleague who was the spokesperson for my fellow graduate students. She asked, "Why hadn't the department chosen a disabled woman if they were to accept a disabled student?" I mentioned that she and others were assuming the department knew about my disability prior to my acceptance. In fact, I had only informed the department about my disability after my acceptance. My explanation was satisfactory for her. However, I remained suspect in the eyes of some other graduate students who continued to question my legitimacy. Unfortunately, no matter what I said, no matter what I did, I remained a person who had achieved my entrance because of my minority status.

Another time I mentioned to a colleague that I was going swimming. He admonished me for trying to achieve the normative body of modernity. He reprimanded me for not allowing my body to deteriorate and become a better "role model" for a new "disabled" body of late modernity. His position illustrates Hevey's (1997) point that often, disabled people's bodies are invoked as a personification of the chaos which threatens order in our society. At other times, this same colleague would introduce me as someone who had "overcome" his disability (poster child for success in modernity) by becoming a university student. Thus, depending on his mood I am invoked as a personification for modernity or late modernity. In his eyes I remained a stereotypical trope or metaphor.

Consequently, Hennessy (1993) argues for a discourse that illuminates areas that have been repressed either within or subliminal to institutions such as the university. She argues against the facile categorization of minority groups and for a validation of their embodiments and lived experience. Yet this validation requires a shift in the thinking of those who implement pedagogical practices and ideologies.

Bogdan and Taylor (1988, 146) conclude that whether severely disabled people (people with severe and profound developmental handicaps or multiple disabilities who sometimes soil themselves, drool, and cannot walk or talk) are considered human is dependent upon their interaction with the non-disabled other. If the non-disabled other accepts the severely disabled person as human, communication is achieved. If the non-disabled other assumes that the severely disabled are less than human, then communication is impossible. In either situation one cannot definitively prove that one's perception is flawed because of a faulty belief system.

Reflecting the perspective of the non-disabled, Lorraine Code (1995, 51) argues:

> Claims to know a person are open to negotiation between the knower and known, where the "subject" and object positions are always, in principle, interchangeable. In the process, it is important to watch for discrepancies between a person's sense of her own subjectivity, and a would-be knower's conception of how things are for her; yet neither the self-conception nor the knower-conception can claim absolute authority, for the limits of self-consciousness constrain the process as closely as

does the interiority of mental processes and of experiential constructs, and their resulting unavailability to observation.

Because of the certainty of their able-bodied sensibility, the self-conception of the able-bodied, coupled with their knowing belief that many disabled people are irrational and illogical, constrains or even prohibits interaction with disabled people.

Sullivan (1997) argues that this overlap occurs when we impose our own familiar meanings upon them without considering the other person's uniqueness and specificity. When our embodiment and our subjectivity become the standard for our interpretation of others, the notion of intersubjectivity is problematic. Sullivan (1997, 13) writes, "When dialogue is only a covert form of ventriloquism, my intersubjective world turns out to be a solipsistic one in which I encounter only myself and my own meaning." Agreeing with Sullivan, I would argue that a disabled person's subjectivity is perceived as pathological and that this results in questionable and illegitimate interpretations of "what the world means," whereas a non-disabled person's subjectivity is normative, resulting in "certain" interpretations of "what the world means."

Validating the Wisdom of a Disabled Embodiment Within Education

In the following sections I will explore how a disabled sensibility deriving from an embodied wisdom can expand the concept of education. Oliver (1996, 88-89) agrees with the new view of integrated education which postulates the notion of normality as false. Moreover, the concept of normality was developed to impose a commonality where there was only difference. Thus the education system must accept that the "difference" of disability does not detract from an educational experience but can enrich it for all involved (although the inclusion of the difference of disability is not dependent upon whether it is either beneficial or detrimental for others).

For me, the essence of education is communication. Booth and Booth (1996) have helpful insights in communicating with supposedly inarticulate subjects. They write, "Too often the problems of interviewing inarticulate subjects are seen in terms of their deficits rather than the limitations of our methods. Such a "deficit" model of informant response is rooted in a view of disability as a problem of the individual" (1996, 67). This exclusionary practice mirrors their exclusion from a wider society.

Booth and Booth (1996, 67) believe that conventional research methods often create obstacles for inarticulate subjects instead of overcoming other barriers that impede their involvement. Moreover, conventional research methods can create obstacles for inarticulate subjects in terms of the demands they make on their inclusion. According to Booth and Booth (1996, 67), researchers should attend more to their own deficiencies than to the limitations of their informant. In the same manner, I argue that educators must examine their own deficiencies in terms of their notions of intelligence and wisdom and be open to pupils who communicate their wisdom in other ways. For educators the process is not a matter of actively discovering embodied wisdom by following conventional methodologies or pedagogical practices. Rather it is a matter of educators being open to the possibilities that may arise from the acceptance of various embodied wisdoms.

Agreeing with Booth and Booth's (1996) hypothesis, as an educator of disabled adults in a rehabilitation center, I attempted to examine the deficiencies of a rehabilitation system that, like most educational systems, privileges logic and rationality. As I taught some disabled people who were deemed lacking the ability to communicate or articulate, I remembered my experience of being tested many years ago.

Through my readings of Bogdan and Taylor (1988) I began to realize that a successful process of education for my inarticulate students is dependent upon my belief that they are communicating with me. From this perspective, any initial "lack" of communication can be reframed as an inability on my part to receive their communications. I must be open to my clients' worldviews and the expressions those views assume through language and communication. It is not enough for me to step out of the metaphorical "box" of rationality and logic because if my authority or knowledge base is challenged I can easily step back into this privileged space. Instead I must metaphorically consider my knowledge base as a porous box that can be permeated by other ways of knowing.

By allowing myself to be open to other means of communication and knowledge, I was able to gain the trust of my clients. Without the worry of being labeled inarticulate, my clients were able to "risk" communication on their terms. Often I was the one who had difficulty in making myself understood, as I was unfamiliar with their communication styles and embodied wisdoms. Working our way through our [mis]understanding and [mis]communication allowed for us to meander down different paths that may have remained hidden, which often led to us to experience different views of what intelligence and wisdom mean.

Creating a Space for Unrecognized Wisdom
in the University Through Teaching

A broadening of the notion of intelligence would be beneficial to non-disabled as well as disabled students. The privileging of rationality and logic often leads to adversarial debates within academia. By demonstrating superior logic and rationality, one academic scores pugilistic points over another. Shotter (1997) argues there are two different ways in which we relate to one another. The first, the intellectual way, is characterized by abstraction, distance and observation that apply within the confines of a disciplinary space. The second, the conversational way, is more relational with an exchange of lived experiences between individuals. This latter style of communication is "an open, unfinalized, and dialogical form of talk in which new spaces may be opened up and others closed down, freely moment by moment" (Shotter 1997, 21). Shotter (1997, 22) explains that what happens in this "interactive moment" is to be ascertained by a non-intellectual, embodied knowledge that eschews both predetermined means of communication and institutionalized formulations which confine discourse.

I would like to apply both my lecturing experience with "inarticulate" disabled people and Shotter's (1997) observations on overcoming textual violence to my experience of lecturing at the university. Usually the lecturer conveys knowledge to her or his students who in turn demonstrate their understandings by responding in a logical manner. Thus, the communication pattern is an endless loop of rational and logical discourse from encoder and decoder. The positions of encoder and decoder are fluid not fixed, but the logical and rational loop remains intact. Any interference with this feedback loop is considered "noise" to be eradicated or at least ignored.

Agreeing with Shotter (1997), I believe that the embodied interactions between, and among those who communicate primarily by making noise (the unrecognized wisdom), along with those who primarily communicate rationally and logically, would create a rich creative environment. Whether within the university or the rehabilitation center, my responsibility as a teacher is to facilitate a space for such interactive moments. In creating such spaces I am not interested in developing consensus because I feel that consensus too often falls back on familiar patterns of rhetoric and rationalization that stifle noise (the unrecognized wisdom). Instead, I am interested in nurturing desire and passion that may or may not result in conflict and contested claims. But, as the lecturer, my job is to ensure that such conflicts and contestations do not result in textual violence whereby communication is reduced to gamesmanship as students score pugilistic points on others by showing their prowess at following certain patterns of intellectualism.

Can the Desire to Validate Embodied Wisdom in University Override the Risk Involved?

As my experience with supposedly inarticulate clients demonstrated, the noise stemming from embodied wisdom allowed us to experience interactive moments that continued successively and created differing paths of intelligence. As a disabled person I have a unique opportunity to facilitate these openings by my presence within the university. When I entered the academy I began my education as an outsider who lacked the control and embodiment usually associated with "rational" intelligence. Bauman (1993, 162) argues that the "outsiders" are ascribed traits that signify ambivalence, irrationality, uselessness. They epitomize the chaos that all social spacing, including academia, aims staunchly yet vainly to replace with order.

Now as a doctoral candidate who has credentials, I have moved beyond the position of outsider and have become what Bauman (1993) refers to as a "stranger." As a stranger I must continually reinforce my legitimacy at the university by proving that I have the "intellectual rigor" required to remain within academia (Bauman 1993, 179). If I choose to validate my embodied wisdom, my colleagues may question my legitimacy within the university.

I have to constantly determine to what extent I can validate embodied wisdom without jeopardizing my position within academia. On the one hand, my presence gives validation to the unrecognized wisdom and might create a space for the articulation of this wisdom. But as an instructor I have moved from the position of an outsider to that of a stranger and to the extent that I allow other voices or communication may put my own presence at the university at risk. There is tremendous pressure on me to keep the noise down.

Yet the memory of that young boy who had to disguise his embodied wisdom and the memory of other disabled students whose embodied wisdom remained unrecognized by the non-disabled world linger in my body. Daily within my spasms the feelings of fear, shame, and ridicule are recalled. Since that day of testing I have had a perhaps unspoken desire to make the conditions possible for unrecognized wisdom to come to fruition, no matter what the risk.

Like Nietzsche (1984, 90), I stand on a footbridge stripped of preconceived notions of what is truth, wisdom, and intelligence and invite others to engage in a polylogue with me. In doing so I leave my porous body vulnerable to other notions of truth. The risk is well worth it as together we might rid ourselves, or at least loosen the holds, of the convictions that bind us. I invite you to join me.

References

Bauman, Zygmunt. 1993. *Postmodern ethics*. Cambridge, MA: Blackwell.

Best, Steven, and Douglas Kellner. 1991. *Postmodern theory: Critical interrogations*. New York: Guilford Press.

Bogdan, Robert, and Steven J. Taylor. 1988, April. Relationships with severely disabled people: The social construction of humanness. *Social Problems* 36: 135-48.

Booth, Tim, and Wendy Booth. 1996. Sounds of silence: Narrative research with inarticulate subjects. *Disability and Society* 11(1): 55-69.

Claridge, Thomas. 1995, 17 February. Don't segregate disabled pupils, appeal court says. *The Globe and Mail*, A1-A2.

Code, Lorraine. 1995. *Rhetorical spaces: Essays on gendered locations*. New York: Routledge.

Davis, Lennard J., ed. 1997. Constructing normalcy: The bell curve, the novel, and the invention of the disabled body in the nineteenth century. In *The disability studies reader*. New York: Routledge.

Erevelles, Nirmala. 1996. Disability and the dialectics of difference. *Disability and Society* 11(4): 519-537.

Foucault, Michel. 1984. Panopticism. In *The Foucault reader*, edited by Paul Rabinow. Toronto: Random House.

Hennessy, Rosemary. 1993. *Materialist feminism and the politics of discourse*. New York: Routledge.

Hevey, David. 1997. The enfreakment of photography. In *The disability studies reader*, edited by Lennard J. Davis. New York: Routledge.

Hoskins, Keith. 1990. The crypto-educationalist unmasked. In *Foucault and education: Disciplines and knowledge*, edited by Stephen J. Ball. New York: Routledge.

Huspek, Michael. 1997. Communication and the voice of other. In *Transgressing discourses: Communication and the voice of the other*, edited by Michael Huspek and Gary P. Radford. Albany: State University of New York Press.

Kristeva, Julia. 1982. *The powers of horror: An essay on abjection*. Translated by Leon S. Roudiez. New York: Columbia University Press.

Leicester, Mai, and Tessa Lovell. 1996. Disability voice: Educational experience. *Disability & Society* 12(1): 111-118

Lonsdale, Susan. 1990. *Women and disability: The experience of physical disability among women*. Hampshire, England: MacMillan.

Nietzsche, Fredrich Wilhelm. [1887] 1974. *The gay science: With a prelude in rhymes and an appendix of songs*. Translated by Walter Kauffmann. New York: Vintage Books.

Oliver, Michael. 1990. *The politics of disablement: A sociological approach*. New York: St. Martin's Press.

Oliver, Michael. 1996. *Understanding disability: From theory to practice.*Hampshire, England: Macmillan.

Shotter, John. 1997. Textual violence in academe: On writing with respect for one's others. *In Transgressing discourses: Communication and the voice of the other*, edited by Michael Huspek and Gary Radford. Albany: State University of New York Press.

Sullivan, Shannon. 1997, Winter. Domination and dialogue in Merleau-Ponty's phenomenology of perception. *Hypatia* 12(1): 2-19.

Wendell, Susan. 1996. *The rejected body: Feminist philosophical reflections on disability.* New York: Routledge.

Young, Iris Marion. 1990. *Justice and the politics of difference.* Princeton, NJ: Princeton University Press.

Merleau-Ponty's Work and Moral Education: Beyond Mind/Body, Self/Other, and Human/Animal Dichotomies

Darlene Rigo

DARLENE RIGO is a doctoral student in the department of philosophy at York University in Toronto. She is currently living in New Orleans working on her dissertation, which focuses on the phenomenological aspects of Simone de Beauvoir's work and the influence of Merleau-Ponty.

Abstract. Drawing on the work of Merleau-Ponty, this paper suggests an alternative approach to moral education. By contrast with the traditional, rule-bound, and externally imposed kind, this version is grounded in a spontaneous embodied experience of continuity with others. I discuss the conventional conception of morality as premised upon transcending our animality, and to elucidate the moral orientations at issue, consider the imposition of meat-eating on children who are averse to it. I argue that for an ethical alternative beyond abstract and deadening dichotomies, more attention to children's relations with animals is needed, and that Merleau-Ponty's work gestures in a promising direction.

Keywords. Merleau-Ponty, Moral Education, Children, Animals, Mimesis

Acknowledgments. I wish to thank the supportive audience at the Bodymind Conference where I presented this paper in Vancouver, in May 1999. Also, in addition to my many nonhuman friends and family members, from whom I have learned much over the years, one last acknowledgement must go to all the human ones whose tales of childhood experiences with animals also inspired and helped to sustain my interest in this project.

Merleau-Ponty's Work and Moral Education: Beyond Mind/Body, Self/Other, and Human/Animal Dichotomies

Darlene Rigo

[W]hat has to be done is to show that philosophy can no longer think according to this cleavage: God, man, creatures...Hence we do not begin *ab homine* as Descartes (the 1st part is not reflection) we do not take Nature in the sense of the Scholastics (the 2nd part is not Nature in itself, a philosophy of Nature, but a description of the man-animality *intertwining*)....

Maurice Merleau-Ponty (1968, 274)

Both canonical Western philosophies and dominant Judeo-Christian religions tend to regard the body as inferior to, if not separable from, the mind or soul. Consistent with this traditional outlook, morality is believed to arise in opposition to natural inclination, and as a reminder of our animality, the body is considered to be a hindrance to moral education. In this paper, I suggest that a less dualistic understanding of human life recasts the problem of moral development and does not necessarily dismiss or derogate the body. Drawing on the work of Maurice Merleau-Ponty, I address the embodied experiences of children, including how they learn in relation to others, in order to question the conventional understanding of morality as purely rational and prescriptive and premised on transcending our animality. I discuss David Michael Levin's reliance on Merleau-Ponty to outline an alternative approach to moral education based on the child's experience of empathic connection to embodied others, and argue that if it is to be viable, children's feelings of kinship with animals need to be taken into account and pedagogically fostered. Tracing the implications of Merleau-Ponty's philosophy not only for challenging rigid mind/body and self/other binaries, but most controversially, for undermining the human/animal dichotomy, I endeavor to elucidate the distinction between the moral orientations at issue by discussing the imposition of meat-eating on children who are averse to it. While this common practice may seem insignificant, and has generated scant empirical study, appealing to published and personal examples, I suggest that it may be worthy of further investigation. It is relevant to exploring moral postures and ethical dimensions beyond the limits of dualistic thought, in which children's experiences of intercorporeality are valued, and "flesh" no longer refers to *mere* matter, but to the elemental living unity of the world.

I

Merleau-Ponty's work poses an extended challenge to dualism and is a testament to the significance of embodied life. His phenomenological undertakings describe and thereby attempt to retrieve the primordial experience not only of a somewhat obscure carnal existence, but also of a pre-personal intercorporeality in a shared world of flesh. In his essay "The Child's Relations with Others,"[1] Merleau-Ponty maintains that the child learns not through piecemeal intellectual operations or cognition proper, but through a prior organizing activity that incorporates totalities through bodily attunement and habituation. Deemed mimesis or mimicry (le mimétisme ou la mimique [Merleau-Ponty 1958]), this mode of learning involves a "postural impregnation" through which a perceiver incarnates the behavior of another without intellectual mediation or translation.[2] Based on an experience of intercorporeality previous to the birth of the "I," mimesis enables the child to develop and restructure its manner of being in relation to other embodied beings, both human and animal.[3] Yet, as Merleau-Ponty characteristically propounds, the experience of childhood "is never radically liquidated," and the unbounded relations between self and other upon which mimesis depends are pushed farther away rather than entirely suppressed (1964b, 138,153-54). Beneath the divisive structures of adult experience reside those more continuous modes of being in the world.

Levin relies on Merleau-Ponty to support his contention that moral guidance needs to be aligned with the child's implicit corporeal sense of value. He contrasts the dualistic and punitive morality of "our centuries-old 'patriarchal' religion of shame, guilt and remorse, which not only justifies, but even requires, the most vehement mortification of the flesh," to a more holistic gentle approach, which would foster the development of autonomous humans who care about other embodied individuals, rather than those who simply learn to follow cognitively-prescribed rules (Levin 1985, 227).[4] Levin agrees with Nietzsche's view that empathy with the souls of others is originally nothing "moral," at least not in any strictly cognitive sense, but has to do with a "physiological susceptibility to suggestions," with the communication of movements and mimicking of signs, rather than the intellectual comprehension of thoughts (Levin 1985, 238; Nietzsche 1968, 428). Following Merleau-Ponty in pointing back to this embodied origin, Levin attempts to sketch out a phenomenology of moral experience that is grounded in the child's corporeal attunement to others.

According to Levin, this bodily attunement provides the basis of genuine compassion, which he deems the "fundament of moral life." He argues that moral teaching should aim to

> heighten the rudimentary, and still undeveloped, bodily felt
> sense of our intercorporeality. Every...body-subject already
> inheres in an elemental, pre-existent matrix of flesh which is
> inherently social, and which already sets down each subject's

incontestable and inalienable kinship with all other sentient and
mortal beings long before there is the reflective life of an
individual person. (1985, 239)

Levin asks how we may contact and develop this sense of intercorporeality,
and holds that Merleau-Pontian mimesis, developed into a "lesson in moral
sensibility," has the most potential for doing so (1985, 240). In order to teach
compassion, he claims that mimetic play could become more explicitly focused
on developing a deeper experience of being coupled with the other, bringing
about an intertwining, bodily feeling of being "moved" by the other.
Eventually, he holds, it would come to fruition in a "well-grounded, bodily felt
sense of extensive kinship, basis for the articulation of our natural fulfillment
through a life of compassion." (1985, 240).[5]

Although Levin does not refer to the tendency of children to mimic animals as
well as humans, it is significant that Merleau-Ponty draws no clear separation
between the phenomena, and in fact highlights children's experience of
animals in early life. Merleau-Ponty states that

> Not only the perception of another child but even that of an
> animal quite different from the child himself shows up, thanks to
> the postural function, in attitudes which resemble those of the
> other and have their same expressive value. (1964b, 145)

He describes the experience of mimesis as "the ensnaring of me by the other, the
invasion of me by the other; it is that attitude whereby I assume the gestures, the
conducts, the favorite words, the ways of doing things of those whom I
confront" (1964b, 146). Although the reference to "words" seems to be limited to
the parroting of other humans, the example Merleau-Ponty provides features a
child mimicking a chirping bird. He claims that after this boy perceived the bird
for a time, he experienced a "postural impregnation," and proceeded to
reproduce the sounds and bearing of the animal. The process is described as a
bodily capacity for meditation, which gives rise to sympathy, or living in the
expressive behavior of another as the other lives in one's own (1964b, 146).

Merleau-Ponty also includes animals when discussing children's precocious
awareness of their bodies as consonant with those of others. He states:

> The child's extraordinary facility in recognizing the parts of the
> body in a drawing or an even rougher sketch, the promptness
> and skill with which he identifies parts of his own body in the
> bodies of animals that scarcely resemble the human body or
> familiar domestic animals, the plasticity of vision that allows
> him to recognize homologous structures of the body in quite
> different organisms—all this can be explained by the state of
> neutral indistinction between self and other in which he lives.
> (1964b, 149-50)

According to Merleau-Ponty, there is no conceptual abstraction in such recognition of mutually shared parts, and the child, tending to "recognize himself in everything," does not essentially distinguish between its own body and that of animal others (1964b, 150).

Moreover, to demonstrate how a child resolves a developmental conflict stemming from the ensuing arrival of a younger sibling, Merleau-Ponty cites the example of a girl who finds her experience represented in the sight of a dog nursing her litter. The girl identifies with one of the puppies who will have to share the mother, and the experience helps her to prepare for the approaching upset in her life (1964b, 111-12). Although Merleau-Ponty does not elaborate on the child's identification with the animal, Freud provides some insight into what he sees as a pattern characteristic of childhood:

> Children show no trace of the arrogance which urges adult
> civilized men to draw a hard-and-fast line between their own
> nature and that of all other animals. Children have no scruples
> over allowing animals to rank as their full equals. Uninhibited
> as they are in the avowal of their bodily needs, they no doubt
> feel themselves more akin to animals than to their elders, who
> may well be a puzzle to them (Freud 1960, 126-27).

II

It is well-known in the contemporary West, almost to the point of invisibility, that children feel a profound affinity for animals. Early experiences of wonder, curiosity, and joy in the presence of animals meaningfully engage us in the world and may even remain unparalleled in later life. In my own experience, besides my earliest recollections of the marvels of my first visit to a zoo and of an injured bird I helped my brother nurse back to health, I recall with gratitude my animal family members as a child. Among the many of them was a black speckled cat, whom I named at the age of three, and later the affectionate and loyal shepherd who became my best childhood friend. While the first taught me how to gently attune myself to another's state (including how one may otherwise inflict harm), as well as the joys of mutual play and sharing ice cream, the latter also guided me in lessons about trust, responsibility, autonomy, and love. It is perhaps in memory of their teachings that I am interested in alternative conceptions of moral development that take children's experiences seriously.

Despite the lack of theoretical literature on the subject, early education exploits children's interest in other species, and they become the bearers of a range of life's lessons. Nurseries and classrooms are filled with their images, which decorate the walls, are manifest in toys, and cover the pages of children's books. Their pedagogical value is suggested by animal guides like Smoky the bear, the "Give a Hoot and Don't Pollute" owl, and Elmer the safety elephant, figures who came to life in my childhood as well as in the plethora of moral fables which provide accounts of their exemplary actions. In less didactic educational modes, all caregivers and teachers know that children love to behave like their favorite species and to mimic animal actions in play, experiences that are ubiquitous in childhood.[6] On the intellectual front, we may even learn to name and classify by comparing and contrasting animals,[7] and it has been argued that they are necessary for human cognitive development, with self-reflectivity and awareness of human difference emerging out of a more basic perception of continuity (Shepard 1978; Mason 1993; Myers 1998). Although more research is perhaps needed to firmly establish these claims, it seems relatively uncontroversial to maintain that animals play an important role in early life with far-reaching educational significance.[8]

However, children, at varying ages as they make their way out of infancy, are taught that they are emphatically not like other creatures, and their education, manifest both posturally and cognitively, becomes centered less on imitating other animals than on emulating conventional adult behavior. To differing degrees of strictness, they are encouraged to get up off the ground, stand up straight, and eat with manners. (For instance, it was conveyed to me more insistently after the age of five that it was no longer appropriate for me to play or sit on the floor with the pets, let alone to share my food with them.) Against the background of experiences with benevolent animal figures, children are taught that human/animal relations are not as continuous or amicable as they may have previously believed.

To those who accept the traditional Cartesian view that bodies and animals are simply mechanistic matter, children who persist in treating animals like equals or expressing concern about their well-being may be deemed foolish and sentimental. They might be seen as corrupted by naive sympathies or bodily passions. According to Descartes, there is no other error which

> leads weak minds further from the straight path of virtue than that of imagining that the souls of the beasts are of the same nature as ours...When we know how much the beasts differ from us, we understand much better the arguments which prove that our soul is of a nature entirely independent of the body. (1985, 141)

According to Merleau-Ponty, however, dualism is not the whole story nor is it the unambiguous truth. Beneath the abstract physiological characterization of the body as a mechanistic mass of cells and tissues, there is a primordial phenomenal body of perceptual and motor experience which "understands," and in which children are immersed. "Under these conditions," Merleau-Ponty explains in the *Phenomenology of Perception*, "the antinomies of objective thought vanish" (1962, 351). There is no longer a mind/body problem, a rigid subject/object dichotomy, or the difficulty of ascertaining the consciousness of others. He asks why, if my consciousness inheres in its body and its world, should other perceived bodies not be similarly endowed (1962, 351). From a child's perspective, previous to any indoctrination that teaches otherwise, the question does not arise.

Merleau-Ponty maintains that the pre-*cogito* experience of childhood provides the foundation for intersubjectivity, and seems to present it in opposition to an adulthood characterized by alienation and relations of mastery.[9] He claims that the "perception of other people and the intersubjective world is problematical only for adults. The child lives in a world which he unhesitatingly believes accessible to all around him. He has no awareness of himself or of others as private subjectivities" (1962, 355). He criticizes Piaget's view that with the achievement of the *cogito* at age twelve, the individual reaches the truths of rationalism, and achieving an independent objectivity, leaves the naiveté of childhood behind (pp. 354-56). For Merleau-Ponty, we are in the first place and always situated in a world shared by others, and the thought of adulthood is neither self-sufficient nor ideal. He states:

> [It] must be the case that the child's outlook is in some way
> vindicated against the adult's and against Piaget, and that the
> unsophisticated thinking of our earliest years remains as an
> indispensable acquisition underlying that of maturity, if there
> is to be for the adult one single intersubjective world. (1962, 355)

He holds that the *cogito* and the master/slave dialectic to which it gives rise are based upon our primordial experience of intersubjectivity: "For the struggle ever to begin, and for each consciousness to be capable of suspecting the alien presences which it negates, all must necessarily have some common ground and be mindful of their peaceful coexistence in the world of childhood" (1962, 355).

The *Phenomenology*, in the words of Monika Langer, "paves the way for a concrete morality which is adequate to the demands of our age" (1989, 154). In her estimation, as well as my own, it provides the foundation for an ecological approach to our environment, and an orientation to the world that is at once a belonging to it (Langer 1990). Its descriptions and thoroughgoing critique of Cartesianism call for an ethics of harmonious coexistence to combat the alienation of modern life. As Merleau-Ponty states, defending the text before the *Societé française de philosophie*:

> If we admit that our life is inherent to the perceived world and
> the human world, even while it re-creates it and contributes to its
> making, then morality cannot consist in the private adherence to
> a system of values. Principles are mystifications unless they are
> put into practice; it is necessary that they animate our relations to
> others...[We] need to act in such a way that our action cannot be
> considered by others as an act of aggression but, on the contrary,
> as generously meeting the other in the very particularity of a
> given situation...Just as the perception of a thing opens me up
> to being...the perception of the other founds morality (1964c, 25-26)[10]

III

In accord with Langer, I think that Merleau-Ponty's work provides a rich resource for an alternative understanding of morality, and I agree with Levin that it suggests a novel approach to its education. However, if we are to aspire to a moral ideal grounded in the child's experience of intercorporeality, beyond Cartesian dualisms and a disincarnate cognition, then perhaps more attention to animals is required. In this section, I consider the imposition of meat-eating on resistant children in order to distinguish the moral orientations at issue: the traditional dualistic and rule-bound model which is imposed from without, and a more holistic one, which emerges spontaneously and is consistent with experiences of intercorporeality. Appealing to examples of children's responses to the discovery of the origin of meat, I suggest that it would undermine efforts to nurture children's compassion for other carnal beings if the killing of animals, with whom they empathize and identify, is treated as a necessity or a good beyond question.[11]

For some children, consistent with Merleau-Ponty's account of the child's attunement to homologous bodily forms, after the initial shock of discovering the link between meat and animals, the corporeal comparisons between the child's ribs, legs, blood or skin, and the configurations of the cooked pork, lamb, beef or chicken, may range from squeamishness to horror. One woman, a vegetarian since she was a small child, claims, "I began to connect that it was flesh, I felt it was like eating your own body." Another refers to the comparison between her own skin with goose pimples and that of chicken skin (Willetts 1997, 122). Yet, such revelations are often treated as foolishness by parents, a matter of course if not an annoyance, and among professionals, rarely a problem worthy of theoretical elaboration. In my own case, it was the rib cage and blue veins on the underside of a breast of chicken that prompted me to make the connection. When I refused to eat the remainder of the meal, my mother deemed it silly; when I subsequently rejected all meat, she threatened that I would "whither away to nothing" and resorted to the imperative. I eventually succumbed to her pressures while still refusing to eat anything that resembled an animal. However, my nascent vegetarianism was again fueled by the shocking discovery that a platter of stew delivered by the neighbors was composed of the remains of my lost pet rabbit. In that case, my horror was somewhat affirmed by my mother's insistence that even she would not partake.[12]

Now, I am not suggesting that all children experience the discovery of the origin of meat negatively, or see meat eating as an expression of violence. In contexts where food is scarce, or in rural environments where children may be exposed to animal slaughter before they are able to question it, the issue would seem less likely to arise. Yet, even though the revelation may not be universally troubling, it appears to be a sufficiently widespread phenomenon to warrant more exploration than it has yet received, particularly in the context of exploring ethical alternatives based on fostering bodily continuity. It suggests a certain discomfort over our treatment of animals, which other cultures seem to more openly address, and to which the lack of investigation of the issue may attest. For example, even among meat-eating traditions which span the globe, like that of the Cherokee, Inuit, Ainu, and Barsana, there are beliefs in animal souls and rituals which serve to appease the guilt induced by killing one's animal kin.[13] At present, there are no comparably widespread beliefs or overt mechanisms in the West that help to maintain a coherent moral framework. Instead, if we are led to question the ever less tenable view of animals as mere matter, which is germane to dualism and tends to condone the exploitation of animals,[14] we likely wrestle with the contradictions between its still potent legacy, and the vestiges of an empathetic bodily kinship with animals more evident among children.

Gene Myers, the author of the only study that I have found on children and animals that addresses meat eating,[15] indicates that our primary modes for dealing with the practice are distancing mechanisms like detachment, concealing the harm, and constructing animals as an out-group (1998, 153-54). His research suggests that children are only in the process of acquiring these defensive aptitudes, and thus, that their refusal to eat meat because of its animal origin is an expression of a moral dilemma. It arises from a conflict between culturally accepted views and their own experience of empathy and core relatedness with animals. He claims that

> Children's concern about animals reveals an inherent and self-
> organizing dynamic of morality. It does so more vividly than
> does their moral development toward other humans, because in
> the case of animals the culture encourages a discontinuity—or at
> best, a complexity that is hard to navigate with moral sensibilities
> intact. (1998, 154)

Myers claims that children's attitudes toward eating meat provide intriguing evidence of how this basic moral sense may be countered by conflicting messages from the environment.[16] Maintaining that moral conflicts about the status of animals may be unavoidable, he nonetheless concludes that they may be minimized by fostering means of continuity and respecting children's concerns (1998, 153-54).

Consistent with Myers, I think that the imposition of meat eating on reluctant children, at best, poses a difficult dilemma for them. At worst, it might contribute to tendencies toward "psychological rigidity," to dogmatism, conformism, or intolerance, which Merleau-Ponty and Levin trace to defenses against authoritarian modes of teaching (Merleau-Ponty 1964b, 100-108; Levin 1985, 234-45). Rather than supporting or enhancing feelings of empathy and nurturing their autonomy, forcing or encouraging reluctant children to eat meat would more likely teach them that their own embodied sense of moral values is skewed, and compel them to adopt an alien system of doctrinaire, cognitive ones.[17]

A telling example comes from Lawrence Kohlberg, a theorist influenced by Kant and Piaget, who is well-known for drafting stages of paradigmatic moral development (Kohlberg 1981; Adams 1990, 123). His model was notoriously opposed by Carol Gilligan's ethic of care (1982), which takes relationships and emotions into account, rather than privileging rules and abstract reasoning alone.[18] Kohlberg recounts the first moral action of his four-year-old son who "joined the pacifist and vegetarian movement and refused to eat meat because, he said, it is bad to kill animals." His parents relied on logical arguments contrary to the child's experience, and set out to convince him that there is a difference between justified and unjustified killing (1981, 14, 46, 143). In order to accept the parental rationale for meat eating, he would have to renounce his own moral inclinations and substitute them with a set of abstract precepts resting on authority. Remarkably, the child managed to hold his vegetarian ground for six months.

Carol Adams cites another example of a boy of four who objected to his parents' meat eating, the killing of seals, and the hunting of stags, and thought that the police should put a stop to these practices (1990, 214). Upon being told that people are allowed to kill animals, he exclaimed: "Allowed, allowed? People are not allowed to take other people and kill them." He was then informed that people think that there is a difference between killing humans and killing animals. Rather than seeing any merit in the child's moral outlook, the author, from whom Adams takes the example, refers to the boy as struggling with "the dreadful 'must' which turns men into killers," and notes that during this transitional period, the child also learns to see soldiers in a positive light. Eating meat is associated with war, and neither is questioned. Adams, however, insightfully directs our attention to a child's possible response: "Once we get in the habit of killing animals, we may find it hard to stop when it comes to people" (1990, 214). The statement implies a child's view of the continuity between animals and humans, and the need for an ethics that values the lives of both.[19]

My point here is not to show that eating meat is wrong so much as to argue that not eating meat because of a felt sense of continuity with animals merits more attention, and overall, to show that questioning the controversial issue of human/animal relations has potential for charting alternate ethical space. There is increasing evidence which correlates violence against animals with violence against other humans (Ascione and Arkow 1999; Hellman and Blackman 1966; Felthous and Kellert 1986), and thus, even if one were not concerned with the plight of animals per se, there may still be good reasons to nurture children's empathic concern for them. If teaching was consistently directed to sustaining children's feelings of continuity with other species, this sense of connection could be more coherently extended to other embodied humans. Working with children's interest in and concern for animals, educators may try to provide non-exploitative access to them (ideally in their natural habitats and excluding practices like dissection)[20] and encourage children to develop a sense of their humanity in relation with other species. As recommended for deepening feelings of empathy among humans (Hoffman 1993), positive interactions with animals may be affirmed, and negative ones may be met with questions about how the child might like to be treated in the same way. Given that we tend to show more concern for those perceived to be similar or close to us (Deaux and Wrightsman, 1984), reinforcing such primary experiences of continuity with animal others might then undergird more peaceful negotiations of our relatively less conspicuous differences from human ones.

IV

Considering the themes he addresses, Levin oddly evades the issue of children's relations with animals. He speaks at length of a connection between moral uprightness and upright posture, but makes no reference to animals, against whom human posture is paradigmatically contrasted. Insisting on the importance of how adults respond to the child's first efforts at standing and walking—claiming that they may encourage "postures of lordly insolence and aloofness," give rise to psychological rigidity, and have an influence on the child's "entire future development as a moral agent"—he nonetheless does not refer to the associations of moral lowliness with animality (Levin 1985, 240-42). This oversight is curious considering the treatment the phenomenologist Erwin Straus gives to the problem, whose work Levin cites, and Straus' view that upright posture is the defining characteristic of the human species (Straus 1966, 137-40). Thus, children who must gradually struggle to achieve this difficult posture, by virtue of their early inability to walk, feel closer to other animals than adults. In some respects complementing Freud's account of this affinity, Straus explains, "A child creeping on his hands and knees not only keeps contact with the ground but is, in his all-fours locomotion, like the quadrupeds, directed toward immediate contact with things" (1966, 144). Remoteness from "Mother Earth" transforms the child's contact with things from grasping, to looking, creating distance, and giving the child the feeling of standing alone. The "I" is born in this posture, according to Straus, defying animality and gravity, and enabling the individual to stand aloof from others. It gives rise to a particular attitude toward the world that one might describe as a detached mode of being in it (1966, 140-44).

It is suggestive that Straus links the child's acquisition of upright posture to the acceptance of table manners. Proposing that standing-up-and-eating rituals mark the threshold into human civilization, he states:

> A young child is close to the ground; to him the stars are far off.
> He does not mind picking things up from the ground; but,
> growing older, he will learn to accept our table manners, which
> remove even food to a distance. We set the table; we serve the
> meal; we use spoon and fork. Our feeding is regulated by a ritual,
> which we like to discard at a picnic. Artificiality and tools inter-

fere with the direct satisfaction of hunger. The mouth is kept
away from the plate. The hand lifts the food to the mouth. Spoon
and fork do not create distance; tools can only be invented and
used where distance already exists...Pointing likewise pre-
supposes distance. It appears to be a human activity. Animals do
not easily, if at all, understand pointing to distant things.
(1966, 145)[21]

Although the passage only briefly refers to animals, they seem to nevertheless
haunt its borders. One of the central features of Western eating rituals is the
presence of meat on the well-laid table, its prominent placement at its head,
traditionally before the man of the house, its precise carving and primary serving. It is perhaps one of the effects of the adult experience of distance from others and food that Straus attributes to achieving uprightness that enables most
adults to eat meat without much thought. Not only do we see ourselves as
more erect and superior to the animals we eat, but also we are often, especially
in urban settings, distanced from the origin of meat. Children who feel closer
to animals and are less habituated to the custom of meat eating often question
it. Should their reluctance to eat it be interpreted not as the presence of moral
value, but of weakness or lowliness?

Straus traces the connection between upright posture and moral uprightness
as expressed in the following phrases: not to stoop to anything, to stand by
one's convictions, to be in good standing, or to hold to one's ideas of rightness
and rectitude (1966, 137). According to him, the upright stance is contrary to
the languid lying down during sex, of lazy sloth, or of the infirmity of addict
and drunk. He contrasts the exalted heights of Sinai from whence Moses
receives the commandments with the shadowy underworld, and notes that in
Milton's terms, Adam and Eve are created "God-like erect," clearly distin-
guished from other living creatures (1966, 137, 142). Yet, he does not refer to
the Fall, and the association of animals with decline is here implicit. The whole
story of Genesis portrays the couple in Eden, initially made in God's image
and granted all plants and trees to eat, yet who, upon tasting of the fruit of carnal knowledge, fall from grace. They become ashamed of their animal naked-
ness as a sign of their alienation from God. As punishment, humanity is forced
to give up its inherited rule, and it is not until after the Flood that God makes
clear his plan that humans, beginning with Noah's clan, should have dominion over the earth and its creatures. The domestication, killing, and eating of
animals are henceforth sanctioned by divine right. Yet, in atonement for its
original sin, humanity is expected to make sacrifices to God, and as often
taught, is enjoined to rise up above its flesh (Sandmel 1976, Noske 1997, 46-47).

V

In my view, in order to open up alternate ethical space, that age-old conception
of flesh as the degraded carnality, which humans are to transcend, needs to be

challenged. In this respect, Merleau-Ponty leads the way. In *The Visible and the Invisible*, making his departure from dualist categories clear, he defines flesh as an element of Being:

> [F]lesh [*la chair*] is not matter, is not mind, is not substance. To designate it, we should need the old term "element," in the sense it was used to speak of water, air, earth, and fire, that is, in the sense of a general thing...(Merleau-Ponty 1968, 139)

Emphasizing its conceptual novelty, he claims that flesh "has no name in any philosophy." It is beyond any rigid subject/object division, but as a more vital primeval unity, is not simply a union of opposites (1968, 147). As body, in our irreducible corporeality shared with animals, we are of the flesh of the world. Immersed in its densely interwoven tissue, we are body-subjects, not absolute minds perusing the world from high above with an abstract disincarnate view (1968, 248). Merleau-Ponty reminds us that vision, though it sustains the illusion of distance, is concrete like all manner of perception, and we can see and touch only because we ourselves can be seen and touched. Humanity is thus brought down to earth, to a primordial intertwining with animals, other humans, and the world.

Nevertheless, perhaps because of our upright posture, which may be morally overrated, we are not on the same experiential level as other sentient creatures. Merleau-Ponty claims that it may be no accident that the rational being, among other "contingencies," is the one that carries itself upright and has an opposable thumb, the means for manual dexterity (1962, 170). We can hardly imagine what it would be like to be predominantly oriented by scent rather than vision, as are dogs, or by sonar as are dolphins, who have perceptual access to the insides of what we see as solid and opaque.[22] But the consciousness of animals cannot be denied on this basis, and as far as I know, Merleau-Ponty, with his firm belief in the primacy of perception, never hazarded to do so. Nor would human language provide adequate support for such a categorical denial given Merleau-Ponty's view that it is primarily gestural, carnal and emotive, features not necessarily foreign to animal expression (Merleau-Ponty 1962, 174-202; Abram 1996, 73-81). David Abram, addressing the radical nature of Merleau-Ponty's bodily view of language and the thinking subject as one of the earth's animals, reminds us that without this body, without tongue and ears, as well as sensory contact with others and oneself, we could not speak or hear another person's voice, let alone have anything to think or talk about (Abram 1996, 44-47).

Although I have spotlighted Merleau-Ponty's descriptions that suggest continuity between humans and other animals, particularly evident in childhood, he nonetheless often designates divergences between them. For example, he maintains that one does not feel embarrassed under the gaze of a dog (1962, 361); animals do not experience their reflections in a mirror in the same way as humans (1964b, 126); we mutually haunt other humans "like no animal ever haunted those beings of its own species" (1964a, 161); and the "adamantine body" of certain animals is not like the flesh of human beings (1964a, 163). Hence, Merleau-Ponty is not attempting to simply reduce humans to other animals, let alone to a childlike state, but to reawaken a less abstract and alienating felt sense of peaceful immersion in the world, a bodily attunement that we carry with us from our pre-personal past. Lest one think that his reformulation of the body and flesh risks casting aside human value and dignity, it is worth stressing that he diagnoses the dichotomous thought of abstract rationalism—in that it neglects its own substratum in living experience—as the danger. Without this vital dimension, "reason and liberty are emptied of their content and wither away"(1962, 56-57). By returning to the phenomenal experience of the body, he attempts to restore our rootedness in the carnality of the world so that we may hopefully be able to take up responsible and mutually respectful modes of being in it.

Levin, in his application of Merleau-Ponty's philosophy to moral education, provides compelling suggestions for how we can develop respectful, compassionate ways of living by nurturing the children's basic corporeal sense of value. His proposed project of retrieving our "first body of moral wisdom" through a gentle caring approach, and thereby vindicating our carnality, is insightful, and his critique of conventional moral pedagogy with its punitive, rule-based and body-suppressing tendencies, is on target. Few could disagree with his rejection of an ethics that sought to instill an "always 'guilty' conscience" in children (Levin 1985, 247). However, by neglecting children's relations with animals, which Merleau-Ponty's thought invites us to consider, Levin's account does not venture far enough in its outline for a benevolent intercorporeal kinship. Such a strategy would be compromised by trying to foster an embodied compassion in children, who feel an intercorporeal alliance with animals, while simultaneously teaching them that this sympathetic experience should be limited to humans. It would drive a rift in the felt-sense of bodily continuity with others, which it aims to cultivate. In my view, if an alternative approach to moral education based on bodily continuity is to be successful, children's relations with animals need to be duly recognized and continuously supported. Western culture's understanding of morality is too fundamentally premised upon flight from animality, and detaching mind from body, to expect to overcome its influence without interrogating the human/animal opposition which upholds it. For an ethical alternative beyond abstract and deadening dichotomies, Merleau-Ponty's work gestures in a promising direction.

Notes

1. Merleau-Ponty's analysis in this essay is heavily influenced by Henri Wallon (1987).

2. Suggesting an equivalence between the terms, Merleau-Ponty uses the phrase "mimesis, or mimicry" twice in the essay (1964b, 145, 146). Although a conceptual distinction

between the two might seem to be warranted (with mimicry more evidently designating outward behavior, as in the playing of roles, and mimesis, which is said to be the "equivalent of introjection," as the process through which the conduct of an other is internalized), it is contraindicated by Merleau-Ponty's view of the basic correspondence between perception and motility in the "fundamental and irreducible form" of mimesis or mimicry (pp. 145-48). However, to distinguish between the usual understanding of mimicry that is deepened and extended by Merleau-Ponty, I henceforth use "mimesis."

3. I use "it" to refer to the child (rather than "he" according to Merleau-Ponty's usage, or "she," or "he or she" as might be expected) to maintain gender neutrality, to avoid awkwardness, and for the sake of brevity. It is for the latter reason that I also omit "nonhuman" in reference to nonhuman animals.

4. Levin understands the Judeo-Christian religious tradition to be responsible for the "patriarchal falsehood which shrouds the body and conceals its gifts of wisdom." He recognizes Nietzsche as the first Western philosopher of this epoch to challenge it and claims that in continuing to carry out this critical reflection we are greatly indebted to him (1985, 227).

5. For another attempt to ground moral education in empathy as an alternative to a traditional model of morality based on cognition, see Martin L. Hoffman's "Empathy, Social Cognition, and Moral Education." Hoffman criticizes Lawrence Kohlberg's impartialist theory of moral development (to which I refer in note 18), arguing that moral motives arise from empathy, upon which a comprehensive theory of morality should be based. He claims that empathy arises "naturally" in most humans, as an automatic response, yet that it can also be enhanced with the use of mimicry, and later, with language mediation (1993).

6. Consistent with Merleau-Ponty's account of mimesis, Gene Myers suggests that the imitation of animals reflects children's felt sense of continuity with them. In his study of children's relations with animals, he points out that although it has not been studied cross-culturally, animal pretend play has been reported in the Fang of Africa and in the Asturian region of northern Spain. He also refers to the ceremonial imitation of animals among the Kwakiutl (1998, 141). Jim Mason maintains that animal play is universal (1993, 106-07).

7. Animals are believed to provide the basis for some 5,000 expressions, more than any other set of natural things (Bekoff 1998, 39).

8. In her paper "Minding Animals: The Role of Animals in Children's Development," H. Patricia Hindley refers to the scarcity of sustained experimental research on children's dependency on animals for their early emotional and cognitive development. After reviewing the literature and arguing on behalf of the importance of the issue, she concludes stating: "Surely, what is urgently called for, at the very least, is a strong interdisciplinary research focus in this area" (1999, 196).

9. The cogito is a shortened designation for Descartes' Latin phrase "Cogito ergo sum," or "I think, therefore I am." It represents his first certainty—that of his own existence, and his answer to radical skeptical doubt (Descartes 1984). Here, it refers to the developmental stage at which the individual becomes aware of itself as such a consciousness existing in the act of apprehending itself, as if transparent to itself, detached from the world, and engaged in impartial reflection. The cogito is said to give rise to a master/slave struggle, in that it features the subject positing itself as absolute and alone in the world, as reigning above a private spectacle; any other subject would have to appear as a threat to its

supreme existence. As a result, the subject attempts to defend itself by denying the other's subjectivity and reducing it to a thing. Yet, criticizing this atomistic characterization that informs adult experience, Merleau-Ponty claims that it involves an impossibility. He denies that the mind is absolute, independent of the body, the world, and others, and maintains that if it were, it would have to be God (1962, 369-409).

10. Aware of such gestures toward an intersubjective ethics in Merleau-Ponty's corpus, Levin (1990) also argues that it exposes the groundwork for the project of building a truly just society.

11. As far as I have been able to gather, there is a dearth of research on this subject. I have only come across one ethnographic study, which I describe below. This lack of investigation is surprising given the many anecdotal confirmations of children's shock, dismay, and/or outrage upon the discovery of the animal origin of meat. Carol Adams cites the following examples: a doctor who became a vegetarian at eight claimed, "I began to ask about the fate of the animals, and I began to inquire about the sources of my food, and I discovered to my horror that the lamb, the mutton on my plate, was obtained from the lambs in the fields. I said, in effect, that I liked lambs and I didn't like lamb, and that was the start of it all"; Robert Nozick, a Harvard philosophy professor, credits his two-year-old daughter with prompting his transition to vegetarianism when at Thanksgiving she asked, "That turkey wanted to live. Why was it killed?"; and a vegetarian boy of three insisted that he and his mother inform the local grocers that they were selling "poor dead mommie and baby animals." (Adams 1990, 75-76).
An exception to the empirical inattention to the issue is Gene Myers' ethnographic study of a class of nursery school children in the United States. In addition to parental surveys, he based his findings on a year of in-class observation of twenty-five children, fourteen boys and eleven girls who ranged from roughly three to five years old. Of these, six children expressed conflicts over eating meat (five out of six of them girls), with three of them refusing to eat it when they discovered its origin (two girls and one boy). The boy had stated "Yuck, I don't want to eat cow meat anymore," and told his mother that he did not like to eat dead animals. Two others were said not to like the taste of meat by their parents. Myers reports that although all the parents claimed that they would respect the child's wish not to eat meat, none of them were vegetarian themselves (Myers 1998, 147-54,173-75).

12. A friend of mine shared somewhat similar experiences not only of the disturbing discovery of the underside of a breast of chicken, but of refusing to eat rabbit for dinner. After playing with bunnies all afternoon on a visit to a farm, both she and a companion burst into tears at the table when they realized what was being served.

13. For instance, Native American traditions, including that of the Lakota or Cherokee who believe that animals are their direct ancestors, regard hunting as done in cooperation with their prey, with the spirit of the killed animal giving its consent, and the surviving spirit punishing greedy or disrespectful hunters (Bekoff 1998, 254). This idea of the hunted animal as kin having a spirit or soul, contrary to Cartesianism, which denies it, is common among hunting communities as diverse as the Ainu of Japan, the Inuit, and the Naskapi of the Labrador peninsula (Mason 1993, 107-12). In some African cultures, there are purification rites for hunters, and in others, the hunter will beg the animal for forgiveness. The Barsana Indians of Columbia believe that an animal's flesh that has not been ritually purified is poisonous, while the Moi of Indochina make expiatory offerings for a killed animal, fearing that its spiritual guardian may take revenge (Serpell 1986). In ancient pre-Christian civilizations, there were complex rituals exercised to either relieve the guilt generated by consuming animal flesh or to honor the animal spirits. There were often taboos surrounding the consumption of unsacrificed

meat, and slaughtering and distribution tended to be exclusively controlled by a priest. The ancient concerns with killing animals for food, evident today in Buddhism, Jainism and the yogic branches of Hinduism, were also evident in some classical Greek literature, particularly among the early Orphic and Pythagorean schools of philosophy which affirmed reincarnation. Aristotle's philosophy challenged this more ancient view and influenced subsequent Western thought with the doctrine that humans, unique and superior by virtue of their rational capacity, had a divine right to use animals for food (Bekoff 1998, 76-77).

14. Consistent with his view that animals, like machines, were bereft of reason and the capacity for genuine passions or feelings, Descartes himself performed vivisection (1985, 140, 317-18, 348).

15. There is another study of university students, however, which found a correlation between early feelings of empathy with animals and the reluctance to eat meat. It revealed that those who had grown up with pets were more likely to have greater concerns about the welfare of animals and to manifest "ethical food avoidances" like vegetarianism (Paul and Serpell 1993).

16. As evidence of this spontaneously emerging moral sense, Myers refers to American and Oriya (Indian) five-to seven-year-olds' agreement that "kicking a harmless animal" is wrong. He refers to it as one of the very few moral beliefs cross-culturally shared and an "apparently universal constraint" (Sweder, Mahapatra, and Miller 1987, cited in Myers 1998, 153).

17. Among vegetarians it is often regarded as an injustice to force children to eat meat. Jim Mason holds that it may be a form of child abuse (Mason 1993, 91-117). Another theorist, Brian Luke, who calls for an alternative ethic to those traditionally privileged in the West, refers to it as one of the most "obnoxious" structures or sanctions which "encourage or force us to act against our sympathies." Another example, in his view, is the meat and dairy industries' promotion of their products as two of the four essential food groups needed for health and well-being. Even though such a view has been debunked and revealed as an advertising myth, many parents still rely on it to encourage their children to consume animal foods. Luke states that the "crucial fact that meat is the flesh of slaughtered animals is systematically withheld" from children, and that when it happens to be discovered, and a moral stand is taken up, it is rarely supported. Such incipient vegetarianism is usually quashed by the "power of parental authority" (Luke 1995, 309-11).

18. The following tale is fitting given Gilligan's opposition of Kohlberg's approach to ethical development on behalf of an ethic of care. His theory features six levels from childhood to adulthood that see the child "progress" to stages where relationships are subordinated to rules (four), rules to universal principles of justice (five and six). Gilligan criticizes the claims of universality he makes for this model, which was exclusively based on studies of males, and for its one-sided emphasis on the importance of impartiality and rights. The model follows Kant and Piaget with its privileging of respect for universal, cognitively generated rules, and is traditional in its rejection of caring and relationships as legitimate factors in moral decision-making (Gilligan 1982).

19. Adams recognizes the difficulty of charting new ethical territory, which in her view is constrained by a deeply entrenched, yet difficult to discern, system of institutional violence against animals. It conceals the reality of the killing of animals by distancing us from the origins of meat. According to Adams, the institutional complex of factory farming is supported by an ethical belief in the violability of animals, and in the absence of an

alternate moral framework, children's refusal to eat meat when they learn of its origin cannot be ethically entertained. Even adults' discomfort with either the kind or form of meat sometimes consumed (from a dog or horse, the brain or liver, for instance), finds no available moral context. As a result, in our society, children's explicit objections, and adults' implicit ones, remain "unassimilated and repressed." Adams contends that institutional violence interposes "an ethics of exploitation for any burgeoning ethic of inviolability" (Adams 1995, 28-29,164-65).

20. Acknowledging the benefits of using animals for educational purposes, in the interests of animal welfare, Petto and Russell (1999) provide an inventory of questions for teachers to consider before doing so. Of course, similar concerns should govern choices about pets and animals held in zoos.

21. Denying that a pointer really "points," the footnote to this passage reads: "It is the hunter who understands and interprets the dog's aiming as pointing. The 'point' is the natural outgrowth of the dog's pausing previous to springing the game" (Straus 1966, 145).

22. Barbara Noske provides an interesting account of what it would be like to experience the world as particular animals. She claims that while for us, "seeing is believing," for a dog, "scenting is believing." Though the dog's sight is far from defective, she holds that it would be inclined to trust its nose over its eyes. Questioning accepted beliefs in human superiority, she states: "If we were suddenly confronted with a world constructed in terms of scent, we would be at a complete loss, and a dog might easily come to doubt our consciousness the way some of us worry about the existence of consciousness in animals. Compared with dogs we are absolutely scent-blind." Describing horses' ability to "speak and listen" with their skin, she claims that for them "feeling is believing," and also refers to dolphins' and whales' use of sonar, which she deems their capacity to "see with sound." Rendering the health and mental states of other individuals transparent to them, it enables them to perceive cancers and pregnancy. On this basis, Noske claims that "Dolphin worldviews would never be reductionist and behavioristic the way positivist science is" (Noske 1997, 158-59).

References

Abram, D. 1996. *The spell of the sensuous.* New York: Vintage Books.

Adams, C.J. 1990. *The sexual politics of meat: A feminist-vegetarian critical theory.* New York: Continuum.

Adams, C.J. 1995. *Neither beast nor man: Feminism and the defense of animals.* New York: Continuum.

Ascione, F.R., and P. Arkow, eds. 1999. *Child abuse, domestic violence, and animal abuse: Linking the circles of compassion for prevention and intervention.* West Lafayette, IN: Purdue University Press.

Bekoff, M. ed., with C.A. Meaney. 1998. *Encyclopedia of animal rights and animal welfare.* Westport, CT: Greenwood Press.

Deaux, K., and L.S. Wrightsman. 1984. *Social psychology in the 80's,* 4th ed. Maunder: Brooks/Code Publishing.

Descartes, R. [1641] 1984. Meditations on first philosophy. In *The philosophical writings of Descartes, volume II,* translated by J. Cottingham, R. Stoothoff, and Dugald Murdoch. Cambridge: Cambridge University Press.

Descartes, R. [1637] 1985. Discourse on the method of rightly conducting one's reason and seeking truth in the sciences. In *The philosophical writings of Descartes, volume I,* translated by J. Cottingham, R. Stoothoff, and Dugald Murdoch. Cambridge: Cambridge University Press.

Feltous, A.R., and S.R. Kellert. 1986. Violence against animals and people: Is aggression against living creatures generalized? *Bulletin of the American Academy of Psychiatry and the Law* 14.

Freud, S. [1913] 1960. *Totem and taboo: Some points of agreement between the mental lives of savages and neurotics.* Translated by J. Strachey. London: Routledge and Kegan Paul.

Gilligan, C. 1982. *In a different voice: Psychological theory and women's development.* Cambridge: Harvard University Press.

Hellman, D.S., and N. Blackman. 1966. Enuresis, firesetting and cruelty to animals: A triad predictive of adult crime. *American Journal of Psychiatry* 122.

Hindley, M. P. 1999. 'Minding animals:' The role of animals in children's mental development. In *Attitudes to animals: Views in animal welfare,* edited by F.L. Dolins. Cambridge: Cambridge University Press.

Hoffman, M.L. 1993. Empathy, social cognition, and moral education. In *Approaches to moral development: New research and emerging themes,* edited by A. Garrod. New York: Teachers College Press.

Kohlberg, L. 1981. *Essays on moral development, volume I: The philosophy of moral development.* New York: Harper and Row.

Langer, M.M. 1989. *Merleau-Ponty's phenomenology of perception: A guide and commentary.* Tallahassee: Florida State University Press.

Langer, M.M. 1990. Merleau-Ponty and deep ecology. In *Ontology and alterity in Merleau-Ponty,* edited by G.A. Johnson and M.B. Smith. Evanston: Northwestern University Press.

Levin, D.M. 1985. Moral education—The body's felt sense of value. In *The body's recollection of being: Phenomenological psychology and the destruction of nihilism.* London: Routledge and Kegan Paul.

Levin, D.M. 1990. Justice in the flesh. In *Ontology and alterity in Merleau-Ponty,* edited by G.A. Johnson and M.B. Smith. Evanston: Northwestern University Press.

Luke, B. 1995. Taming ourselves or going feral? Toward a nonpatriarchal metaethic of animal liberation. In *Animals and women: Feminist theoretical explorations,* edited by C.J. Adams and J. Donovan. Durham: Duke University Press.

Mason, J. 1993. *An unnatural order: Uncovering the roots of our domination of nature and each other.* New York: Simon and Schuster.

Merleau-Ponty, M. 1958. *Les relations avec autrui chez l'enfant: Introduction.* Paris: Centre de Documentation Universitaire.

Merleau-Ponty, M. [1945] 1962. *The phenomenology of perception.* Translated by Colin Smith. London: Routledge.

Merleau-Ponty, M. [1961] 1964a. Eye and mind. In *The primacy of perception, and other essays on phenomenological psychology, the philosophy of art, history and politics,* translated by C. Dallery. Evanston: Northwestern University Press.

Merleau-Ponty, M. [1960] 1964b. The child's relations with others. In *The primacy of perception, and other essays on phenomenological psychology, the philosophy of art, history and politics,* translated by W. Cobb. Evanston: Northwestern University Press.

Merleau-Ponty, M. [1947] 1964c. The primacy of perception and its philosophical consequences. In *The primacy of perception, and other essays on phenomenological psychology, the philosophy of art, history and politics,* translated by J.M. Edie. Evanston: Northwestern University Press.

Merleau-Ponty, M. [1964] 1968. *The visible and the invisible, followed by working notes.* Translated by A. Lingis. Evanston: Northwestern University Press.

Myers, G. 1998. *Children and animals: Social development and our connections to other species.* Boulder: Westview Press.

Nietzsche, F. 1968. *The will to power.* Translated by W. Kaufmann and R. J. Hollingdale. New York: Random House.

Noske, B. 1997. *Beyond boundaries: Human and animals.* Montreal: Black Rose Books.

Paul, E.S., and J. Serpell. 1993. Childhood pet keeping and humane attitudes in young adulthood. *Animal Welfare* 2: 321-37.

Petto, A. J. and K.D. Russell. 1999. Humane education: The role of animal-based learning. In *Attitudes to animals: Views in animal welfare,* edited by F.L. Dolins. Cambridge: Cambridge University Press.

Sandmel, Samuel, ed. 1976. *The new English Bible with the Apocrypha, Oxford study edition.* New York: Oxford University Press.

Serpell, J. 1986. In the company of animals: A study of human-animal relationships. London: Basil Blackwell.

Shepard, P. 1978. Thinking animals: Animals and the development of human intelligence. New York: Viking Press.

Shweder, R.A., M. Mahapatra, and J.G. Miller. 1987. Culture and moral development. In The emergence of morality in young children, edited by J. Kagan and S. Lamb. Chicago: University of Chicago Press.

Straus, E. 1966. The upright posture. In Phenomenological psychology: The selected writings of Erwin W. Straus. New York: Basic Books.

Wallon, H. [1949] 1987. Les origines du caractère chez l'enfant: Les prèludes du sentiment de personnalité. 2d ed. Paris: Presses Universitaires de France.

Willetts, A. 1997. 'Bacon sandwiches got the better of me:' Meat-eating and vegetarianism in southeast London. In Food, health and identity, edited by P. Caplan. London: Routledge.

Educating Nature:
On Being Squeamish in Science

Sonia MacPherson

SONIA MACPHERSON is currently holding a Killam post-doctoral position with the International Forum on Education and Society at the University of Alberta in Edmonton, Alberta, Canada. She is working to develop a cross-cultural, ecological understanding of creativity, with a focus on the Buddhist view of creativity and its implications for education. Her doctoral research examined education in a Tibetan Buddhist monastic institution for nuns in the Indian Himalayas.

Abstract. This chapter examines the control of human and non-human bodies in classrooms through the lens of the author's own experience as child in a grade six science classroom. Through an ecofeminist perspective that illustrates the processes whereby "nature" and the body are *abjected* in modern classrooms, she shows how this leads to the marginalization of girls in particular from science education. She proposes a re-imagined education of *attention of values* that would support and cultivate children's love and pleasure of animals and the human body, including their own; and which respects, rather than dominates, the natural world we are all a part of.

Keywords. Dissection, Ecology, Ethics, Gender, Ecofeminism, Nature, Science Education

Acknowledgment. I would like to acknowledge the generous support of the Social Sciences and Humanities Research Council of Canada, the Killam Trusts, and the Shastri Indo-Canadian Institute, all of which made the writing and researching of this work possible.

Educating Nature:
On Being Squeamish in Science

Sonia MacPherson

...I took my body anyplace with me.
In the thickets of abstraction my skin ran with blood.
Adrienne Rich, "Late Ghazal," 1995

I. A Girl, a Boy, a Butterfly and a Mantis

In grade five, academically ahead of my peers, I was invited to join the grade six class for science and literature. The teacher of this class was a man—my first male teacher. One morning during the science lesson, a boy named Jamie presented a large jar with a creature poised inside among long stalks of weeds and grass. The teacher had us file past the jar to observe what sat still and immobile among the greenery—a praying mantis, a large yellow-green stick insect with front pod-like appendages that folded forward as if in prayer, giving the creature its name.

The following class, with the mantis now safely ensconced in a terrarium, Jamie brought in another jarred creature. This time, it was something more familiar—a monarch butterfly. I used to watch monarch butterflies among the flowers as I walked home from school, and unlike the rather haunting and uncanny image of the mantis, the butterfly, to my eyes, was beautiful. Before I had time to enjoy its beauty, however, the teacher announced we were to view the praying mantis while eating the monarch butterfly. [So, it would seem that the "praying" pods of our mantis were in fact for "preying," and the butterfly, who might well escape in the wild, was to be forced into a death in which I was to be complicit.]

The students were told to file by to witness the spectacle, and all obeyed except another girl student and me; we both refused. The teacher insisted that we follow the other students to the terrarium. Eventually the other student acquiesced, I continued to hold my ground. I felt embarrassed as a "squeamish girl" among these older students, but nonetheless I continued to refuse. The teacher taunted and teased me, and in the end ignored my resolute refusal by ordering two boys in the class to force me physically to witness the death. The boys dragged me by the arms until I agreed to go on my own, but as I walked past the terrarium, I shut my eyes to avoid the sight/site.

Abjecting the Natural from the Human:

We have in this narrative from a (1967) sixth-grade science classroom the simultaneous attempt to manipulate human and non-human bodies. On the one hand, there is an activity to introduce, display and control what is conceived to be the natural, biological world through the housing of an "other" of the insect world. On the other hand, and significantly entwined with this event, is the attempt to manipulate the bodies and senses of students through controlling and directing our attention, experience, and what we are asked or forced to observe. This is accomplished through treating our bodies as objects to be disciplined and forcibly directed or restrained, purportedly for the sake of "learning," which is assumed to be conceptual, abstract, cognitive and intentional. Yet, what is driving such abstract learning, or at least accompanying it, is the education of the body through the disciplining and controlling of attention and bodily desires and movements. This, I would contend, is what drives us into abstraction—a by-product of the abjection of the body and nature from formal education. This, in turn, generates a preoccupation with abstract principles and concepts *about*, rather than experiences *within*, the "natural world."

This personal and local classroom experience is political and global insofar as it exemplifies the tendency to split the natural world of living beings into "objects" (concrete bodies) to be manipulated and "subjects" (observers/concepts) to be disciplined and organized in a way that interrupts their underlying cohesion. In this way, subject/object distinctions established through disciplinary behavior inside classrooms lead to an exaggerated disjuncture between the natural, biological domain and the institutional world of human societies. Such patterns continue to re-enact, and in so doing reinforce, a reified subject/object dualism. While some degree of subject/object distinctions is formed on the basis of the organization of human sensation and perception, such distinctions are accentuated through the interactions, inter-relations, and resulting socialization within institutionalized education. In the following pages, I consider some of the factors and processes whereby the natural becomes dissociated from the human through schooling, with particular attention to my own schooling experiences. I then reflect on the implications from an ecological (in this case, eco-feminist) perspective.

II. Educating Against "Nature"

Something of the butterfly and the mantis *are* the child's body, insofar as they arise within an internally generated perceptual world (Maturana 1999). The popularity of teddy bears, animal themes in children's literature, and the contents of Saturday morning cartoons all attest to children's tendency to identify with animals and nature. Some of this identification may stem from the child's perception of their shared *abjection* with animals. *Abjection* arises when something that cannot be literally rejected is nonetheless cast in ambiguity and left "outside" what symbolic culture deems legitimate. One might think of faeces or corpses as protypical "substances" that are abjected in modern, urban culture, where they are treated as both repulsive and in need of control. To a lesser extent, we find animals and living bodies similarly abjected in modern education. Just as the Otherness of animals and insects is excluded from the disciplined, abstract world of classrooms, so is the child's body, which is disciplined to conform to an abstracted, disembodied "student body." Julia Kristeva (1982, 4) describes *abjection* as that which is "jettisoned out of that boundary, its other side, a margin...It is thus not lack of cleanliness or health that causes abjection but what disturbs identity, system, order. What does not respect borders, positions, rules."

Natural objects, processes, and phenomena are prone to violating such borders, and so become a target for *abjection* because they tend to be defined in opposition to culture. Yet, no matter how much the *human* domain becomes equated with *culture*, we are an embodied species and as such will never be severed from "nature" and its oft-perceived anarchic forces. So, while attempts may be made to ritually control, discipline and even expel the *abject* from classrooms, such rituals cannot really enact the elimination of what is feared. As Kristeva suggests (Oliver 1993, 55), *abjection* is "a revolt of the person against an external menace from which one wants to keep oneself at a distance, but of which one has the impression that it is not only an external menace but that it may menace us from inside." When this split between the objectified "natural" body and the subjectified "human" abstract identity is reinforced through education, the very presence of the *abjected* "object" (as body, organism or environment) in classrooms is controlled, if not ignored or eliminated.

To our modern sensibilities, "educating nature" may sound like an oxymoron. We are conditioned to view human beings as cultured, rather than natural, subjects, and so assume that what is educated is abstract thought and culture rather than nature. In using the term "nature," I am intentionally playing with the ambiguity of its referents—as wilderness, ecosystems, and that part of our world not generated by human invention, as well as bodies, instincts, autonomic functioning, and genetics—to refer to all that appears determined outside our conscious, rational control or influence (as in, *nature* vs. nurture). In all these nuances of meaning, nature conventionally appears as something fixed and impervious to conscious, human development. Yet, if we interrogate the word *education* itself, we discover etymological roots that suggest a "drawing out" of pre-existing proclivities or natural inclinations. This contrasts starkly with what is suggested by processes of *instruction, indoctoration,* or *inculturation.* My own interest in nature's educability arose from studies of Buddhist pedagogy, where meditations and philosophical reflections educate—that is, intentionally draw out—what is termed "Buddha Nature," which is the urge to learn and natural enlightenment inclination immanent in all sentient beings.

I am writing against those who assume that what is of significance in education is abstract language—reading, writing, and arithmetic—rather than education's impact on our natural conditions. These assumptions drive considerations of autonomic and sensory learning to a hidden, unacknowledged curriculum, where bodies, desires, feelings and sensory attention become vulnerable to manipulation by systemic forces of sometimes dubious motive and effect—for example, to produce disciplined workers who demand little but consume a lot. In the process, "nature" is dissociated from human culture, and it is assumed that nature is what arises as an object of observation and study, rather than being implicit in any act of observing and studying. We do not sufficiently appreciate that to educate a human being into culture is to educate nature, because we are inseparably interrelated with Earth's biotic community. To educate a human being *is* to educate nature, both because we are nature and because of our profound impact on the life of the biosphere. Furthermore, our relations with what might be deemed natural in our own existence—body, sensation, feelings—condition how we perceive and interact with the natural "other." If we perceive our own bodies, sensory experience and feelings as simple resources in the service of our abstract and rational egos and intellects, we will tend to treat all nature similarly as a resource for abstract human economies and cultures.

In spite of the known value of direct experience in learning (Dewey [1916] 1944), activities involving direct sensory and physical engagement with the world tend to be limited, controlled, and successively circumscribed as one progresses through modern education systems. One graduates with a type of disengaged, rational abstraction achieved by excluding rather than incorporating (*in/body*) the felt, sensed, and experienced world of the child. The presence of more and more "dead" animal bodies in science classrooms as students "progress" through the system is emblematic of this disengagement, alongside the noticeable reduction in field outings and naturalistic observations of living creatures. Likewise, the tendency to abject the biological livingness of student bodies is evident in the gradual disregard of aesthetics and comfort in classroom environments as one moves "up" the ladder of education. Just compare the carpeting, overstuffed chairs, colors and art of kindergartens with most high school or university classrooms, which tend to be dominated by varying shades of grey on hard plastic and arborite. Students are *scaffolded*—in Bruner's (1983, 60) description of apprenticed learning—progressively out of their bodies and senses, to be graduated with time into an abstract, disembodied state in which sensory experience, aesthetics and pleasure become irrelevant.

As a consequence, by the time student teachers complete their training and return to classrooms to teach, they have been conditioned "out of their senses" and the assumption is ingrained that nature is something that transpires outside classrooms. The void created by the disembodiment of what is living in classrooms is filled with an obsessive preoccupation with technologies well beyond their limited pragmatic applications in elementary and even secondary education. Technologies have emerged in human culture largely to take the place of human bodily (and now mental, with computers) parts, services, and functions, and in this respect can be considered abstractions—models, designs—of bodies and mental capacities fashioned into inanimate machinery. Likewise, as students pass through the education system and have to negotiate more technologies, they themselves become disembodied institutional "*subjects*" where they were once integrated (objective-subjective), sensing, and feeling human body-minds. Yet, to be human *is* to be of the natural world...like *humus*, the earth...it is with us even as we reach into the abstract, socialized and technological world of human culture. This "humus" is abjected biologically in the treatment of living bodies and the senses in classrooms, but so too is it abjected phenomenologically when knowledge becomes disembodied from experience and excessively, frenetically consumed as unlived bits of *abstract* "information."

Abjecting Girls-As-Nature from the Scientific World

Beyond the obvious demonstration of force applied against me in my grade six science experience, there is evidence of a more subtle coercion—to accept a certain scientific world view and its accompanying ethic. Part of the stereotypes girls have to live with is that they are "squeamish." In this case, my squeamishness came from neither wishing to witness nor to support one sentient being killing and eating another. From the perspective of the science teacher, it may have appeared as if I was resisting a "law" of nature—living beings eat and are eaten. Yet this "law" is used to bolster as "natural" a competitive and aggressive patriarchal norm projected on nature and natural history, reinforcing the notion that we have "survived" because we have killed off or succeeded at the expense of other species and individuals. What this presentation of nature neglects are the deep roots of cooperation and love that secure survival and wellbeing, and nowhere more than in the human species. As Maturana (1997, 1999) suggests, women appear to have assumed a greater role in cultivating cooperation and love in human biological history (e.g., in child rearing), and so our experience and conditioning may lead us to experience nature differently. The squeamishness I and other girls experience may arise from an ethical instinct or inclination—a feeling of repugnance at harming others. Even noted female scientists (e.g., Candace Pert 1999) have recounted feeling squeamish when killing and dissecting creatures during their early laboratory training, but pressures to conform to Science as a discipline led them to suppress such discomfort. Regardless of their origins, such feelings are worth conserving in children for ethical reasons, to help to remedy the desensitization to life suggested by youth violence and suicide.

In my case, I attempted to resist the aforementioned lesson—a lesson I understood to be about controlling and killing nature—by closing my eyes. Nonetheless, I did in fact learn aversion for insects, and consequently how to abject and even kill them. Such is the power of situated learning—we learn our environment whether or not we want to—even when we steadfastly ignore it and make great efforts to keep it out of sight. In the ensuing years, I developed an insect phobia toward hard-shelled insects and bugs and would beg my father and others to remove or kill any bugs that approached me. The phobia was so severe that in a grade ten biology class, the context no doubt significant, I began crying in terror when one winter day I looked down and found a big bug resting on my torso. It was only in my early twenties when I went to live in a village in Crete that I healed the fear by holding wood lice in the palm of my hand. In this way, I began to feel genuine affection for these bugs and, with time, extended this feeling to include other insects.

An Eco-feminist Perspective

My story demonstrates how certain aspects of the sentience of nature (e.g., the suffering of the butterfly), human feelings, and the sensibilities of women in particular can be disregarded in scientific culture. Indeed, a growing body of contemporary feminist and historical literature identifies ways in which nature became equated with women while significant aspects of rational culture became masculinized (e.g., de Beauvoir 1952; Haraway 1991; Kristeva 1987; Massey 1985; Merchant 1983; Noble 1992). In this body of criticism the prevailing thesis is that women share with nature some fundamental forms of oppression within contemporary society. The eco-feminist view integrates strands of constructivist and essentialist feminist positions by recognizing, according to Ynestra King (1989, 23),

> that although the nature-culture dualism is a product of culture,
> we can nonetheless *consciously choose* not to sever the woman-nature
> connection by joining male culture. Rather, we can use it as a
> vantage point for creating a different kind of culture and politics
> that would integrate intuitive, spiritual, and rational forms of
> knowledge, embracing both science and magic insofar as they
> enable us to transform the nature-culture distinction...

Feminist analyses of the domination of women-as-nature tend to identify science as one principal agent of the shared oppression of women and nature (e.g., Merchant 1983; Harding 1991; Noble 1992). These authors have systematically critiqued science from their diverse perspectives, both as an instrumental rationalist project with in/human practices and as a history characterized by exclusion and domination. Indeed, feminists and environmentalists constitute two of the principal contemporary sources of social and political opposition to science, and, alongside post-structuralism, serve as its principal intellectual opposition as well. There is, of course, substantial and significant overlap between the feminist and environmentalist communities, as is explicitly the case in eco-feminism and implicitly suggested by the gendering of the environmental movement.

As the gap between eco/feminists and the scientific establishment deepens and becomes more public, the scientific community itself is beginning to acknowledge gender integration as a major challenge facing their field in the coming century. This is being echoed within the scientific establishment itself, as when Nobel laureate Dr. Michael Smith (1998, 22-23), reflecting on the Swiss plebiscite to ban genetic engineering, commented: "Schatz...makes a very thought provoking observation. And that is that the science establishment is male dominated and that the role of highly educated and prominent Swiss women in opposing genetic engineering suggests that 'increasing female leadership in science is essential to ensure acceptance of science by the public'." Dr. Smith cautioned that this calls for more than co-opting women into the discipline; it demands that the scientific establishment change its culture and practices in significant ways to accommodate women's difference, which he identified as being more cooperative and less competitive and aggressive.

Many eco/feminist intellectuals have concentrated their critiques of science on instrumental rationalism in particular. Val Plumwood (1990, 18) called for

> a reconceptualization of the human side of the human/nature
> dualism, to free it from the legacy of rationalism...Also in need
> of reconceptualization is the underside of this dualism, the
> concept of nature, which is construed in polarized terms as
> bereft of qualities appropriated to the human side, as passive and
> lacking in agency and teleology, as pure materiality, pure body,
> or pure mechanism."

Similarly, deep "ecologists" like Neil Evernden (1985) argue that ecology itself, as a rational science, has conserved the separation between humans and nature in a manner that has perpetuated some of the problems behind the current environmental crisis. He calls for a more phenomenological approach to the study of the complex relationships between the purportedly human and natural worlds. This approach would examine our felt and experienced relations with nature, including with our own bodies, and how we can significantly shift the way we construct our identity and, ultimately, actions with respect to nature. This, in turn, requires an understanding of the roots of social domination, because, as King (1989, 24) points out, "without a thorough feminist analysis of social domination that reveals the interconnected roots of misogyny and hatred of nature, ecology remains an abstraction: it is incomplete."

III. Towards a Women- and Nature-Friendly Education

In my own life, the healing of my insect phobia came when I interrupted my university studies to travel to rural and semi-rural locales to practice Buddhism. This provided me with sufficient calm, concentration, and awareness to begin to sense the dissociation—and dislocation—from my body, sensory experience and the natural world. Through training in Buddhist meditation and analytical reflection, I cultivated mindfulness and examined experiences that revealed my conditioned patterns of thinking and feeling about the world. It was not that I didn't experience desire and aversion any longer, but that I discovered a space of refuge where such feelings and thoughts could arise without necessarily compelling me to act. No longer buttressed by forces of attraction and aversion, I learned to see the world for what it is—to see a bug as a bug, and awfully small at that! In turn, Buddhist practices of compassion and loving-kindness gave me the courage and direction to include these creatures in the sphere of my care and concern.

When I returned to complete my undergraduate studies with a rekindled interest in biology, I enrolled in various neurological psychology and, later, pre-medicine courses. These efforts proved, however, short-lived, for some of the same reasons that I rejected my childhood lesson in science. First, I soon discovered that to pursue my interest in neurology would require that I mutilate a considerable number of rats in the process, if not cats or monkeys. When I raised this concern with my professor, he answered by confessing to intentionally and sadistically harming rats in his lab as a graduate student. So, my interest shifted to the seemingly more benign science of medicine, where in Biology 100 one morning thousands of dead swallows were presented to us in buckets so that each of us—whether elective, premedical, or general science students—could dissect one bird on our own. No efforts were made to encourage us to observe such birds in the wild, leading to the spectre of students knowing more of the wing structures of birds than of their ability to fly. Indeed, at the time, there was only one course that involved any fieldwork in the entire undergraduate biology program.

Of course, part of the problem may be situating the study of natural phenomena within the discipline of science in the first place. Instead, nature studies might be better accommodated in the fields of literature, writing, drama, and physical education, where more accommodation is made for experiential engagement with nature. In another vein, educators could benefit from relying on non-scientific experts to glean understanding of nature—ethical or religious leaders such as HH the Dalai Lama or Father Thomas Berry, or naturalists and nature writers like Annie Dillard or Gary Snyder. Even more important may be the inclusion of learning activities to educate children's awareness of their own bodies, senses, and experiences as part of the natural world. The difficulty with such strategies is that they may not significantly shift the political landscape where science holds a privileged position in the public for validating knowledge. In this role, it exerts considerable power over decision-making about our collective treatment of "nature," from the fate of fish to birthing practices to the forcible restraint and medication of persons undergoing unconventional experiences. So long as science is the lens through which knowledge about "nature" is legitimated, then it is in all our interests to address the exclusion of communities and perspectives from the discipline and education of science.

While women have suffered from being equated with nature (Merchant 1983), they have been historically marginalized from the study and field of science, where so many decisions concerning the fate of nature tend to be negotiated. Exacerbating this is the fact that science has exorcised the personal and subjective from the object-as-such, and accordingly became structured to resist the interests of people who prefer a personal, felt subjective experience. In this respect, we might ask: What might the study of life (i.e., biology) look like if women participated equally?...if other cultures participated equally? One vision is offered in *Women Look at Biology Looking at Women* (Hubbard, Henifen, and Fried 1979, 209):

> Science is a human construct that came about under a particular
> set of historical conditions when *men's* domination of nature
> seemed a positive and worthy goal. The conditions have changed
> and we know now that the path we are travelling is more likely
> to destroy nature than to explain or improve it. Women have
> recognized more often than men that we are part of nature and
> that its fate is in human hands that have not cared for it well. We
> must now act on that knowledge.

The issue at stake is not restricted to integrating women and nature into scientific communities. More important is the need to integrate more effectively those marginalized aspects of women and nature within modern and scientific culture's norms and values, and hence to make those qualities accessible to members of our society at large. This vision promises to develop whole human beings recognized as constituted within an unbroken continuum of nature and culture. As currently practiced, education drives us to *abstraction*, not just *distraction*, and is organized to scaffold children's attention progressively away from sensory experiences towards a more disembodied and abstract literate and conceptual world. I in no way intend to vilify abstract thinking and literacy. Instead, my aim is to encourage more integration between sensory and conceptual knowing, to enhance and enrich rather than suppress our connection to nature (i.e., the body, sensation, identification and connection with animals). As it is, abstract thought and literacy are viewed, re/presented and taught as superior to direct experience, with the possible exception of those experiences that are empirically controlled and measured.

At root is the question of trusting what lies outside our conscious control. Abstract culture has constructed a view of nature that perpetuates a sense of mistrust and danger towards what is natural (including our own bodies, hence our mother's bodies, and hence women). Science has constructed a story of our history that is biased as all stories are by the experiences and views of the authors. In a recent *Scientific American* (January 2000) cover story on evolution, for instance, only one identifiable woman and girl were depicted in over 46 representations of hominids. The article itself reflects a similar gendered bias in its focus on the production of tools as the principal cause of our species' advantage, purportedly leading to the extermination of competing hominid species. As if an afterthought, the article concludes with a paragraph identifying language and symbolic culture as somehow complicit in this violence. Such a gendered account of human "natural" history has tended to bolster the view that human survival depends on technology, competition and aggression—i.e., on eating and avoiding being eaten—for which women could be seen in a disadvantaged position. It ignores the fact that through evolution, female hominids (human or otherwise) began to have sex outside of physiologically determined cycles, and that children remained with their mothers for extended periods of time, thereby creating the social circumstances to foster language development. Love, more than aggression, and a love evolving within natural relations (rather than through technologies) may have been the key to the evolution of distinctly human characteristics (Maturana 1999). This is a narrative line that is only possible to arrive at when women are included in the story of our natural history, which is itself more assured when women are included as authors of the story (i.e., as scientists).

The story that our history and species evolved on the basis of an aggressive application of technological culture tends to normalize human violence. It also reiterates the sense that nature, simultaneously one's own body and sensation yet "other" to what is deemed human, is an unsafe, mistrustful place, driving us to technology for refuge." In this manner, scientific culture and education as both contents and practices have facilitated the abjection of nature. If, instead, science education started with the assumption that loving, cooperative relations played a significant role in the unique evolutionary differentiation that gave rise to human beings, this might alter dramatically the way we perceive the world, our species, and our own bodies: as loving, rather than aggressive, violent "places." Such is the view of the neurobiologist Maturana (1997, 9) who suggested, "Children are born in the biology of love. They are not born 'defenseless,' as one may be tempted to say in our patriarchal culture in which all relations are seen as aspects of a struggle for existence. Children are born in trust, in the operationality of trust...."

The squeamishness I experienced and expressed in my science classrooms might well have been an attempt to protect this biological space of trust and love. It is my hope that this essay has at least hinted at the more subtle effects of the way we treat human and animal bodies in classrooms. If so, the task now is to re-imagine a science education and education of values that would support, cultivate, and "draw out" children's love and pleasure of animals and the human body, including their own. This re-imagined education would include more outdoor education, and more education to control the *quality* rather than contents of experience—e.g., mindfulness, ethics, and attention and skills in observation and questioning. Furthermore, such an education of attention needs to extend to include the lived experiences we carry in our own memories, which continue to impact so significantly the way we view natural "others," our own bodies, and learning in general. Such an education of attention asks us to attend to all those diverse butterflies living on in our body-minds long after their predators have passed. Only in healing ourselves, and discovering our own love and trust of the natural world, can we hope to mend others and the world we share as home.

References

Bruner, J. S. 1983. *Child's talk: Learning to use language.* New York: Norton.

de Beauvoir, Simone. 1952. *The second sex.* Translated by H.M. Parshley. New York: Bantam.

Dewey, John. [1916] 1944. *Democracy and education: An introduction to the philosophy of education.* New York: Simon and Schuster.

Evernden, Neil. 1985. *The natural alien: Humankind and environment.* Toronto: University of Toronto Press.

Haraway, Donna. 1991. *Simians, cyborgs, and women: The reinvention of nature.* New York: Routledge.

Harding, Sandra. 1991. *Whose science? Whose knowledge? Thinking from women's lives.* Ithaca, NY: Cornell University Press.

Hubbard, R., M. Henifen, and B. Fried, eds. 1979. *Women look at biology looking at women: A collection of feminist critiques.* Cambridge, MA: Schenkman.

King, Ynestra. 1989. The ecology of feminism and the feminism of ecology. In *Healing the Wounds: The promise of ecofeminism,* edited by Judith Plant. Toronto: Between the Lines.

Kristeva, Julia. 1982. *Powers of horror: An essay on abjection.* New York: Columbia University Press.

Kristeva, Julia. 1983/87. *Tales of love.* New York: Columbia University Press.

Maturana, Humberto. 1997. Biological foundations of morals and ethics in education. Unpublished paper.

Maturana, Humberto. 1999. Lecture notes. Schumacher College course, UK, March.

Massey, Marilyn Chapin. 1985. *Feminine soul: The fate of an ideal.* Boston: Beacon Press.

Merchant, Carolyn. 1983. *The death of nature: Women, ecology, and the scientific revolution.* New York: Harper Collins.

Noble, David. 1992. *A world without women: The Christian clerical culture of western science.* Oxford: Oxford University Press.

Oliver, Kelly. 1993. *Reading Kristeva: Unraveling the double-bind.* Bloomington, IN: Indiana University Press.

Pert, Candace. 1999. *Molecules of emotion: The science behind mind-body medicine.* New York: Simon and Schuster.

Plumwood, Val. 1990. Nature, self, and gender: Feminism, environmental philosophy, and critique of rationalism. *Hypatia: Special issue on ecological feminism* 6(1): 3-27.

Rich, Adrienne. 1995. *Dark fields of the republic: Poems 1991–1995.* New York: Norton.

Smith, Michael. 1998. Killam Lecture. Presented at the AGM of the Killam Trust, Vancouver, British Columbia, Canada.

Ecological Interplay— Humans/Nature in Freefall

Dia(log)ing peels the bark off conversation
Stripping the fibers for words
Re-con(text)ualizing carbon for ink spots
a languaging of tree/world.

(Johnna, March 2000)

Ecological Interplay—Humans/Nature in Freefall

Ecological Interplay

...[T]raditional theories have separated life from nature, mind
from organic life, and thereby created mysteries.... Since both
the inanimate and the human environment are involved in the
functions of life, it is inevitable, if these functions evolve to the
point of thinking and if thinking is naturally serial with biological
functions, that it will have as the material of thought, even of its
erratic imaginings, the events and connections of this environment.
(Dewey 1929, 227)

Johnna: This quote from John Dewey illustrates an important emphasis of this book: the notion of ecological interplay. Ecological interplay requires us to move beyond the breathlessness that we experience as we re-circulate in life's holes. In other words, we often prefer to stay in the familiar (life's holes) instead of risking the unknown. I came upon this notion of a hole when I was stuck upside-down in my kayak in a surfing hole (where water pours over a rock) in the middle of a river last summer.

So the notion of interplay relates to a connection—a passion for living and breathing deeply. Allowing this sense of connectedness to emerge means allowing oneself to encounter the unexpected. Earlier in our first conversation I briefly introduced the term *freefall*. I use this to describe pedagogical possibilities that embrace the emergent, unexpected happenings that occur while paddling the rivers of life. We need to open our chests and smell the earth bringing body, mind and spirit noticeably alive. "Living is a way of being, where worlds unfold, and we push into the unknown, welcoming its unmarked slippery paths" (Haskell 2000, xvi). The continuity embodied in the uncertainties of knowing emerge in our experiencing through the world and with/in education. The following chapters embrace imag(e)inings of text that allow us to enter into an interplay of ecological interstandings and to embody theorizing.

Warren: Your prompting about a "continuity embodied in the uncertainties of knowing" that "emerge in our experiencing through the world" and education brings to life an important knowing that I wrote about in 1997 during our Enactivism and Education class the three of us took together.

As arranged, all of the students met at the head of the trail on the outskirts of campus in the midst of an old-growth forest. One by one they followed each other into the forest. I remember the long line of graduate students ahead of me walking down one of the paths. I was at the end of the line and was struck by the speed of the walking. The previous week I had just finished a 73 km journey over 6 days through mud, ocean flats, and across streams on the West Coast Trail, another path. I remember going through some particularly muddy sections, marveling at the ocean landscapes, the roaring surf, the gray whales just offshore. My companions had been just ahead of me, slowly making their way through large wet swampy mud holes. Now, having returned to the city, all I remember is their backs. The pace of this UBC group amazed me. I gradually fell back and watched this line of humans, in lockstep, each person looking at a back in front of them, in a steady pace, almost at the speed of a march. Did this group of students only stop and look around them once in a while, then move on again?

We come to a crossroads. The group turns right; I go left.

The chattering recedes off in the distance, replaced by chirps of birds and the silence of the green West Coast forest. I begin to smell the earth, watch the trees, and listen to the sounds. No longer aware of the rumble of cars not half a mile away, I became immersed in a solitude, which, if I am willing to be patient, "like a long love, deepens with time" (Sarton 1977, 14).

Alone in the forest. The rapidly scurrying line (of students led by one professor on a breakneck pace for...)

had gone ahead of me.

Moments pass.

Meandering along the forested trail

into that moment, between happiness at being alone and the desire to be part of the group that I had left/had left me, came a *squee ek*. I turned back to try and determine the source of the sound.

squee ek,

squee ek

I stop

squee ek, squee ek

It is an odd sound I have not heard before.
I see C O M I N G Toward Me a mountain cyclist.
Who may be the source of this sound.
  (*It sounds like a whoopee cushion*)
(*or an infant's plastic squeeze toy*)

squee ek, squee ek

Perhaps it is the sound of a rusty saddle...or his bell ringing his presence to me. As he passes, the sound does not change in volume or pitch like the sound of a train would make when it approaches, passes by me, and goes off into the distance. There is a runner behind him, gasping and panting as he sweats his way through a post-work jog. Could it be his running shoes? The sound of feet softly hitting dirt?

All these thoughts occur in the brief seconds of puzzlement I feel as I listen to this unfamiliar sound. There

Up in the tree

A squirrel, four small feet, gripping the trunk, then moving up.

squee ek, squee ek

I had stopped there a long second ago to examine a small beetle scurrying amongst the needles strewn on the forest floor. I had heard its tiny feet as it traversed the path. The squirrel had been there then but had not made a sound. It was only, I concluded, as the cyclist and runner had approached that the squirrel had made its plaintive squeaks. Why had I tried to categorize that sound? To attribute it to human/machine origins?

Earlier I had heard another squeak; one sounding like a woodpecker or a tree rubbing against its neighbor. There again. Categorization. Labels. Cataloguing my experience.

Brent: Pinpointing desire and curiosity
                    to worlds beyond our own
                    Worlds of shift and flow
                    carrying us with them.

                    We reach, hands extended
                    trying to stop movement
                    So we might catch our ground
                    A ground that reassures
                    but eludes.

                    A walk in a forest
                    is full of grounded
                    and ungrounded worlds
                    Worlds of Squirrelness
                    and Cyclists,
                    Categories and Labels.

Johnna: Our inquiries into and interpretation of experiencing are often thought of as a categorization or labeling. What happens while experiencing the squeak of the invisible? Are we "in fact" trying to fixate the squeak, interstand the squeak, or to embody an awareness of the squeak? How do we breathe in the sounds of the forest while participating with a community in the making? Instead of trying to grasp an ultimate ground, groundlessness is revealed "in knowing how to negotiate our way through a world that is not fixed and pregiven but that is continually shaped by the types of actions in which we engage" (Varela, Thompson, and Rosch 1991, 144).

Warren: Ted Aoki (1991) refers to a "knowing known bodily," which is different from the more logical knowing that knows action only as description. Knowing known bodily

in that moment   of listening to what I heard in the forest;
in the moment   between me hearing the sound

       before I started to categorize what I was hearing;

in that moment   of tension where the sound spoke to me;

that momentary stretching into a taut tenseness the world surrounding me
       resonates within me to this day.

Ted talks of how we have become beholden to our eyes. He wonders
if our enchantment with the eyes limits our horizons.

Couldn't I just "be" with that squirrel *squee ek*, avoiding the
temptation to look beyond it for an explanation?

He calls for a polyphonic curriculum that de-centers vision by allowing a
legitimate place for sound;

the sounds of the squirrel *squee ek* and the rusty seat;

the sounds of the runner's breath and the beetle's scurry;

the sound of our blood rushing adrenaline as the clock nears twelve.

I had been trying to perceive what I was seeing and, in the attempt, making it more difficult to perceive. Questing precision preventing achievement of that preciseness.

I look up, up, way up. I see hear feel breathe more. "Alone" (though not alone as the world accompanied me) out there in the forest, lost from the group I had begun this journey with, enabling me to experience

Squee ek Squee ek

Scurry Scurry

Up
the
Tree

There is a moment of fear. Where has the group gone? Where am I? Lost in this reverie, or lost on the trail? No matter.

I make my way towards the sounds of the city. I reach the street and cross over to the parking lot where I await the rest of the class.

Brent: Your story of this outdoor hike from our Enactivism and Education course catches my eye and my curiosity. I want to connect it with Johnna's description of freefall as moving from the familiar into the unknown. I too shared the walk into the forest with you, Warren, with you, Johnna, and with our classmates. I remember feeling as if I were marching in grand procession, an army of centipedes trudging through the wilderness. Could it be that this path was a little too well-known, so well trod by other human feet that it prevented us from striding freely?... Instead, it seemed to carry us into

A
perfect line
like
the letters of
the alphabet
Straight backs and
rounded stomachs
set off against one another
Telephone poles
along a dusty wheat field.

Or did the difficulty lie in our expectations for the walk? Urban creatures that we are, we tend to assume that a walk in "nature" will bring us into contact with new bodies. But those we encountered—the cyclists and joggers—were of the human variety. Perhaps the wilderness we were seeking was further afield than we would have liked.

Why do we need to leave well-trod trails in order to find our humanness? Is it because we have forgotten how to live with our surrounding environments? Have we, in our drive to become technologically "literate," abrogated the senses as vital sources of knowing?

Like walking trails, the paths we encounter in the classroom often direct our focus away from the senses into places of abstraction where computers have replaced primordial forms of bodily contact. I wonder how our perception might take in living bodies, so that the very acts of knowing/interplay might become, in Johnna's words, opportunities for freefall?

Johnna: Maybe we are not used to classrooms in/around the outdoors. How do we interact with, choose to participate in, and perceive the classrooms of ecological interplay? How do we interstand human/nature relationships? Can we pay attention to nature within/around outdoor educational environments or within our environments of learning/living?

Visitors From Nature

The other day, a huge bumblebee with a bright orange abdomen came flying in and out of my closet and the bathroom and began

BuZZing

around my naked ankles. The bee soon found the window again and I opened it wide to allow it back outside.

Yesterday, a bird perched right outside my window looking in at me for a bit before flying off to its calling mate. I was playing music loudly. Could she hear it from her perch? Is this what attracted her? Now I sit in front of my computer with heart beating. I assume it was my little friend from yesterday, a house finch with red head and neck, coming in my other window and proceeding to

H

O

P

from plant to plant while calling its partner to come in and check things out. She likes the plant sitting atop the light fixture on the wall.

Then she tries to fly out of my room. I wonder if she will remember her entrance or perceive the window as open air. Dizzy...

from hitting the window
and all in a fluster about where to go, she finally perches up on a ledge of the window frame, calling her friend.

I smoothly walk over and move a hanging plant and open the window wide again. With a burst of energy she starts smashing into the window again.

Ping...

ping.

The finch and I can hear all the noises from the outside world, including that of her mate flying outside the window. This time she ends up on the window ledge just inches from the opening. I watch, as she seems stunned at first. I don't dare move from my seat—wanting to remain quiet while she rests. We look at each other for quite some time, she blinking her eyes, confused. I keep silently urging her to listen to the sounds outside the window. She hops up onto the window bottom and flies out to a white birch tree. She stays there for a long time; I suppose recovering from her wildly beating heart, the stunned dizziness of pounding into a window, and the panic of trying to reach her mate.

I wanted to freeeeze...

my memory and the intense passion in my own wildly beating heart, to bring back those blinking eyes and little chirps of energy.

Experiencing Freefall[1]

Johnna: Freefall moments are those we experience that "stop familiar interaction and provide freshness to perception" (Haskell 2000, 19). In trying to articulate my notion of experiencing as groundless flow, I recall an excerpt from my dissertation (Haskell 2000, xix):

> In my research, I focus on the phenomena of "experiencing" which is not a fixed event, but actions flowing in a continuously unfolding process.... I use the active word "experiencing" as introduced by Dewey (1929) in *Experience and Nature*. He indicates that the shift in emphasis from what is experienced to the embodied relational ways of experiencing opens capacities for perceiving "unattained possibilities" (p. 151) and promoting respect for the potentialities of human experience (p. 36). He argues that the process of experiencing such as breathing[,] which includes an interaction of both air and the function of the lungs[,] cannot be separated (p. 13). It is this notion of object-subject separation that we come to believe and accept in education through [its] traditions and habituations, which Dewey's theory of experiencing attempts to bring into question so that we may welcome the unknown, invisible and ineffable of experiencing.

Warren: It is interesting that Dewey wrote all this in the early part of the 1900s. Dewey said in his book *Art and Experience* that, "experience occurs continuously, because the interaction of live creature and environing conditions is involved in the very process of living" (1934, 35).

I have a friend now in his late 60s whose father as a teacher in Michigan in the 1930s was heavily influenced by Dewey's philosophy. My friend tells me that Dewey was considered quite controversial at the time. His ideas may have temporarily lost some of their appeal with the growing popularity of behaviorist learning theories. It is interesting, therefore, to note the resurgence today of similar philosophies that connect to Dewey's. It's not that Dewey's ideas on experience were necessarily all-encompassing...but their renewal (at least in part) converges with ideas re-emerging with/in the social and environmental conditions in which we are living today. It is also the type of philosophies that have evolved within these contexts to allow us to revisit Dewey's thinking.

Johnna: Dewey's thinking is consistent with interstandings of ecological interplay. In this volume such interplays embrace bodily experiencing, re-experiencing (reflection), and languaging. Franc Feng, for example, inquires into our connectedness with nature through a critique of colonial practices while David Jardine opens us to the suffering of the human condition, earthly relationships, and the importance of classroom "placefulness." Lyubov Laroche offers us a holographic vision for connecting classrooms/humans with the universe. My chapter shows how some students' learning through outdoor adventure education become aware of their connections through interactions as well as embodying a respect for the flesh of the world. Brent Hocking's chapter brings forth an ecological vision that presents the need for a shift in understanding of renewal as a site for pedagogic inquiry. Writers in this section offer their own languages and texts of ecological interplay and freefall.

Warren: The authors in these last readings, though they might not all be aware of Dewey's philosophy, are part of that renewal of similar ideas. While Brent is emphasizing renewal, Johnna is inquiring into the phenomena of experiencing and the embodied respect that emerges in outdoor adventure education classrooms.

I also remember Brent Davis and Dennis Sumara speaking a few years ago at UBC about a project they had undertaken with a school near Vancouver. They worked with the teachers and parents and students at this school for quite some time, starting to make a new path together. The project ended. A few years later they returned to the school to see what happened in the intervening years. The interesting part for them was that, not only had the work continued, but the thinking, ideas and questions that were emerging amongst the people they had worked with five years before were similar to what Brent and Dennis were now thinking and doing in their own separate teaching work.

This is what I am reflecting on when I think about Dewey and how, when I read Dewey, I am amazed at how he could have been writing today about the same things we are writing about here.

Brent: Dewey's thinking illustrates how living bodies become the environments of which they are part. In other words, we take on the qualities of other bodies with whom we interact.

This explains why family members, lovers, and twins often seem to orient themselves to the world in very similar ways. Their biologies as well as their manners of living have become embedded in particular networks of relationship—ecological niches—that bind them together. Another example of this twinning has been reported by transplant patients who describe acquiring the tastes and personal dispositions of their donors (See, for example, Sylvia 1997). In all of these instances bodies evolve in concert with the environments that nurture and engage them.

Johnna: Our flesh has been disconnected from place for so long that we must breathe deeply so that we may ward off the penetrating fear of theories that bridge connections with the environment. What is important for me is the continuity of the ecology of nature through, for example, the air we breathe. Fortunately, Lyubov Laroche offers us an example of such a holographic view of the human body/world and the renewal of human relationships through teaching science education.

Warren: We shouldn't forget that we breathe with our whole body—with our arms, our legs, our feet, even though our lungs take a leading role in the process. In other words, our breath is part of our interacting with and becoming the world. We are always breathing, always contributing to the ecology of the world. We are part of the world, yet we are not always aware of it.

Brent: This notion of total engagement was central to the work of Gregory Bateson, someone we have not discussed, but whose thinking anticipated many contemporary interstandings of bodymind. In his work, *Steps to An Ecology of Mind*, he drew on the example of a man cutting down a tree (1972, 317) to show how different bodily systems interact with one another. In order to bring down a tree different kinds of thought processes and muscular actions must be engaged. We are now saying that not only are there interactive networks *within* the body, but also across living systems in general.

Embracing Freefall

Brent: As important as the notion of freefall is to education, it seems far removed from what actually happens in many classrooms. Many educators have come to believe that education is primarily about learning goals, programs, and outcomes. In learning theory, for example, educational discussions have shifted between theories that privilege human behavior to those that privilege mental "constructs" and, more recently, to theories that focus on social contexts and interactions. Our lives as educators and human beings are full of these typologies. If we are to interstand ecological interplay, we need to let go of our tendency to separate theory, practice, and classrooms from "real" life.

Warren: I think it is more than theories. I think it is also the ways in which we *are* in the world. We can say all we want about ourselves being part of the environment. But our theories of separation are connected to a history of disconnectedness while at the same time, a history of connecting. Yin and Yang, Back and Forth.

Brent: Note the ways in which even our senses of relationship are cast into language as connectedness or *dis*connectedness. We have come to believe that we are either *in* the world or *outside* it—in much the same ways we have come to understand structures. As a people, we language ourselves in and out of experience instead of allowing the kind of freefall dynamic that we discussed earlier.

I also find the connection between freefall and inter "play" to be an interesting one. The French word for "inter"—*entre*—is not only a preposition, but an imperative verb that is a type of command or order, meaning "Come in!" For me, the notion of interplay is less dialectical than it is a form of polyphony—an overlayering of sounds that come together as one composition. When we encounter bodies we need to find a way to orchestrate our freefall with theirs. This, I think, is the challenge for thinking bodies in and out of the classroom: to learn how to dance with other freefalling bodies. This is what distinguishes a dynamic theory of interplay from efforts to ground experience through our thinking and actions.

Warren: But in moments of freefall there had better be someone on the ground, serving as an anchor, ensuring that I will survive if something goes wrong.

I remember taking a mountain climbing course years ago. One of the classes was held on some cliffs and boulders just off the British Columbia Railway tracks north of Vancouver. There I was climbing a boulder, pressing my fingertips onto the pebbled surfaces of the rock as I inched my way upward. I was secured in my journey by someone who was belaying me below. This was a total stranger whom I had only just met but was entrusting completely. I was also gradually learning to trust the rock, which to the untrained eye looked like a slick surface that could never be climbed. It was the interplay of the rock, its pebbled surfaces, the belayer and my own embodied trusting that ensured my journey to the top. I guess what I am saying is that freefall can only occur when there is an intertwined network of relations that will support my fall.

Johnna: When is there not an interaction, or something there? Is this an anchoring or a grounding? I think freefall occurs all the time but when it becomes familiar, we need to take a risk to embody awareness of intertwined living relations. We may need to embrace the groundlessness of emergent unexpected happenings that occur through moments of freefall.

Brent: You talk about trusting "a network of relations," Warren, but I wonder how many of us are able to trust that which is invisible and often unfathomable? Many mountain climbers seem to rely on the intricate planning and know-how that precedes an expedition. They realize the need to be humble in the face of more-than-human challenges, but they often attempt to anticipate their journey as much as possible. There is a lesson in this for educators. Teachers are notorious for overplanning and forecasting what might happen in the course of their interactions within a classroom. I would argue that engaged relations are too fluid to predict. What we can learn to do, however, is to move with their choreographies as they emerge before our eyes.

Warren: Richard Mitchell (1983), in his wonderful book *Mountain Experience*, characterizes planning as both creation and calculation. It is a process of "fantasy and dream, of imaginatively constructing future and potential experience" (p. 3). It is also forecasting, as you mentioned, in that there is an enumeration of possible outcomes and preparation for contingencies. But that forecasting is based on the experiences of the mountaineer and involves preparation for contingencies of weather and terrain and the teamwork necessary to summit.

Secondly, I take it you are speaking as someone who hasn't climbed. Even in my limited experience of climbing in that course I realized that I was beginning to trust my body, my partners, and my relation with the rock. I hadn't taken the course in order to take up the sport of climbing but to learn to trust myself in the outdoors, to become comfortable with the unpredictable and to know, in an integrated way, the skills required to live with the unfathomable, what might be just around the corner, be it a grizzly bear, an unforeseen storm, or broken equipment.

Around the same time I took an outdoor survival course. Again I didn't take it to prove myself in the outdoors but to learn the skillful trusting that enabled me to realize I could "survive" in the outdoors if I had to, if some unforeseen, invisible, unknown event happened. I remember our instructor, a former Outward Bound leader, who kept talking about the outdoor survival course being about learning to see the wilderness as a place we could live with/in with healthy respect, not as some dark unknown that we had to fear or overcome.

My experiencing of these things was a form of immersion, diving into the world of rock climbing in all its splendor; then resurfacing, traveling, re-immersing.

Johnna: Embracing moments of freefall is very much like embracing rock climbing moves. While balancing on nubbins of rock with each foot and one hand on a tiny fingernail indent in the rock, the other hand searches ("no, this won't do"), feels, tries another spot to only finally make a choice to use that minute handhold to move upward. The risk of moving upward is never planned or forecasted, but embodied through the action, the groundless embrace of the emergent, unexpected unpredictableness of inching up a rock face.

After reading all of the chapters in this book we invite you to listen to another conversation by David Abram and David Jardine. In the *Afterword* they share their thoughts about bodies of knowledge, the discovering of the body in the "thick of things" and how sharing the common flesh with the world helps regain our appreciation and fascination with that unfolding world.

Warren: So, we are back to the beginning of our conversations in this book...how we write and what we write are inextricably intertwined with the ecological interplays we are embracing.

Note

1. "Experiencing freefall" is taken from the title of Johnna's doctoral dissertation (Haskell 2000).

References

Abram, David. 1996. *The spell of the sensuous: Perception and language in a more-than-human world.* New York: Pantheon Books.

Aoki, Ted. 1991. Sonare and vidare: Questioning the primacy of the eye in curriculum talk. In *Reflections from the heart of educational inquiry: Understanding curriculum and teaching through the arts*, edited by George Willis and William Schubert. Albany, NY: State University of New York Press.

Bateson, Gregory. 1972. *Steps to an ecology of mind: Collected essays in anthropology, psychiatry, evolution, and epistemology.* San Francisco: Chandler.

Dewey, John. 1929. *Experience and nature.* 2d ed. LaSalle, IL: Open Court.

Dewey, John. 1934. *Art as experience.* New York: Capricorn Books.

Haskell, Johnna. 2000. *Experiencing freefall: A journey of pedagogical possibilities.* Ph.D. diss., University of British Columbia.

Mitchell, Richard, Jr. 1983. *Mountain experience.* Chicago: University of Chicago Press.

Sarton, Maya. 1977. *The house by the sea.* New York: Norton.

Sylvia, Claire, Bernie Siegel, and William Novak. 1997. *A change of heart: A memoir.* Boston: Little, Brown and Company.

Varela, Francisco J., Evan Thompson, and Eleanor Rosch. 1991. *The embodied mind: Cognitive science and human experience.* Cambridge, MA: MIT Press.

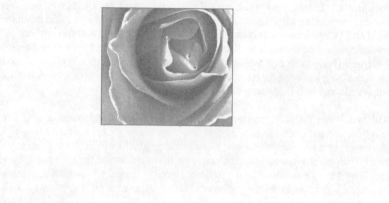

Etude in Green Minor:
On Expanding Ethics, Of Being,
Wholeness, Sentience and Compassion

Franc Feng

FRANC FENG is a doctoral student studying at the Centre for the Study of Curriculum and Instruction, in the Faculty of Education, at the University of British Columbia. His master's degree in Education focused upon the implications rather than the applications of technology, and issues of gender equity in computing, with respects to gender, learning setting, age of learning, and competency. His doctoral dissertation expands upon findings from his M.A. to investigate children's perception of the relationship between ecology, culture, and technology.

Background. The insights of the eco-cultural theorizing I am attempting here were arrived at through combining my coursework with leading postcolonial anti-racist scholars like Ted Aoki and Peter McLaren, and eco-theorists like Chet Bowers, and those of my own postcolonial interpretations of disparate works from social and ecological literature. Although I have been publishing for some time, this contribution represents the first time my theorizing has been coalesced as a chapter within a holistic book on education, sharing empirical work and theorizing of like hearts and minds.

Abstract. When my father passed away, he left a question in my mind, and an existential void that filled me with deep angst, one that was responsible for my re/turn to ecology. His/my story weaves throughout this piece like a bright green thread. In this exploratory piece, I draw upon narrative methodology to weave this green thread through my deep reflections and theorizing. Drawing upon my *subjective* lived experience as postcolonial subject, I theorize towards the possibility of a *meta-subjective*[1] postcolonial experience for all.

In so doing, I argue holism, and the holistic education it represents, must expand and be inclusive and sensitive to cultural history to connect the oppression of culture *and* nature, and healing must be theorized alongside related notions of reclaiming recovery, interconnectedness and wholeness. Moreover, since "society"*and* "nature" are both constructed categories that are intimately interconnected in "lived life," I argue for, and offer, a reconceptualization of the "crisis of modernity" (Latour 1993) as an eco-cultural crisis (Bowers 1993).[2] Drawing together disparate works of Bannerji on oppression (1995), Merchant on epistemological pluralism (1995), Bookchin on natural history (1994) and Nash on expansion of rights (1989), I posit a preliminary model of how holistic education might be reconceptualized to connect social and natural history.

Keywords: Holism, Enactivism, Ecology, Crisis], Eco-cultural, Postcolonial, Community

Acknowledgments. I dedicate this piece to my children, Jasmine and Alexander Feng-Pallot, towards the hope of a better world for them, in memory of their loving grandfather, Feng Yuen Sheng. I would also like to acknowledge my gratitude to Ted Aoki, Walter Boldt, Roger Boshier, Chet Bowers, John Brine, Mary Bryson, Graeme Chalmers, Chan Choon Hian, Jerry Coombs, Pamela Courtney-Hall, Leroi Daniels, Brent Davis, Stuart Donn, Frank Echols, Gaalen Erickson, Jim Gaskell, Hillel Goelman, Ricki Goldman-Segall, Don Fisher, Sharon Fuller, Rita Irwin, Nand Kishor, Carl Leggo, Fred Lewallen, Peter McLaren, Karen Meyer, Steve Petrina, Susan Pirie, Harold Ratzlaff, David Robitaille, Richard Rosenberg, Jim Sherrill, Willard Toliver, Allison Toms, Laurie Ricou, Leslie Roman, Bob Walker, Walt Werner, Marv Westrom, John Willinsky, Doug Wilms, Ian Wright.

Etude in Green Minor:
On Expanding Ethics,[3] Of Being, Wholeness, Sentience and Compassion

Franc Feng

I remember...[4]

I can still hear the sound of typewriter keys filling the still night air, as though in mellow accompaniment to the sounds of Chopin and Beethoven, gently coaxing shut my eyelids already heavy with thoughts that mingle amidst wakefulness and dream. There, drifting off in soft slumber, I remember reflecting on the strange way this gentle man demonstrated his deep love for us, his children, as we lived in poverty, while he struggled to write editorials to put food on our table, clothes on our backs, and shelter from the storms...

I remember him calming my fears, as he gently lowered my little brother and me onto chairs heaped upon smaller tables which themselves stood on more solid wood, even as rushing waters threatened to engulf our little family. I remember watching him bend solid bars that framed windows as he gently lowered us beyond the bent frames to the safety of helping hands as we struggled to escape the mighty ravages of the typhoon. I remember also that next day, the characteristic smell of dank books, the unmistakable odor of a scholar's library, as my father struggled to salvage his precious books, separating each page gently, in a desperate attempt to dry them under the heat of the tropical Asian sun.

I remember my father's involvement in my struggle to learn the foreign language taught in the missionary school I attended. I recall his concern while he patiently taught me the Western alphabet, even as he attempted to balance the teachings of the West with an emphasis on holism of the cosmos, morality bound in narratives, and tales of the old country. I remember him telling me that I am descended from a line of educators, and that my grandfather belonged to the first generation of Chinese scholars schooled in the ways of modernity[5] in the Western academy. I remember my father's great sacrifice in leaving the academy he loved to enter the "real" world of commerce, to care for his little family...

I recall how we eventually migrated to the West, to Canada. I remember him encouraging me to return to academia, and how my return to academia coincidentally marked the start of his brave struggles against an all-powerful force, as he fought against an invisible power that ravaged his being and his humanity. I remember my father leaving his beloved family calmly and bravely, with confused feelings of betrayal, while the life-force was slowly being robbed from him, as he succumbed to the ravages of cancer...I remember the question pursing on his lips as his confused eyes asked the same question...Why?

Holism and the Awakening of Ecological Conscience

Although it may not be immediately apparent, the threads that interweave, hold together, and lend meaning to this sad narrative[6] are highlighted by an existential, ecological worldview. Aside from an appeal through storytelling rather than logic,[7] a characteristic of holistic discourse, the personal story I am sharing is profoundly related to ecology and holism, because it traces the origins of my re/turn to ecology. I have chosen to open my paper with a narrative not only because of its powerful appeal core to holistic philosophy—this is *the* profoundly personal, existential story that provides meaning for me, and reconnects myself to the ecological imperative. This narrative provides the historical, felt backdrop as well as the lived context that creates meaning for my deep commitment to holistic education and alternate ways of knowing. It is also the deep impetus behind my belief in urgent need for healing in the reclamation of our narratives, our families, our cultures, intergenerational communication, and the earth.

The impetus which lay behind my return to holism, re-awakened ecological awareness and conscience, and the reshaping of my ecological identity (Livingston 1994; Orr 1992; Thomashow 1996) was born out of the painful, deep vacuum that emerged as I struggled, grasping for explanations behind my father's "Why" question. It was a state of being that is extremely difficult to convey, as I searched the cosmos in vain—for meaning, for reasons behind my father's untimely and violent passing. Periodically throughout my grief, as I sat beside my ailing father inside the palliative care unit of Vancouver General Hospital;[8] as he was laid to rest; in the days following when I grieved his passing; I had been reading Morris Berman's (1984) *The Reenchantment of the World.*[9] As I searched for "answers," I slowly began to realize Berman's book not only offered a "piece" of cosmic puzzle to my enigmatic question, it opened the way for direct critique of the modern world, and the day-to-day values and priorities functioning at its core. As I reflected on what Berman meant, I experienced a poignant moment. What had once been the unquestionable status of science, the ethic of consumption of modern society and its accompanying mindset, all simultaneously broke down. The import of Berman's critical words filled my innermost feelings and thoughts, and my struggle to interpret them led to what might be described as deep powerful re-awakening almost akin to a type of transcendence.

The above ontological experience that led me to deeply critique scientism, rationality, and the discourse of consumption eventually culminated in the rebirth of ecological awareness and a newfound ecological identity. It also made me realize the power of knowledge claims that rest on foundational premises based on *ontological*, rather than epistemological origins, and implications for knowing situated within a being immersed in a natural/social world. Following Smith (1987), this exemplar highlights not only the importance of locating knowing within the *lived realities* of daily living, but the power of knowledge emanating from felt lived experience. It made me posit knowing bodily, along the lines of Himani Bannerji's (1995) concept of *intersubjectivity*[10] and it made feel as though my existential search reverberated with similar resonance to Rachel Carson's (1962/1994) poignant account in *Silent Spring*.[11]

My experience also offered glimpses into what might have been Carson's deep existential angst that gave birth to our current environmental movement.[12] The core belief that underpinned my struggle for an answer to my father's question was my deep feeling that his passing had not been from "natural causes."[13] I found some validation for this belief in Carson's monumental piece of work. It was as if my feelings about my father's affliction paralleled Carson's own attempt to understand cancer, as she made a connection between an unusually silent spring, the absence of birds, the spraying of DDT, and her own mortality.[14]

Reading Berman's book, I realized the Scientific Revolution had resulted in the disenchantment of the world, the *suppression* of other ways of knowing and healing, and the loss of meaning. Berman argued society itself was sick as a result of the disenchantment at the core of scientific endeavor. It made me think that medicine which has been founded on such a dysfunctional, fragmented, distorted, non-holistic picture of nature might be incapable of putting together the puzzle to solve a force like cancer. Although Berman's book did not provide a direct answer to the deep existential question that I sought, it suggested that "acceptance" of death of one's loved ones from cancer as a consequence of modern life is profoundly problematic.

Berman's critique of a rational society spoke to my injured heart. His words took on a deep resonance, as I wondered if my father's passing was connected to being ill in a society that is embroiled in material considerations, one that conflates happiness with material goods. One motivated by false values that elevate material well-being over spiritual, bodily, and emotional well-being, where economic priorities lie elsewhere...[15] Taken to its logical extension, Berman's pronouncements were for me an ecological indictment against the interconnected global discourses of scientism, rationalism, materialism, and consumerism.[16]

The Turn Towards Culture

Berman's thesis opened the way to a critique of the modern world for me. However, I wanted more. The black mills of Industrial Revolution that blighted the countryside, I reasoned, had not been fueled only by the thinking of the Scientific Revolution, but financed by the labor of slaves and complex machinery of colonialism. I felt there was a connection between my postcolonial experience and Berman's thesis; I needed a more complete story that connected the oppression of culture to the oppression of nature, but for that extended answer I knew that I had to widen my search. I took some key courses[17] and embarked on a journey that combed the ecological literature and socio-historical arguments shaping the concept of modernity.

My above interest in philosophy was in retracing the locus of its movement from traditional formulations towards the liberal impulse paving the way for an environmental ethics and eco-philosophy that *expands* ethics to include the non-human world. It was within this vector that I discovered the lens of culture. My broad readings in ecology, cultural studies, and philosophy made me conclude that environmental studies and cultural studies can and must inform each other. To be inclusive, ecology needs to be located within an understanding of historical, social and cultural practices and processes. Cultural studies, on the other hand, needs to re/embrace ecology to shift its focus from preoccupation with production and the pleasures of consumption thesis (Fiske 1989; McKay 1997) to envirnmental sociology (Catton and Dunlap 1978; Hannigan 1995; Wackernagel and Rees 1996), and the ecological critique of modernity (Naess 1989; Merchant 1994; Bookchin 1995).[18]

The Postcolonial Contribution to Holism

My narrative, besides delving into the sense of existential angst that surrounds the loss of a loved one, began with stories of a happier time, when I was growing up and learning about my heritage and history. However, my story is not just any story, in the sense that it locates my autobiography within oral, ancient tradition, the alienation of postcolonials, and the effects of diaspora (Fanon 1963; Gandhi 1998; McLaren 1995; Said 1979). My narrative attempts to bring a postcolonial standpoint to holistic discourse,[19] a standpoint that argues, since oppression of culture has been historically tied to the oppression of nature, there can be no resolution of the ecological crisis without first taking into account the discourse of colonialism and its effect on both people and ecosystem.[20]

As indicated in the opening, when we speak of holistic discourse education, we reject Cartesian mechanism, dualism, doctrines of anthropocentric humanism, and utilitarianism that forged the picture of "man" [sic] at the center of the universe. We emphasize instead values around compassion, interconnectedness, fullness, deep ecological principles, spirituality, emotions, and body. In so doing, holistic discourse attempts to reclaim values that predated modernity. It is fitting as we re-embrace once marginalized values that we remember that suppression of these holistic ideas was historically *tied* to the suppression of cultures adhering to this alternate worldview. Otherwise, holistic discourse stands open to charges of appropriation, and even more seriously, stinging critiques and charges of racism (Ramachandra Guha 1994). This implies compassion and healing, ideas of interconnectedness and rejuvenation, and theorization of an interconnecting cosmos must be *co-problematized* with the history of colonialism. It is important for holistic discourse to emphasize this sensitivity, framed around an anti-racist and inclusive stance embracing reparation of injured bodies and psyche of marginalized postcolonial beings. Yet how might we approach such complex theorizing? One possible strategy would be to reinterpret the modern ecological crisis as an eco-cultural crisis[21] recast in natural history, in continuity with the past colonial oppression of women, non-European culture, First Nations, and nature, located within a neo-Marxist-Malthusian-cultural critique of political eco-economy.[22]

Etude in Green

My father loved etudes. This piece *is* my etude for him in green minor. The above heading for this passage emerges from my chapter title honoring my father, the green movement, and the values I hold dear of the return to holism and body. My etude for my father reflects my memories of my father, his love of life and music, and the ecological melody that has become central for me as a consequence of his passing—signifying my deep feeling that all was not in vain....

After my father's passing, I recall lamenting I could not appreciate the subtle beauty of brushstrokes of words on the wall, or the deep meanings they held. I remember wishing I had paid more attention to my father's stories...As I began to recall and reclaim my narratives, I also began to realize that the answer to my father's question "Why" might lie in part *within* his *own* words in the stories he told us. I recall beginning to see the world as a story, and myself as a character cast in the continuing story of the making of the modern world....

I remember weeping for my gentle father. I remember wondering *who* will be the person or persons by his side when the hour of his leaving would be nigh upon him. I recall struggling with his ordeal through the night, and being torn in the morning...happy that he was still alive after a terrible night... and sad at the same time...because it meant that he would have to go through all that pain again. I remember well that last flicker before he left, as he temporarily regained clarity.[23] I remember wondering *when*...I remember *that* vacuum, as the palliative nurse awoke my soft slumber as she gently whispered into my ear, "Your father has passed on." I remember mother waking up to the sound of shattering glass that same instant in the next room...even though no broken glass could be found anywhere near his bed....

It was on a gentle summer day; the same kind of summer day when children play in the sand, people revel by the shoreline, and lovers hold hands and walk in quiet mutual appreciation...when they laid my dear gentle father to rest. I recall how nonchalant the world had been in his passing…how the birds still chirped in their merry way, how cars still moved in endless circles outside the cemetery, and how there was still an air of celebration of life…with one significant difference. A good man…my dear father…was no longer part of the mortal world and life he loved. I remember grasping for connection…thinking of the world where all around us, our loved ones are falling, in which value and priorities are set by imperatives of capital and consumption that elevates aggression and scorns humility, turning nature into resource and a sink for waste…I remember contemplating the breadth of the crisis implicated in my father's passing….

The Eco-Cultural Crisis[24]

The modern world stands in crisis. Amidst visions of opulence, plenitude, and free flight of capital, we are troubled by daily visions of those that are without and less fortunate—the poverty-stricken, the disease-ridden, and the homeless. We are reminded as well that the global networking of capital encourages child labor, promotes "sweat shops," and export of labor. Before us stands a society that has glorified material wealth and conflated the individual acquisition of wealth with goodness, at the expense of physical well-being, spirituality, family, community, and connection with nature.

In our quest for energy to power and sustain the infrastructure of corporations and the "better life," we succumbed to the Faustian promise of atomic power and have built massive nuclear reactors near our cities. Our water, soil, and air are poisoned with the toxic waste by-product of our false values and lifestyles, and nuclear spills, chemical accidents, and the daily extinction of species have become the letter of the day.[25]

In our quest to understand nature, and our place in the cosmos, we humans seem to have lost our way, and with it, our sense of humility and respect. We dominate and control nature, and consume and utilize plants, animals, and humans beings as resources to feed the power wheel of wealth. We are immersed within a culture of cyclic violence, as daily images of violence invade our homes, schools, media, and the Internet.[26]

We are losing our connection to our bodies and the natural world around us, as face-to-face human communication, direct immersion in wilderness, and genuine care for other sentient beings is replaced by simulations, representations, virtual reality, and contrived computer-generated imagery that bear little or no correspondence to the original. I am reminded here of David Abram's (1996) poetics, and his speech at the Bodymind Conference, in which he described loss of meaning as bodily encounter and face-to-face meeting being translated into video images on the screen. In the wake of the loss of that vital connection to nature, we watch in horror as our loved ones fall from the threats of previously unknown diseases unleashed in assaults of undisturbed rainforests in our unlimited quest for resources. Spurred by an autonomous race to turn the world into resource, we humans are the authors of not only our own misfortunes, but also those of other sentient beings with whom we share a common home...[27]

Holistic Approaches Towards Analysis

As the "objective" and subjective, macro and micro come together, the emerging picture challenges conceptions of cultural chaos and ecological disaster in isolation. It melds the two inextricably with outlines of what I have argued is an eco-cultural crisis.[28] It hints at fissures appearing in the modern anthropocentric thought experiment that was posited by the Enlightenment, that human life would be emancipated and improved through a combination of rational thought and liberal ideas and the notion of unidirectional "progress." What we see is another picture—that of problematic "progress" and late capitalism at the end of the late twentieth century where the free flight of capital is deeply implicated in the crisis of modernity...where all life and body are reduced to material good, and relevance is framed in the language and imperatives of the market...

Several implications flow from the broader dimensions of the crisis I have attempted to sketch above. The close interconnections between cultural and natural discourse come to the forefront, and cultural chaos construed in this manner falls under ambit of the ecological crisis. The larger picture disputes the *separation* of eco-cultural issues from the discourse of economics, as exemplified by the position held at economic summits[29]—that matters of social equity fall outside purview of economic planning.[30] It suggests the need to fuse the critique of political economy into the language of the ecological crisis, with a holistic approach that includes the elements of both ecology and culture, and sensitivity to the postcolonial world.

Interpretation of ecology, when *expanded* to include health, poverty, and imbalance in distribution of wealth, and its consequential effects, underscores the connection between the domination of cultural and natural worlds. This picture also depicts how accumulation of surplus capital, which forms the fundamental basis of capitalist venture and industry, is achieved upon backs of the disenfranchised and those once colonized—a more accurate portrayal of the Industrial Revolution. This collective imagery ultimately underscores internal contradictions of capitalism built upon the dependence of the earth as "endless" resource, which taken to its logical conclusion, might lead to the collapse of the system.

The sketch above underscores the complicity of advanced capitalism in the culture of violence and the destruction of the environment as consequential results of actions core to capitalist enterprise—around the competition between autonomous human beings, consumerism, and the utilization of resources. It could be argued that the picture suggests violence committed against the natural world is *not* unconnected to violence in the cultural world, and violence to the natural world returns with a vengeance to revisit our society. The parallel oppression of culture and nature and the revenge of nature are core tenets of the Frankfurt School (Horkheimer 1947; Leiss 1972; Marcuse 1964).

Intersecting Ecological and Cultural Theories

Carolyn Merchant's[31] work validating disparate streams within Radical Ecology has been influential in my theorizing towards seeing how elements of seemingly disparate theories of ecology and culture intersect in complementary ways. Building upon a model of inclusion, Merchant bridges disparate discourses, bringing concerns of Deep Ecology and postcolonial standpoints into Ecofeminist discourse. By including Frankfurt thought alongside Deep Ecology, Social Ecology, Ecofeminism, and Spiritual Ecology, Merchant significantly recasts the classical Ecofeminist argument within an inclusive model of holistic ecology and epistemological pluralism (Turkle and Papert 1990; Watson 1985).

Murray Bookchin,[32] taking a cosmic view, posits social impulse as an evolutionary trajectory located within the context of a revised Hegelian (1977) natural history. Through his philosophy of Dialectical Naturalism, Bookchin (1995, 59) brings an evolutionary moment to ecological discourse when he posits "it is nature itself that seems to write natural philosophy and ethics," implying that the evolution of ethics to include the natural world was/is an inevitability *inherent* within nature itself. Echoing Hegel's Spirit, Bookchin theoretically casts the "actualization of...potentiality" (p. 136) of valuing ethical over rational meaning as a form of transcendence in which a "knowing nature" *guides* its own evolution.

The work of Roderick Nash argues for a unified history of cultural and ecological change, insisting that instances of social/cultural change have their counterparts in the ecological movement. Nash's argument fits the epistemological pluralism of Merchant and highlights pivotal events that bring *specificity* to Bookchin's generalized hypothesis on the expansion of rights. Along lines of narrative theorizing of Grumet (1988) and Pratt (1984), I argue that taken together, these elements of the thinking of Bannerji, Bookchin, Nash, and Merchant intersect to produce an example of a *lived*-theoretical framework that addresses the eco-cultural crisis of modernity.

The Ecological Moment and Expansion of Rights to Nature

I remember sobbing within my injured heart, having recurring dreams alternating between remembering my father had passed on, and moments where

he talked to me on the familiar verandah of my youth. I remember being horri-
fied as he appeared bruised in my dreams, and waking up at midday sobbing
deeply because I had at long last embraced his surly form in my dreams. I
remember my father telling me we are children of the wind of modernity,
lamenting we live in a century where we cannot live in freedom from fear...

Albert Camus (1967) tells us the seventeenth century was of mathematics, the
eighteenth of the physical sciences, the nineteenth of biology, and the twentieth of fear. Writing in 1967, perhaps Camus was slightly hasty. True, we are
still living under the shadow of nuclear winter and constant warfare. But on a
more optimistic note, writing on the eve of the next millennium, we can say as
well that our century has also meant the re/awakening of ecology, and the
shaping of an ethics reaching beyond self and species that embraces the living
earth. It appears Bookchin's hypothesis emits a ring of "truth." Perhaps closer
to the "truth," as Nash contends—previous centuries laid down the necessary
prerequisite framework for both the science of ecology and the expansion of
liberal impulse with the opposition of tyranny at its fundamental core, two
events that have at long last propelled human concerns beyond narrow
anthropocentrism.[33]

Although in his work *The Rights of Nature: A History of Environmental Ethics*
Roderick Nash (1989)[34] did not state his thesis in the above way, he implied the
groundwork had to be laid by both the maturing of the science of ecology and
the liberal impulse.[35] In my survey of the ecological literature, aside from
Bookchin's Social Ecology offering a broad "god's eye view" of sociology
within a natural discourse, Nash's seminal classic stands unique in its treatment of the ecological-cultural nexus. For me, Nash's contribution speaks to
both the formulations of Merchant and Bookchin. In particular, Nash ties
oppression of African Americans in slavery, women in domesticated patriarchal society, and colonization to the oppression of nature, citing parallels
between clarion calls by *Uncle Tom's Cabin* and *Silent Spring*. As well, Nash's
thesis connects with my expanded conceptualization of Bannerji's Marxist critique of political economy in his argument that the *common* denominator and
prerequisite for oppression of slaves, women, and subject peoples lies in the
notion of being *propertied*, and accorded lower designation.[36]

Revisiting Roderick Nash's classic work that traced the *legislation of rights* from
the Magna Carta of 1215 to the Endangered Species Act of 1973, I traced the literature that gave rise to these changes.[37] Aligning these changes within histori-
cal context, under the banner of "natural rights," social rights enshrined in the
Magna Carta protected the rights of English barons in 1215. This right evolved
under the pen of Locke and Rousseau to become the right of freeborn
European men. This interpretation of right, which changed further under
Wollstonecraft's argument that extended that same right to women, and
Dubois' extension of that same right to African Americans, culminated when
Leopold finally extended "natural right" to nature itself. Thus the same argu-

ment that began as the act enshrining rights of an English baron, when taken to its logical conclusion, culminated in a persuasive argument not only for the conservation of land, but rights of the ecosystem. Since nature was originally invoked to conceptualize the notion of "natural rights," this ties in with Bookchin's thesis that there may be a connection *inherent* in movement of the awareness of rights from social to natural world.[38] There appears to be a connection between the locus of the notion of right and awareness of self and compassion, supporting the work of Murray Bookchin affirming not only that we are part of nature, but also there may be an evolutionary character to the notion of our self-awareness.

Bookchin's evolutionary interpretation of the Greek notion of *nisus,* advanced by Diderot, takes the form of *sensibilite* or sensitivity, corresponding roughly with Albert Schweitzer's (1994) notion of *reverence for life.* This common concept of sensibilite/reverence for life, apparently arrived at *independently* by two theorists, may represent a significant shift beyond mere sensation and self-awareness. It is *compassion incarnate*, expressed in the act of empathizing with the suffering of others—implying that feelings of deep compassion, of awareness of wrong and sensibilite for sentient beings may be *the* step beyond mere self-awareness. Juxtaposing Bookchin's theory beside the Frankfurt School theory of the revolt of nature embodied as an internal limit[39] suggests human beings embody not only sensibilite to extend sanctity of life to all sentient life, actualized as embodied nature, but also limitations of what is ethical. In realizing the internal limit of nature, in the twilight between twin moments of our deepest capacity—to feel *pain* from domination, as well as *exaltation* in the pleasure of being aware and alive—lies an opportunity for an ecological moment.[40]

I close my essay in the next sections on a more personal hopeful note. Perhaps the ecological moment *is* upon us, and by extending the sanctity of life to all sentient beings, we move from anthropocentric human conceit to a more humble place, as just one part of nature, beyond self and species into the larger context nourishing all life.

Recovery and Reclaiming the Natural World

Just before he left us, almost metaphorically, I remember my father telling me how a small fire can devastate an entire green landscape. I recall feeling guilty, suppressing laughter even after it had returned to the vocabulary of my soul ...not until...my father returned *whole* once again in my dreams, with a smile replacing anguish once etched in his warm face, did he gradually leave my dreams altogether...

I never got a definitive answer, but I did find hints and outlines as my search led me to places that both saddened me and offered hope. My search led me to look deep within my heart, and backwards in time to ancient counter-narratives and memories of happier times when my father played with my brother and me. Stories of diaspora that told me how it was that I was born outside of the mother country. Stories that told me of the mass exodus after the philosophies of the West bifurcated a nascent republic. Stories of conquest and of shame, stories of the blackening of a once green landscape...

I remember wondering if perhaps all is circular, and feeling guilty, thinking that my father's passing and my own grasping for meaning were perhaps connected, as a cosmic lesson to think critically and to write this piece. Perhaps that was the reason for his passing...to immerse me within a deep experience at the existential level that allowed me to wake up and reject a shallow world wallowing in consumerism, to value and recover stories, and to move my heart to speak out against eco-cultural injustice...

The Answer is in the Wind[41]

In the history of change, seemingly insignificant events have catalyzed significant social events. It appears that each time this happened, its significance was not immediately obvious. This happened when Harriet Beecher Stowe wrote about the inhumanity of slavery, when Rachel Carson mourned the silent spring, when Rosa Parks refused to get off the bus, when Henry David Thoreau could not find books that were not ruled, and when Albert Schweitzer felt kinship with a family of hippopotami crossing the Ogowe alongside him. These events in turn led to Beecher's influence in the abolition of slavery, Carson's pivotal role in bringing ecological pollution to people's awareness, Rosa Parks' role in igniting the civil rights movement, Thoreau's acts of civil disobedience to endorse an unjust war and his return to nature, and Schweitzer's formulation of the concept of "reverence for life." As momentum slowly gathers for a planetary shift in ecological conscience amidst a mass call to return to body, I want to argue, along Nash's postulate, that our little green planet may be at another such critical passage.[42]

Ideas, books, manuscripts, and articles of import today in the literature often began as less assuming circles of discourse. For me, the Bodymind Conference may turn out to be a watershed in holism and ecological discourse that embodied and coalesced together the movement back to body, which contributed to the reversal of anthropocentric greed and arrogance, towards a discourse of love, compassion, humility, and reverence for all life.[43]

Notes

1. I need to delimit my conscious use of the term "meta-subjective" here. As critique of Cartesian self, objectivity, and objectivization is core to ecological discourse—I refrain from using the conventionally understood word "objective." In its place, I have inserted

the prior prefix "meta" to the word "subjecive" to indicate a larger sense of self and subjectivity, for learning experience that can benefit the whole earth.

2. Two moves are indicated. The first reconnects social to ecological discourse. The second, following Bowers, argues that since the ecological crisis is the by-product of cultural mindsets rather than the social per se, the crisis is more appropriately termed the eco-cultural crisis. Henceforth in this document, when I refer to the social, I make this cultural turn. Similarly, when I write about the eco-cultural crisis, I am referring to the conventionally understood ecological crisis, albeit re-interpreted within the broader framework I explain here.

3. This essay draws from Aldo Leopold's (1949/1966) early ecocentric thinking, which paved the long road to expanding the circle of ethics, beyond anthropocentrism and human utilitarianism, to include the non-human world, and provide one of the critical impulses that launched the holistic discourse we are engaged in today.

4. These same words "I remember…" are interspersed throughout my entire piece. Although it may seem repetitious when I can alternate between similar words like recall, reminisce, ponder, etc., this is an intentional literary device, in the sense that my memory of my father is like a refrain that lingers on and on, and repeats in my heart. I am grateful to Ted Aoki for validating the ontological basis of my postcolonial knowledge claims, and for connecting my deep existential angst to my research question. This substantially reworked narrative began life as a paper inspired by Ted (Feng 1998), with respect to that connection.

5. Although I am aware there are many denotative meanings of the word "modernity," and the concept is a contested one, the word also carries for me a connotative meaning. Following the thinking of the Frankfurt School (Horkheimer 1947; Leiss 1972), *modernity*, and its correlate, development, has meant for me a term connected to, and complicit in, the concept of *parallel* colonization of nature and subject nations, a concept of which I go into some detail in this piece. It is a concept that goes to the heart of my postcolonial *identity*. As a postcolonial subject (a theme that I develop within this piece), I carry a *subjective* understanding of that experience, which colors my interpretation of the life-world (Habermas 1987). On a positive note, however, I believe that experience, although linked with a history of subjugation, is one that can help to shed new *meta-subjective* insights to forestall similarly disastrous future human endeavors, and one that opens opportunities for richer theorizing along the outlines I am sketching in this piece.

6. The power of narrative and autobiography has been experiencing resurgence in holistic education literature. Knowledge claims based on ontological *lived* experience, rather than epistemological theories, have been steadily establishing validity *over* traditional quantitative claims, and narrative applied towards teaching, research, and theorizing has been validated by disparate works (Giroux et al. 1996; Grumet 1988); Torres 1998). Closer to our holistic interest, Abrams (1996) and Basso (1996) have written about links between stories *place* and *morality*.

7. I am indebted to Carl Leggo (1997), one of my dissertation committee members, for opening the power of the narrative, especially autobiography, to my discourse; his distinction between disparate modes of persuasion; and his emphasis on the power of the appeal from ethos and pathos, *rather than* mere *logos*. The idea of the green thread came from his suggestion for the writing of my comprehensives.

8. I pause at this time to officially express the gratitude of our family, and our indebtedness to the wonderful palliative care nurses at Vancouver General Hospital who taught us how to grieve, and helped us to recover from our sorrow.

9. This was a book I read in a course many years ago, when I engaged the notion of the *non-neutrality* of technology. In hindsight, up until then I only had a mere passing aware-ness of and interest in Berman's book because it did *not* connect with the *lived realities* of my being—this changed radically with the passing of my father. I acknowledge my debt to Berman for his book that launched a critique of modernity and the Scientific Revolution, which also shaped my turn towards holism and ecology.

10. Positing knowing as *identification*, Bannerji invokes this concept to describe her strength she felt through identification as a raced person, that although she was neither Black nor Indigenous, she could identify with Black history, the struggles of people of the Americas, and anti-colonial struggles. Knowing as identification, she theorizes, can be *intersubjective*, across different people joined by the commonality of *experience*, a knowing that can prevail and cut across boundaries, be they geographical, racial, or oth-erwise. For example, although my experience of colonialism was in Malaysia, and Bannerji's in India, the experience of colonialism carries universality, a *commonality* felt intersubjectively between two colonial subjects.

11. Here I draw upon this *identification* concept to posit an explanation for the connection I felt between Carson's pain dealing with cancer and her questioning of the nature of cancer with my own search for meaning behind the cancer that cost my father his life.

12. Bookchin charges the term "environmentalism" does not go far enough to critique underlying assumptions of modernity. Moreover, Roszak (1992) documents corporate backlash, as more and more corporate advertisements appear to co-opt the term. Therefore, following Bookchin, except where unavoidable, I have substituted the word "ecology" in place of "environment."

13. I am aware this claim underscores a debate of philosophical proportions. I am *not* implying that cancer is not natural, rather along lines of contention etched by Carson's thesis, "whether any of the chemicals we are using in our attempts to control nature play a direct or indirect role as causes of cancer" (1994, 222). Carson's words appear to echo the deep ambivalence I felt, that cancer is at once natural *and* social.

14. Extending the implications of Smith's (1987) work, *without* having gone through the bodily soul-searching experience like the one above, I might have only understood Carson's deep questioning at a cognitive level. Having gone through it, however, my understanding is located and validated within felt *bodily* experience and I am able to make this cautionary inference. The current eco-movement owes its origins, in large part, to her thesis and concern. For a better understanding of Carson's struggles, read her moving story.

15. I recall at the time, huge economic concessions were being made to corporations, even as the hospitals ran on a limited budget, and patients had operations on *alternate* days. On this basis, I make the claim that there was a social component around priorities that contributed to my father's passing.

16. This is not meant as a sweeping statement. I recognize that modern science and tech-nology opened doors to understanding and has saved lives with techniques like vacci-nation, better food science, etc., and a rational approach has laid the foundation of a just society. However, that *same* science and technology, and *perversion* of reason, has also opened the door to the risk society (Beck 1992) threatened by the atom bomb, genocide, and destruction of the ecosystem. What I am suggesting here is that the cultural values which result from divorcing Fact from Value, placing *primacy* on science, reasoning, and economy, has been made at the *expense* of holistic values which celebrate body, cultures, families and Earth.

17. Along with organizers of the Bodymind Conference that provided the impetus for this book, I took the course in *Enactivism* first offered with Brent Davis (Davis, Sumara, and Kieren 1996) and Karen Meyer (Fels & Meyer 1997), and later with Karen Meyer, which I augmented with a series of doctoral seminars and interdisciplinary courses that spanned the disciplines of Education, Sociology, and English. My theorizing arose out of this mix and my subsequent readings.

18. It is beyond the scope of this exploratory paper to undertake a fuller examination of cultural studies. Having said that however, I had located this section for four related reasons that I develop within my paper. Firstly, to acknowledge after Bowers, that the eco-cultural crisis is a by-product of cultural mindsets. Second, to emphasize the urgency to correct current overemphasis on consumption, at the expense of under-valuing ecology, in its theorizing. Third, to support my characterization of the crisis as eco-cultural rather than eco-social. Fourth, to act as a bridge to underscore the relevance of the postcolonial experience, the subject of the next section.

19. The beginning narrative is also a postcolonial one. Aside from teaching me my alphabet, my father also enrolled me in a colonial missionary school, St. John Baptiste de La Salle, where I was trained by Jesuits and learned about the story of the West. My Jesuit training provided the historical and ideological framework that formed the backdrop to my historical explorations discussed later in this paper.

20. Elsewhere I have posited beginning a conversation that argues the standpoint of postcolonial experience offers an unique originating point in the articulation of historical ecological destruction (Feng 1999). As an in-depth consideration of the postcolonial experience is beyond the scope of this paper, I make this footnote in passing, to acknowledge necessary rigor and complexity that underscores the introduction of the *discourse of power* (Foucault 1980) into holistic theorizing.

21. The history of oppression of the natural world has been posited by the Frankfurt School to parallel that of historical oppression of culture. Approaching the ecological crisis as an eco-cultural crisis disrupts the artificial reification of nature as something "out there" and the parallel reification of culture as something "in here." These two "constructs" are intimately interconnected and disjoint only as construction of categories. Approaches that do not see the two as integrated run the danger of thinking that "social/cultural disasters" like refugees, bombs, population explosions, and wars hold no ecological significance. Rather than embark on a philosophical tangent in making my case, I provide an exemplar of this conceptualization as I begin to sketch the broader outlines of the breadth of what I have termed the eco-cultural crisis…after a brief interlude in memory of my dear father…

22. Such a theorization might, for example, encompass tenets of Deep Ecology, EcoFeminism and Social Ecology, opening up the possibility of bridging these disparate streams in Radical Ecology, with the political economy of Malthus critiquing the relationship between population, growth and substence (1798/1976). Here I posit merging the ideas of Bannerji's thinking emphasizing culture, social history and political economy with Murray Bookchin's (1995) revised Hegelian natural history, within the Malthusian thesis. On balance however, it is critical to note two qualifications— Bookchin himself argues that his analysis departs from Hegel; and this should not be taken to mean an uncritical acceptance of Hegel and his ideas; anti-racist scholars have arguably found racist aspects within Hegel's discourse (Chukwudi 1997).

23. This phenomenon corresponded with the notion that like the way the candle issues a sudden incandescence before it goes out, life itself resurges with sudden brilliance before it leaves the mortal coil.

24. This section was reworked from the unpublished paper cited earlier (Feng 1998). When we did the copyediting, one of the editors, Warren Linds, remarked how the tone of this section departed from my writing style thus far. He was quite right; I had been too close to my writing to notice the departure. After some introspection, I realized the reason for this departure might lie in the global extent of the betrayal I felt around my father's passing. My words here, in a sense, echo along the lines of Bill McKibben's (1989) timely impassioned plea when he warned of a *new atmosphere*, as he attempted to outline the breadth of the ecological crisis. Thank you Warren for your comments.

25. The Three-Mile Island nuclear disaster and the recent explosion of gas pipelines that run under whole communities in Washington are testimonials to this claim. *Where* do extinct species stand on the balance sheet of progress?

26. Like many attending the Bodymind Conference, the images of the shooting at Columbine High permeated my being and my ecological discourse. The guns promoted by the gun lobby, "justified" for hunting and killing animals, were the *very ones* used on children. It occurred to me since violence to nature has been theorized to be *connected* to violence to people, President Clinton might well include ecologists in his panel of representatives comprised of the gun lobby, software manufacturers, and Internet providers. We might do well to remember Roderick Nash's warning when he cited ideas of John Locke and Henry Bergh that gave rise to the early humanitarian impulse, in his claim that "a nation that did not stop cruelty to animals ran the risk of cruelty extending to people" (1989, 46). For an understanding of the context in which Nash made these remarks see (Nash 1989). The work of (Horkheimer 1947) and Leiss (1972) offer a more theoretical treatment of this connection.

27. In this section, drawing upon a sampling of textual "snapshots" of the modern world, I attempt to trace a few outlines of the complex dimensions of the ecological and cultural implications of modernity to demonstrate how the two might be co-implicated. As unappealing as these images may be, this combined problematic generates the complex image that troubles me—*when I think of its overwhelming burden in the lived daily realities of our children and students.* The magnitude and complexity of the modern crisis sketched above underscores the need for a holistic educational framework to respond to the complex intersections of the oppression of nature and culture.

28. The concept itself is not new. Although not described as eco-cutural to the best of my knowledge, there are extant bodies of work connecting culture with ecological concerns. The scope of the inquiry is quite disparate (Bahro 1994; D'Antonio, et al. 1994; Mander and Goldsmith 1996; Petrina in press). My exploratory piece is intended here as my beginning contribution to this continuing conversation—a task I recognize as a humbling one involving a lifetime of research.

29. *What* do protests against Asia Pacific Economic Cooperative (APEC) in Vancouver, World Trade Organization (WTO) in Seattle, World Bank and International Monetary Fund (IMF) in Washington D.C., Organization of American States (OAS) in Windsor, and homelessness in Toronto have in common? Corresponding to the free flight of and networking of global capital, there has been a rise in non-govermental groups (NGOs)— organized in opposition by activist, labor, environmental, feminist, pacifist, AIDS, anti-poverty groups, that are coalescing together upon a common platform of eco-cultural issues, to dispute this *fundamental* separtion.

30. In the research of Neo-Malthusian, Thomas Homer-Dixon goes even further. Homer-Dixon claims that his research allows him to hypothesize close links between ecological and cultural disasters, and that environmental collapse in the shape of rainforest

destruction, crop depletion, etc., has broad implications on scarcity, population, social violence, and wars. Arguing that "ecological and population factors don't act independently of social, political, cultural and historical factors," in Kingwell (1996, 82), Homer-Dixon posits a *direct* link between ecological disaster and cultural conflict.

31. I subscribe to the Ecofeminist's claims that under patriarchy, in a similar manner, the oppression of women and nature *is* profoundly connected. Merchant's (1980) classic piece linked the marginalization of women to the "death" of nature. Merchant's continuing scholarship has been impressive with her survey of the ecological literature in her expansion of Ecofeminist discourse.

32. Murray Bookchin's (1995) stand includes an Ecofeminist dimension. Bookchin locates the root causes of the ecological crisis in anthropocentric hierarchical systems, which emanates from social structures that have made possible the oppression and exploitation of women by men, young by the old, poor by the rich and colonization of nations.

33. What I mean here is that on balance we have also learned to *care* for animals and the ecosystem. Moreover, our caring is *not* out of prudential human conceit, self-aggrandizement or utility, nor for the sake of their "welfare," but in a trans-human caring recognizing and respecting nature, and right to existence, with minimal human interference (Fox 1995).

34. From my reading of the ecological literature, it appears to me that Nash's powerful *opus magnus* arguing a compelling case for the rights of nature has been *undervalued*. Nash's work has been powerful in informing me of the philosophical issues underlying environment issues, and the connection between the cultural and natural world. I believe that we need to revisit Nash's thesis and re-examine his tenets in these closing days of the twentieth century.

35. Our work stands initially upon the shoulders of earlier pioneers who first lit the spark (Muir 1911; Leopold 1944; Salt 1879; Thoreau 1854), and later on those of Merchant, Bookchin, Nash, etc. As Nash contends, it is important to note that for the first groundbreaking work to emerge there had to be a *prior* sense of the ecological *relationship* of humans to nature, and of *freedom* from oppression as espoused by liberal principles. It took thinkers like Salt, Leopold and Muir to grasp possibilities of expanding the ethical circle to include nature, which became possible only through advancement of the science of ecology and liberal principles.

36. In the book cited above, Nash compares and credits Harriet Beecher Stowe with awakening the abolitionist cause, and Rachel Carson with jolting people's consciences with an environmental impulse, noting that "One-hundred and ten years after *Uncle Tom's Cabin* Rachel Carson wrote another book that exploded traditional American assumptions" (1989, 78). Drawing parallels between the slavery, oppression, domination and exploitation of people and nature, Nash argues that the notion of being regarded as chattel or *property* (as in the ownership of land), and that of being considered a non-person, as a "thing" are key markers of common oppression. This argument coincides with Bannerji's discourse of power in her Marxist critique of political economy. Leopold also posited a problematic relationship between property, ecology, and ethics, when he located the problem in the omission of ethics in land deeds—"The disposal of property was then, as now, matter of expediency, *not* of right and wrong" (my emphasis, 1966, 237).

37. Inspired by Nash's undertaking, I traced the writings of John Locke (1690), to Jean-Jacques Rousseau (1755), to Wollstonecraft (1792), to W.E.B. Dubois (1903), and to Aldo Leopold (1949).

38. Nash opened his book with the chapter *From Natural Rights to the Right of Nature*. This also suggests the idea of right follows an *internal logic* with a *predictable* trajectory, rights that once protected the barons now protect not only those who would have been descendents of his serfs, but the land itself, and the ecosystem of which it is an integral part.

39. Based around a psychoanalytical analysis, the revolt of nature is a postulate of the Frankfurt School. Horkheimer (1947) posited that the domination of external nature reaches a point when it is resisted by human internal nature. This postulate in turn suggests that there is an *internal limit* in humans above which toleration is *not* possible. The reaction of nature in the form of the ecological crisis takes this concept further in that external nature *also* has a limit. Building upon this body of work, Leiss (1972) extended that conception, interpreting the ecological crisis as a physical correlate and manifestation of Horkheimer's earlier concept.

40. I pause to acknowledge an earlier conversation with Kelly Davidson, in which she made a profound statement that "the very fact that we have the capacity to empathize with so-called lesser beings places a greater sense of obligation on us." This extended line of theorization owes its origin to her deep insight.

41. Bob Dylan's prophetic words seem appropriate to title this last section as it ties my existential search for meaning to our quest for holism and embodiment.

42. Although it was not apparent at the time in the nineteenth century, Nash traced how many apparently insignificant fliers, journals, etc., contributed to amass into consciousness that collectively *made a difference* in the fight to abolish slavery. As we approach the turn of the millennium, there appear to be parallels between the grassroots environmental movement of the late twentieth century and abolitionist movements documented by Nash in the nineteenth.

43. It may seem a little far-fetched but along the same lines posited above, history might well recall the Bodymind Conference as an event located in late-twentieth century, in the last days of the second millennium, at the time of the fin de siécle, when consumerism reigned high, and nations exercised discourses of violence against nature and culture. History might remember it as a conference that brought together pedagogical and research concerns in the call to return to body with a universality that transcended disciplines.

References

Abrams, D. 1996. *The Spell of the Sensuous*. New York: Pantheon Books.
Bahro, R. 1994. *Avoiding social and ecological disaster: The politics of world transformation*. Gridgend: Gateway Books.
Bannerji, H. 1995. *Thinking through: Essays on feminism, Marxism and anti-racism*. Toronto: Women's Press.
Basso, K. H. 1996. *Wisdom sits in places: Landscape and language among the western apache*. Albuquerque: University of New Mexico Press.
Beck, U. 1992. *The risk society*. London: Sage.
Berman, M. 1984. *The reenchantment of the world*. Toronto: Bantam.
Bookchin, M. 1995. *The philosophy of social ecology: Essays on dialectical naturalism*. Montreal: Black Rose Books.
Bowers, C.A. 1993. *Education, cultural myths, and the ecological cCrisis: Toward deep changes*. Albany: State University of New York Press.

Camus, A. 1967. Neither victims nor executioners. In edited by F.W. Matson and A. Montagu. *The human dialogue: Perspectives in communication*, New York: Free Press.

Carson, R. 1962/1994. *Silent Spring*. New York: Houghton Mifflin.

Catton W.R. Jr., and R.E. Dunlap. 1978. Paradigms, theories and the primacy of the HEP-NEP distinction. *American Sociologist* 13: 256-59.

Chukwudi, Eze, E. (Ed.). 1997. *Race and the Enlightenment: A reader*. Cambridge: Blackwell.

DiAntonio, W. et al. 1994. *Ecology, society and the quality of social life*. New Brunswick: Transaction Publishers.

Davis, B., D. Sumara and T. Kieren. 1996. Cognition, co-emergence, curriculum. *Journal of Curriculum Studies* 28(2): 151-169.

Dubois, W.E.B. 1903/1994. *The souls of black folk*. New York: Dover.

Fanon, F. 1963. *The wretched of the earth*. New York: Grove Press.

Fels, L. and K. Meyer. 1996. On the edge of chaos: Co-evolving world(s) of drama and science. *Teacher Education* 19 (1), 75-81.

Feng, F. 1998. *Remembering My Father, Answering the Questions: Generative Chiasmic Spaces of Love and Healing for the Curriculum and Our Earth*. Unpublished manuscript. University of British Columbia, Vancouver.

Feng, F. 1999. *An ecosocial moment in extending the ambit of racism: Opening a conversation towards postcolonial ecology theory*. Unpublished manuscript. University of British Columbia, Vancouver.

Fiske, J. 1989. *Understanding popular culture*. London: Unwin Hyman.

Foucault, M. 1980. *Power/Knowledge. Selected interviews and other writings*. 1972-11977. London: Harvester Press.

Fox, W. 1995. *Towards a transpersonal ecology: Developing new foundations for environmentalism*. Albany: State University of New York Press.

Gandhi, L. 1998. *Postcolonial theory: A critical introduction*. New York: Columbia University Press.

Giroux, H. et al. 1996. *Counternarratives: Cultural studies and critical pedagogies in postmodern spaces*. New York: Routledge.

Guha, R. 1994. Radical environmentalism: A third world critique. In edited by C. Merchant. *Key concepts in critical theory: Ecology*, New Jersey: Humanities Press.

Grumet, M. 1988. *Bitter Milk: Women and Teaching*. Amherst: University of Massachusetts Press.

Habermas. 1987. *The philosophical discourse of modernity*. Cambridge: Polity Press.

Hannigan. 1995. *Environmental sociology: A social constructionist perspective*. London: Routledge.

Hegel, G.W.F. 1977. *The phenomenology of the spirit*. Translated by A.V. Miller. Oxford: Clarendon Press.

Horkheimer, M. 1947. *Eclipse of reason*. New York: Columbia University Press.

Kingwell, M. 1996. *Dreams of millennium: Reports from a culture on the brink*. Toronto: Penguin.

Latour, B. 1993. *We have never been modern*. Translated by C. Porter. Cambridge: Harvard University Press.

Leggo, C. 1997. *Teaching to wonder: Responding to poetry in the secondary classroom*. Vancouver: Pacific Educational Press.

Leiss, W. 1972. *The domination of nature*. New York: George Braziller.

Leopold, A. 1966/1949. *A Sand County almanac: With essays on conservation from Round River*. New York: Ballantine Books.

Livingston, J. 1994. *Rogue primate: An exploration of human domestication*. Toronto: Key Porter Books.

Locke, J. 1690/1967. *Two treatises of government*. Edited by Peter Laslett. Cambridge, MA. Cambridge University Press.

Malthus, R. 1798/1976. *An essay on the principles of population*. P. Appleman (Ed.). Norton.

Mander, J. and E. Goldsmith, eds. 1996. *The case against the global economy: And for a turn toward the local*. San Francisco: Sierra Club Books.

Marcuse, H. 1964. *One dimensional man: Studies in the ideology of advanced industrial society*. Boston: Beacon Press.

McKay, H. ed. 1997. *Consumption and everyday life*. London: Sage.

McKibben, B. 1989. *The end of nature*. New York: Anchor.

McLaren, P. 1995. *Critical pedagogy and predatory culture*. London: Routledge.

Merchant, C. 1980. *The death of nature: Women, ecology and the scientific revolution*. San Francisco: Harper and Row.

Merchant, C. ed. 1994. *Key concepts in critical theory: Ecology.* New Jersey: Humanities Press.

Muir, J. 1911. *My first summer in the Sierra.* Boston.

Naess, A. 1989. *Ecology, community and lifestyle; Outline of an ecosophy.* New York: Cambridge University Press.

Nash, R.F. 1989. *The rights of nature: A history of environmental ethics.* Madison: University of Wisconsin Press.

Orr, D.W. 1992. *Ecological literacy: Education and the transition to a postmodern world.* Albany: State University of New York Press.

Petrina, S. (In Press). The political ecology of design and technology education: Toward sustainable practice. *International Journal of Technology and Design Education.*

Pratt, M.B. 1994. Identity: Skin, blood, heart. In edited by R. Schmitt and T.E. Moody. *Key concepts in critical theory: Alienation and social criticism,* New Jersey: Humanities Press.

Roszak, T. 1992. *The voice of the earth.* New York: Simon and Schuster.

Rousseau, J-J. 1755/1984. *A discourse on inequality.* Translated by M. Cranson. London: Penguin.

Said, E. 1979. *Orientalism.* New York: Vintage.

Salt, H.S. 1897. *Cruelties of civilization: Program of human reform.* London.

Schweitzer, A. 1994. Reverence for life. In edited by L. P. Pojman. *Environmental ethics: Readings in theory and application.* (pp. 65-70). Sudbury: Jones and Bartlett Publishers.

Smith, D. 1987. *The everyday world as problematic: A feminist sociology.* Boston: Northeastern University Press.

Thomashow, T. 1996. *Ecological identity: Becoming a reflective environmentalist.* Cambridge: MIT Press.

Thoreau, H.D. 1854/1986. *Walden and civil disobedience.* New York: Penguin.

Torres, C.A. 1998. *Education, power and personal biography.* New York: Routledge.

Turkle, S. and S. Papert. 1990. Epistemological Pluralism: Styles and voices within the computer Culture. *Signs: Journal of women in culture and society,* 16(1): 128-157.

Wackernagel, M. and W. Rees. 1996. *Our ecological footprint: Reducing human impact on the earth.* Gabriola Island: New Society Publishers.

Watson, W. 1985. *The architectonics of meaning: Foundations of the new pluralism.* Albany: State University of New York Press.

Wollstonecraft, M. 1792/1992. *A vindication of the rights of woman.* London: Penguin.

Back to the Future:
Holography as a Postmodern Metaphor for Holistic Science Education

Lyubov Laroche

LYUBOV LAROCHE originally from Latvia, has taught college chemistry and physical science in Russia, the United States, and Canada; produced several science education videos; and published poetry in anthologies and magazines. She has a Ph.D. in science education from the University of British Columbia.

Abstract. Today Western society increasingly understands that modern fragmentary thinking is the underlying reason for the contemporary disaster of modern civilization. As is increasingly acknowledged, to find a pathway from the confusing labyrinth of modernity we need to develop and educate a new spiritually oriented planetary culture that believes in the unbroken unity of person/planet/universe. In this essay, the author describes an emerging unified holographic vision of reality. She speculates about elements of post-modern "holographic" science education which is based upon a constructive postmodern philosophy. This includes, transcends, and creatively synthesizes holistic ancient wisdom with the understandings achieved by avant-garde science.

Keywords. School Science Education, Hologram, Constructive Postmodern Philosophy, Teacher Education, Curriculum Change, Quantum Theory, Holistic Education.

Back to the Future:
Holography as a Postmodern Metaphor for Holistic Science Education

Lyubov Laroche

A Swinging Pendulum and Holographic Science Curriculum

Pendulums are strange creatures. They like to swing backward and forward, to and fro. What makes a pendulum want to swing back? Is it necessity of simple harmonic motion or a nostalgic desire to return to its past? Don't we humans, just like pendulums, often want to swing back into the space-moments of our happiness. But there is no way to reconstruct exactly what has gone forever. Only an ideal pendulum, free from friction force, comes back exactly to the same point. However, ideal pendulums exist only in the universe of abstract mechanistic science. In real life, there is no such thing as an ideal pendulum. It never comes back to exactly the same position. The universe is never the same and never repeatable. Every moment is new and fresh. Even if you try to return to the same point of your existence, you will come to it on a different turn of the spiral, which includes your new experiences and those of the universe.

An exciting time is unfolding. Today, a whole parade of state-of-the-art scientific thoughts, theories and models of physics, biology, mathematics, chemistry and astronomy paint the fascinating revolutionary picture of an emerging living, complex interrelated and mysterious reality. This resembles the enchanted world of ancient perennial philosophy, which "has been the dominant official philosophy of the larger part of civilized humankind throughout most of its history" (Wilber 1998, 7). That perennial philosophy assumed a deep unity between all entities in the world, which were just different appearances of a huge single organism, a living Cosmos.

When the pendulum of human history swung into the modern epoch, the living Cosmos was collapsed into an inanimate Perfect Machine. Modern mechanistic science closed a "black box" and made "objective" scientific conclusions. Everything in nature is ultimately material, dead, predictable, calculable, reducible, and subject to manipulation. There is nothing more to it! The time of mysteries is over. The earth is an inanimate ball. The ancient myths about a living interconnected universe are just that, "ancient myths." Get real! Get material! This is the basic nature of contemporary school science curriculum, which is

> chained to the mechanistic cage
> which contains blind forces

which act upon prosaic passive dead matter
which occupies empty space
which is completely empty
which is why it has a perfect ability to separate all the things
which constitute a modern fragmented world.

A petri dish sits on the windowsill.
An angel passes unnoticed outside the window. (Fels 1999, 106)

Mechanistic science dissected all perennial interconnections with the sharp knife of mathematical logic and chased away medieval magic, spirits, gods, goddesses and angels. The modern universe became a disenchanted world of scattered material fragments. This fragmentation led to antagonistic relationships between humans and nature, created various cultural tensions, resulted in disharmony between the inner and outer human world, and promoted a disjointed educational system, which reinforced fragmentary thinking. Today Western society increasingly understands that such thinking is the underlying reason for the contemporary disaster of modern civilization (Miller 1996).

As William Quinn (1997) writes, in order to find a pathway from the confusing labyrinth of modernity, we need to develop and educate a new spiritually oriented planetary culture that believes in the "homology of person/planet/universe." However, how do we educate such consciousness? Bowers (1995) and Miller (1996) suggest developing holistic education based on the perennial philosophy, on Ancient Wisdom, which reflects holistic perception of reality as a living and interrelated unity. However, as both authors acknowledge, the problem with using perennial philosophy as grounds for contemporary education is that this philosophy comes from pre-modern spiritual traditions, which most people of the atomic age find difficult to accept and articulate.

True, there is no way for us to stop evolution and go back to pre-modern times. Pendulums do not swing back exactly to the same position. We cannot erase the modern coil of the spiral of human civilization's development. If we were to return to Ancient Wisdom, it needs to be a contemporary version. Since we are brought up in a scientific culture, we might readily see "the unity, the sacredness, the oneness of life, owing to its universal acceptance as a scientific fact" (Quinn 1997, 24). The good news is that a state-of-the-art, postmodern version of Ancient Wisdom emerges today in the form of a philosophy, which Ken Wilber (1997) calls neo-perennial and David Griffin (1988) calls constructive postmodern philosophy. Such philosophy includes, transcends and creatively synthesizes visions of both pre-modern and modern epochs. It aligns a holistic spirit of Ancient Wisdom with understandings born on the advances of leading edge science and technology. This is why, I believe, it can provide the philosophical underpinnings for a postmodern version of holistic curriculum, which I propose to call "holographic."

Why holographic? Because a holographic vision of the universe is a remarkable unified new model of reality derived from insights of avant-garde science (Talbot 1991). This model revisits the holistic perennial vision of the world from the most sophisticated scientific vantage point. The pendulum swings back to the future, into a holographic living interconnected universe!

Holographic Thinking as a Radical (re) Enchantment

I know it's hard for you to understand about size, how there's very
little difference in the size of the tiniest microbe and the greatest galaxy.
—Madeleine L'Engle, *A Wrinkle in Time*

Appearances, appearances...
They can be so illusive and deceiving.
They reflect from mirrors what is not!
Sometimes clouds look so substantial, so thick, so inviting,
just like pristine white snow covering the ground.
Come, walk upon this blinding whiteness!
The white color which appears so pure and monochromic,
is in reality a hidden colorful rainbow,
a magic bridge into nowhere that connects nothing...
The light from many distant stars, that appears so real,
is just an echo from a past that is gone forever.
The Earth under your feet that appears so perfectly flat
is actually a colossal curving globe.
Hold on to gravity, don't fall off!
The seed in the palm of your hand seems so tiny, but do not believe it.
A giant tree lies hidden within its tiny body.
Even matter, which seems to be so solid, so firm, and so reliable,
dissolves at the quantum subatomic level
into a semi-real tango of probability waves.
Appearances...What lies behind these cunning masks?
Who makes us play this ongoing "hide-and-seek" game?
Catch me, if you can!

Entering this new millennium, our world has become increasingly holographic. As everyday routine in the very near future, we will enjoy holographic movies, holographic television, holographic computers, holographic art, and the advanced technology of virtual holographic reality. Such holographic popularity is based upon the amazing property of holographic pictures to be three-dimensional or, if moving, four-dimensional. Holograms have the appearance of real things, but their substance is not material. Catch me, if you can!

Another interesting property of holograms is that each part of a holographic film contains all the information of the whole image. For instance, if you cut a holographic film containing the image of a house into several pieces, each piece of film, when illuminated by a laser, will still show the whole house. The smaller the piece of holographic film, the fuzzier the image. From this perspective, the hologram does not contain any parts. It is an undivided unity.

A truly fascinating thought is that our entire universe might well be a giant hologram. Such a holographic model, initially proposed by prominent physicist and philosopher David Bohm (1988), is increasingly accepted by other scientists (Talbot 1991). The idea about the non-mechanistic and possibly holographic nature of our reality sprang from magical properties of the subatomic world revealed through "objective" sophisticated quantum mechanical experiments. These experiments indicated that at a deep subatomic level, our reality does not seem to be material; it seems to hesitate within a mysterious space, somewhere in between reality and non-reality, in the form of superimposed shadowy waves of probabilities. Only ideas in our consciousness can exist in such a potential form. Another truly magical quantum mechanical phenomenon is the *quantum inseparability* or *quantum nonlocality* principle. The mathematics of quantum theory led to a strange conclusion—that if two quantum entities once interacted, they become a single unity even after separation. They continue to communicate instantly without any mediating fields, without any apparent cause for their interactions. Nothing can shield quantum connection, and time or distance does not affect it. In 1982, French physicist Alan Aspect and his group illustrated this phenomenon experimentally.

ELECTRONS' TELEPATHY

[Aspect's experiment described informally]

Electrons (like everybody else) prefer to exist in pairs. In order to "tolerate" each other without unnecessary tension, electron partners usually spin around themselves in different directions. When one of the partners spins left, the other spins right, and vice versa. Very simple! But…if a pair of electrons is separated in the lab by means of a strong magnetic field (against their desire!), a strange phenomenon occurs. Even separated by distance, the partners continue to "feel" each other. If one of the partners is forced to change the direction of its spinning, the other simultaneously and voluntarily changes its spin, too! It is doubtful that electrons use the telephone to call each other, saying something like: "Hey, partner, how are you on your own? These people made me change my spin from left to right, so hurry up, change yours!" How then do they know about each other's affairs? How then do they know so instantly?

Since all particles in the universe are "continually interacting and separating, the nonlocal aspect of quantum systems is therefore a general property of the universe" (Talbot 1991, 53). As physicist Nick Herbert (1993) writes, the nonlocality phenomenon is "a cosmic crazy glue" which connects the universe into an undivided unity, where its every element knows what the others are up to.

The idea that our world instantly communicates within itself as an unbroken wholeness and accumulates information through the experiences of all of its entities is derived not only from physics, but also from other scientific fields. Experiments with chemical systems indicate that in a state far from equilibrium, at the edge of chaos, a new order of organization may spontaneously jump into existence. As Prigogine and Nicolis write, such a process illustrates an amazing correlation between a huge number of particles: "[E]verything happens as if each volume element was watching the behavior of its neighbors and was taking it into account, so as to play its own role adequately and to participate in the overall pattern" (1989, 114).

Biologist Rupert Sheldrake (1990) proposes the existence of morphic fields that "contain a kind of collective memory." For example, when laboratory rats learn something new in the United States, rats in laboratories throughout the world "show a tendency to learn it faster." How do they know? Or, there is a well-known tendency for new drugs to crystallize with greater difficulty the first time than after some repetition: "as time goes on, they tend to appear more readily all over the world" (Sheldrake 1990, 89).

It seems that all universal information is transmitted instantaneously throughout the entire world. One of the founders of constructive postmodern philosophy, Alfred North Whitehead, writes that all entities "internalize" the rest of the universe, "creating a unity which is unique to it" (Whitehead 1978). In such a world, every tiny atom enfolds the information about the whole universe. If so, our world has the property of a hologram, where every tiny piece of a holographic film contains the entire image.

> The hologram suggests a new kind of knowledge and new
> understanding of the universe, in which information about the
> whole is enfolded in each part and in which the various objects
> of the world result from the unfolding of this information.
> (Bohm 1988, 89).

The experiments of psychotherapist and researcher Stanislav Grof provide another testimony on behalf of a holographic model of the world. He describes his own and other participants' experiences in an extraordinary state of consciousness, which he calls holotropic (1988, 1998). Using psychedelic drugs, particularly the hallucinogen LSD, can evoke such a state of consciousness. Grof also developed non-drug techniques, which yielded the same results.

When participants enter a holotropic state of consciousness, they have "authentic and convincing experiences of conscious identification" with other people, animals, ocean waves, plants, mountains, atoms, planet Earth, and even the entire Cosmos. It seems there are neither limits nor boundaries as to who or what participants could become. Such experiences strongly suggest that each human might well enfold information about the entire universe. After years of conceptual struggle and confusion, Grof became convinced that his data from holotropic research strongly "indicates the necessity to change drastically our image of human nature, culture, history, and of reality"(Grof 1988, xiii). He came to the conclusion that his experiments support a holographic version of reality.

The emergent model of reality as a living hologram is truly exciting. If every little corner of the holographic universe enfolds the information of the whole image, it means "that if we knew how to access it, we could find the Andromeda galaxy in the thumbnail of our left hand" (Talbot 1991, 50). All entities of the holographic world, continues Talbot, are manifestations of the "one thing," unbroken wholeness, one "enormous something that has extended its uncountable arms and appendages into all the apparent objects, atoms, restless oceans, and twinkling stars in the cosmos" (1991, 49).

No doubt, there is something undeniably holographic about our world. Genetic engineering has been able to produce a replica of a parental organism, a clone, from the nucleus of a single cell. Life itself embraces holographic properties, since each living cell contains the information of a whole organism! Also, according to quantum theory, our seemingly solid and reliable world is not what it seems to be. Perhaps it is just an appearance, a holographic image …the interesting question is, an image of what? What lies behind all these cunning masks that we "objectively" observe? What is this "something" of which our world is a holographic image? Bohm speculates that our physical world is perhaps the *explicate* or *unfolded* order of a deeper, single, and vast nonmaterial reality, which he calls hidden *implicate* or *enfolded* order. This deeper implicate order of reality might well be pure consciousness.

Bohm's holographic universe is dynamic. It constantly evolves through ongoing processes of *enfoldments* and *unfoldments*, which Bohm calls *holomovement*. The "river" metaphor can help us to understand the nature of such a reality. The little vortexes, eddies, and whirlpools of a flowing, running river have their own separate forms, sizes and shapes, but they are still just water in the river. It is the same with us. While having unique identities and appearances, we all are manifestations of a single running river of a deeper reality. This river unfolds into the physical world through innumerable entities with different "ratios" of mind and matter. Holographic reality is therefore a multileveled matter-mind continuum, and as such, it resembles understandings achieved recently in ecological psychology about the mind as a process that spreads itself widely throughout entire ecosystems (Varela, Thompson, and Rosch 1993).

Welcome back to the future! The holographic vision of the universe is similar to the enchanted ancient vision of reality, in which an organic macrocosm was reciprocally reflected in every human-microcosm. After centuries of a modern mechanistic divorce between humans and the world, the holographic vision of reality brings us back to the synergy of the alchemists' adage, written in the Emerald Table: "As Above as Below." In the holographic universe, the status of a human being is elevated from being merely a bolt in the machine into a microcosm, a mini-universe! In a holographic world, human life has a cosmic meaning! To me, the image of a living, holographic universe is emotionally appealing. Why? Perhaps the voice of an ancient memory deeply enfolded in me, which is older than the Big Bang, whispers that I am a holographic "One." *"The psyche is not entirely a consequence of inhibitions, its original pristine sense being mythic, holographic, and poetic"* (Ahsen 1991, 71).

Holographic thinking, just as much as spiritual holistic thought, can provide grounds for developing harmonious, non-destructive relationships between humans and the rest of the world:

> *Tired from a lonely world*
> *where everything is separated*
> *where no one cares*
> *where everyone is imprisoned*
> *within their own cocoon*
> *which has absolutely no value*
> *in the context of a cold infinity,*
> *I imagined a different universe*
> *where my life is worth an entire Cosmos*
> *where each drop of rain on the roof is me*
> *where the wind swiping away autumn leaves is me*
> *where a whispered mountain echo is me...*
>
> *I am this star, I am this crying child,*
> *I am an enigmatic atom*
> *puzzled by the question: to exist or not to exist?*
> *as a mountain, I enjoy my dialogue with clouds*
> *as a cloud, I like to rest on the peak of the mountain*
>
> *I am a seed from which the whole world grows,*
>
> *I am the world,*
> *and being the world,*
> *would I hurt myself?*

Holographic thinking is a radical (re)enchantment since it enables us

> to see a World in a Grain of Sand
> and a Heaven in a Wild Flower,
> hold Infinity in the palm of your hand
> and Eternity in an hour
> —William Blake (Talbot 1991, 50)

All in all. Unbroken wholeness. As above as below.

Teaching Science in a Holographic Universe

Researchers in many different fields are joining together to present startling and thought-provoking perceptions of reality which teachers can no longer afford to ignore. (Alistair Martin-Smith 1995, 11)

Holography's biggest impact is yet to come—holographic principles being applied to the arts, sciences, and humanities. (Frank DeFreitas 1999, 3)

To teach science in a holographic universe? It sounds quite exciting, because the main purpose of a holographic science curriculum is not to develop a highly skilled work force, but "to re-unite humanity with the rest of the Kosmos, to see the same currents running through our human blood that run through swirling galaxies and colossal solar systems" (Wilber 1997, 60). In the holographic universe, the most important mission of science education is to educate a sense of holographic oneness with the rest of the world. For this purpose, we can incorporate into science lessons Grof's (1998) breathing exercises combined with music, which evoke a *holotropic* state of consciousness in which participants identify themselves with other experiencing beings. Or, perhaps, in the future, as physicist Nick Hebert speculates, the mind-link technology might be able to acquaint us with the senses of other experiencing beings.

> What would it be like to experience the world via the sonar sense of a dolphin or a bat? Or sense electric fields as certain fishes do? How does a plant feel while it is gazing on photons of light? If you could directly experience the sizzling sensation of photosynthesis, how would you describe to someone else the taste and smell of sunlight? (1991, 74)

Wouldn't it be exciting to plug yourself into a sophisticated apparatus and have every experience of a butterfly's flight! However, since no such apparatus has been invented yet, we can use our bodily imagination. This way of knowing, as Martha Heyneman (1993) writes, is familiar to us from childhood. Bodily *architectonic* imagination enables us to turn temporarily into someone or something, helping us to develop an intuitive holographic sense of oneness with the world:

> Without changing position, it [body] can sense itself in any size or any shape—curled up in a ball, or with an arm poking out here, a leg there, creating a pattern of wrinkles, stresses, and strains in the field of sensations—so long as there is some shape. This faculty of intentional bodily imagination underlies our capacity to put ourselves in the place of another person or thing and know, not theoretically but in the sensation of our own bodies, what it feels like to be that other. (1993, 23)

Imagine yourself a butterfly. How wonderful it must be to ride the wind and fly from one colorful flower to another. How beautiful a butterfly's world must be!

Have ever you ridden the wind?

Studying a unit on butterflies, we learn their parameters, habits, and life cycles. But we should also learn to imagine how it might feel to be a butterfly. Exploration of the butterfly's experiences by means of our imaginary senses is legitimate scientific inquiry of holographic science education. When we merge our story with the imagined butterfly's story, a new caring science might leap into existence (Leggo 1997). If you were a butterfly, how would you feel if you had to exist in captivity?

The inhabitants of the enchanted land of childhood are literate in the language of bodily imagination, a language that was long ignored and uneducated by mechanistic science education.

You will be okay...

The park was so beautiful. It was newborn after the rain. It shone in the sun with a myriad of tiny drops. My little daughter and I walked through this sparkling kingdom. Suddenly, the child broke away from me. In an instant, she was hugging a little, half dry, seemingly ill tree. While hugging the tree, she was saying: "You will be okay..." I asked her later why she had done that. She imagined how the little tree felt. It was lonely and ill. It desperately needed a hug.

If my daughter had not told me, I would definitely have passed by the little tree without even noticing it.

But...the little tree was screaming for a hug! The child heard its cry!

I did not. Is there something that I knew in my childhood and then forgot? Teaching the chemistry of cellulose, I have never imagined or invited my students to imagine what a tree might experience. I know about the structure of long-chain molecules of cellulose or about burning as a reaction of oxidation, but somewhere, in abstract lands of mechanistic science education, I lost my intuitive language of bodily imagination.

Turn temporarily into something!

Quantum leap:

what do I teach
and
what do I unteach
when teaching science?
Is my teaching worth unteaching?

Writes Heyneman (1993, 24):

We have today to gather our dismembered hearts, piece by piece from where we left the fragments deposited long ago, hidden in the forgotten particular sensations of childhood.

Turn temporarily into something or someone, and you will be able to tune into "vibrations" from others at the level of your feelings, at the level of the emotional intuition of your soul (Miller 1996). Your vibrations and the vibrations of others, resonating into holographic patterns, could harmonize themselves into a symphony of empathy, which is "a truly social interchange at the holographic level" since it "stretches forth to objects and draws them into itself" (Ahsen 1991, 66).

How might it feel to be an unpretentious stone lying unnoticed on the ground? What memories are stored in its stony body? What desires and dreams lie within its stony spirit?

In the West I call a black stone friend
Friend, I will send a voice, so hear me.
Friend, I will send a voice, so hear me.
     (Shaman chant)

How might it feel to be a little dog in an animal shelter? How might it feel to be our planet Earth? What could her life be about? What kind of news could she discuss with other planets? What does she think of a modern human civilization that makes her so ill? How might it feel to be an entire Cosmos? Since in the holographic universe each of us is a mini-cosmos, we can learn about cosmic experiences by becoming attentive to our own. Such an approach resonates with visions of Ancient Wisdom.

Ancient Tantric texts suggest that the human body literally is a microcosm that reflects and contains the entire macrocosm. If one could thoroughly explore one's own body and psyche, this would bring knowledge of all the phenomenal worlds. (Grof 1998, 58)

A Soap Opera "Days of a Teacher Education Course"
PHYSICAL SCIENCE IN ELEMENTARY SCHOOLS

The whole day was an ongoing parade of experiments with sound: echoes, singing bottles, tuning forks, different mediums, tape recorders, self-made musical instruments. At the end of the lesson the meaning of the concept of sound emerged.

Sound is a form of energy. It travels as a mechanical wave. Sound is produced by very fast back and forth movements called vibrations. These vibrations produce sound waves in the air by pushing and pulling it to produce changes.

Teacher: There is something else about sound, however. To explore it, let's dance! While dancing, be aware of your body. What does it do and why? Be mindful of your bodily movements. To concentrate better, close your eyes and listen to your body.

Chorus: The body resonates with sounds; it responds to rhythms.

Teacher: Now, redirect your mindfulness. Be aware of your emotions as they arise when your body moves in accordance with sounds.

Chorus: Enjoyment, sense of intrigue, lightness, elevated spirit.

Teacher: Is our knowledge of sound limited to defining it as a form of energy that travels as a mechanical wave?

Chorus: No...

Teacher: Sound is not just mechanical waves. It is also our music and our poetry. The mechanistic universe was deaf to these human realms. In the holographic universe, you are Cosmos, and if so, Cosmos knows what music and poetry is. Now redirect your mindfulness into an imaginary dimension. Listen to the music. Respond to it with your body and with your soul. Try to imagine an incredible cosmic symphony of rhythms, which you perhaps cannot grasp with your ears, but your heart may be able to hear it. Look deeply into your inner dimension, look inside yourself, and you might see unimaginable cosmic flowers, colors, forms, shapes, and dimensions dancing in an ocean of unthinkable cosmic music. Then draw what you have seen inside yourself.

Thirty-four different inner Cosmic appearances leaped into artistic expressions. Among them were

abstract shapes and forms
a sun and planets
stars
strange creatures
a medieval lady on a balcony
blue flowers
colorful butterflies

-What about angels?

-What about them?

-There were no angels in the students' drawings. Do they really exist?

-To be honest, I do not know. Personally, I have never met one, although I wish they existed because our world would be cozier if angels lived in it.

-In a century or two, advances of genetic engineering perhaps will enable humans to splice "the genes for wings onto a human back. That means humans could become angels if they want to" (Kaku 1997, 239).

-Angels are not about wings, but about souls. In the holotrophic state of consciousness, people sometimes identify themselves with non-material beings made from pure energy. These beings emit love, warmth, and compassion, and this is what angels are supposed to be all about. The holographic model of the universe can account for the existence of such beings. They might exist at a different, higher frequency level of holographic reality (Talbot 1991; Sheldrake 1990).

In the holographic universe, there is enough space for humans, for angels, and for the universal Spirit, which may well be the pure consciousness of an implicate order. The otherworldly realm of spirits, goddesses, and angels was a definite "no-no" for mechanistic science education. Today, this realm hesitates at the door that has been opened by cutting edge science.

> *What is the knocking?*
> *What is the knocking at the door in the night?*
> *It is somebody who wants to do us harm.*
> *No, no, it is three strange angels.*
> *Admit them, admit them.*
> —D.H. *Lawrence* (Nachmanovich 1990, 23)

Realistic materialistic teachers and curriculum makers "may agree or disagree with new paradigm(s), [but] one conclusion unmistakably emerges: at most new science demands spirit; at least, it makes room for ample spirit" (Wilber 1985, 4).

Inconclusive Conclusion

My mechanistic realistic "self" craves for a conclusion, but my (re)en-chanted postmodern holographic "self" rejects rigid conclusions as characteristic of a static and idealized world. In a real, complex and dynamic universe, "truth keeps happening" (Davis 1996). The trick is to balance at the very edge of chaos, to capture a place of junction between "stillness and motion," between "time arrested and time passing" (Capra 1996). I have speculated here about elements of postmodern holographic science education, the story of which is yet to be inscribed onto holographic patterns of reality.

I recall a science fiction film, "The Sphere"...

There was a strange pulsing and shining Sphere inside a spaceship, which had acciden-tally "dropped" in from the future. If you went through this Sphere, all your wishes, dreams, and fears, all your thoughts and images materialized into reality. The people who first found this strange apparatus nearly destroyed themselves, since the Sphere materialized into existence all of their destructive images. They were clearly not ready for the Sphere!

A fantastic time is approaching, a time when science might become such a "Sphere" for humanity.

> [I]n front of us lies a new ocean, the ocean of endless scientific
> possibilities and applications, giving us the potential to
> manipulate and mold the forces of Nature to our wishes.
> (Kaku 1997, 4)

Is consciousness, which strives to "manipulate" and "mold" Nature, ready for the Sphere (powerful science)? If humans are to have such a scientific "Sphere," they must outgrow their fragmentary thinking, their destructive images, thoughts, and actions. This is the core of postmodern holographic sci-ence education for the twenty-first century: to prepare humans and their powerful new science for each other, by developing nondestructive non-mechanistic holographic thinking. We are Nature. All in all. Unbroken whole-ness. As above as below. Unity in multiplicity. Uniqueness in oneness.

Just as a huge tree grows from a tiny seed, the entire amazing living universe can grow out of each young human being. The responsibility of holographic science education is to prepare the ground and to fertilize this Holomovement of Becoming.

> "I see. Now I understand. You were a star, once, weren't you?"
> Mrs. Whatsit covered her face with her hands as though
> she were embarrassed, and nodded.
> —(Madeleine L'Engle, A Wrinkle in Time)

References

Ahsen, A. 1991. Imagery and consciousness: Putting together poetic, mythic, and social realities. *Journal of Mental Imagery* 15(1): 63-83.

Bohm, D. 1988. Postmodern science and a postmodern world. In *The reenchantment of science: Postmodern proposals,* edited by D.R. Griffin. Albany, NY: State University of New York Press.

Bowers, C.A. 1995. *Educating for an ecologically sustainable culture: Rethinking moral education, creativity, intelligence, and other modern orthodoxies.* Albany, NY: State University of New York Press.

Capra, F. 1996. *The web of life: A new scientific understanding of living systems.* New York: Bantam Doubleday Dell.

Davis, B. 1996. *Critical educational practice. Teaching mathematics. Toward a sound alternative.* New York: Garland.

DeFreitas, F. 1999. Holograms. http://www.holoworld.com/holo/editorial.

Fels, L. 1999. *In the wind clothes dance on line. Performative inquiry—a research methodology of possibilities and absences within a space-moment of imagining a universe.* Ph.D. diss., University of British Columbia.

Griffin, D.R., ed. 1988. *The reenchantment of science: Postmodern proposals.* Albany, NY: State University of New York Press.

Grof, S. 1998. *The cosmic game: Explorations of the frontiers of human consciousness.* Albany, NY: State University of New York Press.

Grof, S. 1988. *The adventure of self-discovery.* Albany, NY: State University of New York Press.

Herbert, N. 1993. *Elemental mind: Human consciousness and new physics.* Australia: Dutton.

Heyneman, M. 1993. *The breathing cathedral: Feeling our way into a living cosmos.* San Francisco: Sierra Club Books.

Kaku, M. 1998. Visions: *How science will revolutionize the twenty-first century.* New York: Doubleday.

Leggo, C. 1997. Knowing from different angles: Language arts and science connections. *Voices from the middle* 4(2): 26-30.

L'Engle, M. 1973. *A wrinkle in time.* New York: Bantam Doubleday Dell.

Martin-Smith, A. 1995.Quantum drama: Transforming consciousness through narrative and roleplay. *The Journal of Educational Thought* 29(1): 33-38.

Miller, J.P. 1996. *The holistic curriculum.* Toronto: OISE Press.

Nachmanovitch, S. 1990. *Free play: Improvisation in life and art.* Madison, WI: Penguin Putnam.

Prigogine, I., and G.Nicolis. 1989. *Exploring complexity: An introduction.* New York: W.H. Freeman.

Quinn, Q.W. 1997. *The only tradition.* Albany, NY: State University of New York Press.

Sheldrake, R. 1990. *The rebirth of nature: The greening of science and God.* Sydney: Random Century Group.

Talbot, M. 1991. *The holographic universe.* New York: HarperCollins.

Whitehead, A. 1978. *Process and reality: An essay in cosmology.* Corrected edition. Edited by D.R. Griffin and D.W. Sherburne. New York: Free Press

Wilber, K. 1985. *The holographic paradigm and other paradoxes: Exploring the leading edge of science.* Boston: Shambala.

Wilber, K. 1997. *The eye of spirit: An integral vision for a world gone slightly mad.* Boston: Shambala.

Wilber, K. 1998. *The marriage of sense and soul: Integrating science and religion.* New York: Random House.

Varela F.J., E. Thompson, and E. Rosch. 1993. *The embodied mind: Cognitive science and human experience.* Cambridge, MA: MIT Press.

Unable to Return to the Gods that Made Them

David W. Jardine

DAVID W. JARDINE is a professor of education in the Faculty of Education, University of Calgary, and his interests lie in the intersections between hermeneutics, ecology and the lived realities of pedagogy.

Abstract. This essay is an exploration of the idea of experience-as-suffering as found in the intersections between ecology, Buddhism, and an ecopedagogical reading of Gadamer's hermeneutics. It is suggested that releasing things into their "suffering" is a releasing of things into all their co-arising relations and that without such a release, pedagogy is worse than unnecessary. It is impossible.

Keywords. Ecology, Interdependency, Memory, Pedagogy, Curriculum, Experience, Suffering

Unable to Return to the Gods that Made Them

David W. Jardine

> [T]the sound of water implies...the eye and the ear of a recluse
> attentive to the minute changes in nature and suggests a large
> meditative loneliness, sometimes referred to as *sabi*: the sound of
> the water paradoxically deepens the sense of surrounding quiet.
> (Shirane 1996, 51)

Late May, foothills of the Rocky Mountains, and the banks of the Elbow River
are starting to shift again under the weight of water and the billow of spring
runoff. Funny how the banks and shores and waters and airs have, once again,
in this mysterious perennial arc, attended each other so perfectly. *Not one stone,*
however meticulously small, is anywhere at all except exactly where it should
be, perfectly co-arising in a big, goofy Alberta Sunblue Grin of interdependence.

Things have warmed up enough that you can start to smell the pine trees.
Evening grosbeaks andpine Grosbeaks grosbeaks and red crossbills. Sickly new
apsenleaf sour smell. I remember these smells. *But this is not quite right.* This
place has taken perfect care of a bodily remembering that I had since forgotten.
This place spills my own most intimate memory out into an Earthbody greater
than this sheath of skin.

Memory, here, alludes to a deep mutuality with this place. I remember these
smells, then, but not single-handedly.

A mating pair of harlequin ducks in a bit of a stillpool on the far shore up
against warm cliff-faces.

We've been spotted!

But we'd already been spotted by the aspensmells. Not the Great Alertness of
this duck eyeing. But still *there*. A felt awareness of being placed by this place
into place in a way I could not have done alone, could not have even imagined.

How can it be that none of these things is ever elsewhere than *precisely* where it
is, following the silent mysteries of the ways of water and steepness and volume or the tangled clutters of bushwillowy roots that hold just like *so*, with
their long trailing underground reddish rootedness through loose gravel
shoals holding as fast as is possible and no faster? How is this possible, that
their attentions to all their relations is so acute?

Some have endured this winter's end.

Some have passed and gotten pushed up onto silty bars or edges alongside a downed age-old spruce whose banksoils failed and in such failure did precisely what was possible. There can be no grieving here except for that sweet fact that all life is One Great Suffering, One Great Undergoing, One Great Passing.

In the presence of such a fact, there are the fragile beginnings of a release from the odd self-containedness, the odd, desperate and understandable holding-on-holding ourselves away from the fact of suffering—that we humans have hallucinated as self-identical substances.

As Rene Descartes says in his "Meditations on First Philosophy," "a substance is that which requires nothing except itself in order to exist" (1640, 1955, 255). An ecological nightmare, this simple step of envisaging that the reality of something, its "substance," is what it is independently of everything else, any of its relations, any of its sufferings. So clearly the great Cartesian task of understanding the substance-reality of any thing is the great task of severing its relations and forcing it to stand alone under the colonizing gaze of objectivism (Jardine 1992, 1998), a gaze which demands of things that they "shape up" and conform to the logico-mathematical certainties that modern[ist] science demands of all things. This is one more step along a path (Jardine 1990, 1998), inherited by Descartes from Thomas Aquinas and before him, Aristotle, towards what biologist E.O. Wilson has named the new era: Nemozoic, the Age of Great Loneliness.

But this is not the loneliness of a great, empty (*sunyata*) spaciousness full of dependent co-arisings (*pratitya-samutpada*). It is not the meditative loneliness of *sabi*, which is aimed at the increase of such releasing spaciousness around the restlessness paranoia of any seemingly isolated thing (think, for example, of Chogyam Trungpa's (1990, 44) "restless cow" image of meditation and the meditative task of making its meadow larger and larger and richer and richer "so that the restlessness becomes irrelevant" (p. 44).

Rather, this is the venerated Protestant-Eurocentric-Neo-North American Loneliness of Individuality, of one's self existing estranged of all its relations (like some independent, immortal soul caught through some awful accident in the messy, bloody, dependent squalors of the flesh). Following from such a sense of estrangement, we then demand such isolationism of earthly things if they are to be properly and substantially understood, thus reproducing our own loneliness in all things. A perfect example is an isolated "math fact" on a Grade One worksheet: 5+3= __, isolated from the "x" that would make it sensible (Jardine and Friesen 1997), isolated from subtraction that would make it meaningful, memorizable but never especially memorable. A horrible little thing—one more "wanting and doing" (Gadamer 1989 xxviii)—that only needs to be *done*. Little wonder that a Grade Seven boy recently told me that he used to want to get his mathematics questions correct "because if I do, I won't have to do any more."

I have never heard a more damning condemnation of what schools can sometimes (seemingly unwittingly, witlessly) do.

In beginning to release ourselves from such self-contained holding-on, we necessarily begin to release ourselves to suffering, to undergoing, to experiencing each thing (even things like [seemingly] isolated math facts) as in the earthly embrace of every other, one Great Dharma Body, turning, wheeling. It is little wonder we rarely pursue such release and enjoy the full consequence of its sweet and sensuous spell, because this spell portends our own suffering, our own shit and piss mortalities.

This is the sweet agony of interpretation: every thing thus begins to appear as a luscious, spacious, standing-in-itself moment of repose in the midst of a great and heralded topography of relations and dependencies and belongings. With the grace of interpretation, we begin to stand in the vertigo of the movement of "opening," of "clearing." And yes, even that little math fact that seemed so lifeless, so inept, so isolated, so unmemorable, starts to howl with the "multifarious…voices" (Gadamer 1989, 284) of all its lost ancestors.

More fearsome yet is the glimpse we suddenly get that this previously seemingly isolated little math fact *is* that multifariousness, and to the extent it is presented to our children as an isolated "fact," understanding its real, earthly *facere*, its real "make up" is no longer possible at all.

We can only understand this river edge in the middle of its attunement to and thereby witness of the waters and skies that it has endured. It *is* its endurances, just as we are ours, just as Pythagorean Theorem is the attentions it has deservedly endured in order to have come down to us thus (the real mathematical question to ask of Pythagorean Theorem is thus not "how do you do it?" but "how has it come to be entrusted to us?" and "*now* what are we going to do?").

Thus I become visible, here, too—"[my] self in its original [earthly] countenance" (Nishitani 1982, 91). Spotted, smelling aspens and also sniffed on passing winds *even if I don't know it*. In the midst of all these things "claiming, *but not* requiring [my] witness." (Hillman 1982, 78)

Spring moon crouched here near river vents that breathe when waters roll over rocks and capture oxygens from airs above.

These places of song, where rivers sound. Perfectly so, just like the arcs of rock and the drumskins of waters over white turbulences allow.

In places like this, the old Zen adage finally makes some sort of sense, some deeply bodily sense in the wet middles of this deep Earthbody: that if this twirl of dust bootkicked up off the path did not exist, *everything* would be different.

Suddenly, this odd crown of human consciousness gets turned around, turned inside out, caught in the giddy belly giggle of how wonderfully ridiculous is this dribbling trail of words.

This is, of course, the great *converse* that is at the centrer of a true conversation—that we are turned around: addressed, not simply addressing ("Understanding begins when something addresses us. This is the first condition of hermeneutics" (Gadamer 1989, 299); claimed (Gadamer 1989, 127), not simply making claims; spotted, witnessed, not simply bearing witness: "not what we do or what we ought to do, but what happens to us over and above our wanting and doing." (Gadamer 1989, xxviii). This animate upsurge of the worldbody (not precisely an "unmotivated upsurge" as Merleau-Ponty suggested in an early work (1962 xiii), but an upsurge surely beyond the horizon of merely human motivation) is one of the greatest and most fearsome insights of David Abram's beautiful work (1996).

No. Perhaps the greatest and most fearsome is the moment of knowing I am this Earthbody *and nothing besides*.

My consciousness that turns this attention here and there is not different in kind from the lure that pulls these flowerheads to face the sun.

Sit squat in the open forest arc. Spending my passing days listening to the eerie auditory spaciousness of grosbeak whistle echoes off the foothill to the west.

The ear of the other animal was always already open and even though I'd forgotten to listen, I've been heard.
I sit flower-headed facing Sun.

Pulled now, beyond my wanting and doing, into an effort, these words, at air-bubble rockcast riversinging.

II

The unnoticeable law of the Earth preserves the Earth in the
sufficiency of the emerging and perishing of all things in the
allotted sphere of the possible which everything follows and
yet nothing knows. The birch tree never oversteps its possibility.
It is [human] will which drives the Earth beyond the sphere of
its possibility into such things that are no longer a possibility
and are thus the impossible. It is one thing to just use the Earth,
another to receive the blessing of the Earth and to become at
home in the law of this reception in order to shepherd the
mystery and watch over the inviolability of the possible.
(Heidegger 1987, 109)

The thing is, I've been living under a hood of depression and distraction and exhaustion for the past several months. Somehow, somewhere, I've lost track of the things that might sustain my life, sustain this writing, this *entheos*, things like stomping along this river edge and feeling my breath surge up again out from under winter's dark dip.

How is it possible to forget such things? Worse yet, how is it possible to forget such things *again*? No sense pretending that this hasn't happened before, feeling a bit like a dirty little math fact caught in perpetual self-isolation. Loneliness. So here are the riverbanks and waters remembering all their living relations exactly, remembering the pitch of aspen smells, with an exquisiteness and a relentlessness and an inviolability that is sometimes almost terrifying, and I'm left, goofing again, forgetting again, fumbling again.

Thank the gods at least that Hans-Georg Gadamer (1989, 15-16) reminded me that the dialectic of memory and forgetting is part of what constitutes the building of character, what constitutes the great and terrible human enterprise of becoming *someone*. This is why the first part of his *Truth and Method* speaks so often of *Bildung*: I become someone because of what I have been through, what I have endured in losing and gaining, in remembering and forgetting, in venture and return.

Thank the gods, too, that he was able to admit out loud that "every experience worthy of the name" (p. 356) involves suffering. It involves opening ourselves to the open-ended sojourn of things, their ongoingness perpetuation and fragilities and sometimes exhilarating, sometimes terrifying possibilities and fluidities (interpretation "makes the object and all its possibilities fluid" [Gadamer 1989, 367]). This is central to the arguments in his *Truth and Method*: that experience (*Erfahrung*) is not something we *have*: it is something we *undergo*, and, to put it more intergenerationally, something we just might *endure*. It therefore has to do with duration, with what lasts, and therefore with what can be cultivated, taken care of: experiences worthy of the name are not interior mental events had by a self-same subject, but are more like places that hold memory, topographical endurances (like these river edges) full of ancestry and mystery and a complex, unrepayable indebtedness. Full of dependencies, full of "it depends," full of dependents. And more, experience therefore links with my own endurance, what I can live with, which, in part, means where I need to be, in what "space," (in what relations) to endure.

That, of course, is why these last months have been so humiliating coupled as they have been with a forgetting of what I need to endure. The question seems to be, again, how could I have forgotten this, again?

It may be, however, that such earthbound forgetting is inevitable as may be having to endure such forgetting again and again.

This gives human experience the character of a journeying (another meaning buried in *Erfahrung*), becoming someone along the way, but never in such a way that suffering is simply overcome or finished, but only in such a way that, perhaps even for a moment, the stranglehold of consciousness may be gracefully interrupted by the dusty world and the unanticipated plop and peep of an American dipper off a mid-river rock.

So here's the rub. Forgetting these things that sustain me is akin to Martin Heidegger's terrible idea, cited in the long passage above, that we can somehow sometimes do the impossible. Human will—our "wanting and doing" (Gadamer 1989, xxviii)—with all its consequent unearthly Cartesian dreams of an earth full of isolated substances, isolated "objects" bereft of relations, can push us beyond the allotted sphere of the fleshy, earthy relations we need to sustain us, into doing things that overstep the allotted sphere of the possible, and, are thus impossible.

We can, that is, work against the conditions under which our work might be actually accomplishable.

I can, like this darkening winter mood, "not be myself."
And even though I may then still be on Earth, I can act out of a forgetting of this given, this gift, worldless mumbling a soft cocoon of merely words that have lost their sensuous spells, their fleshy referents, their hum and rattle on the breath.

III

> All things show faces, the world not only a coded signature
> to be read for meaning, but a physiognomy to be faced. As
> expressive forms, things speak; they show the shape they are
> in. They announce themselves, bear witness to their presence: "Look,
> here we are." They regard us beyond how we may
> regard them, our perspectives, what we intend with them,
> and how we dispose of them. (Hillman 1982, 77)

So what of those odd things we often surround our children with in schools? Odd objects that have lost their body, their richness, their rigor, their recursiveness, their relations (Doll 1993)? Objects that seem to have no ancestors, no place, no topos, no topographies, no lives; objects that might be memorizable but not memorable, that don't bear remembering, that don't require our suffering the journey of coming to understand them and therefore coming to understand ourselves differently having understood them?

What witness do such things bear on us and our doings? Not "what do we have to say about them" but "what do they have to say about us."

(Spotted!)

Many of the things our children are surrounded with in school are simply isolated activities (simply our own "wanting[s] and doing[s]" (Gadamer 1989, xxviii) instead of places to go full of their own wantings and doings, places to inhabit, places to take care of and cultivate, places the travelling of which might require us to become someone in the presence of others who travel with us and in the presence of this place which itself will shape our character (Jardine 1997c).

Many of the things we all surround ourselves with are unable to show their suffering, their care, their relations, their topographies.

Consider this Styrofoam cup I'm just about to throw away. It is produced as part of a standing reserve (Heidegger [1954] 1977) for something else (just like math facts are produced as part of a standing reserve for the accumulation of marks and grades). It (and from here on, we're speaking of the Styrofoam cup but also imagining at the same time the frantic little do-its of mad math minutes) is so disposable (so without position or place, without composure, one might say) that any relations of it or to it cannot be cultivated, chosen, cared for, remembered, enjoyed, either by us or anything else that surrounds it. I cannot become composed around such a thing. There will be no mourning at its loss or destruction. It does not show its having-arrived-here and we have no need to try to remember such an arrival. All trace of relations and endurance are gone. In fact, it does not endure. It does not age.

It breaks.

In fact, it is produced deliberately in order to not hold attention, not take on character, not arouse any sense or possibility of care or concern. It is deliberately produced in order to not be remembered. *It is deliberately produced for forgetting.* It is *Lethe.* It is lethal.

It is what we use so that our ability to remember the care and suffering that constitutes the interdependencies of the earth (and therewith the possibility of remembering our own suffering) is not visible and seems to be not necessary. But worse, it "is" in such a way that care is not even possible.
It is impossible.

And, to the extent that our human life and this great earth life is constituted by the attentiveness and suffering of all its relations (Heidegger's [1962] understanding of care as *Sorge* and his insistence, along with Gadamer's [1989], on our "finitude"), to that extent, this Styrofoam cup is impossible, even though *there it is.*

So the problem with such things—and therefore the problem with surrounding ourselves and our children with such things—is their impossibility. Human will has produced something that has spiralled out of the order of relations. The problem with the disposability of this cup is not simply the products or by-products of its manufacture or the non-biodegradability of what remains of it after its use (this is ecological consciousness at its most literal mindedness). The deep ecological problem with it is that it is unable to be cared for, and living in its presence therefore weakens, undermines or occludes our ability to see how our lives and this Earth are constituted by such suffering. (And, too, the problem with the disposability of isolated math facts is that they are unable to be cared for, and living in their presence therefore weakens, undermines or occludes our ability to see how we might understand mathematics as a living place, a living inheritance with which we have been entrusted, full of its own hidden agencies that live "beyond my wanting and doing (Gadamer 1989, xxviii), and therefore that can, potentially, release me from my (schooled) isolation out into a *world* of relations."

This Styrofoam cup becomes a perfect example of a Cartesian Substance: something that is bereft of any relations. This Styrofoam cup thus stands there in the world "by itself," as an object produced of bereaving. But it also promises to help us get over our sense of loss through a relentless, ever accelerating stream of consumptiveness: one faceless, bodiless, placeless, careless cup after the other (just like one faceless, bodiless, placeless, careless schooly math activity after the other), all bent to the satisfaction of our "wanting and doing" (Gadamer 1989, xxviii).

And then, of course, we excuse the existence of such cups by pointing to our own convenience, never once suspecting that our sense of convenience has been manufactured by and is now housed in the very cups that use our sense of convenience as their excuse. And, just as evidently, we inundate our children with relentless streams of one activity after the other and excuse it by referring to their short "attention spans," never once suspecting that many of the things they are inundated with in schools *are not worthy of attention*, because they have been stripped of their imaginative topographies (their living "ecologies," we might say). We thus become caught in producing rushed, impossible activities to service the very attentions we have violated through such production. A *perfect* image of knowledge-as-consumption-and-production, knowledge as a scarce resource, and school as commodified exchange processes bent on producing consumers in a forgetfulness of the original given, the original gift (Jardine, Clifford and Friesen, in press; what Matthew Fox [1990, 23] called "the original blessing" of the earth). Since, in such an economy of consumption, "time [itself] is always running out" (Berry 1987, 44), the only hope, in the midst of such a rush of activities is not slowing down and opening up rich fields of relations. Rather, hope is found only in *accelerating* the rush (Jardine 1995, 1997b, 1997c) in a grand eschatological race for the End Times: a time when wholeness will be achieved once all the scattered bits and pieces of the curriculum are finally, finally "covered." These impossible, consumptive, isolated, never really satisfying bits and pieces thus always leave us looking longingly for the last days when all will be redeemed and we can finally rest, assured. Differently put, our relentless consumption is premised on a desire for it to end in the full satisfaction guaranteed of our "wanting and doing."

IV

In the summer of 1998 I taught a course on hermeneutics at the University of Victoria, and we spent our last class considering James Hillman's "*Anima Mundi:* Returning the Soul to the World" (1982). There is a certain point in this essay where the image of an object cut off from all its relations is brought up, an object unable to return to the gods that made it, an object unplaced. In our class, I offered up the image of a fragment of Styrofoam cup buried ten feet underground in some long-forgotten dumpsite.

Darkwormyness. The roiling relief of decays, where all things begin to return to the gods that made them, begin to empty out from their illusion of self-containment into all their relations. And then, right in the midst of these rich, dark, moist underworlds, these rich sufferings, this dry brightlit brightwhite self-contained, "clear and distinct" (Descartes [1640] 1955), fully present, unreposing, utopian thing, is unable to let go of its self, unable to find its lost relations (excuse the Heideggerianism, but unable to *world*).

Oddly impossible, having overstepped something unutterable, now condemned, it seems, to never re-turn, never to con-verse, never to breathe out into its topography...

Hillman says that this image of an object that has "no way back to the Gods" is precisely an image of a "figure in Hell" (1982, 83).

V

In *Truth and Method* (1989), Hans-Georg Gadamer insists that "Youth demand images for its imagination and for the forming of its memory. [We must, therefore] supplement the critica of Cartesianism with the old topica" (1989, 21). The *"critica* of Cartesianism" are essentially methodological and procedural. As Martin Heidegger (1972, 66) has noted, in this fulfillment of the modern age, "the matters at hand become matters of method." Once this Cartesian inheritance is enacted in schools, isolated, anonymous, disembodied, clear and distinct, methodologically reproducible and assessable math facts become understood as more "basic" than the troublesome, roiling, ongoing, irreproducible, ambiguous, highly personally and bodily engaging conversations we might have with children and colleagues about living mathematical relations. Ideologically, under the hood of Cartesianism, such living conversations blur and despoil and contaminate and desecrate what is in fact objective and certain and self-contained.

"We are living out a logic [of fragmentation and isolation] that is centuries old and that is being worked out in our own lifetime" (Berman 1983, 23). Against this modernist logic, Gadamer insists that understanding and its memorial formation require the productive supplementation of topographical imagination, thus placing what might have seemed to be isolated "math facts" back into the sustaining relations that make them what they are, that keep them sane, that make them rich and memorable. "The old *topica*" is thus essentially not methodological but substantial, full of smells and names and faces and kin, full of ancestral roots and ongoing conversations and old wisdoms and new, fresh deliberateness and audacity and life. It is also necessarily and unavoidably multifarious, contentious, ongoing, intergenerational, and unable to be foreclosed with any certainty because, for example, as a *living* discipline, mathematics endures. Therefore, topographically-hermeneutically-ecologically, "understanding mathematics" means going to this living place and getting in on the living conversation that constitutes its being furthered.

Understanding is thus not method: it is *learning to dwelling in the presence of this river edge, or learning to dwell in the presence of Pythagorean proportionality* and, under such witness, becoming someone because of it.

VI

As unhidden, truth has in itself an inner tension and ambiguity.
Being contains something like a hostility to its own presentations.
The existing thing does not simply offer us a recognizable and
familiar surface contour; it also has an inner depth of self-
sufficiency that Heidegger calls "standing-in-itself." The
complete unhiddenness of all beings, their total objectification
(by means of a representation that conceives things in their
perfect state) would negate this standing-in-itself of beings and
lead to a total levelling of them...A complete objectification of
this kind would no longer represent beings that stand in their
own being. Rather, it would represent nothing more than our opportunity for using beings, and what would be manifest would
be the will that seizes upon and dominates things. [By this river
edge] we experience an absolute opposition to this will-to-control,
not in the sense of a rigid resistance to the presumption of our
will, which is bent on utilizing things, but in the sense of the
superior and intrusive power of a being reposing in itself.
(Gadamer 1977, 226-27).

The project of hermeneutics requires that we strive to "overcome the epistemological problem" (Gadamer 1989, 242-64). The healing art of interpretation is not concerned simply with knowing things differently than Cartesianism allows. Rather, it requires that we strive to "break open the *being* of the object" (p. 362) we are considering. Things, taken up interpretively, *exist differently* than the logic of self-containedness and self-identity allows. The healing art of interpretation is thus first and foremost *ontological* in its movement.

Living things in this world are all their vast, ancestral, intergenerational, earthly relations. *This* is the greatness and power of their "repose." They *are* all the ways, all the voices, that have handed them to us, a great and vast receding spaciousness, where "beings hold themselves back by coming forward into the openness of presence" (Gadamer 1977, 227). This river edge *is* all its relations sounding outwards into all things and back and forth in the cascades of generational voices faded and to come. It isn't first some thing and somehow "then" in relation (which gives rise to "the epistemological problem"). "Only *in* the multifariousness of such voices does it exist" (Gadamer 1989, 284). And it resists objectification—it "holds itself back" in repose—because it is unfinished. It is open to the endurances and sufferings to come which that can never be fully or finally "given." "The whole" is never given (Gadamer 1989, 38) and it is therefore never fully present or presentable or representable (this is the great "critique of presence" that Heidegger initiated as a critique of the Being of things, not an epistemological critique).

And, if the whole is never simply given, health is never given. Healing and wounding, like memory and forgetting, like *sol stasis* and return, are never done. Again, suffering, endurance, furtherance:

> This ultimately forces an awareness that even [a simple thing like a twirl of dust kicked up from the path, or a seemingly isolated math fact, or the seemingly pristine givenness of Pythagorean Theorem] possesses its own original worldliness and, thus, the center of its own Being so long as it is not placed in the object-world of producing and marketing. Our orientation to [such things, unlike our orientation to the object-world] is always something like our orientation to an inheritance. (Gadamer 1994, 191-92)

The act of understanding such things is not a matter of utilizing or control or making fully present and objective or making completely clear. It is the act of participating in the work of "handing down" (Gadamer 1989, 284) such things. However, we must also cultivate in ourselves the ability and the desire to adamantly *refuse* (Jardine 1994) some inheritances, those that toy with impossibility and despoil our ability to dwell in the suffering of things (that despoil our ability to *experience [Erfahrung]*). We must refuse the levelling that violates the deeply ecopedagogical repose of things.

So even when a young child simply counts up to ten, to *understand* such an event means to allow ourselves to experience (*Erfahrung*) how they are standing with us in the middle of a great human inheritance, a great human endurance, full of arcs of ancestry and memory that define mathematics as a living discipline. This is one of us, one of our kind, one of our kin, counting out in an act that is of a kind with the measured pacing of birdcalls heralding the sun's arcing higher and higher.

Under such an image of our work as educators, the task of learning the ways of a place like mathematics becomes akin to the task of becoming native to a place, developing

> the sense of "nativeness," of belonging to the place [see the
> detail with which Gadamer (1989, 462) deals with the idea of under-
> standing-as-belonging and the relationship between
> belonging (*Zugehorigkeit*) and hearing (*horen*)]. Some people
> are beginning to try to understand where they are, and what it
> would mean to live carefully and wisely, delicately in a place,
> in such a way that you can live there adequately and comfortably.
> Also, your children and grandchildren and generations a
> thousand years in the future will still be able to live there.
> That's thinking as though you were a native. Thinking in terms
> of the whole fabric of living and life. (Snyder 1980, 86)

Thus it is that there is a great kinship between hermeneutics, ecology and pedagogy. They are each, in their own ways, concerned with returning us to our suffering and to the suffering we must undergo to understand our place in this great earthly inheritance, full as it is with both river edges and the graceful beauty of Pythagoras—these two now no longer different in kind, both understood as finally able to return to the gods that made them.

Endbit

"Understanding is an adventure and, like any adventure, it always involves some risk" (Gadamer 1983, 141). In fact, *"understanding proves to be"* not a method but an *"event"* (Gadamer 1989, 308), a moment of the fluttering open of the meticulous co-arisings that repose around any thing.

This is what hermeneutics understands as "truth": *Alethia*, the opening of what was previously closed (and therefore, like the necessary dialectic of memory and forgetting, the necessary closing off of things as well, part of the "hostility towards full presentation" that Gadamer alluded to above), the remembering of what was forgotten (*Lethe* as the river of forgetfulness and our living in the wisdom that "only by forgetting does the mind have the possibility of seeing things with fresh eyes, so that what is familiar fuses with the new. 'Keeping in mind' is [thus] ambiguous" [Gadamer 1989, 16]), the making alive, the livening up, of what was dull and levelled and therefore deadly (lethal) and morose.

As for me, I'll sit here a bit, near solstice, facing Sol's perennial high-pitched summer stasis over the Tropic of Capricorn.

Sun's re-turning (*tropos*) in the sign of the Goat.

Undergoing, with fresh eyes, my own "slower, more miraculous returns" (Wallace 1987) to the gods that made me.

References

Abram, D. 1996. *The spell of the sensuous: Language in a more-than-human world*. New York: Pantheon Books.

Berman, M. 1983. *The reenchantment of the world*. New York: Bantam Books.

Berry, W. 1987. *Home economics*. San Francisco: North Point Press.

Descartes, R. circa [1640], 1955. *Descartes' selections*. New York: Scribner's.

Doll, W. 1993. Curriculum possibilities in a "post"-future. *Journal of Curriculum and Supervision* 8(4): 277-292.

Fox, M. 1990). *Original blessing*. Santa Fe: Bear and Co.

Gadamer, H.G. 1977. *Philosophical hermeneutics*. Berkeley: University of California Press.

Gadamer, H.G. 1983. *Reason in the age of science*. Boston: MIT Press.

Gadamer, H.G. 1989. *Truth and method*. New York: Continuum Press.

Gadamer, H.G. 1994. *Heidegger's ways*. Boston: MIT Press.

Heidegger, M. 1962. *Being and time*. New York: Harper and Row.

Heidegger, M. 1972. *Time and being*. New York: Harper and Row.

Heidegger, M. [1954] 1977. The question concerning technology. In *Basic writings*. New York: Harper and Row.

Heidegger, M. 1987. Overcoming metaphysics. *The end of philosophy*. New York: Harper and Row.

Hillman, J. 1982. *Anima mundi:* Returning the soul to the world. *Spring*.

Jardine, D. 1990. Awakening from Descartes' nightmare: On the love of ambiguity in phenomenological approaches to education. *Studies in Philosophy and Education* 10(1): 211-232.

Jardine, D. 1992. Immanuel Kant, Jean Piaget and the rage for order: Hints of the colonial spirit in pedagogy. *Educational Philosophy and Theory*. 23(1): 28-43.

Jardine, D. 1994. "Littered with literacy:" An ecopedagogical reflection on whole language, pedocentrism and the necessity of refusal. *Journal of Curriculum Studies*, 26(5): 509-524.

Jardine, D. 1995. The stubborn particulars of grace. In *Experience and the curriculum: Principles and programs*, edited by B. Horwood. Dubuque, IA: Kendall/Hunt Publishing.

Jardine, D. 1997a. Reprint. "Under the tough old stars:" Pedagogical hyperactivity and the mood of environmental education. *Clearing: Environmental Education in the Pacific Northwest* 97 (April/May): 20-23. Original edition, *Canadian Journal of Environmental Education* 1 (Spring 1996): 48-55.

Jardine, D. 1997b. "All beings are your ancestors:" A bear Sutra on ecology, Buddhism and pedagogy. *The Trumpeter: A Journal of ecosophy* 14(3): 122-131.

Jardine, D. 1997c. The surroundings. *JCT: The Journal of Curriculum Theorizing* 13(3): 18-31.

Jardine, D. 1998. *"To dwell with a boundless heart:" On curriculum theory, hermeneutics and the ecological imagination*. New York: Peter Lang Publishers.

Jardine, D., with S. Friesen. 1997. A play on the wickedness of undone sums, including a brief mytho-phenomenology of "x" and some speculations on the effects of its peculiar absence in elementary mathematics education. *Journal of the Philosophy of Mathematics Education 10*.

Jardine, D., P. Clifford, and S. Friesen. In press. Globalization and the pedagogical prospects of the gift. *Alberta Journal of Educational Research*.

Merleau-Ponty, M. 1962. *Phenomenology of perception*. London: Routledge and Kegan Paul.

Nishitani, K. 1982. *Religion and nothingness*. Berkeley: University of California Press.

Shirane, H. 1996. *Traces of dreams: Landscape, cultural memory and the poetry of Basho*. Stanford: Stanford University Press.

Snyder, G. 1980. *The real work*. New York: New Directions Books.

Trungpa, C. 1990. *Cutting through spiritual materialism*. San Francisco: Shambala Press.

Wallace, B. 1987. *The stubborn particulars of grace*. Toronto: McClelland and Stewart.

Experiencing Unknown Landscapes: Unfolding a Path of Embodied Respect

Johnna G. Haskell

JOHNNA HASKELL, Ph.D., is a lecturer in the faculty of Teacher Education at the University of Southern Maine. Her research interests explore outdoor experience, ecological and enactive perspectives, and freefall pedagogy. Her passion in education is to search for pedagogical possibilities that, while promoting environmental sustainability, foster communities of inquiry for a compassionate world.

Abstract. The ideas found in this chapter come from an inquiry into students' unexpected moments in an outdoor adventure education classroom. The theme of embodied respect emanates out of five months of research with Grade 10 students in western Canada. Embodied respect arises through emergent interactions with the environment bringing forth a continued freshness of perception. As our embodiment of action is not separate from our social history of experience, embodied respect emerges as a way of being with/in the world. My hope is that this chapter opens possibilities for thinking about emergent ways of interacting and pedagogies that lead to unfolding embodied respect for humans and the natural world. Furthermore, my hope is that a curriculum of wilderness experiences within unknown landscapes may evolve to foster embodied respect among our nation's children.

Keywords. Embodied Respect, Awareness, Perception, Experiencing, Bodyworld, Emergent Interaction, Action

Note. Portions of this chapter are currently in print in the *Australian Journal of Outdoor Education* 4 (2).

Experiencing Unknown Landscapes: Unfolding a Path of Embodied Respect

Johnna G. Haskell

Prelusion to Unfamiliar Landscapes

In education, stories and images of wild landscapes inside books shape how children come to know the world. One of the dilemmas with using books to depict wilderness landscapes, however, is that these images overlook the sensuous and dynamic nature of human experience. Despite a few whale watching trips or excursions to visit science museums, students experience little interaction with the natural world in education. How is it that we have become so separated and disconnected from the beauty of our unfolding world? What opportunities or possibilities might allow us to experience a deep respect not only for each other but the living landscape?

Perhaps pondering my own experience will serve as a guide for responding to these questions. I have come to know the world through interacting with various outdoor environments. Fascinated by the ocean landscape, I watch attentively while kayaking toward an island of land on the horizon. Huge boulders appear to move atop immense slabs of rock rising out of the ocean. Some are brown, others black. A sense of wonder and inquiry pulsates through my body. Now I catch the wind filled with loud incessant barking blowing offshore.

Rrrrrarkk   rrrrk,

I paddle with my fellow kayakers into a channel of water, communicating via hand signals over the roar of activity. Two other kayakers who ventured into these waters are leaving, afraid of the sea lions swimming too close for comfort. I confront my fear of wilderness landscapes by interacting with them, heeding a respect for the animate bodies and sensuous waters flowing over my body. I move forward, embracing the unexpected and unfamiliar.

The possibilities found in unknown and emergent ways of interacting bring forth a freshness of perception. I ease my boat forward with slow paddle strokes toward a gigantic California sea lion lying up on shore. We eye each other wordlessly. Next, expelling a loud Rrrrrr—this animal sits up, towering above me. I sit still! The deafening noise and fetid rich air around us disappear as we engage in a conversation of sorts and then, slowly, I back-paddle, leaving this sleeping giant basking in the sun. The world opens a new sensual awareness. I inhale it slowly, attentive to my emergent, perceptual interplay with the breathing landscape.

A view of perception as participatory and embodied is not grounded in the human body but arises through one's unfolding actions with the world. Embodied awareness emerges while experiencing unfamiliar or unknown landscapes, whether they be forests and fields enclosing a schoolyard or the untamed wilderness surrounding my sea kayak. Experiencing unknown landscapes is that journey where we walk forward, not following a path, but "laying down the path in walking" (Varela, Thompson, and Rosch 1991). When we interact with/in unfamiliar spaces, we do not walk in a path that we see before us. Rather, we open paths with each step (or paddle stroke) forward or back, bringing a freshness and wonder through our embodied experiencing.

> In this sense, how might a "path" of embodied respect unfold through experiencing unknown landscapes?

Embodying Respect

Embodied respect is an awareness that emerges while interacting within emergent spaces. At a time when so much of education seems to disembody what we know and learn, alternative ways of perceiving and inter-standing[1] embodied respect are critical. Typically, students find out what they need to know to do well on tests, find a way to remember it for a moment and regurgitate this information only to forget. We have become adept at disconnecting ourselves from the living, sentient world. We are fast moving away from a time when families worked with the land and each other to feed themselves and build shelters. We need to revitalize fresh ways of embodying our experiences within our cultural communities and the natural world. Indeed, in a world so "disembodied," our fragile ecosystem depends upon an inter-standing of how embodied respect unfolds. Embodied ways of knowing that are connected to the land and each other are vital for education and the health of the our earthly relations.

Such embodied ways of knowing embrace the inseparability of body and mind. They pay close attention to how our bodies experience the world through hands-on, or what I refer to as "bodymind," activities in education. These opportune experiences often facilitate a respect for animals and for the everyday world, one that includes the living land and its resources.

If embodied respect is critical for discerning our web of relations with all "experiencing forms" (Abram 1996), then how might we foster a pedagogy to engage the sentient (land)scape around us? How do we open possibilities for our earthly children to experience and mindfully interact with a "more-than-human" world (Abram 1996)? How might they realize their dreams and aspirations in a global system of infinite chaos? There are no "tidy" answers to these questions. I can, however, begin to imagine pedagogical possibilities that might foster embodied respect with/in educational communities. These possibilities are further linked to my experiences of wilderness environments in outdoor environmental and adventure education programs. These programs heighten students' awareness and enable them to lay down new paths as they interact with each other and the natural world.

Experiential awareness is never one fixed event but a temporary, elusive, and ever-evolving interplay of relations. It is a journey that unfolds choices and actions through "sensing" the familiar in unfamiliar ways. These choices are themselves in constant flux: they emerge through experiencing and re-experiencing.[2] Such embodiment of actions through experiencing the unknown opens our human bodies to an interplay of respectful actions and choices.

As already mentioned, embodying respect arises while interacting in emergent spaces such as we might find in the natural world. Consequently, finding theories that recognize and honor human experience as fluid and ecological is important for fostering embodied respect within educational communities.

Ungrounding Educational Experience

I am inspired by the enactive approach found in *The Embodied Mind* (Varela, Thompson, and Rosch 1991). This theoretical perspective "disrupts" traditional representationalist views of experience.[3] An enactive approach offers an interpretation of human experience that does not separate our previous experience, social history, or interaction with the environment (Varela et al. 1991). It is an ecological view that opens possibilities for how bodymind experiences arise through a world of interrelationship. "New possible worlds" are breathed into being as individuals experience unexpected and unknown landscapes.

Unexpected happenings arising through inquiry or the momentary flux of experience can not be grounded in any one act or described in any one event. They are continuously evolving. Such groundlessness is found in everyday experience, "that is, in knowing how to negotiate our way through a world that is not fixed and pre-given but that is continually shaped by the types of actions in which we engage" (Varela et al. 1991, 144). Embodied awareness emerges during acts of inquiry and educational adventures within traditional classrooms as well as outdoor education programs.

I recently explored Grade 10 students' perceptions of experiencing in an outdoor adventure and environmental education program in western Canada.

The program introduces students to a wide range of outdoor pursuits and experiences that develop leadership, self-confidence, personal responsibility, environmental awareness, love of the outdoors, and group cooperation skills. Students participate for one semester in a combination of outdoor activities including sea kayaking, rock climbing, biking, and winter backpacking trips. The following semester in this one-year program offers a school-based intensive math and science curriculum.

In the first month of the outdoor semester, students learn the skills of camping, cooking, self-rescuing, and belaying. Students are randomly assigned tenting/cooking partners and are responsible for packing all their own signed-out gear and food for outdoor trips. A path of embodied respect emerges as students articulate their perceptions of their experience in interviews, journal entries, poetry, and conversations with me throughout the program.

During my inquiry I focused on students' unpredictable moments and unexpected conversations that occurred while out on trips. As the project unfolded, I noticed shifts in their awareness, prompted by their engagements with peers and the surrounding landscape.

I was particularly interested in students' evolving inter-standing of respect through embodying an interplay of relations with the breathing landscape. My interaction with course participants was important in that it unfolded a trusting relationship for some students to share their stories and poetry. I was drawn to some narratives of experience more than others because of their heightened senses of respect for the land. Students' articulations of their journeys unfold a web of relations emerging as embodied respect.

Journeying Unfamiliar Paths

Journeying unfamiliar paths requires orientation to, and unfamiliar actions with, new landscapes. Students, particularly at the beginning of their first outdoor trip, seem to be asking all the same questions. *Can I last a week in the wilderness? What happens if I fail, if I can't handle it?* Despite their disorientation, on the first of several planned outdoor trips, students, with compassion and openness, seek new footings. They struggle with simple tasks such as cooking and tarp construction, yet embrace these unfamiliar paths with a positive attitude. Students talk of "not wanting to bring the group down" so, instead of focusing on their misery and fears of failing, they set positive goals and assist others. This positive energy and attitude is contagious, enacting a respect for each other, themselves, and the wilderness landscapes. Alli describes a memorable experience in which students, even though they are struggling with skiing in eighteen inches of powder, try to encourage each other.

> My best days in the program were today.... I couldn't believe how well people worked. People weren't putting each other down at

all they were being really supportive, like come on you can do it
as they were falling down [while skiing]. Everyone was positive!
... It was fun. I really enjoyed today, people connections were
good, weather was great and the scenery was beautiful.
(Alli, taped conversation, December 8, 1998)

The path of interactions with which we engage requires choosing and listening to our actions differently. We not only listen to the world of other humans, but we incorporate an open attitude of listening (to all bodily views). Like a buzzing nighttime mosquito seeking flesh to pierce, my ears search the stillness of day for how students are embodying struggle. How does this manifest into being respectful of one another? As human flesh, we are open to experiential happenings, which, in turn, evoke relational acts of encouragement and persistence. While laying down this path in walking (or skiing), we may espouse not only a practice of positiveness but also respect.

Journeying unfamiliar paths or adventures in the outdoors involves embracing our fears of uncertainty. The unknown adventures of learning may also open fresh perspectives, but we must risk experiencing the unexpected and unfamiliar.

It also follows that all thinking involves a risk. Certainty cannot be guaranteed in advance. The invasion of the unknown is of the nature of an adventure; we cannot be sure in advance. (Dewey 1916, 148)

It was within the uncertainty of unfamiliar landscapes while sea kayaking or hiking that most teenagers in the program became aware of their efforts to embody listening and acting in respectful ways toward each other and the environment. It is through these fresh interactions and experiences with the natural world that students begin...

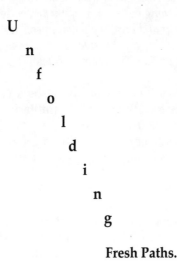

U
  n
    f
      o
        l
      d
        i
          n
            g

Fresh Paths.

A group of twelve students, two instructors, and myself are on a sea-kayaking trip out exploring the beaches and tide pools next to our campsite. Walking on algae-coated rocks, my boots turn into roller skates. As I carefully totter, slipping and sliding across the rock ledges exposed by the escaping tide, I finally hit the soft comfort of sand stabilizing my feet. My ankle length cagoule protects my entire body from the wetness of the day. The sea life on the West Coast is growing before my eyes, huge in size compared to the East Coast, with which I am more familiar. I peer into a pocket of water on one of the rock ledges and am welcomed by the most elegant three-inch-long tubeworms waving up at me. We find sea sponges, crisp purple sea urchins, and bright orange sea stars firmly attached in various patterns all over the rocks at the lowest edge of the tide line. And Holly, a student in the program, writes

Dawn of a new era

with a stick in the sand near the water's edge.

The rising tide slowly nibbles at her neatly carved words. Holly's experience is pertinent as she is not very comfortable in the outdoor environment and questions whether she will make it through the program. Although she often separates herself from her peers, I discover in my conversations that she is spending this time interacting with the wilderness around her and trying to articulate her evolving interactions through poetry and journal writings.

In response to her assignment to compare herself with nature, three to four days into the sea kayaking trip, Holly writes in her journal the following:

> Before [the program] I was like a piece of driftwood, in one place until
> something moved me, full of water, but still strong inside. Now I am
> like the tides, strong but unsure of my power, sometimes calm but
> often lashing out and breaking down uncontrollably. In the future I
> hope to be like a Douglas Fir tree: strong, proud, content, beautiful,
> and not afraid to stand on my own. (October 3, 1998)

In our conversations Holly expresses how she loves to engage in these analogies as she continues to talk about her similarity to animate and inanimate forms. She describes water as powerful enough to kill or maim, but also as beautiful. Water flows everywhere with an intensity it may not be aware of. She looks at the trees as living a long time but always in impending danger—a notion of herself as fragile even though she may look strong. As she herself is trying to do on her first trip, she views the sea creatures as always striving to survive, always in struggle. Her experience of writing poetry is embodied in the shape of characters in the sand reshaped by the changing tides. Holly draws parallels between her experiences in nature with other experiencing forms, an embodied awareness that evolves through her outdoor interactions.

Perceptual Inter-standing

Holly's perceptions arise out of sensual or synaesthetic experience. Synaesthesia, referred to as the "flowing together of different senses into dynamic and unified experience,"(Abram 1996, 125) requires active participation to form the structures of perception (p. 130). As such, perception is

> a communication or a communion, the taking up or completion
> by us of some extraneous intention or, on the other hand, the
> complete expression outside ourselves of our perceptual powers
> and a coition, so to speak, of our body with things.
> (Merleau-Ponty 1962, 320)

Merleau-Ponty (1962) refers to perception as a chiasm between the senses, which cross-over, couple, and collaborate with one another. This chiasm opens a cohesive perceptual intertwining of human flesh and the flesh of the world where embodied respect unfolds. Perceptions are "experiential, consensual, and embodied: they depend upon our biological and cultural history of structural coupling" (Varela et al. 1991, 171). While embracing the experiential world, a system of emergent interaction, embodied respect permeates human actions.

Our experience is not grounded in the body but arises through our movements, our perceptual inter-standing and embodied awareness. I refer to the awareness that arises in forming perception through experiencing as an embodied respect with the flesh of the world. This holistic perspective corresponds with the enactive approach, in which we embody awareness through our bodymind experience with the world embracing a mindfulness of our interactions. Bodies, whether of flesh, water or land, exist as experiential networks. Embodied respect arises in the interstices of our footsteps laying down a path of learning and possibility. The intertwining of humans/environment brings forth a capacity for acting, an interconnecting of sentient webs arising as embodied respect.

Articulating Possibility

Consider how such awareness and respect can arise through experiencing our natural world. Holly's "Ocean World" poem expresses such sensual awareness.

Ocean World

Standing on the sandy beach,
I realize how small I am.

The world is powerful,
Threatens to crush me if I don't respect it.

I'm glad I can respect this place,
The trees older than I will ever be,
The land purer than anything I have ever known.

I breathe in the smells of the ocean,
Wishing I could live on the air alone.

The world watches me and,
I watch the world,
And I am no longer small.

It is clear from her writing that her experiencing of the outdoors through kayaking, beachcombing, and camping has evolved an embodied respect for the unfamiliar landscape of barnacled tidal pools and windswept shorelines.

Through interpreting, conceptualizing, and re-experiencing Holly's sea kayak journey, we begin to see the possibilities of an embodied, respectful way of knowing. This knowing is where experience, action, and awareness flow into/with perception. It is not only the feeling of actualization that can be experienced, but also the merging of action and awareness into a spontaneous, poetic wording. Such expression taps into an intuitive reflection or what I refer to as a re-experiencing. Since each moment abounds with previous experience, reflecting on such experience is a re-experiencing, which continues to bring forth fresh awareness.

Should we be asking how our bringing forth of words on the page taps into the intuitive or embodiment of actions? By intuitive, I am referring to what is embodied through experience yet not in language. As Petitmengin-Peugeot (1999, 76-77) asserts:

> Intuition does correspond to an experience, that is, a set of
> interior gestures which involve the entire being.... it is
> possible to encourage its appearing.... It consists of emptying
> out, in giving up our habits of representation, of categorization,
> and of abstraction. This casting off enables us to find spontaneity,
> the real immediacy of our relation to the world. For, astonishingly,
> our most immediate, most intimate experience is also the most inacces-
> sible for us. A long detour is necessary before we receive awareness of it.

Expressing intuitive awareness through words is an embodied detour, co-emerging with our present experiencing through the action of writing—a coupling of interactions. The ways in which our students seek their potentials often requires further experiencing, struggle, and "walking" into the unknown intuitive landscape. Articulation of experience into words is very much a tapping into an embodiment of evolving and flowing interaction.

However, words are not a way to ground or represent experience. Words open us to possibility, while re-imagining and re-experiencing the emotions of a previous experience. Our immediate relations with the arising world are an emergent network of interactions between our body and the world. In other words, our bodyworld structure emerges from the coupling of human experience and social history (Varela et al. 1991). If experience is not grounded in the body, but arises through our movements or embodied actions, how might we connect to the experiential flow of sentient webs? How might we pay attention to this unfolding landscape of interaction?

Intertwining Bodymind/world

The flow of interaction in the wilderness is a time spent with an intense focusing of attention (Csikszentmihalyi 1990). Educational experiences that utilize the outdoor environment open paths toward awareness of bodyworld interactions. As evidenced in Holly's poem, "Ocean World," she uses the words of world and self as though they are separate. *The world watches me and/I watch the world/And I am no longer small.* However, she begins to intertwine what we see as her body and the ocean body or body of air. Such interpretations are difficult to express, thus we often resonate with quotes from others. Another student, Alli, shares a quote by Einstein in her journal that entertains a rethinking of the human body towards an embodied respect of the whole living world.

> *A human being is part of what we call the universe, a part limited in time and space. [They] experience [themselves], [their] thoughts and feelings, as something separated from the rest—a kind of optical illusion of [their] consciousness. This illusion is a person for us. Our task must be to free ourselves from this person by widening our circle of compassion to embrace all living beings and all of nature.*
> Albert Einstein
> —Alli's Journal, September 27, 1998

Hence, embodied respect never separates the mind from the body from the world (environment), but embraces all three in an interactive hug.

Our bodymind in relationship with our world is an organic breathing organism as Merleau-Ponty so eloquently explains:

> The body is our general medium for having a world. Sometimes it is restricted to the actions necessary for the conservation of life, and accordingly it posits around us a biological world; at other times, elaborating upon these primary actions and moving

from their literal to a figurative meaning, it manifests through them a core of new significance: this is true of motor habits such as dancing [climbing]. Sometimes, finally, the meaning aimed at cannot be achieved by the body's natural means; it must then build itself an instrument and it projects thereby around itself a cultural world.... In it we learn to know that union of essence and existence.... (1962, 146-47)

In our bodyworld, perceptions intermingle with body systems, emerging as embodied capacities for action or compassion (Dreyfus and Dreyfus 1999). Embodiment emerges through our capacity to climb mountains while also gaining physical and cultural skills. Merleau-Ponty uses the terms "intentional arc" and "maximum grip" to describe such embodiment. He refers to intentional arc as a union of cognitive, sensing and acting bodies, and to maximum grip as our embodied motivation. Intentional arc reinforces the coupling of bodyworld/experience that comes through embodied actions and skills in such activities as driving a car or rock climbing. Maximum grip is the choice or the way the body brings this embodiment into flow in our living or activities. As in climbing or most outdoor activities, we learn basic skills, moving through stages of novice, advanced beginner, competent, proficient and expert (Dreyfus and Dreyfus 1999) where one can distinguish actions which meld with the situation intuitively.[4] As the climber moves through the skill stages, attempting more difficult climbs, a desire or motivation is embodied not as a concrete goal but as "self-actualization" (Maslow 1968/1999).

Self-actualization (defined as ongoing actualization of
potentials, capacities and talents...as a fuller knowledge of...
as an unceasing trend toward unity, integration or synergy....)
(Maslow 1968/1999, 31)

It is this coupling of intention, motivation, and actualization that embodies a capacity for action which opens an awareness and respectful intertwining of bodymind and world.

Embodied respect, the awareness that arises through forming perception while experiencing, guides actions or choices, bringing forth a capacity for embracing interactions of the unknown. If we remain open-minded, that is, open to views, interactions and intuition, then climbing mountains or scripting words emerge through the flow of actions in conversation with the flesh of the world.

One does not need a goal or intention to act. One's body is simply
solicited by the situation to get into equilibrium with it.
(Dreyfus and Dreyfus 1999, 111)

As with many of our experiences, to attain a flow of interactions we embody a respect—a letting go of trying to grasp each moment. Thereby, through freefall, we release a positive energy of actions. Our bodies flow to new and unfamiliar bodily ways of attunement. For example, when climbing on a glacier of moving rock, our bodily actions attune with the moving scree,[5] as rock and body dance through each step. Fresh goals, ambitions, hopes, continually emerge as a continuation of this dance, bringing forth an unknown landscape we refer to as "our" world.

Re-experiencing the Breathing Landscape

Holly articulates well in her writings her respect for the human-made and natural parts of the world. She acknowledges what humans have achieved and how they have impacted nature. She remarks on her ability to enjoy city life, the city being "just as good" as untamed nature. She likes to think of herself as connected to the rawness of nature, yet she also accepts how she changes nature through her presence. Holly compares the wilderness to dreams with no distractions, a tuning out of things in the "stillness of nature."

> *When everything else is silent, your head is speaking to you a lot louder than it usually does, and all your thoughts are there and they are not going anywhere soon.   (Holly's Journal, January 22, 1999)*

And in the pausing between thoughts, we enter into a breathing landscape, our breath the heartbeat of the water, the air, the rocks. David Abram (1996) describes the silent conversations we have with the animate and inanimate. For example, in his writings, he relates a perceptual dialogue or sensual exploring of the world:

> When my body thus responds to the mute solicitation of
> another being, that being responds in turn, disclosing to my
> senses some new aspect or dimension that in turn invites
> further exploration...Whenever I quiet the persistent chatter
> of words within my head, I find this silent or wordless dance
> always already going on—this improvised duet between my
> animal body and the fluid, breathing landscape.... (pp. 52-53)

Holly's experience, as well as Abram's, speaks to the opening of the sensual, the invisible, the embodied awareness we are experiencing in the outdoors. And through the opening of the sensual, an embodied respect for the flesh of the world resonates between the lines of our writing...

Deep in the Woods

Deep in the woods,
I learn to be afraid for real.

On the water,
I find the true meaning of serenity.

In the darkness.
I learn to find light.

At the end of my knowledge,
I learn to know myself.

When I find my dependence,
I learn to rely on myself.

Deep in the woods,
I find a better person.

(Holly's Journal, October 7, 1998)

As Holly pointed out in one of our conversations, the "outdoors is dangerous and risky...safe, not harmful...not avoidance, it smacks you in the face. It's not an illusion." Likewise, her poetry expresses the "potential for experiencing the world in profound and dramatic ways" (Neumann 1992, 189).

Each encounter, participation, and interchange brings about an experiencing of the natural world. However, an embodied respect for, while out in, the natural world is important. As Abram (1996, 69) suggests,

> [W]hen consciously acknowledged...surroundings are experienced as sensate, attentive, and watchful, then I must take care that my actions are mindful and respectful, even when I am far from other humans, lest I offend the watchful land itself.

In being mindful to remain connected with the natural world, we embody a respect for the intertwining of our flesh with the flesh of water and land. Our web of intertwined experience incorporates infinite bodies, embodying wordless perceptions and sensations. Such capacity or potential "choice" of actions is synaesthetically performed in the gurgle of moving water, the watchful eye of the eagle, the glitter of smooth rock and the movement of the kayaker paddling with the flow of the tides. Thus, the wilderness of our interactions expressed poetically opens us to an embodied awareness of our attunement with the living landscape. Choosing a path respectful of the world's watchful "eye" invites passion and an unending flow of interaction—a limitless body-world of experiencing unknown landscapes.

Wilderness

This is beauty at its best.

The powerful ocean crashes the fine sand,
Lit by the light of a cloudy moon.

Slowly clouds roll by...
The trees outlined by a sky of velvet silk.

A bird perches to sleep on a branch,
Observing all that goes by...

I sleep and breathe in the peace of the water,
And the life of the forest,
Undisturbed in the night.

(Holly's Journal, October 2, 1998)

Embodying Respect: Pedagogical Possibilities

Pedagogy that opens us to experiencing unknown landscapes provides a space to continually unfold a freshness of embodied respect. As students' experiences in the outdoor program indicate, respect cannot be attained like a diploma, but emerges through the actions of doing. Alex, a former student now out of the program for nine years, talks about the interplay of embodied respect:

> *In the program, you also learn self respect, respect for others, and respect for the environment.... If you respect our environment, you are respecting the environment you live in, therefore you respect yourself and you are respecting that of your peers and whoever lives in the environment.*
> *(January 15, 1999)*

Learning in the outdoors unfolds the intricate web of connections to embody respect, bringing to light a recognition of the consequences of actions within the bodyworld. A great respect develops in this interactive journey along each step into the unknown. Students begin to talk of their actions and interactions as connected to the environment and each other. This connective web vitalizes a positive attitude and perceptual openness.

How can we as educators teach/facilitate a perceptual awareness or embodied respect? What pedagogical possibilities provide opportunities for inquiry and an awareness of students' choices/actions? The possibilities found in emergent ways of interacting in the wilderness open the human body to choices/actions and the unfamiliar which may be found all around us in educational environments. For example, the outdoor landscapes around our built school environments may provide opportunities for re-connecting and experiencing the familiar in unfamiliar ways. Our challenge is to encourage students to explore the unknown within breathing classrooms.

In schools, students come to know the world as a fixed landscape. Journeying into the outdoor natural world opens them to the unexpected waters of possibility. Ocean landscapes are classrooms where, like Holly, students may have the opportunity to explore possible connections and different ways of interpreting/interacting/learning, and embodying a respect for one another and the environment. My hope and invitation to you is that we provide our students opportunities in education for emergent ways of interacting that foster an embodied respect and a freshness of perception through a curriculum of experiencing unknown landscapes.

Notes

1. Inter-standing is relational where understanding is not grasping what lies beneath but gives emphasis to what lies between and amongst (Taylor and Saarinen 1994, 1, 8). For example, when braiding strands of hair, the focus is not only on the strands and how they are woven but the tension and spaces between the strands. It goes beyond just a conceptual view and stresses the significance of a relational "view."

2. I use the word re-experiencing instead of reflection to stress the point that reflection is not just in the mind but an embodiment of experience through the bodymind.

3. Representationalist views depict experience as fixed events. Experience is presented as something apart from the bodymind and disconnected from our constant evolving interactions.

4. See Dreyfus and Dreyfus (1999) for a better understanding of Merleau-Ponty's notion of intentional arc as they describe the acquiring of the skills of playing chess or driving a car.

5. Scree is the accumulation of loose stones and rocks at the bottom of a cliff or mountain.

References

Abram, David. 1996. *The spell of the sensuous: Perception and language in a more-than-human world*. New York: Vintage Books.

Csikszentmihalyi, Mihaly. 1990. *Flow: The psychology of optimal experience*. New York: Harper and Row.

Dewey, John. 1916. *Democracy and education*. New York: The Free Press.

Dreyfus, Hubert L., and Stuart E. Dreyfus. 1999. The challenge of Merleau-Ponty's phenomenology of embodiment for cognitive science. In *Perspectives on embodiment: The intersections of nature and culture*, edited by G. Weiss and H. F. Haber. New York: Routledge.

Maslow, Abraham H. 1999. *Toward a psychology of being*. 3d ed. New York: John Wiley and Sons.

Merleau-Ponty, Maurice. 1962. *Phenomenology of perception*. Translated by Colin Smith. New York: Routledge.

Neumann, Mark. 1992. The trail through experience: Finding self in the recollection of travel. In *Investigating subjectivity: Research on lived experience*, edited by C. Ellis and M. G. Flaherty. London: Sage.

Petitmengin-Peugeot, Claire. 1999. The intuitive experience. In *The view from within: First-person approaches to the study of consciousness*, edited by F. Varela and J. Shear. Thorverton, UK: Imprint Academic.

Taylor, Mark C., and Esa Saarinen. 1994. *Imagologies*. New York: Routledge.

Varela, Francisco J., Evan Thompson, and Eleanor Rosch. 1991. *The embodied mind: Cognitive science and human experience*. Cambridge, MA: MIT Press.

Touched by Gentle Breezes in Spring: An Ecological View of Renewal in Teaching

Brent Hocking

BRENT HOCKING is an educator and doctoral candidate with 18 years of teaching experience. His academic background reflects his interests in writing and the arts, second-language instruction, conflict resolution, and adult and higher education. For the past several years, he has explored enactive approaches to pedagogy and curriculum. His doctoral research focuses on themes around bodily cognition and participation to emphasize the need for thoughtful and inclusive understandings of university teaching and learning.

Abstract. This essay is contextualized by ongoing discussions about renewal as a framework for educational participation. I present the need for ecological perspectives that honor the complex, embodied nature of cognition. I explore this view through images of personal experience and analyze their significance for classroom pedagogy.

Keywords. Renewal, Embodied Cognition, Ecophilosophy, Pedagogy

Touched by Gentle Breezes in Spring: An Ecological View of Renewal in Teaching[1]

Brent Hocking

Invoking Spring through Narrative: (Em)bodied Memories of Renewal

Every spring my body experiences a profound transformation as if it were being renewed. I become part of an unfolding landscape that catches me in moments of wonder. Familiar, everyday streets turn into fragrant showcases of cherry tree blossoms. Row upon row of pink and white petals animate the city, filling the air with soft, sweet-scented perfumes.

The oceanside park where I jog also awakens. For the first time in months shoots emerge on plant stems, squirrels wander lazily out of the woods, and light, soft and translucent, filters through dense, overhead branches of old-growth forest. I feel the environment playing with my senses in strange, delightful ways. Even the smell of sea salt invigorates my body.

These memories belong to my home in Vancouver, a complex landscape of snow-encrusted mountains, high-rises and houses, and winding coastal inlets. This place holds different images from my childhood setting in north central British Columbia...

For many years I lived inland in a village surrounded by wilderness across mountain, valley, and waterway. Long before winter ended, while chilling gusts of snow and heavy afternoons of darkness still burdened the landscape, there was a contest to see who could predict when the lake would thaw. Spirits soared with each red-bellied robin sighted and each ray of sunshine that began melting snow piles stacked high on country roads. Every fuzz-covered pussy willow, every cadenced trickle of icicle dripping from rooftop gutters, and every gentle breeze on the cheek announced the passing of one era and the inauguration of another. In this clime of snow and ice the tracking of seasons, like the tracking of moose, called on every fleshly sense and intuition.

These are the images of renewal that linger in my body as it moves from one landscape to another. Although my place of residence has changed, my experiences of spring continue to inspirit my thinking with "radical aliveness" (Moss 1986). I feel the sensuous coupling that links my bones to other earthly beings. Sometimes this sense of connection is so powerful that my whole being is transformed. I identify myself with Laura, an individual in Moss's (1986, 1) introductory chapter, who is transported beyond the limits of her biological body:

> For several hours [she] had been singing a childhood hymn, repeating it over and over. Suddenly the quality of her singing changed. She felt as though she were no longer singing. She *was* the song. She found herself lifted to her feet, her arms raised toward the sky, her head arched upward. She said her hands did not end at her fingertips, but continued into the air and sky.

I too feel this sense of transcendence in spring. I lose track of that which separates my body from its encompassing worlds. It is difficult for me to discern what is renewing and what is being renewed. Ordinary, perceptual boundaries that I would use to make this distinction dissolve. For a brief instant, I am transported, moved beyond the spaces of my head and limbs like Laura, to become many bodies at once: a sky that beckons, a robin that warbles, an icicle that melts.

Spring as a Framework for Educational Inquiry: Nuturing Ecological Sensibilities

How might images of spring serve as a framework for thinking about renewal in education? What significance is there in the rhythmic flight of the robin and the fresh fragrance of the cherry tree petal? How might we carry their sense of mystery and delight into the classroom, so that it too will be the terrain of vital, generative forms of teaching and learning—forms that breathe with intrigue and possibility?

These are the points of inquiry that inform this essay. Underlying them is the issue of how and what educators should know in order to understand renewal through the language and gestures of the body within certain landscapes. My opening narrative suggests that some views of knowledge and cognition are more "embodied" than others. How these views inform teaching and learning is critical. There are three goals that serve as paths of possibility for my writing and thinking: (a) to explore notions of embodied cognition, (b) to identify them with ecological understandings of renewal, and (c) to discuss the resulting implications for pedagogy. I will relate all three areas using a series of images from my journey as a teacher and from current personal experience. Before focusing explicitly on education, however, I will describe qualities of knowing and engaging that are integral to an ecological view of renewal.

These qualities are illustrated by my recollections of spring. They draw attention to knowing as a dynamic phenomenon characterized by tension, transformation, and possibility. This is an important first element associated with ecological thinking. Feelings of sensuousness in spring are connected to the ongoing dance of life, one that shifts and flows through space and time. This dance in education as in life transforms bodies like Laura's and mine. Although it is

possible to analyze this change retrospectively, it appears that when the transformation is under way the body cannot escape the phenomenon in which it
participates; there is no felt separation between the perceiver and that which it
perceives.[2] As Abram (1996, 33) says, "The world and I reciprocate one another.
The landscape as I directly experience it is hardly a determinate object; it is an
ambiguous realm that responds to my emotions and calls forth feelings from
me in turn." It is the interplay between the world and my perceiving body that
is the site of transformation and therefore the site of understanding and possibility. Such is the nature of their interaction that my body feels overcome,
caught in a spellbinding symphony of the senses.

This connection between the body and its encompassing environment gives
rise to a second consideration: the need for ecophilosophical frameworks that
honor knowing as an interactive phenomenon. An ecological view reminds us
that earthly bodies in spring as in other seasons are structured and formed
through complex relationships, including those that allow us to be mindful of
transformations in the first place. These connections are shaped through the
sensuous particularities of communities and their ecosystems. Although it
might seem that I recalled two different sets of memories *about* spring from the
comfort of my adult years, my thinking played an active role in determining
how and in what contexts the landscapes presented themselves. This recontex-
tualization was essential for immersing me in the images that have played a
central role in my life—images that carry rich associations and legacies.
Attention to this level of detail is crucial for developing authentic understandings of a landscape and its bodies.

My participation within the landscape ensures that my images will remain
vital and alive. One criticism of my narrative might be that it over-romanti-
cizes my experiences and, as such, tends toward abstraction. Although spring
has always cleared my nostrils and invigorated my flesh, it does so as part of a
mottled landscape of sights, sounds, feelings, and smells. The same gentle
breeze that caressed my body as a child also carried nonhuman scents from
newly born tadpoles and salamanders that lived in dank, dark ponds by the
railway tracks. Rays of sunshine that melted the snow also flooded my front
yard. For every nascent, joyful sign of renewal, there is another less glamorous
but essential quality of spring as a textured landscape.

To speak of knowing as *deeply* ecological is to further acknowledge the importance of the spiritual as well as physical, affective, and intellectual dimensions
of cognition. This is a third quality revealed by my narrative description of
spring. Capra (1996, 12) identifies spirituality with the ethics of interconnectedness and says that "if we have deep ecological awareness, or experience, of
being part of the web of life, then we *will* (as opposed to *should*) be inclined to
care for all of living nature." Compassion for others is underscored in the work
of Varela, Thompson, and Rosch (1991). Unlike Capra, they maintain that compassion cannot be understood in terms of "an axiomatic ethical system nor

even...pragmatic moral injunctions. It is completely responsive to the needs of the particular situation" (Varela, Thompson, and Rosch 1991, 250)—in other words, to the moment-by-moment interactions between one perceiving body and another. My awareness of the environment in spring kindles heartfelt compassion for worlds that allow me to breathe and embrace the fullness of life.

An emphasis on embodiment means that thinking *about* a phenomenon and thinking *through* a phenomenon will result in different forms of knowing and being. The significance of an ecological view is that it challenges me to understand renewal as an unfolding, a dynamic interplay of possibilities that catches me with the other. Thinking through renewal as an educational phenomenon opens delightful possibilities for teaching and learning...

Renewal in Educational Discourse and Literature

I have been inspired in my thinking by the works of enactive theorists (Maturana and Varela 1992; Varela, Thompson, and Rosch 1991) and ecophilosophers (Abram 1996). Their writings offer fresh insight into the nature of cognition as complex and embodied. The term *embodied* signifies "both the body as a lived, experiential structure and the body as the context or milieu of cognitive mechanisms (Varela, Thompson, and Rosch 1991, xvi). The nature of embodiment is such that it simultaneously involves and implicates us in worlds beyond our own. How and in what form this embodiment unfolds is what distinguishes one living body from another. Ecophilosophy and enactive theory offer new possibilities for understanding teaching and learning as vital, bodily forms of participation that orient us to the world. To the extent that pedagogy is a breathing life form it has the potential to reawaken felt senses of embodiment in and beyond the classroom.

The need for embodied understandings of renewal in education is supported by works that analyze teaching, faculty development, and the place of the university in contemporary society. Illustrative of this literature are texts by Boyer (1990) and Frost and Taylor (1996). Both portray renewal as a vital but complex focus of inquiry in education. Boyer (chap. 4) argues for an enlarged view of scholarship that considers faculty development across individual life cycles, disciplines, and institutional demand structures. Frost and Taylor (1996, 436) note, "Investment in personal renewal can be of significant benefit to individuals and to their institutions." Their discussion, like Boyer's, is framed as part of a general inquiry into the professoriate and the relationships that inform scholarship, teaching, and research.

More engaging arguments for rethinking educational renewal appear in a special section of a recent issue of *Phi Delta Kappan* (Soder 1999). According to its contributors, discussions about renewal in public schooling incite wholly different languages and worldviews from those associated with the languages of reform. Goodlad (1999, 574) characterizes this distinction when he says, "The language of reform carries with it the traditional connotations of things gone wrong that need to be corrected.... This language is not uplifting. It says little or nothing about the nature of education, the self, or the human community. Through sheer omission it dehumanizes." Notions of renewal, by contrast, are described as "multidimensional, relatively free of good guys/bad guys and (to the frustration of many reformers) of the linearity of specified ends, means, and outcomes" (p. 575). Sirotnik (1999, 607-08) adds that renewal thinking is ecological and dynamic:

> *Renewal* is about the process of individual and organizational
> change, about nurturing the spiritual, affective, and intellectual
> connections in the lives of educators working together to under-
> stand and improve their practice. Renewal is not about a point in
> time; it is about all points in time—it is about continuous, critical
> inquiry into current practices and principled innovation that
> might improve education.

Whether or not one accepts these views about reform and renewal, it is inter-esting to note their authors' underlying senses of knowledge and cognition. The language of reform for them connotes the need to *do* something that is, to change education through planned intervention. Appeals to renew, on the other hand, are based on a deep awareness of the consequences one's actions might have within the web of life. This awareness may arise during times of doing as well as *not* doing—a point of significance in schools, universities, and other institutions of learning where activity often seems to privilege reflective forms of engagement. Frost and Taylor (1996) argue for consideration of the ways in which different types of activities, including rest and reflection, might contribute to a felt sense of renewal. They discuss this in relation to the sabbat-ical as a time for faculty renewal:

> Our own "drivenness" to produce and to be constantly active
> also makes the more reflective aspects of a sabbatical period
> difficult to envisage or to implement. Nevertheless, we think
> that we and our fields benefit when some significant part of
> our sabbatical periods is devoted to "nondoing," to listening to
> ourselves at rest. (Frost and Taylor 1996, 436)

The reform view of engagement is instrumentalist and prescriptive while the renewal perspective is prompted by concern for the growth and well-being of vital, sustained relationships within a community.[3] There are two implications of the reform/renewal discussion that have immediate significance for this essay. First is the confirmation that educational philosophies of renewal will be well served by thoughtful and informed understanding of knowledge as eco-logical and embodied. Second is the awareness that such understanding will resist oversimplification.

Pedagogic Enactments Unfolding

While engaging with this essay, I have been moved to simultaneously experience and re-evaluate renewal as a rhythmic interplay within my worlds of educational research and elementary school teaching. For several weeks I have savored the languages of renewal, allowing them time and range to sit on my tongue and wake my body. I have opened myself to worlds beyond my own, worlds that interrupt my thinking and reach under my skin. I wonder if the senses of energy and renewal that animate my body as a writer might offer insight into the senses I long for in my teaching? Perhaps this is the place at which my thinking *about* might become a thinking *through*, a site for energy and transformation, reinvigoration and creativity?

To help me understand this tension, I have reflected on my journey as a teacher. I remember thinking that teaching and learning are and should be about innovation, change, and new beginnings. Perhaps I have long believed in renewal because I have been a firm advocate of education as a critical framework for personal and collective transformation and well-being. At 24 years of age when I enrolled in a teacher education program, I longed to work in an area where I might be able to make a difference in people's lives. Dreams to remake the world became aspirations to renew. These dreams have attracted me at various times to the youthful promises of child-centered curricula, the dynamic languages of active and liberatory pedagogies, the lucid glows of critical thinking, and the rejuvenating qualities of progressive schooling—discourses which hinge on the transformative potential of teaching and learning.

I am still lured by discourses of this type, but am inclined to rethink the values and intentions that inform my world-making. I am less willing to accept an instrumentalist view of renewal; that is, the notion that I need to impose change on the world. Although I still prepare comprehensive instructional units and lesson plans, my manner of engagement with them has shifted. Instead of teaching *from* them I teach *with* them. I also think about my body and the classroom environment. Notions of reform that once seduced my thinking have given way to a much greater seduction: the recognition that I too am part of the text, that my body as teacher participates reciprocally with other classroom bodies through time and space to renew and be renewed. It is a fertile, generative space where every moment, every animate being, fully breathes with possibility. It is a space where language, gesture, and performance enfold unto one another and where the actions and interactions of classroom participants are choreographed as teaching and learning in a "more-than-human" (Abram 1996), more than seasonal spectacle of birds, flowers, and icicles.

To the extent that ecological and embodied views of knowledge have heightened my bodily awareness, they have shaped my senses of connection and complicity in the world.[4] The transformation of my body, I realize, is never wholly self-directed, but enacted from a background of meaning in which person and environment co-mingle. To renew is to understand that my teaching body is subject to change in the course of instructing others. This body that I know as mine is a critical link to the surrounding life-world. A pedagogy of renewal that resonates with the breaths and heartbeats of students and teachers is one that catches me with the other—the other engaged in classroom content and activities, the other inspired by the challenges of research, and the other who has not yet entered formal education or who has graduated. This pedagogy of renewal has transformed my body so that I might open myself to "the nourishment of otherness"(Abram 1996, ix).

With any transformation there remains the possibility that such nourishment will be withheld, that elements of the choreography will fail to unfold as expected. Movements and engagements that allow my body to connect *with* the other are precisely those that keep it *from* her, suspended midcourse in abeyance. Transformative processes, by definition, are always in process, shifting and sliding. It is not only the classroom that changes, but my perceptions of it—the instances that bring *me* into contact with *them*: instructor into contact with student, theory into contact with practice, and intent into contact with action. To speak of classroom renewal as a dynamic is to honor the absences and movements of the unknown and not-yet-there. It is to recognize moments when teacher and learner, person and environment, body and mind, seem to dance joyfully as one. Participant actions and interactions can never be abstracted out of context or reified in language because at every moment possibilities to nurture and be nurtured are always *en route*— emerging, travelling, and renewing teaching and learning through possibility as well as desire, similarity as well as difference.

For this reason, renewal is less a formulated plan of action than a quality of knowing and living that spills over into pedagogy, curriculum, and research. An enactive view of knowledge does not privilege one form of inquiry over another. To inquire is to make known, to enter into a body of knowledge and reveal its connections to other knowing bodies. It is this interplay of idea and understanding, text and subtext, entry and entanglement, that speaks to renewal as an embodied and authentic, life-sustaining phenomenon worthy of inquiry from a variety of perspectives. This is the nature of complicity, an embodiment that catches individuals in their knowing. A challenge for me has been to become mindful of the ways in which my body engages with its encompassing worlds.

Images of Renewal from Recent Experience

While I was thinking about renewal in the context of my daily activities three images came to mind—two from the classroom and one from my home environment. They challenged my ability to engage across their similarities and differences. Their bodies were vital and alive but they kept sliding into spaces of being and non-being, opaqueness and transparency. I summoned the images again, so that I might feel them incarnate in my bones and study their rhythms.

Time to Renew...A Letter from the Principal

For the past seven years I have worked part-time as an elementary teacher while pursuing graduate studies. Although my doctoral research embraces enactive understandings of pedagogy and participation at the university level, the first set of images that appeared when I thought about renewal were from the school where I teach. I was reminded of the energy, excitement, and confusion that characterize the beginning of each academic year.

This September when I returned to school I noticed a welcome letter from the principal in each teacher's mailbox. I pulled out my copy and read:

> Dear All...
> So what a difference a summer makes...travel, falling into our
> "preferred" daily rhythms, having a myriad of choices available
> to us. We each have our unique indicators that we really have
> "come down" from the last school year. I knew I was beginning to
> relax when, about three weeks into the summer, I asked, "What
> day of the week is it?" (Do we ever ask ourselves that question
> during the school year??) Nevertheless, there is an excitement
> that comes from the opportunity for "fresh starts." I think we
> are probably in one of the few fields where we experience this
> annually. (P. George, personal communication, August 1999)[5]

This letter describes different space-moments of renewal. There is reference to the summer holidays, a time for relaxation and for preferred bodily rhythms and freedoms. The seasonal view of time in the opening sentence gives way to a feeling of timelessness as one day becomes another. In the closing paragraph there is a return to summertime energies again, but in the space-moments of September when school begins.

This felt sense of falling in and out of time is crucial to how educators perceive and engage with renewal. Formal education follows a linear structure based on the calendar year and the cycle of seasons. Within this structure September is often perceived as a time of fresh starts because it allows teachers to contemplate possibilities for their students' learning. Next to September, January seems to be a month for new beginnings. At both times teachers often seem motivated to develop a course of action for the weeks of instruction ahead.

Yet, I wonder if thinking about the school calendar in these terms may be a little too rational—even contrived? What spaces do we leave as instructors for the unanticipated? Sirotnik (1999, 607) argues that an ecological conception of renewal "places much more emphasis on chance, serendipity, unanticipated circumstances and events, and ongoing interpretation rather than on predetermined goals, planned interventions, designated outcomes, and causal explanations." The consideration here is on renewal as process and unfoldment rather than a particular product. Educators' perceptions of renewal are directly related to their understandings of time.

For those who subscribe to a linear view of time and simultaneously hold to a view of September and January as periods of renewal—a fundamental contradiction emerges, for the months that these teachers cherish as opportunities for fresh starts are experienced by many non-educators and wild animals as periods of reduced activity.[6] As September becomes October summer dew is replaced by frost. Birds fly south to warmer feeding grounds. Leaves once green and silky transform into brittle, color-stained parchment. In Vancouver the heavy flow of traffic to beaches subsides and fewer joggers show up for their daily exercise. A sun that once generated soft, opulent streams of light loses its energy and warmth. These are the signs of summer-turned-autumn for many bodies outside the classroom.

Does the academic calendar disrupt the body's felt sense of time? In thinking about the letter from my principal I am reminded of the order educators impose on their lives, so that they might go about the "real" business, some would say, of planning and delivering lessons and assessing learning outcomes. Yet, if we think about newness as an annual phenomenon, we are bound to overlook the needs of our bodies. The reason summer may stimulate a felt sense of renewal is not because it occupies a particular time of year, but because it creates spaces for the body to discover its own rhythms. Thinking about summer as a season is different from participating in summer as a timeless phenomenon. The latter speaks to an embodied sense of renewal.

Understanding rejuvenation as an embodied phenomenon poses challenges in academic institutions regulated by timetables. One challenge is the need to consider individual differences. What stimulates and renews one body may not stimulate and renew all bodies. Another challenge is that opportunities for rest and relaxation as well as activity will trigger multiple responses. A question here is not whether one form of participation facilitates change more than others—renewal can happen in both instances. The more critical issue is whether classroom participants are aware of the rhythms and conditions that leave their bodies feeling revitalized. Developing an awareness of one's body de-emphasises a prescriptive view of time while challenging the notion that pedagogy and curriculum can be fully planned.

Enactive understandings of the body carry important implications for classroom instruction and learning, including concern for the ways in which living "organism and environment enfold into each other and unfold from one another in the fundamental circularity that is life itself" (Varela, Thompson, and Rosch 1991, 217). It is through our embodied webs of connection with other living bodies that our perceptions of the world change. To know, enactively speaking, is to bring forth new worlds at each moment through our living in spaces with others (Maturana and Varela 1992, 11).

It is because our perception of the world is mediated moment-by-moment from one body to another that teaching and learning are continuously re-enacted. When the worlds we create improve our lives or stimulate our thinking we may feel renewed as educators. Sometimes the worlds we co-enact, however, will disrupt classroom relationships. In their work on socially situated learning, Lave and Wenger (1991, 114) explain how participants within communities of practice "are replaced (directly or indirectly) by newcomers-become-old-timers...This tension is in fact fundamental—a basic contradiction of social reproduction, transformation, and change." Any discussion about embodied cognition as a dynamic process of renewal must consider these moments of separation and displacement as well as those that rejuvenate and revitalize classroom participants.

Senses to Renew: Children's Interactions with the School Environment

The principal's note led me to reflect on renewal as an embodied phenomenon and the need for dynamic understandings of seasons. My second image carries more energy. It is my recollection of children returning to school. Like my images of spring, it reminds me of the sensuous coupling between the body and its environment—a sensuousness that shapes perceptions of renewal. For all of teachers' conscious efforts to structure the school year, something wonderfully spontaneous and chaotic happens whenever young minds enliven the classroom and little feet fill the hallways. I picture the sounds and laughter of my students playing off one another in my imagination. I see the nervous, animated bodies of children sitting in their desks during the first day of school. I sense their anticipation while they wait to discover who their new teacher will be.

This image of young learners highlights the importance of interplay, of dynamic engagement between the sensing body and its encompassing world. When watching elementary children it appears that they have as much influence on the school environment as it has on them. It is the tension between the two that bears witness to the generative and vital processes of life—processes that create spaces for learning and rejuvenating the body. There is depth as well as breadth to children's engagements with the environment. These interactions are not based on any one sense but on the orchestration of many senses coming together as one dynamic response. This "synaesthesia," or fusion of the senses, says Abram (1996, 62), is integral to the ways we know and experience the world:

> My various senses, diverging as they do from a single, coherent
> body, coherently *converge*, as well, in the perceived thing, just as
> the separate perspectives of my two eyes converge upon the
> raven and convene there into a single focus. My senses connect
> up with each other in the things I perceive, or rather each
> perceived thing gathers my senses together in a coherent way,
> and it is this that enables me to experience the thing itself as a
> center of forces, as another nexus of experience, as an Other.[7]

Therein lies the significance of interplay, a playfulness that catches the senses at once. This is what my body experiences in spring.

Synaesthesia highlights the importance of direct sensory experience for under-standing renewal. Seasoned instructors often make reference to "teaching in the moment." Typically, this means laying aside preconceived notions about what might happen as instructors involve themselves in a particular lesson. It is the opportunity to fully engage their senses *in* the moment rather than thinking *about* the moment that presents so many possibilities. As adults we have much to learn from the ways in which children immerse themselves com-pletely in the world.

A synaesthetic view of classroom participation underscores the immediacy of lived experience. This is crucial to an understanding of renewal. Although the reform view is directed towards future change, the ecological view reminds us that renewal is always present in the bodies around us. According to this sec-ond perspective, renewal not only speaks to what might or should be, but that which already is an integral dimension of educational inquiry and classroom participation. Even as instructors strive to develop lessons, the bodies they are attempting to change are already deeply immersed in life-changing events through the ecologies of relationship that constitute classroom cultures. One implication for instructors is again to be mindful of their responses within these relationships.

Like adults' bodies, children's bodies do not return to school according to a standard format. Some children return enthusiastically or matter-of-factly, oth-ers, with tension and trepidation. Some arrive punctually at the beginning of the year; some arrive late after an extended holiday. Some study over the sum-mer; others abandon formal learning and return as if it were their first time in school. Most children come back as expected; some move away over the sum-mer holidays. Even if they wished, educators could not predict all of these pos-sibilities. A complex, dynamic view of renewal calls for imaginative ways of re-experiencing and relanguaging the world—ways that honor wonder and creativity. A pedagogy based on "the possibilities for transformation inherent in human experience" (Varela, Thompson, and Rosch 1991, xv) acknowledges that educational programs "will make the world a different place" (Cervero and Wilson 1993, 60). This difference arises through animate bodies and the fusion of their senses.

A Tree Beyond Seasons: Interrupted Space-Moments of Possibility

The third and final image of renewal was the most unexpected and hence the most dissonant for me. It was not from the classroom, but from a familiar stretch of space outside my living room window. I remembered the tree that has been my companion and source of inspiration since moving into my apartment. It is a tree that changes seasonally. Bleak and barren in winter, it comes to life once again with its cherry blossom petals in the warm airs of spring. In the autumn, leaves that were once home to swallows and other birds metamor-phose into fiery red flames before falling onto the sidewalk and into the street.

I have contemplated the importance of this tree in other contexts (Hocking 1998).[8] Yet, when I first moved into my apartment I was oblivious to its existence. At the time its branches were silhouetted quietly against the cold December sky. Then it snowed. Branches that had once been naked suddenly became a centerpiece of winter's magic, captivating my senses and imagination. A tree once invisible had suddenly pushed itself into the foreground of my perception. Following that experience the tree has served to remind me of the ways in which my body extends into a more-than-human landscape.

On this occasion, however, I perceived the tree's presence as an intrusion. *What did a tree in mid-autumn have to do with an essay on renewal?* I wondered. Why was I not dreaming about the tree in spring with its soft, fragrant petals—a metaphor more consonant with revitalization? I reflected on my dilemma and then realized that without autumn and winter, there would be no fragment profusion of petals in spring, no bright colors to grace the eye.

Similar patterns can be found in the renewal of classroom bodies. As learning unfolds, different patterns of growth and development manifest themselves from one individual to another. Very often learning seems to be in a state of non-renewal, a period of quiet repose until a series of actions or interactions trigger that which has been tacit and unnoticed. Like the tree and my relationship with it, classroom bodies form a web, a backdrop for individual transformations. As the individual is renewed, so too is the web. Yet, bound as we are by our own silky threads, we may not notice the threads around us. Our entanglements as teachers and learners may prevent us from sensing blossoms that are latent—the blooming that will bring new learning and new worlds into the classroom.

Not once but twice the tree caught me off guard and interrupted my thinking while I wrote this chapter. I waited for its green leaves to turn color in October. Several weeks passed. Still they remained on their branches while dervish windstorms and early dark nights replaced warmer, summer breezes. It was the end of November before a banner of red leaves set the street on fire.

Old rhythms shift; new rhythms evolve. While I was thinking about the tree and its rhythms I had inadvertently become part of another transformation, the unfolding and shifting transformation of tree-in-the-world and me-in-the-tree, a choreography which, like teaching and learning, caught my body in new and unexpected places.

Towards an Ecological Understanding of Renewal: Implications for Teaching and Learning

In this essay I explored the connections between embodied forms of knowing and an ecological perspective of renewal. Although I have referred to enactive theory and ecophilosophy, my primary emphasis has been on personal and professional images of experience that speak to the sensuous, engaged nature of my bodily encounters with the world. I reflected through the writing rather than on the writing as a way to re-enact my understandings.

It may be helpful to review key characteristics of the ecological or *ecophilosophi-cal* view at this point. The first is a heightened sense of the relationships underlying personal and collective experience. Spring air feels incisively warm and inviting; cherry trees seem to bloom ever more gloriously. In both cases my senses are alerted to subtle, yet important transformations in the environment. A second quality is the interplay between the knower and known. This was discussed in relation to the notion of reciprocity. This engagement in time and space is dynamic—a third characteristic. Understanding of the world is, fourth, shaped by the histories and legacies of organisms that transform their bodies over time. This movement is nonlinear and generally unpredictable. A fifth quality is the importance of direct sensory experience as a primary means of engagement. The fusion of the senses brings together diverse bodies, each with their embodied rhythms. Finally, notions of renewal as *deeply* ecological raise questions about the ethical dimensions of human inquiry and knowledge. How one participates in the world cannot be separated from the beliefs, principles, and motivations underlying one's actions.

These are the qualities that are compatible with an ecological view of renewal. This view identifies learning as an ongoing process. It acknowledges participation across multiple bodies of knowledge. It allows for different kinds of transformation according to the self-organizing capabilities of living organisms within a particular environment. And it speaks to the tensions and possibilities of human existence on Earth.

Such a view will have important implications for classroom participation and pedagogy. Different areas of teaching, including program planning and implementation and the evaluation of learning will be affected. A primary consideration in the first instance will not be how instructors should forecast change, but rather how they might engage with emerging interactions among classroom bodies. This will include the biological bodies of participants as well as disciplinary bodies of knowledge. A key question in terms of implementation will not be how to teach to instructional overviews, but how to be mindful of the ways in which plans are animated and reshaped by classroom encounters. Attention to assessment methods and evaluation criteria will be vital for making sense of learning.

An ecological view of renewal will require snapshots of children's learning through different stages to honor knowing as a dynamic process. The snapshots should address bodies that learn individually and in concert with other learners. Unlike much of the current literature on evaluation, I believe that teachers must search for indicators of learning that go beyond ocularcentric, that is, observation-based, representations of knowledge. Evaluation should be based on varied forms of sensory experience that speak to how children make sense of the world. These are the kinds of practical considerations that will be important when shifting from a reform orientation to an ecological view of renewal.

Embracing this perspective will require teachers to be mindful of their own bodies and to seek images of renewal that have special significance for them. What are those images? What are their shapes and contours? Following this initial level of inquiry, a second level to place the images in context will be needed. At this stage a challenge will be to identify relationships among certain images and their respective classroom ecologies. Finally, teachers will need to explore their emerging understandings by re-embodying them in everyday classroom experience. All these forms of inquiry will heighten instructional sensibilities to renewal as a dynamic phenomenon. To understand renewal in education is not only to focus on the particularities of knowledge and the idiosyncrasies of living organisms, but to be mindful of one's body researching new pedagogic worlds, transformed and enlivened by classroom rhythms and connections.

To the extent that teaching and learning are informed by complex cycles of change, they call for a vital, full understanding of the body—one that speaks to the constraints as well as freedoms, continuities as well as ruptures, impasses as well as possibilities of human relationships with the earth. An ecological view of renewal reminds us that our capacities to know and be are possible because of the air we breathe and the trees that solicit our wonder.

Notes

1. My use of the term "ecological" in this paper is meant to be synonymous with the term "ecophilosophical." The latter "insists that the human project is a rediscovery of human meaning, related to the meaning of the universe" (Skolimowski 1981, 1) and encompasses a broad range of ecologically influenced perspectives. My own understandings of ecophilosophy have been heavily influenced by the work of David Abram (1996). I use the term "ecological" because it is shorter and consistent with Sirotnik's (1999, 607) description of renewal.

2. This is a critical principle of enactive theory and 'ecophilosophy'—areas that will be introduced later in the essay.

3. In addition to their conceptual differences, notions of reform and renewal have also played vital roles in the history of North American education. There is some evidence to suggest confusion between understandings of reform and understandings of renewal as illustrated by the following statement from the Task Force on Education for Economic Growth in the United States: "If the progress of education renewal in our country could be judged solely by the number of states that have either implemented or are developing state plans to improve the public schools, one would have to say renewal is well under way" (1984, 5).

4. For a discussion of complicity and complexity in education, see Sumara and Davis (1997).

5. Quoted with the consent of my principal, Pam George. I have maintained the original punctuation when copying her words.

6. This tension between a seasonal view of time and the academic calendar was discussed at a presentation I attended during the 19th Annual *JCT (Journal of Curriculum Theorizing)* Conference on Curriculum Theory and Classroom Practice, October 15-18, 1997, in Bloomington, IN. The presentation was entitled *Engaging "Mind"fulness: Spirituality and Curriculum Connections* by Elaine Kent Riley from Louisiana State University. The discussion took place among participants in attendance at this particular session.

7. The notion of synaesthetic perception is derived from Merleau-Ponty, the French phenomenologist. See his work, *Phenomenology of Perception,* 1945/1962, pp. 228-229.

8. Copies of the text from my conference presentation and the texts of my co-presenters are available at the following website address: <http://eduserv.edu.yorku.ca/~dav&sum>.

References

Abram, D. 1996. *The spell of the sensuous: Perception and language in a more-than-human world.* New York: Pantheon Books.

Boyer, E.L. 1990. *Scholarship reconsidered: Priorities of the professoriate.* Princeton, NJ: Carnegie Foundation for the Advancement of Teaching.

Capra, F. 1996. *The web of life: A new scientific understanding of living systems.* New York: Anchor Books.

Cervero, R.M., and A.L. Wilson. 1993. *Power and responsibility in planning adult education programs.* Paper presented at the 34th Annual Adult Education Conference (AERC). University Park, PA: Penn State University.

Frost, P.J., and M.S. Taylor. 1996. *Rhythms of renewal.* In *Rhythms of academic life: Personal accounts of careers in academia,* edited by P.J. Frost and M.S. Taylor. Thousand Oaks, CA: Sage.

Goodlad, J.I. 1999. Flow, eros, and ethos in educational renewal. *Phi Delta Kappan* 80(8): 571-578.

Hocking, B. 1998. Troubling subjects: An ecological view of teaching and learning. In B. Davis (Chair), *Troubling education: Enactivism as a theory for teaching.* Symposium conducted at the Annual Meeting of the American Educational Research Association, San Diego, CA.

Lave, J., and E. Wenger. 1991. *Situated learning: Legitimate peripheral participation.* Cambridge: Cambridge University Press.

Maturana, H.R., and F.J. Varela. 1992. *The tree of knowledge: The biological roots of human understanding.* Revised ed. Boston: Shambhala.

Merleau-Ponty, M. 1962. *Phenomenology of perception.* Translated by C. Smith. London: Routledge and Kegan Paul (Original work published 1945)

Moss, R. 1986. *The black butterfly: An invitation to radical aliveness.* Berkeley, CA: Celestial Arts.

Sirotnik, K.A. 1999. Making sense of educational renewal. *Phi Delta Kappan* 80(8): 606-610.

Skolimowski, H. 1981. *Eco-philosophy: Designing new tactics for living.* London: M. Boyars.

Soder, R., ed. 1999. Educational renewal [A Kappan special section]. *Phi Delta Kappan* 80(8): 568-610.

Sumara, D.J., and B. Davis. 1997. Enlarging the space of the possible: Complexity, complicity, and action-research practices. In *Action research as a living practice,* edited by T.R. Carson and D. Sumara. New York: Peter Lang.

Task Force on Education for Economic Growth. 1984. *Action in the states: Progress toward education renewal: A Report.* Denver, CO: Education Commission of the States.

Varela, F.J., E. Thompson, and E. Rosch. 1991. *The embodied mind: Cognitive science and human experience.* Cambridge, MA: MIT Press.

All Knowledge Is Carnal Knowledge: A Correspondence

David Abram and David W. Jardine

What follows is a reconstruction of an e-mail correspondence that took place between November 1999 and February 2000.

David Abram: Greetings, David! Here I am at last. My sweetheart and I have been wandering through the American West, snooping around for a potential community, and although no place reached up through our feet and grabbed us, we've landed for a time in the high desert of northern New Mexico—in the midst of a mongrel community of activists I know fairly well from years spent living and loving in this dusty terrain before moving to Washington State three years ago. We had hoped that island realm would claim us, but the combined effects of Boeing, Microsoft, and the city of Seattle generally sprawling all around us, sprawling up into our noses and our ears, finally forced us to flee. We embarked on this most futile of quests in turn-of-the-millennium America: the quest for wildness—wildland and wild, earthy, close to the ground community. Slim pickin's these days. Development everywhere, clear-cuts even in the back of the backcountry, streams ravaged by effluent from abandoned mining operations. It's not all hopeless: there's still plenty mystery out in them thar hills, but I was mostly shocked by how *the same* all the towns are becoming. Ah well…I suppose Canada's a decade or two behind the States, and if only we could get visas to live and work in Canada, we'd prob'ly be there in a flash.

Anyway, David, I've just finished reading for the second time in three days your little essay "Birding Lessons and the Teachings of Cicadas" (Jardine 1998). I read it again only because, on reading it a few days ago, it brought me such pleasure, and I wanted to experience that pleasure again. And did. That whole little essay just makes me really happy—to know that someone is thinking and writing like that, saying these things as gently and gracefully as you are. I mean, I was really struck by the writing style that you've been forging for yourself, and it got me thinking about the ways of languaging that seem to reign within academia, and within Western education generally, and ultimately within our civilization at this curious moment.

Seems that you and I both are engaged, whether implicitly or explicitly, in trying to nudge the collective language—to loosen it up, perhaps, in hopes of making room for various other non-human voices to enter and influence the general conversation. No matter that these other voices do not speak in words (but rather in honks, or trills, or croaks, or whispering rattles)—what's important, as your essay on birding lessons seems to show, is that our own words be awake to these other styles of expression, these other bodies, these other shapes of sentience and sensitivity. But to let my words and my thoughts stay awake and responsive to these other voices entails, it seems, that I speak more as a body than as a mind—that I identify more with this breathing flesh (this skin and these hands and this ache in the gut) than my culture generally allows, and that I let my words and my thoughts blossom out of my limbs. That I acknowledge and honor my own animal presence, this curiously muscled form with its various affinities and cringes, and its apparent ability to echo, or reverberate off of, any other body it encounters—a sandstone cliff, or a water strider, or a wolf howling out in the forested distance.

For me, the whole reason and worth of reclaiming the body—or rather, of letting the body reclaim us—is so that we may find ourselves back inside this delicious world from which schooling had exiled us, rediscovering our embedment in the thick of things, remembering our real community and being remembered by that community. I mean, how long did we think we could go on without the necessary guidance that herons and toads have to offer?

David Jardine: So, what if we try to think of our human inheritances, cultural, disciplinary, textual…our mathematics, our buildings, our schools of art with their pulls of paints, the oddly named "language arts" found in schooling…as somehow, somehow *bodies of knowledge?* Given (and it is perhaps this seeming "given" that is the sorest point) the mandates of schools and the entrusting of the human disciplines to teachers and children, can we draw into those places the earthly, bodily images and the sorts of sensuous, bodily encounters you suggest? What often happens when "environmental education" penetrates the school is that we come to understand the earth as a special topic (distinct from but still) among others (language, mathematics, social studies, the fine arts, each with their own curriculum guide alongside the "environmental education" curriculum guides). We then pursue the delicious thick of things like sandstone cliffs, or water striders, or wolf howling and the guidance of herons and toads, but we have such a hard time finding our human works bodily delicious. All the rest of schooling is left behind (in the wake of "environmental education's" desire to "get outside") and, to be brutal about it, school subjects are drained of their body and life and blood. They have, in a weird way, been abandoned.

So, is it possible, is it even feasible, is it even *desirable* that Pythagorean Theorem become something off which we can echo and reverberate? That it, too, might be a *body of work* we might remember and be remembered by, a real, living community of conversation, of struggle, of shared and contested histories, of shoals and sediment layers and evidences of erosion and restoration and endurance, of signs, tracks, pointing, a place that must be entered with care if it is to show itself and not be scared off by our interloping, leaving only math worksheets in its wake? I'm not sure where it is from: someone suggested that "it is language all the way down," and someone responded, "If it is language all the way down, then it is also Earth all the way up."

David Abram: Um, I vaguely remember that it was my philosophical colleague Jim Cheney (1989), responding to a statement by Richard Rorty that "it is language all the way down," who said something to the effect of "well, yes, but it is also Earth all the way up."

Earth all the way up—of course! So there's really no realm of our experience, no layer of reflection so rarefied that it definitively breaks free of the earth's influence. No artifact that has not also been authored, or at least enabled, by the curious mix of minerals, winds, and waters that comprise this wild planet, no "virtual" reality so virtual that it is not tacitly informed by the tastes and textures of *this* reality. Not even language is immune to the influence of gravity! All of which becomes apparent as soon as we return to our senses and acknowledge the sensuous, corporeal character of all our experience. Even the most outrageous visions are still visual, still granted—that is, by the bodily eye in its dreaming or delirium—and hence already infected by the visible.

And so why not mathematics, too—I mean how could it be otherwise? Does not all our mathematics grow out of the proportion between our bodies and the round earth? Is not "geometry," as the very word suggests, the measure of Ge or Gaia—the way the earth measures itself in relation to the human body?

I find rather odd the common assumption that another thoughtful species evolved on some other planet would somehow come up with the same mathematics that we have. Heck, even another species on this planet, if they chose to codify their sense of order, would surely incubate a different mathematics than this that we've hatched. Indeed, the sea urchin who once inhabited the delicate calcium matrix that now rests on my windowsill, to say nothing of the giant undulating jellyfish I once came upon (while diving off the coast of Thailand) who had a whole school of hundreds of little, fluorescent blue fish living under the protection of her transparent and pulsing umbrella—these radial folks seem already to be practicing a mathematics very different from the one we two-leggeds seem to be pursuing. It is our breathing body—with its symmetries, its rhythms, its vertebral sequences and distances and digits—that infiltrates us into the field of numbers and numerical relations, and so of course the body will lend something of its character to the mathematics that it glimpses and explores.

And yet the sea urchin's mathematics would not be entirely alien; indeed it would be weirdly complementary to any human mathematics we might devise, intimately familiar in its strangeness, since both we and the urchins, for all our corporeal differences, can only dream in relation to the same earth, the same sphere, the same vast and spherical flesh. Our small bodies are so different, yet our larger body—our larger flesh—is the same.

Or so I have always imagined it. I mean, it's plenty obvious that even different *human* cultures (China and Europe, for example) can come up with different sciences, different mathematics, different ways of relating to the common earth. And so I am in utter agreement with your sense that these institutions are *bodies* of knowledge—that our schools, our sciences, our most refined arts are all living bodies of knowledge, with particular habits, rhythms, and styles of comportment that have been grappled over and handed down from generation to generation. That these are not fixed and finished sets of facts but corporeal practices, styles of engagement, ways of seeing, active ways of knowing. Of course this does not mean that they are arbitrary, since they are ways of relating to the actual earth. They are not merely "socially constructed," at least no more than they are constructed by the earth the particular grasses we eat.

In this sense your notion seems important to me, radically so—that we should teach even such a taken-for-granted truth as the Pythagorean Theorem as a living body of knowledge, a richly sedimented bunch of fleshly encounters and contested practices that we have inherited and, perhaps, can reactivate and contribute to. What a shift that would bring to contemporary culture, if mathematics began to remember itself as a sensuous, breathing, carnal field of earthly interactions! I mean, what were Pythagoras and his secretive sect up to if not cultivating a set of bodily practices, of ways of looking and listening—to the world, to numbers, to the night sky studded with lights.

But then again, wasn't it Pythagoras himself who was early among Westerners to so segregate the realm of number and proportion from the sensuous world to which our animal bodies give us access? Wasn't it Pythagoras who, in our tradition, first insisted upon the purity and eternal nature of mathematical truth relative to the shifting, dangerous, and hence less real world of generation and decay in which we find ourselves bodily ensnared? Wasn't it he, enamoured of numbers and their apparent generality, who first set the human mind lusting after a purity that was not of this earth?

David Jardine: "Lusting after a purity that was not of this earth?" Think you've got it there. Maybe, to really understand mathematics as a body of knowledge, we need to understand something of the lust for immortality that hides in its axiomatic allures. Wouldn't it be something to meditate upon this sort of thing with our children in schools? I remember one grade seven kid out in the school yard, near winter solstice, talking about how low the sun had gotten, and how, even so, even with *this* sort of bodily evidence of the grand circles of change, somehow, the tree and its shadow casts still carry Pythagorean proportionalities. What is this strong allure of mathematics, *as a lure*, as a *bodily* allure? Hmm.

Been thinking the odd similarity our work has, that both of us tell bodily tales, but we both also share a philosophical tradition that, for me anyway, handed me back my fleshy life out of a career in philosophical ideation. Phenomenology, the sensuous presence of the lived world, hermeneutics and the embodiment of ancestry and a seriously finite human subject…it is clear in your book (Abram 1996) that your tale is somewhat similar. When, in your work, you take up Merleau-Ponty and his visibilities and invisibilities (or Plato and his), it becomes clear that the ancestors can help us experience more deeply, more thoroughly. That is the feel I get from your book, that knife edge, where what presents itself to the critterbody, the sensuous spell, the sensuous *Speil*, is not just felt, but mulled over, taken seriously enough to not just be stimulating, but thought-provoking as well. For me, this is really the knife edge that I want my own work to have—the felt immediacies of the ancestors howling in the flesh. Robertson Davies once suggested that the outcome of education is that you become haunted by more ghosts. So when I think back to your words about Pythagoras and his motley, secretive crew, their work, even their formulae, become like old, odd inheritances passed down through many warm hands, and even though he might have aspired to otherworldliness, I can feel the flesh-heat of that aspiration as a deeply human one.

So, let me try this.

When Merleau-Ponty states that the eye that gazes out at the visible terrain is also visible, and hence is entirely a part of that visible field, so that, as you've written in *The Spell of the Sensuous*, the world and I share a common *flesh*—a common animate element that is at once both sensible and sensitive, perhaps even sentient—well, as we read and ponder this, it is some aspect of our embodiment that takes in these words of his and yours: we read them, we speak them out loud, we remember them and they affect our thinking. Similarly, when we turn away from our books and tune in to the cicadas thrumming outside, well, some aspect of our bodies takes in that experience as well. To be sure, the latter experience has a different character; it is less verbal and more auditory, having to do with the dips and volumes of air and its humidity between these trees and me. But the tales told are analogous, some-how, even akin.

When some theorists speak of "embodied knowing" they want to set up some sort of fight at this juncture, claiming, without often saying so in so many words, that academic work (like reading Merleau-Ponty), is *in principle* "dis-embodied," that all those ancestral-bibliographic searches in what James Hillman (1991, 101) called "the old place" are to be disparaged in favor of some image of immediacy. But I don't think these two encounters are necessarily at odds here, or that one is any less embodied than the other. They are simply two different aspects of the body, or two different ways of being body.

David Abram: This must be a quick missive: I am in the grip of some intense sickness misery at the moment and trying to fathom how to deal rightly with it before it deals overmuch with me, so I ask your patience for a few days. I'll climb back into the conversation as soon as I can think straight (or better, curved—as soon, that is, as I can curve my thoughts again without flying into a tailspin).

But your last comments about "disembodiment," and how maybe what seems "disembodied" within the academic world is perhaps not really disembodied at all, unquiets me. I mean sure, a lot (or at least some) of that scholarly textual tracking of phrases and forgotten foibles and bibliographic peering after "who was quoting who and why and where" is indeed a kind of marvellous mudra for the muscles—a way of communing with long-dead ancestors and ancestral haunts, and of learning from them how to haunt the library stacks in style when we, too, have transmogrified into a trail of traces. I mean *of course* everything felt or sensed or even thought is felt and thought by a body (whether that body is furred or feathered or made of bricks). But shucks, man! The question is whether that body blossoming into song is singing in a way that blesses the other bodies that abound, or whether it's proclaiming only and endlessly *ITSELF*, at the expense of all else, by pretending it's not a body in blossom but a burst of brilliance from beyond Alpha Centauri, a burnished piece of bombast that wants to blast the bodily world to bits, despising its own density and texture for being vulnerable to the wind and the wet (and the withering away). The abstract intelligence, I think, is a sheer delight when it's in service to the earthly dance, but reckless and stiflingly mean when it strives to certify its dominion, terrified of noticing that it's enmeshed in the world it seeks to control. The terror of being vulnerable, and the consequent wish to disembed oneself, to stand forever outside the sensuous world—to possess the world in thought, to comprehend it and own it and finally to control it: that is the sad dance that I'd call "disembodied." It's still a dance, yes, but one that has forgotten the pleasure of the thing.

Drat! I seem to have forgotten my resolve to hold off on these thoughts till I'd felt a bit better in my limbs, and a bit more limber in my brain—feel free to ignore the above paragraph if it's just ranting without grokking yer main point, which I sense is a kindhearted one. The problem, David, is this: schooling did indeed hurt me, wounded me bad. The schools I went to didn't leave any room between their four walls for such folks as myself— "dyslexic" they'd probably call it now, and maybe also "attention deficit disorder" or some other dysfunctional label—'cause they didn't recognize any value in the sort of delicious somatic empathy I inadvertently felt in relation to creatures and grasses and rock faces, and in general, every sensorial thing I met and pondered. Which translated into a kind of slowness in regard to less tangible matters like logical theorems and abstract principles. And so I guess I've got a chip on my shoulder, one that sends splinters into my flesh every time I remember sitting, shaking, and sweating in front of yet another timed test while the clock on the wall ticked away, or whenever I remember the frogs pinned to the dissection boards by students who'd never gazed at a live frog in wonder (classmates laughing as they flung a few severed limbs around the lab).

Yes indeed there is a rich kind of scholarship and a yearning to learn that knows knowledge is a way into a deeper relationship with things. But there is also a type of learning that accumulates knowledge solely in order to acquire a new power over things, a kind of scholarship that by its exercise hopes to avoid and indeed to vanquish the difficult ambiguity of relationship (with all its attendant vulnerability and responsibility). This is a strategy one can pursue only by denying or forgetting one's bodily embedment in the thick of things. This is what I'd call a disembodied approach—the approach of a body trying to pretend its not there.

Crisp, crisp stars out tonight...

David Jardine: Hey, look, get better. Actually loved your last message because it broke something for me and is precisely the sort of slap I often need in my work and my life. I used an image ages ago in a paper about the loss of the fourth R in environmentalism (Jardine 1994). We've still got "recycle, reduce, reuse." The R that got lost was "refuse": not simply "refuse" in the sense of "garbage" but refusing some things. Your lovely ire in your last message—that is the sword that compassion required to prevent what you graciously called "gentle and graceful" above from being what Chogyam Trungpa (1995, 122) called "idiot compassion." You're right: some of what the academy suggests is ecologically and spiritually insane and must be refused. Much of what goes on in schools is horrifying in its violence against children and against this great inheritance and great task of bodily remembering. That is why Merleau-Ponty's words of flesh are worth our love and attention, because of their character, because of what they say and what they ask of us and our lives. We must learn again to refuse, to say "no" now from deep down in the belly breath.

Your school wounds are tethered to wounds in what could have been the sensuous beauty of geometry, for example—itself, like you, in a schooled desk, tied down to tests that hate the lovely ambiguities and allures of its body, as much as school hated you and your body. School(ed) child/school(ed) mathematics: each bears a wound.

I've attached another recent paper called "All Beings Are Your Ancestors" (Jardine 1997). The title is from Hongzhi Zhengjue (1091-1157), in a text called *Cultivating the Empty Field* (1991): "Transforming according to circumstances, meet all beings as your ancestors."

Enjoy. Later.

David Abram: Thanks for the paper, David—it's an interesting piece, written with style and precision. As in this line of yours, "Giddy sensation, this. Like little bellybreath tingles on downarcing childgiggle swingsets." Hah! What a precise muscleskin memory in my belly, yet not named from outside before.

David Jardine: That line you mentioned is one I also really like, because, as you say, it voices such an intimate bodyplace that is so rarely said out loud. It is such a schoolyard image, as if children, out of school, had some secret not-school knowledge they were secreting away into bodily recesses at recess.

Each of us knows something of this, down on hands and knees with yer snout in the tall grasses in intimate bug worlds and dirt smells, knowing something, something carnal, that no one seems able to admit. So we experienced it, all of us, and never ever *ever* said anything at all about it. Secret knowledge. Perhaps something we shouldn't leave to schools, perhaps we shouldn't even let them know, given what they've often done with so many other things.

David Abram: Yeah. I call it "shadow knowledge," since it's gathered or gleaned outside of the officially sanctioned spaces, away from the gaze of the adults, out of the spotlight cast by those ostensibly in charge of what's worth knowing.

Here's another thing I thought I would mention, in case you've met other kids like this. You know, as a kid I actually loved numbers and their mysteries, but I got befuddled by the way mathematics was taught in high school. I mean, I was unable to just memorize formulas and simply plug 'em into equations wherever needed (though I certainly tried to), because, for some reason I felt I had to work those formulas out afresh every time, feel it out in my body before I could deploy them in any particular instance. Which made it utterly impossible for me to finish any test in the allotted time (although whatever I did finish I always got right). I simply had to experience each formula in my muscles, had to feel how it moved, how it acted, in order for it to *make sense* to me. (Similarly with reading: I was and still am unable to abstract the meaning of a printed phrase directly off the page, but rather have to feel it in my body, have to sound it out or at least feel it in my tongue muscles, and it is this *bodily* experience that discloses the meaning to me. Hence I am a very slow reader compared to everyone else that I know—I read at about the same speed at which I could read aloud, and indeed any text I'm really interested in I do read aloud.) If mathematics had been taught to me more in the way that you advocate—as a living body of knowledge, with a corporeal history—well, it sure would've opened mathematics up to me and others like me, instead of effectively closing it off to us. It took many years before I was able to regain my appreciation and fascination with that world.

David Jardine: You ask if I've met other kids like that. Can you keep a secret? I'm that other kid. And so are many of the children I see squatted in desks, and many of the teachers I meet, their eyes bloodshot with trying to keep up the charade they don't even know they are in.

Let's rest here for a bit.

References

Abram, D. 1996. *The spell of the sensuous: Language in a more-than-human world*. New York: Pantheon Books.

Cheney, J. 1989. Postmodern environmental ethics: Ethics as bioregional narrative. *Environmental Ethics* 11: 117-134.

Hillman, J. 1991. *Inter Views*. Dallas: Spring Publications.

Hongzhi, Z. 1991. *Cultiviating the empty field: The silent illumination of Zen Master Hongzhi*. Translated by T. D. Leighton and Y. Wu. San Francisco: North Point Press.

Jardine, D. 1994. "Littered with literacy": An ecopedagogical reflection on whole language, pedocentrism and the necessity of refusal. *Journal of Curriculum Studies* 26(5): 509-524.

Jardine, D. 1997. "All beings are your ancestors": A bear Sutra on ecology, Buddhism and pedagogy. *The Trumpeter: A Journal of Ecosophy* 14(3): 122-23.

Jardine, D. 1998. Birding lessons and the teachings of cicadas. *Canadian Journal of Environmental Education* 3: 92-99.

Trungpa, C. 1995. *Cutting through spiritual materialism*. San Francisco: Shambala Press.

Subject Index

Name Index

Perhaps the issue is not a fixed knowledge of the good, the single focus that millennia of monotheism have made us idealize, but rather a kind of attention that is open, not focused on a single point. Instead of concentration on a transcendent ideal, sustained attention to diversity and interdependence may offer a different clarity of vision, one that is sensitive to ecological complexity, to the multiple rather than the singular.

—Mary Catherine Bateson

About the Editors

Brent Hocking is a public school teacher in Richmond, B.C., Canada and a doctoral candidate at the Centre for the Study of Curriculum and Instruction at the University of British Columbia.

Johnna Haskell is an outdoor educator and lecturer at the University of Southern Maine. She graduated with a Ph.D. in curriculum studies at the University of British Columbia.

Warren Linds is a community educator and facilitator in Regina, Saskatchewan, and a doctoral candidate in language and literacy education at the University of British Columbia.

The Foundations of Holistic Education Series

Vol. 1 *Caring for New Life: Essays on Holistic Education*
Ron Miller

Vol. 2 *Education for Awakening: An Eastern Approach to Holistic Education*
Yoshiharu Nakagawa

Vol. 3 *"Under the Tough Old Stars": Ecopedagogical Essays*
David Jardine

Vol. 4 *Unfolding Bodymind: Exploring Possibility Through Education*
Edited by Brent Hocking, Johnna Haskell, and Warren Linds

Vol. 5 *The Primal, the Modern, and the Vital Center: A Philosophy of Holistic Experience & Place, the Cultural Preconditions of Education*
Donald W. Oliver, Julie G. Canniff, and Jouni Korhonen

Vol. 6 *Holistic Education: A Pedagogy of Universal Love*
Ramón Gallegos Nava; translated by Madeline Newman Ríos and Gregory S. Miller

For more information write to the
Foundation at P.O. Box 328,
Brandon, VT 05733 or visit us
online at www.great-ideas.org.
1-800-639-4122 or 802-247-8312